D1756462

Public–

Public–private
policies and ser
perspectives on
ment from aro
evaluation of t
number of diffi
of public–priva
formance in an

public
retical
anage-
for the
from a
anding
ir per-

Stephen P. O
the Research
University. He
profit manager
Review.

ctor of
Aston
d non-
agement

Routledge Advances in Management and Business Studies

Public–Private Partnerships

Theory and practice in international perspective

Edited by Stephen P. Osborne

London and New York

First published 2000
by Routledge
2 Park Square, Milton Park, Abingdon, Oxon, OX14 4RN

Simultaneously published in the USA and Canada
by Routledge
270 Madison Ave, New York NY 10016

Routledge is an imprint of the Taylor & Francis Group

Transferred to Digital Printing 2007

Typeset in 10/12 Monotype Baskerville by Steven Gardiner Ltd

British Library Cataloguing in Publication Data
A catalogue record for this book is available
from the British Library

Library of Congress Cataloging in Publication Data
A catalogue record for this book has been requested.

ISBN10: 0–415–21268–5 (hbk)
ISBN10: 0–415–43962–0 (pbk)

ISBN13: 978–0–415–21268–7 (hbk)
ISBN13: 978–0–415–43962–6 (pbk) ✓

Printed and bound by CPI Antony Rowe, Eastbourne

For Maddy

Contents

List of figures

List of tables

Contributors

Helmut K. Anheier is Director of the Centre for Civil Society at the London School of Economics, England.

Peter Carroll is Professor of Management at the University of Wollongong, Australia.

Gerard Clarke is Lecturer in Development Studies at the University of Wales (Swansea), Wales.

Sven-Olof Collin is Professor of Business Administration at Lund University, Sweden.

Richard Common is Senior Lecturer in Social Policy at London Guildhall University, England.

Gavin Drewry is Professor of Public Management at Royal Holloway College, University of London, England.

Teresa S. Encarnación Tadem is Assistant Professor in Political Science at the University of the Philippines, the Philippines.

Peter K. Falconer is Senior Lecturer in Public Management at Glasgow Caledonian University, Scotland.

John Hailey is Director of Research at Oxford Brookes University Business School, England.

Lennart Hansson is Head of Management Control of the Swedish Association of Local Authorities, Sweden.

Chris Huxham is Professor of Management at Strathclyde Graduate Business School, Scotland.

Brian Jacobs is Professor of Public Policy at Staffordshire University, England.

György Jenei is Professor of Public Policy and Management at the University of Economic Sciences, Budapest, Hungary.

Erik-Hans Klijn is Senior Lecturer in Public Administration at Erasmus University, Rotterdam, the Netherlands.

David Lewis is Lecturer in Development Management in the Centre for Civil Society at the London School of Economics, England.

Kathleen McLaughlin is lecturer in local Governance in the Institute of Local Government Studies, University of Birmingham, England.

Ronald W. McQuaid is Senior Lecturer in Economics at Napier University, Scotland.

Lynne Moulton is an independent researcher in the United States.

Vic Murray is Adjunct Professor of Public Administration at the University of Victoria (BC), Canada.

Stephen P. Osborne [editor] is Reader in Public Management in Aston Business School, Aston University, England.

Peter Steane is Senior Lecturer in Management at Macquarie University, Australia.

Geert R. Teisman is Professor of Policy Science at the Catholic University of Nijmegen and at Erasmus University, Rotterdam, the Netherlands.

Mike Tricker is Senior Lecturer in Public Services Management, Aston University, England.

Siv Vangen is Teaching Fellow in Management at Strathclyde Graduate Business School, Scotland.

Anna Vári is a Researcher in the Institute for Social Conflict Research of the Hungarian Academy of Sciences, Hungary.

Introduction

Understanding public–private partnerships in international perspective: globally convergent or nationally divergent phenomena?

Stephen P. Osborne

The 1990s has seen the establishment of public-private partnerships (PPPs) as a key tool of public policy across the world. Not only have they become seen as a cost-efficient and effective mechanism for the implementation of public policy across a range of policy agendas, they have also been articulated as bringing significant benefits in their own right – particularly in terms of developing socially inclusive communities. Examples of both kinds of PPPs include:

- in the UK, PPPs are a cornerstone of the developing *stakeholder society* of the 'New Labour' government and an essential tool to implement significant social policies, such as the regeneration of urban areas (the Single Regeneration Budget) and the struggle to combat youth unemployment (the *welfare to work* programme) (Falconer and Ross 1998);
- in Hungary, PPPs are being seen as a means through which both to restructure the provision of public services to meet social needs and to develop *a civil society* in the aftermath of the communist regimes (Osborne and Kaposvári 1997, 1998);
- within European Union policy development, PPPs are an essential integrative mechanism both to combat social exclusion and to enhance local-community development (Jones 1998); and
- in the US, PPPs are central to national and state-government initiatives to regenerate local urban communities, as well as often arising out of community-led attempts to deal with the crisis of government in American communities (Aspen Institute 1997; Podziba 1998).

Indeed, PPPs do offer exciting opportunities to achieve a number of public policy outcomes, including

- a means by which to combat social exclusion by integrating the public and private components of local communities – including local government, local politicians, local community and voluntary groups and the local community itself;

- the chance to reform local public services, making them more accessible to the local community and more responsive to their needs;
- the opportunity to develop cost-efficient ways of providing local services to meet social needs which are able to utilize resources from both the public and private spheres and to build upon local networks for their implementation;
- more responsive and flexible public policy making, by utilizing the community and business links offered by PPPs in order to improve the quality of the policy making process; and
- a route both to the reform of the political basis of government and to the creation and sustenance of *civil society* – whatever this contested term may mean.

Notwithstanding these important potential community gains from PPPs, their successful realization is a significant challenge in itself, however. There is a wealth of both theoretical and empirical literature on these challenges. Five literatures are especially important. First, there is the theoretical literature on the nature of organizational collaboration, which raises, amongst other issues, the significance of structural issues on collaboration (Huxham and Vangen 1996) the resource-dependency thesis on collaboration (Benson 1975) and the institutional paradigm (DiMaggio and Powell 1988; Singh *et al.* 1991). Second, there is the public management literature which has developed within Anglo-American experience. This has emphasized the significance of management arguments and focused upon issues of the contractual relationships, their management and costs and the impact of trust upon them (Williamson 1988; Osborne 1997). Third, there is the public governance perspective on public–private partnerships which has emphasized the primacy of the governance of relationships within networks and the importance of the interrelationship between the political and the social context of such networks (Kooiman 1993; Kickert 1997).

Fourth, there is a substantial community-development literature which explores public–private partnerships within the context of the needs of the local community as well as the impact of the former upon the self-learning capacity of local communities (Oakley 1991). Finally, there is an empirical literature which has sought to describe the process and impact of public–private partnerships upon the provision of local services and upon the development of the local community (Taylor 1997).

All these literatures are significant in their own right. However, a weakness is that each has often been developed in isolation of the others. This has limited both the extent to which lessons can be learned across these approaches and also the extent to which new syntheses can be developed which surmounts their narrow disciplinary basis. Further, there has been a narrow national focus to much of the literature.

This book is intended both to reflect the issues and literatures identified above and to consider their import for the management and impact of PPPs across the world. It is not, however, intended to offer one unified body of theory. The perspective held here is that PPPs are a divergent phenomenon in terms of

- the theoretical models available for understanding and evaluating them;
- the different partners – government, business, the voluntary and non-profit sector and the local community – which can be involved in PPPs; and
- their prevalence and impact in different parts of the world.

This diversity is essential to their understanding and is reflected in this volume. It invites you, as the reader, to draw your own conclusions about the nature and import of PPPs.

I.1 Structure of the book

This book is in four parts. The first part offers a number of key theoretical perspectives for understanding the nature, process and management of PPPs. The second part explores the divergent public-policy contexts, internationally, for PPPs and argues for the need to understand such PPPs within these regional and national contexts. The third part presents a series of case studies of the management and outcomes of PPPs, each highlighting a key issue. The fourth part explores the issue of the evaluation of PPPs both in terms of their outcomes and their processes, and tries to identify some core characteristics of successful partnership processes. The concluding chapter then asks the question of the extent to which PPPs are solely a policy implementation tool, or whether they have an important role in the design of policy initiatives.

I.2 Guide to the chapters

Part I commences with a fundamental review by *Ronald W. McQuaid* both of the rationale for, and the strengths and weakness of, PPPs. *Peter Carroll* and *Peter Steane* then explore the prevalence of PPPs across the governmental, business and non-profit sectors. *Gavin Drewry* takes a legal perspective upon PPPs and suggests that they raise some important legal considerations, both about the boundaries between public and private law and the nature of accountability. In the final two chapters in Part I, the processes of PPPs are examined. First, *Stephen P. Osborne* and *Vic Murray* present a model of the process itself. Then, *Erik-Hans Klijn* and *Geert Teisman* ask some key questions about the nature and management of the governance of the PPP process.

In Part II, two separate contexts for PPPs are contrasted. In Chapters 6 and 7, the context for PPPs in the Western-style market economies are examined. *Lynn Moulton* and *Helmut Anheier* explore PPPs in North America, with its focus on the market as the key governance mechanism for PPPs. By contrast, *Peter Falconer* and *Kathleen McLaughlin* explore the evolving community-governance (Ross and Osborne 1999) framework for PPPs in the UK, under the 'New Labour' government. In Chapters 8 and 9 this is contrasted with the context of PPPs in the East and South-east Asia region. Both *Richard Common* and *Gerard Clarke* argue that the cultural basis for PPPs is far less established in this region. Whilst many global pressures are encouraging PPPs, the local political and sectoral cultures are far less amenable to this plural model of service delivery.

Part III explores a range of case studies of PPPs, highlighting key issues. *Geert Teisman* and *Erik-Hans Klijn* offer a detailed examination of the use of PPPs in the field of transport policy in the European Union. It demonstrates the gap between policy rhetoric and the reality of PPPs and how this impacts upon their management and effectiveness. *Teresa S. Encarnación Tadem* provides a different perspective from the Philippines. Here the focus is on community–government partnerships both for economic regeneration and the sustenance of civil society. She explores the roles that NGOs can play in developing such partnerships, the importance of personal relationships in their management in the Philippines – and some of the difficulties of their development and sustenance. She makes the timely point that PPPs, by themselves, are no guarantee of successful policy implementation.

Following on from this point, *Sven-Olof Collin* and *Lennart Hansson* explore the important case of the failure of PPPs to gain significance in Sweden; where the culture of cooperative development might have been expected to spawn a plethora of such arrangements. They argue that it is important to view PPPs not as a discrete phenomenon but rather within the wider institutional framework within which they operate. When this institutional framework in Sweden is explored further, then the strength of government within it is apparent, as are the key reasons for the failure of PPPs to gain a greater significance. *Brian Jacobs* then raises the vital issue of the evaluation of complex organizational arrangements such as PPPs, with a fascinating example of a complex community initiative in Pittsburgh in the US. This issue is pursued further in Part IV.

In Chapters 14 and 15, *Mike Tricker* and *David Lewis* examine the ability of PPPs to be a tool for social inclusion and community capacity building in two varying contexts. In the former case this concentrates on capacity building in the context of the rural regeneration programme in the UK. In the latter case, the focus is upon rural regeneration in Bangladesh. Finally in Part III, *György Jenei* and *Anna Vári* focus on the contribution that PPPs can offer to the policy-making process. This is a particularly interesting example in that it focuses on the experience of a transitional nation of Eastern Europe (Hungary) and argues that PPPs have the potential both to improve policy making and to contribute to the sustenance of civil society in such nations.

The three chapters in Part IV focus on evaluation. In Chapter 17, *Vic Murray* examines the differing perspectives of success of both the funder and fundees of PPPs and questions whether evaluation can ever be more than a contested issue between these two parties. This part concludes with two chapters which evaluate the impact of PPPs as policy-implementation mechanisms and which seek to establish some core conditions for their maximum impact. *John Hailey* does this in the context of the developing world, whilst *Chris Huxham* and *Siv Vangen* focus on the Western experience.

The book concludes with a discussion by *Kathleen Ross* and *Stephen P. Osborne* of the relationships between PPPs, policy making and the policy implementation. It argues whilst the latter issue has often been the focus for PPPs internationally, they have a great deal to offer to the policy-making process. This contribution is detailed here, as well as the key preconditions for its achievement.

References

Aspen Institute (1997) *Voices from the Field*, Washington: Aspen Institute.

Benson, H. J. (1975) 'Inter-organizational networks as a political economy', *Administrative Science Quarterly* 20(3): 229–49.

DiMaggio, P. and Powell, W. (1988) 'The iron cage revisited', in C. Milofsky (ed.) *Community Organizations*, New York: Oxford University Press, pp. 77–99.

Falconer, P. and Ross, K. (1998) 'Public–private partnership and the "new" labour government in Britain', in L. Montanheiro, B. Haigh, D. Morris and N. Hrovatin (eds) *Public and Private Sector Partnerships: Fostering Enterprise*, Sheffield: Sheffield Hallam University Press, pp. 133–48.

Huxham, C. and Vangen, S. (1996) 'Managing inter-organizational relationships', in S. Osborne (ed.) *Managing in the Voluntary Sector*, London: International Thomson Business Press, pp. 202–16.

Jones, R. (1998) 'The European Union as a promoter of public–private partnerships', in L. Montanheiro, B. Haigh, D. Morris and N. Hrovatin (eds) *Public and Private Sector Partnerships: Fostering Enterprise*, Sheffield: Sheffield Hallam University Press, pp. 183–94.

Kickert, W. (1997) 'Public governance in the Netherlands: An alternative to Anglo-American "managerialism" ', *Public Administration* 75(4): 731–52.

Kooiman, J. (1993) *Modern Governance*, London: Sage.

Oakley, P. (1991) *Projects with People*, Geneva: ILO.

Osborne, S. (1997) 'Managing the coordination of social services in the mixed economy of welfare: Competition, cooperation or common cause?', *British Journal of Management* 8: 317–28.

Osborne, S. and Kaposvari, A. (1997) 'Towards a civil society? Exploring its meanings in the context of post-communist Hungary', *Journal of European Social Policy* 7(3): 209–22.

—— (1998) 'Non-governmental organizations and the development of social services. Meeting social needs in local communities in post-communist Hungary', *Public Administration and Development* 18(4): 365–80.

Podziba, S. (1998) *Social Capital Formation, Public-Building and Public Mediation: the Chelsea Charter Consensus Process*, Dayton, OH: Kettering Foundation.

Ross, K. and Osborne, S. (1999) 'Making a reality of community governance: Structuring government–voluntary sector relationships at the local level', *Public Policy and Administration* 14(2): 49–61.

Singh, J., Tucker, D. and Meinhard, A. (1991) 'Institutional change and ecological dynamics', in W. Powell and P. DiMaggio (eds) *The New Institutionalism in Organizational Analysis*, Chicago: University of Chicago Press, pp. 390–422.

Taylor, M. (1997) *The Best of Both Worlds. The Voluntary Sector and the Government*, York: YPS.

Williamson, O. (1988) *Economic Organization*, Brighton: Wheatsheaf.

Part I

Understanding public–private partnerships

1 The theory of partnership
Why have partnerships?

Ronald W. McQuaid

1.1 Introduction

This chapter explores some of the theoretical and policy issues concerning the reasons for developing and operating partnerships. In particular partnerships to promote urban and rural regeneration or economic development are analysed as these involve a wide range of actors (including central or federal government, local government, the private sector, and local communities) and the underlying issues that they deal with are multifaceted. Many case studies of such partnerships exist (see e.g. Wannop; 1990); however, the more general theoretical basis for understanding and analysing them remains poorly developed.

Partnership approaches have received widespread support from across the political spectrum, including policy makers, officials and local communities. They are likely to remain high on the policy agenda at all levels (see e.g. Audit Commission, 1991). At the supra-national level the European Union (EU) promotes partnerships as it operates with and through member states and more local agencies to achieve its policy aims, taking account of national rules and practices (CEC 1996). At the national level in many countries, including the UK, there has been government pressure to move away from public provision of services towards joint private–public partnerships or greater private provision.

At the local level continued or greater involvement in partnership approaches is likely between public bodies and/or private bodies and non-governmental organizations because of pragmatic factors such as resource constraints, as well as more ideological factors (see Leach *et al.* 1994). These factors include: a belief in the overall advantages of a partnership approach; the move towards enabling local government (where publicly funded services are implemented by private or not-for-profit bodies rather than by the public sector); a recognition that any one local actor often does not have all the competencies or resources to deal with the interconnected issues raised in many policy areas; and greater agreement that urban regeneration should include the genuine participation of the local community. However, the theoretical and empirical validity of these views needs further analysis. Indeed, in order to fully understand the behaviour and policies of organizations involved in economic development and regeneration it is necessary to consider the nature of their relationships with networks of and partnerships between other actors, including the flows of resources, power, and information within these networks.

While each partnership is a function of particular historical, economic, social and political contexts, there are many common trends. The natures of partnerships, particularly 'private–public partnerships' but also partnerships between quasi-public and/or public agencies, are altering because of changing global economic patterns, government funding and changing economic structures, in both the US (Weaver and Dennert 1987) and the UK (Harding 1990; McQuaid 1994, 1999). One broad context for the growth of partnerships is the transformation of central–local government and changing state–private sector relationships, in which partnerships may be the result of, but in other cases the cause of, such changing relationships. Indeed this has given rise to a paradox concerning the fragmentation of publicly funded agencies and the multifaceted nature of issues that government must deal with. This apparent paradox is that there has been a move in recent decades for many government functions to be delivered through quangos or other agencies with a narrow range of objectives so as to increase focus, accountability and effectiveness. Yet as a result of the multifaceted nature of the issues and problems being dealt with, these agencies must generally work in various forms of partnership to effectively tackle the issues. However, as discussed below, these partnerships cloud accountability, reduce focus and influence overall efficiency and effectiveness unless the partnerships are carefully designed and operated.[1]

The remainder of this chapter explores some of the factors that are useful for understanding partnerships in different circumstances. Section 1.2 discusses what is meant by the term partnership. Section 1.3 sets out a framework of typologies for analysing them. Sections 1.4 and 1.5 consider why urban economic development policies might use partnerships, by analysing their potential advantages and disadvantages respectively. Section 1.6 considers some of the theories concerning why different actors with differing motivations and objectives may work together in partnership and the implications of the theories for the development of partnerships. Section 1.7 presents the conclusions and discusses areas for future research.

1.2 Definitions of partnership

The term 'partnership' covers greatly differing concepts and practices and is used to describe a wide variety of types of relationship in a myriad of circumstances and locations. Indeed, it has been suggested that there is an infinite range of partnership activities as the 'methods for carrying out such (private–public) partnerships are limited only by the imagination, and economic development offices are becoming increasingly innovative in their use of the concept' (Lyons and Hamlin 1991: 55).[2] This section considers some general and policy-orientated definitions of partnership in the context of economic development and regeneration.

There are a number of assumptions underlying definitions of partnership. First, the potential for synergy of some form, so 'the sum is greater than the parts'. Second, the partnership involves both development and delivery of a strategy or a set of projects or operations, although each actor may not be equally involved in all stages. Third, in public–private partnerships the public sector are not pursuing purely commercial goals. So a criteria of partnership is the presence of social partnership (so excluding purely commercial transactions).

Partnership involves cooperation – i.e. 'to work or act together' – and in a public policy can be defined as cooperation between people or organizations in the public or private sector for mutual benefit (see Holland 1984). Harding (1990) sets out a similar general definition of 'private–public partnership' as 'any action which relies on the agreement of actors in the public and private sectors and which also contributes in some way to improving the urban economy and the quality of life' (Harding 1990: 110), although he argues that this has limited conceptual value. Bailey (1994) provides a working definition of private–public partnership in urban regeneration as 'the mobilisation of a coalition of interests drawn from more than one sector in order to prepare and oversee an agreed strategy for regeneration of a defined area' (Bailey 1994: 293).

Taking an economic development perspective, Sellgren (1990) defines partnership as a scheme with involvement or funding from more than one agency. Bennett and Krebs (1994) similarly stress the joint objectives of the bodies and defines partnership as cooperation between actors where they agree to work together towards a specified economic-development objective and draw the key distinction between generalized policy communities that develop a broad local vision for the area or local economy and the specific networks (or partnerships) that are necessary to support individual projects.

There are a number of further definitions which take a policy perspective. One that shows the wide scope of partnerships and the contributions of partners is from the Commonwealth (State) of Massachusetts which says '(A) partnership is a collaboration among business, non-profit organizations, and government in which risks, resources and skills are shared in projects that benefit each partner as well as the community' (Stratton 1989). Other policy definitions may try to define more closely the range of actors involved, the geographical areas covered and any power that is devolved.

Within the context of urban development in areas of multiple deprivation, the UK Government has defined the partnership approach as involving the 'voluntary commitment by the wide range of bodies with a contribution to make to urban development or regeneration (including local communities, the local authorities, Government departments and agencies and the private sector) to an agreed comprehensive long-term regeneration strategy for their areas' (The Scottish Office 1993: 6). This approach incorporates a range of issues which will be further considered below. These include: the voluntary nature of the relationships; the wide range of participants, ranging from the community to the private sector (the voluntary sector is only mentioned elsewhere in their document), local government, national-government departments and quasi-autonomous non-governmental organizations; the need for an agreed strategy; the long-time scale; and agreed contributions of resources (presumably in a variety of forms) to the process, although it omits the sharing of risks.

At European Union level, one of the European Commission's three main principles in its guidelines for its structural policy was 'to implement a partnership with all the parties involved in structural policy, especially the regional authorities' (CEC 1987). It went on to define the term partnership in its framework Regulation for Reforming the Community's Structural Funds as 'close consultation between the Commission, the Member States concerned and the competent authorities designated by the latter at national, regional, local or other level, with each party acting as a partner in pursuit of a common goal' (CEC 1989: 15; CEC 1996). Hence this type of partnership implies both consultation and action at a local level, as will be discussed further below.

Others, such as Atkinson (1999), argue that there are varying meanings of words such as partnerships and the meaning assigned to partnership in urban and rural regeneration in the UK is an exercise in power which reinforces social relations. He argues that there is no single authentic mode of assigning meaning to terms such as partnership and that their meaning is constructed in the context of power and domination where official discourses have privileges over others. However, while such analysis is useful the degree of influence of such official discourses or documents may vary in different circumstances, and what is omitted from the documents may often be fundamental to its operation. Also the real level of influence by different actors at the local level is dependent on many factors beyond those set out in documents. It is usually the underlying relationships which develop before, during and after any strategy document is written that are more significant than the documents themselves. In addition different actors within a partnership may have different views on its purpose, operation and power structures (McQuaid and Christy 1999). Hence, partnership remains a varied and ambiguous concept.

In order to refine the concepts underpinning differing types of partnerships it is necessary to consider some of their key dimensions or characteristics. Otherwise we may be left at one extreme with such a wide level of generality that few lessons can be learnt, or at another extreme with a series of specific case studies which do not fully consider the external environment and possible underlying principles and pressures affecting partnerships. The next section sets out some key dimensions which help define broad types and characteristics of partnerships.

1.3 Types of partnership

This section considers a range of parameters which are useful for analysing partnerships or developing models of them, in the context of urban regeneration and economic development. Each partnership has many dimensions. In order to try to capture the richness of various forms of partnership this section sets out a range of dimensions to partnerships which can be combined to form a set of characteristics of a partnership. Hence any individual

Table 1.1 Components of partnerships

Range/examples	Components	Range/examples
Purpose		
Exogenous (external resources)	Focus	Endogenous (internal resources)
Employment creation	Aims	Employment redistribution
Single project	Range of activities	Long-term programme
Strategic	Level	Programme cooperation or one-off project collaboration
Who is involved		
Public agencies	Range of actors	Private, voluntary, 'third sector'
Formal (legal contracts– general agreements)	Structure	Informal (overlapping networks)
Top-down	Process of mobilization	Bottom-up
Unequal power	Power relationships	'Fair' power relationships
When		
Pre-development/ development	Phase/stage	Operation
Close partnership	Decision points	Continue partnership
Where		
Geographical area (e.g. small urban area)	Area/group	Client group (e.g. young unemployed in the region)
How		
Stand-alone partnership organization	Implementation mechanisms	Agreements influencing existing services

partnership is a combination of these different dimensions and there are large differences between partnerships and within a partnership over time.

Five main dimensions of partnership are now discussed: (a) what the partnership is seeking to do – i.e. its purpose and whether it is strategic or project driven; (b) who is involved – i.e. the key actors and the structure of their relationship in the partnership; (c) when – i.e. the timing or stage of development of the partnership process and changing relationships and activities over time; (d) where – i.e. the spatial dimension; (e) how the activities are carried out, the implementation mechanisms (Table 1.1). A further set of characteristics, the expected benefits of the partnership, are considered in the next section. Each of these dimensions for analysing partnerships also have themselves a number of axes, or sub-dimensions. However, there is a balance to be drawn between increased complexity (and realism) and clarity of any typology of partnerships. Finally each of these components will have direct implications for the efficiency and effectiveness of a partnership and for the balance of power within it, and so can help form a basis to analyse these issues.

(a) What is the partnership seeking to do?

Purpose   The main dimension along which we can classify partnerships is their purpose. The purpose of entering into a partnership may be to gain extra resources for an area, project or organization, to release synergy through collaboration and joining various types of resources, or to transform one or more of the partner organizations. This may include letting them act more entrepreneurially through loosening some constraints and introducing new ways of doing things which are more effective or efficient (see e.g. Mackintosh 1992; Hastings 1996).

The implicit purposes of the partnership are also important. These may be to improve effectiveness or efficiency, to attract additional resources into the area, to manipulate one of the partners to supporting your activities, or to overcome local opposition. Clearly issues such as how and by whom the components making up the overall remit are set are important. Differences in focus between partners are not necessarily mutually exclusive, although conflicts between aims are common and it is crucial for each partnership to be clear where its priorities lie.

The focus of a partnership may hence range from being exogenous to being endogenous. In broad terms then a purely exogenously focused partnership may seek solely to attract extra resources from outside the partnership, while a purely endogenously focused partnership would seek only to maximize the efficient use of existing resources and the synergy between these resources. Of course, most partnerships will have a combination of these purposes, but the relative importance of each will vary.

Strategic or programme/project driven   Partnerships may also be strategic, covering the broad aims of the organizations and dealing with major long-term issues or project/programme driven, involving only specific programmes or projects. For example, a partnership may seek to create and agree a broad development strategy for an area or it may be set up to develop and/or implement a particular project (such as the development of a business park).

Linked to the strategic or project focus is the range of activities or programmes the partnership is involved in. It may focus on a single project (e.g. the redevelopment of a particular building) or a series of programmes affecting a range of factors influencing the 'quality of life' for residents in an area. They may also focus on a narrow range of activities (e.g. building a business park, or business development) or a wide range. For example, the Scottish Office (1993) sets out a range of economic and non-economic aims for partnerships to help regenerate urban areas, which include improving incomes and the quality of life for residents.

The underlying basis of the partnership   The underlying basis of the partnership may be a high level of trust, as in the view of partnership as a marriage which develops over time but is underpinned by trust and a mutual belief in the positive gains for both partners. Hence one partner may accept reduced short-term benefits if this leads to considerable gains for the other partners, although in the longer term there may be some expectation of a quid pro quo. There may be an expectation that the partnership will continue even if its focus and rationale changes over time; that is, the partnership process may be seen as almost an end in itself. Other partnerships may be termed real-politik and based on self-interest of the partners, so that partners may leave or the partnership disintegrate once their gains cease or reduce. The rationale for partnerships is further discussed below.

(b) Who is involved?

Key actors A second dimension of partnerships considers the key actors. One issue is the range of actors. These include the key agencies such as central and local government, government-funded agencies, voluntary-sector bodies, the local community (groups or individuals), and the private sector, but may include 'significant' individuals also. However, each of these groups may contain a variety of types of actors (see Ahlbrandt and Weaver 1987). For instance, the role of the local community is accepted as essential in part-nerships for areas such as those suffering multiple deprivation but the form of this contribution may vary and is discussed below.

The 'private sector' is far from being monolithic and covers many types of organization with differing motives and resources such as: firms located in or linked to an urban area, firms whose 'business' is urban regeneration, paternalistic firms, and organizations concerned with corporate social responsibility, or employer representative organizations (see e.g. Askew 1991). Types of firms also vary by control (locally owned or controlled firms to branch plants), size, or types of tie to the area (such as those tied to the local community for their income or labour supply, say, small shops or estate agents or those dependent on wider markets). Also some firms have urban development and regeneration as a core business and seek partnerships, with the public sector or others, as a means of expanding their market. Others may be involved in partnership for less directly commercial reasons as they have a tie to the area. Within the private sector more informal social networks may, however, be more common than formal partnerships (McQuaid 1996). It is therefore important to identify precisely the types of actors and the manner in which they contribute to a partner-ship.

Structure of the partnership Another continuum for considering key actors and their relationships in partnerships is the formal structure of the partnership, which may range from formal legally binding contracts, to unenforceable public agreements or general agreements to cooperate. Formal partnerships generally include specific objectives and mechanisms.

The Wester Hailes Partnership Agreement in Edinburgh provides an example. It sought to 'maximise the number of local residents able to secure and retain employment both within Wester Hailes and in the wider Edinburgh economy and thus increase local income ... etc.', through a mechanism which included 'a new organization that will provide and improve access to jobs, training, learning ...' (Wester Hailes Employment Initiative 1986). Later the partnership suffered internal tension because of the lack of consensus that the area itself was an appropriate choice (as there had been strong political pressures for its selection compared with some other areas in the city), a lack of clarity of rights and duties of the partners and the place of the community within this, too many committees to attend (a significant resource cost for all, including the community) and uncertainty over the role of the professional support team (McGregor *et al.* 1995).

A more rigid set of formal partnerships may be based upon a legally binding contract, particularly where there is a direct commercial transaction. In many cases partnerships are moving towards a legal basis with legal contracts binding partners to specific inputs and actions. However, there are dangers with this approach – as exemplified in the USA where the 'contract culture' has often led to a 'bureaucratic paperchase' – and may reduce voluntary cooperation as each organization seeks to protect itself from legal repercussions of it failing to meet the contract terms even if the situation has changed and a more appropriate activity could be carried out (Gutch 1992: 73). This emphasis on contracts also permits funding to be reduced with the implications, and sometimes blame, for this falling upon the contractor. There is also a question of whether contracts can help lead to increased trust by creating certainty and commitment and reducing the risks for the partners, or to a breakdown in trust as a result of each party retreating to the conditions of the formal contract.

Besides the formal relationships between organizations, there are often a series of informal networks interlinking individuals in the organizations. This is common, especially as those involved in partnerships – say in a community repre-sentative capacity – may have political or social links with key decision makers in some of the agencies (Perrucci and Pilisku 1970). These informal structures can have a significant impact on the operation of partnerships, particularly bypassing or influencing official or agreed decision-making procedures. Although these overlap with the informal working agreements between agencies and their staff, in this context informal structures can be seen as relating to indi-vidual actors participating in different networks.

Less formal agreements, which may be termed organizational networks rather than partnerships, may be more appropriate for relationship building between actors and information sharing. These take various forms and often simply involve regular meetings of agencies who can then formally or informally report back to their own organization.

Top-down or bottom-up development   An important aspect concerning key actors has been termed the process of mobilization (Bailey 1994). This is the process of creating partnerships through a top-down process (e.g. the initial impetus from a higher level of authority such as central government) or a bottom-up catalytic process. The latter may mean seeking more autonomous control by local communities through locally based and developed strategies which use local resources, address local needs and reduce external dependency (Friedmann and Weaver 1979). While many initial projects start with a top-down approach, the development of individual projects may have bottom-up characteristics. There have been many instances of the UK central government funding key community workers to aid local-capacity building so that local communities can generate their own initiatives and draw relevant bodies into partnerships. Bailey (1994) goes on to develop a typology of partnerships covering development, development of trust, joint agreement/coalition/company, promotional, agency and strategic partnerships, based on level of mobilization (local/national, etc.), geographical area of coverage, range of partners, and remit.

(c) When?

A third set of dimensions is time. Over time key individuals may move or change their views and peoples' and organizational priorities change, so their role in a partnership may change. The stage of an initiative or policy at which there is cooperation can influence the balance of power within the partnership and contributions of partners. Holland (1984) separates the policy dimension in which the goals of the community are articulated and the operational dimension in which those goals are pursued. This can be termed policy formation with agreements focused on the overall aims, specific goals and implementation or how they are to be achieved, resource inputs, implementation mechanisms and organizational structure and monitoring and evaluation (see also Lyons and Hamlin 1991).

Some of the main stages of developing a partnership includes the pre-development stage when the nature of the problem is investigated and the need, or otherwise, of a partnership is identified. During this stage trust between prospective partners needs to be created or developed and working relationships built. The following phase may be the development of the strategy and the formation of some form of partnership agreement. Next, the appropriate strategy and agreement may be selected, along with the main projects and implementation mechanisms. The partnership and strategy then need to be implemented (arguably the most difficult part of the process). This is followed by *ex-post* evaluation which feeds back into improving the strategy and partnership and helps when the decision point is reached to continue, modify or close the partnership. Clearly these are only broad stages and each may overlap with others (e.g. experience during implementation may reinforce or damage the trust between the partners).

At different stages of a partnership there will be different balances of power between actors. For example, in the early stages when an initiative is being developed, all those 'around the table' will have potentially large influence as their involvement will often be considered important for getting the initiative started. However, the environment within which the key funders operate is very influential (e.g. in ruling certain approaches out of discussion). When the initiative is agreed, then the views of the main funders are likely to become relatively more important; that is, there may be a shift from the influential power of some actors (such as voluntary groups) towards a relative increase in the authoritative power of the main funders. Once a specific organization has been set up to deliver the service, then that organization's management becomes very powerful, even when there is a management board of the partners. Once the review stage of the initiative is entered, then the main potential funders regain much of their power as they have greatest influence over whether or not the initiative continues.

(d) *Where or whom?*

Partnerships may focus on different scales of geographical area (e.g. concentration on a small area of urban deprivation or on the wider travel-to-work area). Others may focus on a particular client group within the area or across a wider area. They may focus on national-level policies (or attempts to influence policy), such as social exclusion, discrimination or urban regeneration in a national context, or may focus on such issues at a local or regional level. Clearly the likely partners or other key actors will differ in each situation. There may also be tensions between local and national perspectives within each type of partner.

(e) *How? Implementation mechanisms*

A fifth dimension, or group of dimensions, of partnerships concerns implementation mechanisms, which involves who does what, including who provides resources and who controls them. The partnership may agree to co-ordinate and alter priorities of the partners' existing services or, at another extreme, they may operate through a stand-alone unit. These and hybrid mechanisms are common, although the latter will usually require a formal agreement. An example of the latter is the development and operation of a free-standing not-for-profit company to act as the secretariat of the East of Scotland European Partnership which helps coordinate and implement a major European Union funding programme in partnership with local actors and central government (McQuaid and Christy 1999).

In summary, given the huge diversity and ever-changing nature of partnerships in urban economic development, one line of enquiry in order to get greater understanding is to narrow the focus down to individual or subgroups of partnership along the dimensions discussed, while a complementary approach is to seek some general principles that may be applied to partnerships. A typology of partnerships should incorporate all of these factors. So, for example, if a partnership is described as 'exogenous' in order to add depth to this description it may also be seen as a strategic, formal, national partnership involving the public, 'third' and private sectors and operating through a stand-alone executive. This chapter now considers some possible reasons why a partnership may be set up.

1.4 Potential advantages of partnership

An important question is why should an organization use a partnership rather than carrying out the activity by itself? This section considers some of the arguments in favour of forming and implementing urban economic-development policies through partnerships. The main assumption for using partnerships is that the partners are not in a zero (or rather constant) sum game. By cooperating the total output is increased for a given level of resources (see Section 1.5 for more detailed discussion). Also they are seen as allowing each partner to gain the benefits from cooperation, while still retaining their autonomy.[3] In general, partnerships can be argued to be an effective way of overcoming market imperfections that are caused by externalities. Although if the market imperfections are overwhelming and permanent, the product indivisible, economies of scale are large, externalities are enormous, information is bad or impossible, and the market becomes monopolistic then Lyons and Hamlin (1991: 61) argue that the government should provide the good or service directly. The main advantages of partnerships can be grouped as: resource availability; effectiveness and efficiency; and legitimacy.

(a) Resources

First, the nature of the problems facing local economies are multifaceted requiring a combined response from a number of private and public key actors in order to be effective and efficient. The economic, social and environmental and other problems faced by urban areas, particularly those areas suffering from multiple deprivation, are often interrelated, overlapping and mutually reinforcing. Hence solutions aimed at one part of the system are unlikely to be fully successful because of the counteracting impacts of other factors. Partnerships between key actors are therefore essential in order to tackle the various causes (in so far as these can be tackled locally) as well as the symptoms of the problems of the local economy. Also formal or informal joint working or partnerships are important mechanisms to achieve complementarity and avoid wasteful duplication of effort.

Such a view has underpinned much urban policy. In the case of the EU, there is an insistence upon partnerships between the agencies it helps fund to tackle poverty. One underlying principle of the Third Programme to Combat Poverty was the '... need for operations integrating every facet of poverty. Such integration should be achieved through coordinating policies and various public and/or private measures geared to encourage independence which is the basis for social reintegration of the poor' (CEC 1988: 9). The Programme specifically called for the schemes requesting assistance to be '... managed by a Steering Committee composed of representatives of all the bodies involved in carrying out the scheme . . . who will undertake to complete a joint programme to combat all facets of poverty in their . . . town' (CEC 1988: 13) and this partnership should contain the active participation of the representatives of the disadvantaged. More recent EU policy approaches have generated partnerships of local actors to develop and support urban and regional-development programmes.

For separate partners, advantages include resources, effectiveness, legitimacy and conflict avoidance. Partnership allows a pooling of resources so that larger projects, or more aspects of a project can be tackled than is possible for an individual agency (or it allows the agency to devote some resources targeted at one policy to be released for use elsewhere). This is particularly important for UK local authorities who have seen their resources and flexibility of movement reduced since the 1970s (see Harding 1990 for a brief review). While the agency may lose total control of its own resources, it may gain influence over a larger set of resources. Such 'leverage' of resources is often also a performance measure of local economic-development agencies.

In addition to increasing the scale of available resources, partnerships may bring it different *types* of resources, such as information and expertise not available in an organization. This may include legislative power, land, finance, or knowledge, alternative perspectives on the issues and contacts from local-community participants or the private sector. Organizations such as Business in the Community in England and Wales and its sister organization in Scotland have increased the capacity of the private sector to provide such resources to participate in partnerships. On the other hand, commercial partnerships with the private sector (such as development firms or perhaps local employers seeking to increase investment) may be used to increase the level of financial resources available for economic development in the community. In general, a partnership may enable the partners to gain the benefits of economies of scale (e.g. in terms of finance, marketing, administration or production), but with the advantages of the smaller scale organizations and avoidance of some of the diseconomies of scale. Countering this will be the transaction costs incurred and the loss of control by the organizations.

(b) Effectiveness and efficiency

Depending upon the nature of the problem, partnership can greatly increase an individual organization's effectiveness and efficiency, especially through improved coordination between (and within) organizations (see e.g. Webb 1991), hence creating a synergy between the various bodies and reducing wasteful duplication. Therefore, both greater output and cost savings might be achieved.

Partnerships may reduce the confusion faced by people in identifying the appropriate agency by acting as an umbrella for people to approach. Also many initiatives use community activists and groups to become more responsive to user needs and so, for example, increase participation rates in training initiatives, as prospective trainees have greater confidence and trust in such groups and will respond to them rather than to an 'outside' agency. Hence, this should increase the efficiency of the economy rather than being only a redistributive policy (especially when shortages for certain types of labour occur).

For certain policies – such as promoting a city or area – partnership between the various bodies and between public and private sectors is crucial to create a positive external perception (Kotler *et al.* 1993). Partnerships also play an important role in breaking down the stereotypical views of partners towards one another, building trust and making joint working easier and more efficient, as well as improving understanding and knowledge of each other's organizations opening the possibility of better coordination and creation of synergy and new ways of joint working. Partnerships may also improve effectiveness, especially in the long term, through creating stability, building local confidence and minimizing risk for partners and potential investors, and may be an important mechanism for building local capacity for action and control by the local community and other actors.

(c) Legitimacy

Partnerships can also allow greater legitimacy for policy as they may involve participants from the local community directly rather than through the representative democracy of central and local government. Certainly where many policy-implementation decisions are being made by employed officials of an elected central or local government or unelected quasi-autonomous non-governmental organizations, then the legitimacy of the policies as seen at the local level can be enhanced through community participation (although this raises questions about the form of participation). However, partnerships may sometimes be used by government to bring in their supporters to influence local policies; for example, by bringing in the business community or, on the other hand, community activists.

The creation and sharing of risks and rewards and incentives towards creating and participating in partnerships apply in varying degrees to different actors. For instance, McQuaid (1993) argues that strong incentives for local authorities to enter into partnership are provided by the possibility of bringing external resources into the area (e.g. funding, property, expertise, links to national support schemes, etc.), avoidance of duplication, replication of good practice in other joint initiatives, and hence more effective and efficient policy development and implementation. The local authorities themselves also provide resources, statutory powers and democratic legitimacy to such partnerships.

This leads to wider questions concerning representative democracy, with, for example, shifts in control from an elected body (such as a local authority) to a non-elected new agency, even though it may have (unelected) community participation. This can, however, be interpreted in terms of representative and more direct forms of democracy. Partnership may also result in strategy compromise with each partner concentrating upon its own perception of important issues, perhaps leaving gaps of unmet needs. These and other potential disadvantages of partnerships are now considered.

1.5 Potential disadvantages of partnership

There are many problems in working through partnerships (McQuaid 1994; Hastings 1996), which may vary according to the form of partnership. These include unclear goals, resource costs, unequal power, cliques usurping power, impacts upon other 'mainstream' services, differences in philosophy between partners and organizational problems.

(a) Goals

A lack of clear aims or goals is often cited as a major cause of the failure of partnerships. Many partnerships have agreed broad aims, but their detailed goals may be unclear or the partners may have differing understandings of what the goals mean. This can rapidly lead to misunderstanding, lack of co-ordination, and possible conflict between the partners. This could be accentuated if some partners had undeclared, or 'hidden', agendas and were deliberately seeking to gain advantage over the other partners or seeking to achieve their own organizational goals, without supporting or reciprocating the efforts of their partners. Lack of clarity of goals and the means of achieving them may increase the likelihood or perception of other partners having a 'hidden' agenda.

In general, each of the dimensions of partnership discussed earlier presents possibly difficult choices. For instance, how the term 'community' is defined may have significant implications for the distribution of power. It may be difficult to identify the appropriate nature and level at which the community or private sector, or other, participate (e.g. at the strategic or operational levels). National or regional agencies or representatives of the private sector may participate at the strategic level and have greater power than more local actors if the latter only participate at the operational level.

(b) Resource costs

Next, there are considerable resource costs; for instance, in terms of staff time in discussions and making agreements, and in delays to decisions as a result of consultation with partners. It may be difficult to close an inefficient or unsuccessful partnership, or even one whose objective has been achieved if all partners do not agree, as this may sour relations elsewhere. There can also be problems of accountability as no single partner feels fully accountable for the actions of the partnership because of the split between responsibility and control (see McQuaid 1997).

If each partner 'claims' the full success of the partnership (e.g. in terms of jobs created) but only considers its own costs then this may distort decisions. Hence the full social costs of the partnership need to be aggregated and compared with the full social benefits, rather than each partner focusing upon its own costs and benefits.

(c) Unequal power

In most partnerships there is unequal power (as discussed above). As Syrett (1997) argues, conceptualizations of partnerships often fail to recognize the unequal power relations between social partners. Cadbury (1993) argues that the terms consultation and public partnership are often used interchangeably, but that partnership is a more involved form of participation with a wide range of meanings, and implies power being shared equally among all partners. She notes that while Partnership with the Community has been a crucial part of government policy in the UK, it is not a legislative requirement (e.g. with the City Challenge policy).

Bennett and McCoshan (1993) argue that the partnerships between agents may be unequal as it may be more important for one partner than the other(s) or one partner can coerce or mandate the others (e.g. through providing or withholding finance). This, however, may cause considerable tensions as one body seeks to alter another's priority (e.g. to alter education provision to reflect economic needs), particularly where a non-elected partner seeks to coerce a democratically elected body.[4] This issue of balance of power between partners is developed further in the subsections on disadvantages of partnerships (Subsections 1.5(*d–g*)).

However, the presence of unequal power should not imply that all partners should necessarily have equal power. Some may have greater legitimate claim – e.g. because of their greater involvement in the area – or have greater political legitimacy in the case of elected bodies. Also who should have equal power may be difficult to determine (e.g. should the voluntary sector as a whole or each individual voluntary organization have equal power to, say, local government or the local community within the partnership?). Although there are different types of power, greatest power generally rests with those controlling resources. Often this will be a body far from the urban area itself (e.g. the national government or the EU). They are likely to dominate those in the local area who may have the greatest understanding of what is relevant and effective, albeit from a local rather than macro-perspective, and whose feeling of 'ownership' can be crucial to the initiative's success.

(d) Cliques usurping power

A further set of dangers lies in the operation of the partnership. For instance, the objectives or operation of a partnership may be usurped by some actors, cliques or groups (e.g. professional or community groups), resulting in outcomes that increase their benefits rather than overall welfare. There is also the familiar problem of decision-making difficulties in groups whereby they may make irrational or suboptimal decisions which the individuals themselves would not have done. Similarly, there may be a problem of the partnership lacking momentum as each actor relies on the others to push activity forward, resulting in none doing so. This is often countered by having a 'product champion', to use management jargon, or a separate or a dedicated/assigned unit to develop the project.

(e) Impacts on other services

Another set of problems involves impacts on other services. There is a wider problem for many urban economic-development initiatives of marginalization from the mainstream activities of the key agencies. Partnerships (especially those with stand-alone implementation units) may be seen as an alternative to realigning mainstream services to deal with the issues, and yet the scale of and integration between mainstream services may be far more significant, especially in the long run. Conversely the partnership may draw resources from other mainstream services or confuse the services in the minds of users, so reducing their effectiveness (i.e. there may be a significant opportunity cost). This problem is also linked to the scope of partners with, for instance, local authorities having wide ranges of services and responsibilities, while others, such as regional development agencies or community groups, have much narrower responsibilities.

Indeed, the increase in numbers of agencies, often themselves formed out of partnerships, can be argued to have increased the fragmentation of services, with partnerships then being seen as the means to solve the fragmentation. For example, in the UK, the rise of enterprise trusts, regional development agencies, LECs/TECs, trade and innovation support centres and others in providing business support services has caused confusion in the minds of some users (although once 'inside' the system this is often dissipated); so one solution is to set up a coordinating 'one stop' shop in the form of another partnership.

(f) Organizational difficulties

Organizational difficulties inhibiting successful coordination of programmes and approaches, and overcoming the specialist concerns of disparate organizations is a key implementation problem in public agencies working together. Jennings and Krane (1994) found that various barriers hindered coordination. These barriers were: organizational (these include differing missions, professional orientations, structures and processes of agencies); legal/technical (statutes or regulations set down by higher authority, and the technological capacity and practice of the organization); and political (both external political environment but also internal bureaucracy politics). Managers had used a diverse variety of mechanisms to overcome these barriers. They argue that good management characteristics, particularly leadership and interpersonal relationships, are the main ingredients of effective coordination, but also they need to be combined with clear direction (a 'vision of client service') and a clear division over responsibility of functions.

(g) Differences in philosophy among partners

Finally, there may be significant differences in philosophy between the partners, such as in the degree to which they feel the market can solve urban development problems. These differences may become more apparent when difficult circumstances arise. For instance, in many local economic-development partnerships there is a tension between those partners who may emphasize employment and wealth redistribution (e.g. through assisting certain groups to get better access to employment, etc.) and those who emphasise employment and wealth creation.[5] In areas of urban deprivation or renewal the market has often clearly failed, so there is a question as to what degree can the market solve the problem, possibly leading to some conflict between their different philosophies and motivations (and need for varying incentives). This is perhaps a major reason for the generally poor contribution, in financial terms, of the private sector to many urban-renewal initiatives. In initiatives to increase the growth of specific opportunities in an urban area, there may be more support for improving the workings of the market and thus less conflict.

Linked to this, there may be a problem of combining public and private management practices and philosophies within one partnership organization, or a partnership without a clear contract (see e.g. Bryson and Roering 1987). One example is in the area of ethos or stricter ethics of the public sector (e.g. in the interpretation of conflicts of interests, etc.), or in the way aims and objectives are set.

In summary, there are many potential problems in working through partnerships and which may vary by the type of partnership. These revolve around resource costs, power distribution (between bodies and over time), operational difficulties, impacts on other services and the influence of differing philosophies of partners.

1.6 Some theories on partnership development

This section deals with some theories concerning the development of partnerships. In particular the theories of enforced cooperation and game theory are briefly outlined in a very basic form to illustrate the pressures aiding or hindering cooperation between actors in urban regeneration and economic-development policy. There are also a number of other related and overlapping theoretical perspectives that can assist the analysis of partnerships.[6]

The discussion then leads to consideration of some implications of such theories for helping to ensure such cooperation. These issues are especially important in the case of urban economic development as it is concerned with wealth and employment creation (preferably sustainable in economic, social and environmental terms), so the private sector and special-interest groups (e.g. for the disabled) will play a major role. Their perspectives and input will need to be understood and incorporated within policy formation and implementation. Hence it is important to begin to understand those pressures aiding or hindering cooperation among the various actors, particularly where they have differing motivations and objectives.

(a) Enforced cooperation

The main reasons for cooperation are the threat of a central authority, common objectives or (other) self-interest. This threat may have a positive (i.e. coercion) or negative factor. The seventeenth-century philosopher Hobbes (1651) argued that it was difficult to develop cooperation without a strong central authority. However, this philosophical perspective of the need to externally control mankind's nastiness and the usual state of war is countered by Jean-Jacques Rousseau's view of the uncorrupted 'noble savage' and a peaceful state. Adam Smith and Charles Darwin followed the Hobbesian view of competition between individuals. Biologists such as Ridley (1997) argue rather human minds are built by selfishness, but that they were built with the capacity to be social, trustworthy and cooperative, as this may benefit the individual. Hence, our institutions should be designed to draw out these instincts, such as to encourage social and material exchange between equals of enfranchised and empowered individuals.

In local economic development, cooperation can be forced on the public or government funded agency (or community-based group dependent on public finance) through legislation or control of financial resources by central or local government, and increasingly the European Union. Such financial control may be by making resources available (e.g. grants), or through other controls (such as the UK capital-expenditure restrictions on local government or budget controls on other funded bodies).

Many of the bodies involved will have similar objectives and motives which will include (in theory at least) improving the overall welfare of the area, so there will be a strong incentive to cooperate. This is likely to be the case where people in the various bodies share common values, such as officials in different tiers of local government. However, in practice a number of differences in organizational objectives, priorities, timing and other factors (including personal) or competition for power or resources, etc. may inhibit such cooperation. So this alone may be inadequate to foster full cooperation.

Some key actors are not subject to such central authority or common motives. Private enterprises will have commercial pressures making their motives more 'selfish' (as noted in the earlier discussion of types and motives of private-sector organizations), while some pressure groups may be primarily concerned with the interests of their own members rather than the wider community. Although self-interest is a powerful incentive for partnerships offering advantages to the individual partners, these may be insufficient to encourage participation, even though this may lead to increased overall welfare. This would especially be the case if an actor can gain many of the benefits individually without participating. In other words, why should these actors cooperate where there is no effective central control on them or common overriding motive to benefit the welfare of that community?

(b) Game theory

One area of economic theory that can structure the issues of interrelationships and interaction is game theory. This is a huge and complex body of theory and only a brief discussion of the basic application to the Prisoners' Dilemma is possible here (see e.g. Weibull 1995 for more detail). Axelrod (1984) uses this Dilemma to argue that for individuals pursuing their own self-interest, incentives for cooperation will be greater than for selfish behaviour (even without central authority) under a wide variety of circumstances, including where the 'partners' are hostile.

The structure of the Prisoners' Dilemma is based on the story of two accomplices arrested after a crime who are interrogated separately (see Luce and Raiffa 1957 and Axelrod 1984 for more detail and the full assumptions). These two players have two choices: to cooperate with each other or to defect. If one confesses (defects) and the other does not, then (s)he will get free (i.e. a high positive pay-off, although note that these pay-offs are endogenous to the model) but the other prisoner will get a heavy sentence (zero pay-off). If both confess then they both get a medium sentence (low pay-off), and if neither confesses then both get low sentences (medium pay-off). The latter is the best solution for both prisoners together (they maximize their combined welfare). However, for each individual, it is in their interest to confess as: (s)he receives the worst outcome (a heavy sentence) if (s)he does not confess but his accomplice does; while (s)he gets the maximum pay-off (goes free) if his accomplice does not confess. Hence, assuming that neither prisoner has moral qualms or fears revenge from the other prisoner, then each would choose to confess, resulting in a suboptimal outcome for their combined welfare.[7]

However, if the process is iterated, say they are likely to be caught again, then cooperation becomes much more easy as there will be a strong incentive for both *not* to confess as in the future case they will know how the other reacted and base their behaviour (to confess or not) on what happened last time. So, the strategy for success for each depends entirely upon the strategy of their accomplice. If there is a strong central control mechanism – e.g. the accomplices are part of a gang which will punish anyone who confesses – then cooperative behaviour between the accomplices will occur. Provided the game is repeated a number of times, that players can recognize and remember the results of previous encounters, that future pay-offs are not greatly discounted, then cooperation will be mutually beneficial. Even if there is a short-term cost to cooperation it will still occur if future retaliation for current defections is great enough. This forms the basis of a theory of cooperation based upon reciprocity.

Axelrod (1984) tested the Prisoners' Dilemma using a computer competition simulation (where the players were not in total conflict) and found that the most successful strategy was also the simplest: start with cooperation in the first move and then do what the other player did in the previous round (tit-for-tat). Hence the winning strategy was for a player to always cooperate with a cooperative adversary, but if the adversary did not cooperate, then in the next move the player would cease to cooperate, but once the adversary returned to cooperation, the player should also return to it. Axelrod argued that the evolution of cooperation depended upon individuals having a sufficiently large chance of meeting again, so they have a stake in their future interaction (this can be applied to individuals within organizations as well as to the organizations themselves). The cooperation can be based upon reciprocity, but once established this can survive many different strategies used by the individuals and can protect itself from less cooperative strategies.[8] Game theory has developed considerably over recent decades although there is disagreement about interpretations and conflicting evidence (see e.g. Axelrod and Dion 1988 and Zupan 1990), but the purpose here has only been to outline some of the basic notions and applicability of one approach to understanding why partnerships may come about.

(c) *Some implications of theory for partnerships*

The discussion above suggests a number of factors which may promote or hinder partnerships (see McQuaid 1999 for further details). First, enlarging the 'shadow of the future'; that is, to increase the importance of the future relative to the present may aid cooperation. Stable cooperation is aided by frequent interaction between individuals. Organizations and hierarchies are said to promote this by binding people in long-term multi-level relationships which increase the number and importance of likely future interactions. Hence constant changing personnel or their responsibilities may discourage cooperation. However, regional government (such as the Scotland Parliament) suggests greater potential future interaction among key actors.

Second, cooperation can be encouraged by changing the pay-offs, and by making deflections from cooperation more expensive. Where urban agencies or groups are involved in a number of different projects, then ceasing cooperation on one may have negative impacts upon other projects, hence cooperation is encouraged. In order to attract increased private-sector involvement, it is likely to be essential to change existing pay-offs. Also if the costs of failure of a partnership are high (e.g. in terms of future losses, bad publicity, effect on other projects, etc.) then a partnership is less likely to disintegrate.

Third, if, however, the relationship is likely to come to an end then there will be a temptation to hold back, or behave more in your own interests rather than trying to maximize joint gains. Hence joint ventures are more likely to succeed if they are seen as a precursor to more intimate cooperation rather than as finite activities.

Fourth, writers such as Kay (1993) apply the Prisoners' Dilemma to joint-venture business relations, arguing that a long-term relationship can overcome the Dilemma and achieve the optimum outcome. In joint ventures the process is broken down into a sequence of small steps, with early meetings used to explore each others' attitudes, then offering wholehearted cooperation and awaiting a response. If the other side fails to reciprocate, then not much has been lost and you can hold back in the future, but if they do reciprocate then you continue to give full cooperation, so gradually improving trust and establishing a cooperative relationship. Some other general lessons may arise from literature on strategic alliances for companies (Drucker 1992). This also illustrates that cooperation need not be incompatible with competition. Intra-organizational cooperation is, in fact, necessary in order to compete effectively with external organizations and strategic alliances expand this circle of cooperation to incorporate (perhaps only temporarily) former competitors. Cooperation and competition can also remain at the same time (e.g. in sports leagues where teams compete fiercely) but cooperate to fight other forms of entertainment.

Fifth, local characteristics are also important in assisting public–private partnerships. Even where there is a will to cooperate, there remains the question of capacity to make a meaningful contribution; hence there is considerable emphasis on capacity building to enable more local communities to participate in economic-development initiatives. Considerable work has been carried out on local capacity building for local community organizations. National 'social responsibility' private sector organizations have grown in capacity and importance and are often crucial to private inputs to economic initiatives (e.g. Business in the Community leading, with the support of others, to the setting up of the Enterprise Trust network and more recently assisting in other regeneration initiatives). Local social networks may overlap with formal partnerships, and add incentives to them succeeding, although there is a danger of 'favouritism' amongst those in the network. Also numerous private companies have set up specialist divisions to develop partnerships with local authorities and others, especially in economic regeneration involving construction or as a means of getting access to development opportunities.

Finally, Nutt and Backoff (1992) argue that a 'mutualist' strategy by organizations of marshalling external and internal stakeholders is effective for a public agency in responding to turbulent environments in which needs are rapidly changing and collaboration is required to respond. Such a strategy is proactive and responds to a diverse and ever-changing set of needs through actions to meet these needs (which describes the needs-driven approach of much urban local economic development in the last decade). Such a strategy calls for 'organizational relationships which jump across traditional lines of authority, creating complex structures' (Nutt and Backoff 1992: 96). This contrasts with a hierarchical management structure.

Overall, some key aspects of successful partnerships include: clarity of each organization's own objectives and that of the partnership; agreement on the operation of the partnership (structure, resources, who is responsible for day-to-day management and longer term strategy); clear lines of communication and decision making between each partner and the partnership (and each other); clear exit routes (when has the partnership achieved its objectives and then what is to happen to it); a supportive institutional infrastructure; a suitable system of incentives within and between organizations to encourage changed behaviour; and, perhaps most importantly, trust between the partners.

1.7 Conclusions and further research agenda

This chapter considered some of the issues concerning the key dimensions of partnerships in general, and of partnerships in economic development and regeneration in particular. It suggests that there is a need to form frameworks both to allow more meaningful analysis of partnerships, to distinguish differing types of partnerships and to make partnerships more effective. However, this chapter has also indicated that, despite the diversity of partnerships, there are general dimensions that can begin to build towards a more general framework.

Without effective frameworks, there is a danger that much of the research on partnerships may be comprised of useful, but somewhat limited, studies analysing particular individual circumstances. Notwithstanding this, further empirical evidence is needed about the levels of real benefits that partnerships do (or do not) offer. However, one clear conclusion is that care must be taken when trying to generalize about partnership – they are of such diverse forms and natures that generalizations may be treated with caution.

An apparent 'form and function paradox' was set out above whereby the multi-functional nature of policies needed to deal with complex issues conflicts with the single-function nature of the organizations, resulting in the need for new partnership forms of strategy development and delivery which then reduce some of the apparent benefits of having individual organizations. However, partnerships allow the participation of non-public-sector key actors – particularly the private, third sector and local communities – and together with the other advantages of a well-designed partnership discussed in this chapter, these benefits can allow such an apparent paradox to be overcome.

The idea of partnerships deserves wide (but not uncritical) support, and this chapter outlines some factors likely to assist in developing effective partnerships. However, some partnerships may be of an inappropriate type or may not be particularly effective or efficient, while others may consist more of rhetoric than substance. Success will depend upon how partnerships are led, legitimised, resourced, managed and evaluated. These will vary according to local circumstances, the issues to be dealt with, the institutional framework and, of course, the partners themselves. Future directions for research will be in the development of more generalized models of partnership and, linking these to empirical studies, considering if and how the benefits and costs of cooperation and competition can be reconciled.

As this chapter has indicated, there remain many questions about the development and operation of partnerships which require further research. There are a number of roles that such research can undertake. It can help improve our understanding of policy development and implementation; provide models that are useful for practitioners and researchers; help us learn what type of partnerships are appropriate in differing circumstances and indeed if other forms of organization are more appropriate; clarify the advantages and disadvantages of partnership approaches and how can these can be dealt with. This leads to some key questions for research. What is the appropriate type of partnership under different circumstances? What are the conflicts between administrative, functional and economic boundaries for partnerships? How can partnerships be made to work more effectively and efficiently? How can the benefits of partnership working be increased and the costs and potential pitfalls decreased, and indeed, in what circumstances might the costs of partnership outweigh the benefits? Research needs to progress more towards answering such questions in the many different circumstances in which partnerships are used and in developing more robust and useful theoretical frameworks for analysing and improving partnerships.

1.8 Acknowledgements

I would like to thank all those with whom I have worked, as a practitioner and as an academic, in many partnerships in local economic development and regeneration over almost two decades. They have taught me many lessons.

References

Ahlbrandt, R. S. and Weaver, C. (1987) 'Public–private institutions and advanced technology advancement in southwestern Pennsylvania', *Journal of the American Planning Association* 53: 449–58.

Atkinson, R. (1999) 'Discourses of partnership and empowerment in contemporary British urban regeneration, *Urban Studies* 36: 59–72.

Askew, J. (1991) 'Public and private sector partnerships for urban regeneration in Sheffield and Wakefield', *Local Government Policy Making* 17: 37–43.

Audit Commission (1991) *Urban Regeneration and Economic Development: The European dimension*, London: The Audit Commission for Local Government in England and Wales.

Axelrod, R. (1984) *The Evolution of Co-operation*, New York: Basic Books and London: Penguin (1990).

Axelrod, R. and Dion, D. (1988) 'The further evolution of co-operation', *Science* 242: 9 December.

Bailey, N. (1994) 'Towards a research agenda for public–private partnerships in the 1990's', *Local Economy* 8: 292–306.

Bailey, N., Barker, A. and MacDonald, K. (1995) *Partnership Agencies in British Urban Policy*, London: UCL Press.

Bennett, R. J. and McCoshan, A. (1993) *Enterprise and Human Resource Development*, London: Paul Chapman.

Bennett, R. J. and Krebs, G. (1994) 'Local economic development partnerships: An analysis of policy networks in EC-LEDA local employment development strategies', *Regional Studies* 28: 119–40.

Bryson J. and Roering, W. (1987) 'Applying private sector strategic planning to the public sector, *Journal of the American Planning Association* 53: 9–22.

Cadbury, R. (1993) 'The partnership challenge', *Public Policy Review* 1(November/December): 11–12.

CEC (1987) *The Single Act: A New Frontier for the Community's Structural Policy*, Brussels: Commission of the European Communities.

—— (1988) *Establishing a Medium Term Community Action Programme to Foster the Economic and Social Integration of the Least Privileged Groups*, COM (88) 826, Brussels: CEC.

—— (1989) *Guide to the Reform of the Community's Structural Funds*, Luxembourg: CEC.

—— (1996) *Structural Funds and Cohesion Funds 1994–99: Regulations and Commentary*, Brussels: CEC.

Drucker, P. F. (1992) *Managing for the Future*, London: Butterworth-Heinemann.

Friedmann, J. and Weaver, C. (1979) *Territory and Function: The Evolution of Regional Planning*, Berkeley: University of California Press.

Fukuyama, F. (1995) *Trust: The Social Virtues and the Creation of Prosperity*, London: Hamish Hamilton.

Gutch, R. (1992) *Contracting Lessons from the US*, London: NCVO.

Harding, A. (1990) 'Public–private partnerships in urban regeneration', in M. Campbell (ed.) *Local Economic Policy*, London: Cassell.

—— (1991) 'The rise of urban growth coalitions, UK-style?', *Environment and Planning C, Government and Policy* 9: 295–318.

Hastings, A. (1996) 'Unravelling the process of partnership in urban regeneration policy', *Urban Studies* 33: 253–68.

Hobbes, T. (1651) *Leviathan*, New York: Collier Books.

Holland, R. C. (1984) 'The new era in public–private partnerships', in P. R. Porter and D. C. Sweet (eds) *Rebuilding America's Cities: Roads to Recovery*, New Brunswick, NJ: Center for Urban Policy Research.

Jennings, E. T. and Krane, D. (1994) 'Coordination and welfare reform: The quest for the philosophers stone', *Public Administration Review* 54: 341–8.

John, P. and Cole, A. (1995) 'Models of local decision-making networks in Britain and France', *Policy and Politics* 23: 303–12.

Kay, J. A. (1993) *Foundations of Corporate Success: How Business Strategies Add Value*, Oxford: Oxford University Press.

King, R. (1985) 'Corporatism and the local economy', in W. Grant (ed.) *The Political Economy of Corporation*, London: Macmillan.

Kotler, P., Haider, D. H. and Rein, I. (1993) *Marketing Places*, New York: Free Press.

Leach, S., Stewart, J. and Walsh, K. (1994) *The Changing Organisation and Management of Local Government*, Basingstoke: Macmillan.

Lipman, B. L. (1986) 'Corporation among egoists in Prisoners' Dilemma and chicken games, *Public Choice* 51: 315–31.

Luce, R. D. and Raiffa, H. (1957) *Games and Decision*, New York: Wiley.

Lyons, S. T. and Hamlin, R. E. (1991) *Creating an Economic Development Action Plan*, New York: Praeger.

McGregor, A., Kintrea, K., Fitzpatrick, I. and Urquhart, A. (1995) *Interim Evaluation of Wester Hailes Partnership*, Edinburgh: Scottish Office Central Research Unit.

Mackintosh, M. (1992) 'Partnership: Issues of policy and negotiation', *Local Economy* 7: 210–24.

McQuaid, R. W. (1993) 'Economic development and local authorities: The Scottish case', *Local Economy* 8: 100–16.

—— (1994) 'Partnership and urban economic development', *Social Science Working Paper No. 13*, Napier University, Edinburgh, April.

—— (1996) 'Social networks, entrepreneurship and regional development', in M. Danson (ed.) *Small Firm Formation and Regional Economic Development*, London: Routledge, pp. 118–31.

—— (1997) 'Local enterprise companies and rural development', *Journal of Rural Studies* 13: 197–212.

—— (1999) 'The role of partnerships in urban economic regeneration', *International Journal of Public–Private Partnerships* 2(1): 3–28.

McQuaid, R. W. and B. Christy (1999) 'European economic development partnerships – the case of the Eastern Scotland European Partnership', in L. Montanheiro, B. Haig, D. Morris and N. Linehan (eds) *Public and Private Sector Partnerships: Fostering Enterprise*, Sheffield: Sheffield Hallam University Press, pp. 355–66.

Nutt, P. C. and Backoff, R. W. (1992) *Strategic Management of Public and Third Sector Organizations*, San Francisco: Jossey-Bass.

Perrucci, R. and Pilisku, M. (1970) 'Leaders and ruling elites: The interorganizational bases of community power', *American Sociological Review* 35: 1040–56.

Ridley, M. (1997) *The Origins of Virtue*, London: Penguin.

Scottish Office, The (1993) *Progress in Partnership: A Consultation Paper on the Future of Urban Regeneration Policy in Scotland*, Edinburgh: HMSO.

Sellgren, J. (1990) 'Local economic development partnerships – an assessment of local authority economic development initiatives', *Local Government Studies* July/August: 57–78.

Straffin, P. D. (1977) 'The bandwagon curve', *American Journal of Political Science* 21: 695–709.

Stratton, C. (1989) Quoted in: OECD, *Mechanisms for Job Creation*, Paris: OECD, p. 81; and Askew (1991).

Syrett, S. (1997) 'The politics of partnership: The role of social partners in local economic development in Portugal', *European Urban and Regional Studies* 4: 99–114.

Wannop, U. (1990) 'The GEAR project: A perspective on the management of urban regeneration', *Town Planning Review* 62(3): 311–30.

Weaver, C. and Dennert, M. (1987) 'Economic development and the public–private partnership', *Journal of the American Planning Association* 50: 430–37.

Webb, A. (1991) Co-ordination: A problem in public sector management', *Policy and Politics* 19.

Weibull, J. W. (1995) *Evolutionary Game Theory*, London: MIT Press.

Wester Hailes Employment Initiative (1986) *Partnership Agreement*, Edinburgh: Wester Hailes Employment Initiative.

Zupan, M. A. (1990) 'Why nice guys finish last: A comment on Robert Axelrod's *The Evolution of Co-operation*', *Public Choice* 65: 291–2.

Notes

1   Hence it can be termed a 'form and function paradox' whereby the multi-functional nature of policies needed to deal with complex issues conflicts with the single or limited-function nature of the organizations, resulting in new partnership forms of strategy development and delivery which may then reduce some of the apparent benefits of having individual organizations.

2   There is danger of the term 'partnership' losing much meaning beyond that of being a vague, though benign, platitude. Similar lack of clarity in the use of the term can be seen in other areas. It is important to distinguish partnership from collusion where costs may be deliberately imposed on third parties.

3   Also no partner or other sector of the community should be worse off, or at least – applying the Hicks–Kaldor theorem – they could be compensated from the increased benefits for the amount that they are worse off. However, sometimes the benefits of partnerships are seen in terms of benefits for the organizations involved rather than for the wider society.

4   The authors consider this concept of (unequal) partnership to be quite different from concepts of local coalitions, local cooperation or local governance (King 1985; Harding 1991). They stress the need for partnerships to ensure both horizontal integration between agents in different programmes and vertical coordination to ensure programmes are effectively operated and they also stress the importance of learning for organizations within a flexible framework that reflects different local circumstances.

5   Such difference between partners may be disguised in the strategy documents by including general aims and objectives that meet the wishes of all the partners, but the underlying tensions are likely to arise when specific projects are being developed or implemented.

6   These include cooperation as a result of central authority, game theory and trust and altruism (Fukuyama 1995) which particularly may be useful in explaining why partnerships might be developed. Network analysis (John and Cole 1995), theories of bureaucracy, contract theories and strategic alliances literature (mentioned above) can be useful in analysing the setting up and operating of partnerships more effectively; while managerial theories and strategy literature can be particularly useful in considering the setting up and development of partnerships in urban–regeneration theories based on growth coalitions or local-regime theories (Bailey *et al.* 1995).

7   If A = the high pay-off, B = medium pay-off, C = low pay-off, D = zero pay-off, w = chance for future interaction, then if $w \geq \max[(A - B)/(B - D), (A - B)/(A - C)]$, there exists a Nash equilibrium in which all the players will use tit for tat. A Nash equilibrium is that, given what the other player has done, then each player makes the best response. It gives a unique solution meeting four conditions: the solution must be independent of the choice of utility function; both players cannot simultaneously do better than the Nash solution (i.e. a Pareto optimal solution); the solution is independent of irrelevant alternatives; and the solution must be symmetrical (i.e. if players swap over the solution remains the same with the pay-offs reversed). The game can be extended to a non-zero sum, n-player, cooperative (i.e. players communicate and can make binding agreements) game (see Straffin 1977 on voting). Lipman (1986) generalizes the Nash equilibrium results to the game Chicken. He argues that there are strong forces pushing players towards mutual cooperation even when they are self-interested and there is no central authority in a modification of the Prisoners' Dilemma, called Chicken. Here each party tries to prevail over the other party through creating fear, rather than in the Prisoners' Dilemma where establishing credibility means instilling trust.

8   It is worth finishing with a salutary example of cooperation between antagonists' illustrated in the writings of combatants in World War I in northern France and Belgium. For example, one British officer wrote that he was 'astonished to observe German soldiers walking about within rifle range behind their own line. Our own men appeared to take no notice . . .' Both sides apparently believed in the policy of 'live and let live' (Dugdale 1932, quoted in Axelrod 1984). However, much of this cooperation came to an end (and deaths rose) when head-quarter's staff ordered raids, so they controlled the actions and stopped the front-line troops reciprocating only to actions from the enemy, hence preventing tit-for-tat responses.

2 Public–private partnerships

Sectoral perspectives

Peter Carroll and Peter Steane

2.1 Introduction

The broad aim of this chapter is to examine the development of public–private partnerships, with an emphasis on the impact on partnerships of the perspective and expectations of the public, non-profit and business sectors. It is divided into the following main sections. Section 2.2 is a brief section in which definitions of the key concepts are provided. Section 2.3 describes the development of partnerships that highlight significant changes to their extent and nature over time. Section 2.4 examines the changing role of the state in regard to its role in partnerships. Section 2.5 examines the role of business. This is followed by a conclusion in which several key themes are indicated, notably the need for more systematic research.

There can be a variety of reasons why organizations from different sectors enter into partnerships. First, there are external reasons where regulatory systems or competitive forces may necessitate different actors working together in areas previously the responsibility of only one actor. For example, charitable organizations may find compelling reasons to establish a working relationship with privatized housing authorities in a deregulated market in order to service the needs of homeless people. Second, there may be internal factors that stimulate the establishment of partnerships. For example, the involvement of other actors in a partnership can spread the financial risk of an operation or raise the credibility profile of one or other party. A case in point may be a business desiring to link up with a charity in a philanthropic venture.

2.2 Definitions

In a chapter that focuses upon public–private partnerships it is important to indicate the ways in which these terms are defined. Our starting point is that there is no clear distinction between the public and private realms, with any definition being largely arbitrary or designed to meet the particular needs of the authors in question. A case in point is the status of political parties. These are private organizations in the sense that, in liberal democracies, they are created by private persons, but they have a range of public and private purposes, most of which are political in nature. The following definitions are subject to these limitations and are intended to provide a sense of direction for the reader.

The terms public, public sector and state, unless otherwise noted, are used interchangeably, referring to that set of institutions which exercise legitimate authority over populations, for the most part within a given geographical area. The term private or private sector refers to all institutions other than those of the state. The term business refers to organizations the major aim of which is to generate profits for their owners. The owners may be private individuals or a state agency (a public or state enterprise), or a combination of both. In the countries with which we are concerned most businesses are owned by private individuals, with a declining incidence of state enterprise. Non-profit organizations have a variety of objectives but tend to be characterized more by altruistic concerns and less by profits. Any surplus earned is not distributed to those who may exercise control over it (Hansmann 1980: 838). This places them closer to the public than business organizations in terms of their motives, although they do not exercise legitimate authority over populations, other than as agreed to by their members or as delegated to them by a state agency (Mason 1996; Jeavons 1992; Paton 1996).

The term partnership is used in the fashion defined by McQuaid in Chapter 1. Partnerships are cooperative ventures that rely upon agreement between actors in return for some positive outcome for each participant, which could be some economic or social goal or potential for synergy. Hence, public–private partnerships are agreed, cooperative ventures that involve at least one public and one private-sector institution as partners. This definition is broad enough to encompass a very wide diversity in the types of partnerships and the circumstances in which they arise. It can include the loose network of consultative relationships that exist between a government department and a range of peak business associations, as well as partnerships in the narrower, legal sense. Indeed, it is worth pointing out that the phrase public–private partnership has come to be used in a very loose fashion. In the legal sense a relationship with partnership status results in certain legal implications, notably the notions that partners may have a joint and several liability for the obligations of the partnership and that the action of any partner can bind the entire partnership (Kucera 1998). As Kucera notes, the term partnership should be used with discretion if the actors in a relationship are not intending that they should be liable for each other's actions. If they mean that they are working together to provide, for example, a more efficient and economic service,

> . . . then it may be more prudent actually to say that, instead of using buzz words that may imply other meanings.
>
> (Kucera 1998)

Partners have expectations in regard to the benefits of the partnership, with expectations being defined as beliefs and opinions about a partnership. In this sense expectations have, at the least, four major, often overlapping roles: that of motivator, shaper, norm and change agent. First, they are motivators in encouraging actors to enter into discussions about forming a partnership. Each actor may believe that a partnership will bring about benefits otherwise not achievable, or difficult to achieve. Second, beliefs about what should constitute a partnership, including the basic terms of the agreement, are a vital force in shaping the form and content of the agreement. Third, norms of behaviour are determined usually after the agreement by perceptions about what constitutes appropriate and acceptable behaviour, and can influence a partnership as it proceeds. Last, when the terms of the agreement are perceived as no longer adequate, new expectations come into play in modifying or even terminating the original agreement as change agents.

2.3 The development of public–private partnerships

Historical developments

It is difficult to conceive of a time or context in which there were not public–private partnerships. Indeed, it is not too fanciful to conceive of the relationship between the state and the public as, in some respects, a complex, dynamic partnership between those who govern and those who are governed. Recent decades have seen a new focus on the notion of partnerships between the public and private sectors, developing first in the USA during the 1970s then spreading at various rates to other countries. However, in our focus on contemporary development we should not forget that such partnerships have been a constant feature of state–society relationships.

In Australia, for example, there has always been a strong, if variable, commitment to broadly liberal notions of market freedom, competition and managerial prerogatives. However, the Australian state also has played a very active, interventionist role in society and the economy, though this began to change rapidly in the 1980s. The state in Australia, argues Pusey,

> . . . was not excluded from the private economy but rather joined it in a relationship of strong partnership
>
> (Pusey 1988: 30)

Historically, Australian business welcomed the role played by a more activist, interventionist state, either acting on its own initiative, or in partnership with business. In terms of our conceptual framework, it could be argued that the expectations of these actors were working as motivators with a distinctly positive impact on public–private partnerships, such as economic development. The achievement of this as a goal was slowed by Australia's particular physical conditions. The solution, at least in part, was to use the greater resources of the state to overcome these barriers.

Government was to use its resources to gain access to international, largely British, finance and to carry the risk involved, acting as entrepreneur and developer in a fashion readily understandable to nineteenth-century businesses. There was also a clear expectation that, for example, the physical development of the infrastructure would involve the private sector, with the bulk of the work contracted out to individual businesses. In practice the situation became more complex as in several areas the private sector not only lacked the financial resources for large-scale infrastructure development, it often lacked necessary organizational and technical capacities. This was most obvious in regard to the development of railways, where colonial governments frequently had to develop their own, 'in-house', organizational and technical capacities to develop railways at the desired rates (Carroll 1995).

By the early part of the twentieth century, different coalitions of liberal and labour-affiliated groups introduced a wide range of welfare, labour and citizen legislation at federal and state levels (Castles 1985). In terms of our conceptual model, expectations about partnerships changed, resulting in an expanded role for government. Similarly, in the first decade of the twentieth century urban, industrial business interests and labour interests combined to establish a web of tariff, labour, arbitration and general regulatory controls to 'protect' the Australian economy from international competition (Castles 1988; Capling and Galligan 1992; Glezer 1982).

In other words the web of public–private partnerships in Australia increased sharply, to include welfare, labour relations, immigration and trade. However, it was a contentious increase not wholly welcome, with the attitudes of business becoming far more differentiated. In particular, whereas the nineteenth-century use of the Australian state for economic development was largely pragmatic in nature, the early twentieth-century developments saw a distinct ideological dimension enter debates, stimulated by the increasing political success of organized labour.

The Australian state developed economic relationships of a pragmatic nature, concerned more with the 'domestic defence' of industry from the rigours of inter-national competition. These developments stand out in marked contrast to the smaller, European states (Castles 1988; Bell and Head 1994; 9–10). Over a similar period of time, Austria, Sweden and Norway emerged with detailed public policies of microeconomic reform, social welfare, industry development and various labour-market programs, characterized by Castles as policies of 'domestic compensation', as opposed to Australian policies of 'domestic defence' (Castles 1988). The aim in the former case was to continue to expose domestic business to the forces of international competition, not to protect it and run the risk of overly protected, inefficient, domestic monopolies. As Bell and Head describe it, Australian protectionism came without much microeconomic oversight:

In fact, in a range of areas from foreign investment and trade practices to the operation of key utilities and service industries, there was a pattern of neglect in microeconomic policy and very little state scrutiny of the detailed workings of the economy.

(Bell and Head 1994: 11)

Historically, there were clear and largely agreed expectations between elites regarding the role of markets, business and the state, for example,

> The ruling assumption throughout twentieth century Australia has been that markets, not government officials, knew best how to run their firms and industries. Rarely has the Australian state challenged the concept of the autonomous firm or the concept of private management prerogative.
>
> (Bell and Head 1994: 11)

However, from the post-1945 era, there was increasing disquiet about the maintenance of this pattern of public–business partnerships. This period saw a more or less continuous decline in export prices for rural and mineral exports at the same time as the import cost of manufactured imports rose. The result was a severe and continuing difficulty with Australia's terms of trade, exacerbated by relatively inefficient, domestic manufacturing industry, so long shielded from international competition by policies of domestic defence. Uncertainty became a feature of government–business relationships as the earlier, Keynesian-inspired belief that it was possible for governments to engage in successful, macroeconomic demand management fell into disrepute. The broad consensus that supported policies of domestic defence disappeared and the 1970s and early 1980s were marked by substantial conflict between governments, business and labour. Government attempted to bring a new consensus into its economic management with income policies and industry plans. What emerged was a call for a radical change in the role of the state in the economy at a time when the influence of the proponents of neoclassical economics (neo-liberalism or the new Right) was growing both in Australia and elsewhere.

Non-profit organizations have had a different contribution to Australia's economic history. Many of the 'friendly societies' or 'cooperatives' sprang out of liberal sentiments of the nineteenth century or religious beliefs generally. Unlike the relative independence of such groups in the United States, Australian non-profit organizations mimicked developments in Britain, where a dependence upon public funding prevailed. While this is still the case today, the roles played by non-profit organizations is changing. The effects of a general and often negative reassessment of Keynesian approaches to economic management, for example, has had a delayed but increasingly significant impact on the charitable sector. The Industry Commission report of 1995, for example, sought to redefine relationships between the state and non-profit groups by legislative and regulatory changes. The result has been the introduction of public tendering and contracts for clearly defined and accountable services that are legally enforceable. The general tenor of the Commission's report was that a quasi-USA system of non-profits working within a more rigorously market-oriented system was appropriate.

Recent development

The stagflation of the 1970s and early 1980s, combined with budget cutbacks and their impact on local, regional and national economies in the major OECD countries spurred a search for new or revived options to deal with these issues, including partnerships with business and voluntary groups (Walzer and Jacobs 1998). In essence, the 1950s and 1960s had been years of budgetary expansion, combined with an often-unquestioned belief in the capacity of the state to cope with a wide range of economic and social issues. Public–private partnerships existed but had a markedly lower profile than came to be the case. At the same time, economic recession brought increasing demands for solutions, at a time when the capacity of the state, unaided, to meet those demands, was falling.

Business, at least large business, was well aware of this situation and the increasingly competitive nature of local, regional and national-government efforts to stimulate their economies, particularly as regards employment creation. In this context businesses could gain significant concessions from governments in a variety of areas, such as free services, low-interest-rate loans and local tax concessions. The packages of concessions typically were presented as major efforts to promote local economic development in partnership with business (Walzer and Jacobs 1998; Walzer and York 1998).

The realization that such competition could be costly, in turn, stimulated local, regional and national governments to refocus their efforts and attempt to reinvigorate existing businesses and to encourage new business start-ups. In the United Kingdom this took the form, for example, of a series of new government offices for the regions, providing a range of assistance measures under the Single Regeneration Budget and related European Union funds, targeted at economically depressed areas (Mawson and Spencer 1997).

The efforts of public officials to attract and reinvigorate their local or national economies necessarily involved them, to varying extents, in a range of entrepreneurial activities with which most were unfamiliar. In particular, their activities increasingly involved widespread networking and the development of a range of public–private partnerships, the subject of this chapter.

It is likely that public officials would have undertaken such efforts even without any major policy shifts or changes in ideology. However, their efforts were legitimized by the increasing influence of the proponents of supply-side economics and policy prescriptions that emerged out of that school of thought. This, combined with the coming to power of Presidents Carter and Reagan in the USA and Prime Minister Thatcher in the UK (Colman 1989 provides a good summary of the US situation in the 1970s and 1980s) strongly encouraged governments at all levels not only to privatize but to look to the private sector as a role model and potential partner.

The result has been a dramatic growth in the development of a very wide range of public–private partnerships and public policy in regard to such partnerships. As a crude measure of their extent and importance, a search through GOVBOT, the US federal government's database of Web sites using the words 'public private partnership' resulted in 8,830 hits. A similar search through the UK government's CCTA Government Information Service resulted in over 1,000 documents being identified. Influential national lobby groups promoting public–private partnerships have been established in the USA (The National Council for Public–Private Partnerships, the successor to The Privatization Council, established in 1985) and Canada (The Canadian Council for Public–Private Partnerships).

2.4 The state and public–private partnerships

It is difficult to generalize with any degree of accuracy regarding the expectations of the state in regard to public–private partnerships. Expectations vary from state to state, over time within each state (particularly where that involves changes of the political parties in government), from agency to agency within the state and from level to level of the state. However, a few general observations can be made. The first is that, as described above, there has always been a substantial extent of public–private partnership in twentieth-century OECD governments, indicating that, at least in the areas of the partnerships, expectations are positive. Even in the USA, partnerships have long been a feature of government, usually encouraged by the state, from the local, to state government and national levels, as described by Colman (1989).

The second is that there has been a rapid growth in the number of partnerships since the 1970s, especially during the 1980s and 1990s (Colman 1989; Walzer and Jacobs 1998). It has been most obvious in countries that have experienced conservative governments characterized by their antipathy to the expansion of the welfare state since 1945 and an accompanying commitment to privatization, contracting out and regulatory reform. The governments of Ronald Reagan and Margaret Thatcher are the most obvious examples but it is difficult to think of an OECD member that has not been marked to some extent by these characteristics, even when governments of the Left were in office. In Australia, for example, it was the Australian Labor Government that introduced the notion of partnerships for the encouragement of growth in the information-technology sector, with an emphasis upon export development (Department of Industry, Science and Technology 1995). While specific expectations have varied, their growing use clearly indicated beliefs that there were advantages to be gained from such partnerships.

A third trend has been an increase in the types of partnerships created, sometimes to avoid legislative constraints, sometimes on a pragmatic basis in the attempt to ensure that the most appropriate organizational form was adopted (Colman 1989; Jacobs 1998). In the UK, for example, there has been a tendency for local authorities to make increasing use of the legal form of companies for their public–private partnerships. A fourth trend has been the distinct increase in partnerships at the local and regional, rather than national levels, though often initiated and funded by national governments. Their major purpose has been to stimulate or reinvigorate local economic development and a rich literature addressing partnerships at this level has grown up (see e.g. Andersen and Eliassen 1993; Goetz and Clarke 1993; Sudarskis and Edwards 1993; Harding *et al.* 1994; Leonardi 1995; Middlemas *et al.* 1995; Walzer and Jacobs 1998; to name but a few).

In other words the expectations of the state generally have been positive, with a variety of policy developments aimed, at least in part, at providing wider opportunities for the development of partnerships. In the earlier years of the Reagan and Thatcher regimes the emphasis was, at least as portrayed by the media, on providing opportunities for the private, particularly business, sector to undertake work traditionally performed by public-sector agencies. This was the case most dramatically in the UK as the large-scale privatizations of the 1980s took place. More recently, the Blair government's 'Third Way' indicates a tendency where the private sector is less regarded as the sole saviour of society's economic and social interests. Rather, the Blair government has encouraged the use of whatever sector or mix between business, public or non-profit organizations can provide more immediate value for money (VFM).

However, while expectations have been positive, they have not, for the most part, been naive, usually being tempered with the realization that they are not appropriate in all situations for all purposes. The Private Finance Initiative (PFI), in the UK, for example, while strongly encouraging an expanded use of the private sector in the delivery of public services, applied very strict tests governing its use (Hall 1998). In this context it is interesting to note that while the Blair government commissioned a review of the PFI, it accepted the review's recommendations for the retention of PFI, relaxed its requirements in regard to the use of private funds and, in the terms of reference for its Comprehensive Spending Review, called for government departments to examine the scope for greater use of public–private partnerships in the delivery of public services (Hall 1998: 1).

There have been few systematic, empirical studies of the expectations or motives of public servants in regard to partnerships, though the literature is growing. A recent UK study found that:

> ... that the driving force for ... partnership with the private sector had been the desire to secure European and central-government funding. Interviewees listed several reasons for promoting private-sector involvement: a sense that you cannot succeed in economic development without the active participation of the private sector; to allow the public sector to concentrate on its role as enabler, rather than service provider; to bring in investment; to influence public-sector policy, and to bring in an outside view.
>
> (Department for Education and Employment 1997)

The international arena, the state and public–private partnerships

Given the growth in the use of public–private partnerships in key OECD countries such as the USA and the UK, it is not surprising that a similar, if somewhat later, enthusiasm for their use appears in major, international, intergovernmental organizations. In the UNO, for example, the notion of partnerships for development is well entrenched, with an increasing emphasis on the importance of the development role of the private sector in partnership with the state and aid agencies. In 1994, in responding to the recommendations of the Rio Earth Summit on public–private collaboration, the United Nations Development Programme (UNDP) and the Business Council for Sustainable Development (BCSD) initiated public–private partnerships for the urban environment. This global programme to promote public–private partnerships in support of sustainable development goals became operational later that year when UNDP and the not-for-profit Swiss association Sustainable Project Management (SPM, an offshoot of BCSD) joined forces (UNDP 1997).

As early as 1982 the OECD Council authorized a new Programme of Co-operation and Action concentrating on local employment initiatives (ILEs), with the objective of promoting the exchange of experience and information on the development of local employment and enterprise. It later published a text that containing a series of case studies based on experiences from the programme, noting that job creation in OECD countries until the 1970s tended to be a matter for central governments alone, with the private and voluntary sectors rarely directly involved in economic development (OECD 1993). As the authors note, this changed in the 1980s as high levels of unemployment persisted and spread. In response to increasing pressures from their local communities and from central governments, local authorities, private and voluntary agencies and the business community sought new ways to promote economic and social development. They quickly realized that it was essential to work in partnerships with one another, if their efforts were to mobilize maximum resources and make a substantial impact. It was a trend strengthened by political and administrative decentralization (OECD 1993: 7).

The European Union similarly now places considerable emphasis on the use of public–private partnerships. Neil Kinnock, for example, the EU Commissioner, has noted that,

> As far as large infrastructure projects are concerned, the Commission is looking into the ways that it can encourage private/public partnerships as it was asked last December by the European Council at Essen.
>
> (Kinnock 1995: 5)

In summary, the expectations of major, international, intergovernmental organizations in regard to public–private partnerships have been growing and, for the most part, have been positive. This is particularly so for international organizations dominated by OECD members, where they have brought to bear their influence and experience in promoting the greater use of partnerships. Even in the area of aid for developing countries, long dominated by public-sector aid agencies, there has been a rapid growth in support for the value of public–private partnerships in promoting development. This is most obvious in the UNDP's urban-environment program, which has now thrown substantial weight behind its 'PPP' project, following an initial, pilot study (UNDP 1997). This is not to argue that, in the context of developing countries, there has yet been a dramatic shift to the use of such partnerships; it is to argue that the UNDP, as with other agencies, sees an increasingly valuable role for partnerships and is devoting considerable resources to the encouragement of their use.

Local government and public–private partnerships

As noted above, the earliest and perhaps most significant growth in the post-1945 focus on partnerships developed at the local level, notably in the USA (Walzer and York 1998: 52). There has been a long history of government–business partnerships in the USA, if not always favourably regarded (Colman 1989: 173–4). This trend was accelerated in the 1950s and 1960s, stimulated by federal-government programmes regarding slum clearance, urban renewal and economic-development legislation for depressed regions. Perhaps most significant was the Economic Opportunity Act of 1964 and its War on Poverty, built around local-community action agencies. While non-profit bodies were the driving force on these latter bodies, local businesses and business organizations were often represented.

The period 1977–87 saw a sharply increasing emphasis upon the private sector in policy development and implementation by the Carter and Reagan administrations, resulting in an expansion of old and an increase in new partnerships (Colman 1989: 177). Influential reports, such as 'Building Partnerships', released by the President's Task Force on Private Sector Initiatives,1982, recommended that business firms double their level of cash contributions to non-profit organizations engaged in public service, double their level of involvement in community-service activities and that they:

> ... commit themselves to active involvement in the development and enhancement of partnerships between the private and public sectors in their communities.

> (Colman 1989: 177)

In 1984 the National Governors' Association adopted a policy emphasizing the role of state governments in international trade and proposed federal–state partnership actions to educate the public about the importance of world trade to economic well-being and to deliver commercial services and counselling to individual firms entering international markets. In 1987 the National Governors' Association enunciated a set of goals in 'Education for Economic Growth', consisting of eight goals, the second being, 'Creation of broad and effective partnerships among business, labor, and the education professions, including business partnerships with individual schools'. This followed a similar proposal by the National Science Board in 1983 (Colman 1989: 195–9). While some of the partnership programmes initiated by the Carter administration were terminated under President Reagan, President Clinton has re-emphasized the role of public–private partnerships at the local level, with his empowerment zone and enterprise community program, relying primarily on tax credits and reallocated program funds (Clarke 1998).

The development of partnerships at the local and regional levels also has been noticeable in the UK (Jacobs 1998). As in the US, they have been used primarily for local economic-development purposes, with an emphasis on urban regeneration. In 1994, for example, the Single Regeneration Budget required active, three-way partnerships between public authorities, businesses and local communities in urban regeneration. More recently, the Blair government announced its intention to make partnerships a key feature of its plans for regional government in the UK (House of Commons Library 1998).

Not all local and regional governments are unreservedly enthusiastic about the development of public–private partnerships. However, as Walzer and York (1998) conclude in one of the few attempts to quantitatively measure the growth and importance of partnerships at the local level:

- 80 per cent of US local officials surveyed reported partnerships as important or very important to their local economic-development initiatives.
- 60 per cent reported that the number of partnerships had increased in the 1989–94 period, with an average city in the sample with a population of 25,000 or more reporting an average of twenty-eight partnerships.

Most officials reported a high degree of satisfaction with their partnerships and consider a high percentage of them to have been successful, providing a reasonable return to the city (Walzer and York 1998: 66). These findings are mirrored in the UK, where a survey of partnerships engaged in by local governments undertaken by Newchurch and Company Ltd, found that:

> Local authorities recognise the value of involving the business community in developing and implementing policy, although some consider the benefits of consultation to be outweighed by the process involved.
>
> (Newchurch and Company Ltd 1997)

An indication of the high expectations and growing use of partnerships in the UK was the 1996 establishment of 'The Public–Private Partnerships Programme Ltd'. Set up by the Local Authority Associations in England

and Wales, with support from all the major political parties, its aim is to deliver greater investment in local services through partnerships between the public and private sectors. More specifically it lobbies government for changes to the regulations that hinder the development of PFI and other forms of partnership with the private sector and helps identify and assist in delivering existing and new council pathfinder projects. Its efforts, in part, resulted in the UK government's introduction of the 1997 *Local Government (Contracts) Bill* (Department of the Environment 1997).

The local-government lobbying that resulted in the above Bill is instructive, for it clearly indicated that while local governments were positive in regard to the value of partnerships, they were aware of the difficulties, especially the legal difficulties associated with partnerships. In particular, they were uncertain as to the legal standing of partnership-type contracts entered into with private bodies, an uncertainty which was removed with the introduction of the Bill (Department of the Environment 1997).

2.5 Business and public–private partnerships

In general, there seems to be little identifiable business opposition to the principle or practice of public–private partnerships and, on the basis of the existence of a number of national associations created specifically to lobby for the use of these partnerships, substantial support for their use. The Canadian Council for Public–Private Partnerships, for example, lists ninety 'Corporate Members', including some of the largest corporations in Canada and its statement of objectives makes its support very clear:

> The Canadian Council for Public–Private Partnerships is:
> A clearing house for knowledge and information with respect to public–private partnership projects and developments in Canada,
> An information exchange promoting dialogue between public and private sector participants and interest groups,
> An advocate for public–private partnership development with decision-makers at all levels of government in Canada,
> A sponsor of conferences, seminars and publications designed to increase the awareness of the benefits of public–private partnerships for all Canadians.
> (Canadian Council for Public–Private Partnerships 1999)

The National Council for Public–Private Partnerships in the USA expresses almost identical views, describing its mission as:

> ... to advocate and facilitate the formation of public–private partnerships at the federal, state and local levels, where appropriate, and to raise the awareness of governments and businesses of the means by which their

cooperation can cost effectively provide the public with quality goods, services and facilities.

(National Council for Public–Private Partnerships 1999)

It might be argued that statements such as these express the ideal, the goal, rather than the real world of government–business relationships. However, at least in part the actions of both business and not-for-profit organizations over recent years has been strongly supportive of this goal. In the USA, for example, the Federal Government changed the title of the influential National Performance Review, led by Vice-President Al Gore, to the National Partnership for Reinventing Government in 1998. Within the context of the Review the business sector stepped forward to play a significant role in the Review, taking up membership of at least twenty-eight federal executive boards and more than 100 federal executive associations, working with state and local governments to help reinvent government (Kamensky 1999).

While there has been much development at the national level the bulk of part-nerships have occurred at local and regional levels, though often supported or even sponsored by national agencies (see Allen *et al.* 1989; Colman, 1989 and Walzer and Jacobs 1998 for good descriptions and discussions of these develop-ments). As Colman notes,

The seventies and eighties witnessed an expansion and intensification of public–private-sector relationships at both state and local levels. Spurred by national business organizations such as the Committee for Economic Development and the Business Roundtable, corporation boards and chief executives began to devote increased attention and resources to the exercise of 'corporate social responsibility', with particular stress on business partici-pation in and assistance to local government and community betterment. The urgency for strengthened public–private-sector collaboration was height-ened by the decreasing federal role in assisting state–local activities, beginning in 1978 and accentuated by the Reagan administration.

(Colman 1989: 127)

In the 1990s the Clinton administrations added extra weight to these local and regional developments in the shape of the Empowerment Zone and Enterprise Community initiative, intended to play a central part in enhancing job creation and urban redevelopment in economically depressed areas. A central focus of the initiative was the use of local development partnerships (see the EZ/EC Web page at http://www.ezec.gov/About/implemen.html for details of the initiative). In other words, at all levels there have been growing, often realized and positive expectations expressed by business regarding partnerships, expectations that provide a sound basis for such partnerships.

Similar enthusiasm developed in Britain during and following the prime ministership of Margaret Thatcher. An increasing variety of partnerships developed at the local and regional levels. As Jacobs notes,

> In Birmingham and the West Midlands, as elsewhere in the EU, national governments and the private sector create partnerships because partnerships are adaptable when dealing with specific localized problems. They are generally not constrained by the limitations of traditional local government ... Birmingham's 1996–1997 Economic Development Program, therefore, depends upon partnerships to drive economic growth in the city by effectively linking city partners and programs to regional and European initiatives.
>
> (Jacobs 1996: 75)

In particular, the Private Finance Initiative (PFI) was announced by the then Chancellor of the Exchequer in his 1992 Autumn Statement. Its aim was to:

> ... bring the private sector more directly into the provision of public services, with the public sector as an enabler and, where appropriate, guardian of the interests of the users and customers of public services. The initiative developed from several earlier projects in which private capital was used to finance infrastructure projects which traditionally would have required a major public sector capital expenditure. The concept underlying such public/private partnerships is that the government's prime interest in public projects is the service which they deliver to users rather than the specific capital asset used to deliver those services. This is in contrast to the traditional approach to public projects which risks focusing on physical aspects of the design of the capital asset rather than the services to be delivered by it.
>
> (National Audit Office 1998: 1)

While the evidence suggests that business is generally positive about partnerships, especially with the public sector, it is for a variety of motives. A case study of business motives in the Coventry and Warwickshire area of the UK found, for example, that:

> Interviewees expressed a mix of reasons for their involvement in partnership, most powerfully the expectation of direct business benefit. Other motivations included: a chance to meet people in order to gather information about business opportunities; to lobby others about their own wants, needs and expectations; to be part of something, especially if the partnership is successful; a sense that this was something that they should do, having been invited to join; a wish to make a contribution; personal development.
>
> (Department for Education and Employment 1997)

Partnerships involving non-profits

Non-profit organizations can be characterized as distinctive from public organizations because of the emphasis on reputation and trust, sometimes lower labour costs, and attention to vision (Oster 1995). Research from the United Kingdom (Hudson, 1995; Paton, 1996) and the United States (Jeavons, 1992) highlights the importance of non-profit related values in the management of non-profit organizations. Private companies may well manifest humanitarian concerns, just as non-profit organizations may manifest instrumental values. But generally their *raisons d'être* manifestly differ. Private companies are presumed to exist primarily for profit – the general measure of their performance – while non-profit organizations are presumed to be concerned with service for some ideological end.

Partnerships between business, government and non-profits can be problematic when values clash. While non-profits do not hold exclusive rights to ideological and value-related goals, the context of competition sometimes evident in emerging partnerships can be one that favours business-orientated actors with configurations adept at manifesting operations aligned with a 'return-on-investment' (Rose-Ackerman 1996).

The implication for partnerships where one or more actors are overt in referring to values and ideology is that such phenomena are likely to impact on the expectations of actors. This builds on our conceptual framework, to the extent that values or ideology can influence motivations, beliefs, norms of behaviour, and new expectations in managing and delivering a service. In some partnerships, this may take the form of more conscious and overt consideration of the intangibles. For others, priorities regarding efficiencies and transparency may challenge non-profit partners to engage management practices more aligned with the corporate world

2.6 Conclusion

Public–private partnerships bring together parties with somewhat different motives, values and objectives. This does not necessarily pose dangers for the success of partnerships. Partners with differing positions can stimulate a healthy debate leading to innovatory approaches and a successful partnership. Indeed, one of the virtues of the debate regarding the merits of partnerships is that it has encouraged the examination of a far greater range of organizational means for dealing with issues than might have been the case in earlier decades. Similarly, the mere placing together of persons from different sectors with differing values and objectives can be a valuable learning experience for all parties.

However, where the parties involved or potentially involved have not only differing values and objectives, but are inflexible in regard to those values and objectives, particularly where their positions are ideologically embedded, then the potential for conflict is obvious. O'Faircheallaigh *et al.* (1999: 298) concludes that interactions between parties from different sectors often are based on the assumption that the same values and incentives are operative. But what if they are not? Business will usually have a predominantly commercial perspective in a partnership, commonly, but not always, focused on profits. Alternatively the business partner may have a concern to develop market credibility by being associated with government, or may have political motives such as gaining an 'insider' position in policy processes, working to achieve policy outcomes favourable to business. In contrast, government partners may be motivated by values less entrenched in the business sector, such as a greater concern for equity, attempting to provide, for example, telecommunications services to remote areas. Non-profit organizations might enter a partnership for altruistic reasons, with the partnership seen primarily as a means of securing financial support for their activities from government. At other times non-profit organizations may have political objectives, aimed at influencing policy, based on their core values; for example, where conservation groups enter partnerships with business and government regarding sustainable development. With such a variety of motives and underlying values the potential for conflict in public–private partnerships is very real.

Even where the values of the partners are similar, there can be concerns for outcomes. It may be, for example, that all partners in a particular partnership are sympathetic with the neo-liberal economic theories which underpin much of the policy drive associated with privatization, regulatory reform and public–private partnerships (Fischer 1980). Such theories and the policies they inform are by no means value free. They place a high premium on the market, individual enterprise and competition. Where partnerships develop in which, for example, the public-sector partners are imbued with these values, there may be an undue dominance of values associated with efficiency and cost effectiveness, leading to the neglect of values concerning equity and social harmony, which may be more likely to be the case where the public-sector actor in a partnership dominates the partnership (Halligan and Power 1992).

Indeed, there is often likely to be some power imbalance between the members in a partnership. When a partnership is characterized by the resource dependency of one or more partners on another partner (often, but not always, government), for example, there is fertile ground for the development of an organizational homogeneity with the loss of valuable, distinctive, organizational characteristics (DiMaggio and Powell 1983). This can raise serious issues for non-profit, voluntary organizations, where it is the very fact of their particular value base and organizational distinctiveness that accounts for their attraction (Jeavons 1992; Nygren *et al.* 1994).

It is difficult to be precise about the impact of partners' expectations upon partnership performance for two major reasons. One, there is a distinct lack of empirical data available. The little which exists tends to provide either evaluations of the financial and economic costs and benefits of partnerships, or data regarding the attitudes to existing partnerships of public and private partners. It does not measure the impact of expectations upon performance or partners' satisfaction, although some inferences can be drawn from the data. Two, as the range of types of partnership and of partners is so wide it is difficult to generalize with any degree of precision about expectations and their impact.

As the above sections indicate, the views of both public and private bodies regarding partnerships have been generally positive, but not entirely or uniformly so. At one extreme, for example, we have the example of largely negative political and business expectations from South Yorkshire (Chandler 1998). At the other we have the very positive expectations and impacts reported regarding London Underground and its £1 billion partnership with the Transys Consortium (Edwards 1998). Moreover, it is clear that expectations change substantially over time. Even in the South Yorkshire case the mutual and initially very hostile expectations of the local authorities and business groups became positive over time. They were spurred on by changes in the ideology and policies of the Labour Party and a reluctance of central government to award grants and subsidies faced with a lack of partnerships. A similar situation seems to have been the case in Germany, which has lacked the US tradition of public–private partnerships until very recently (Friederichs 1998). German local-government officials are reported as fearing a loss of control and being overwhelmed by business when it comes to partnerships, with the result that progress has been slow, based on more limited, smaller scale partnerships compared with the US (Friederichs 1998: 188).

The political and economic climates that stimulated the creation of today's partnerships may themselves be undergoing changes. The 'hegemony of neo-liberal individualism', as some would see it, arguably is losing its predominance in public discourse and policy (Mulgan 1998). There are now thirteen governments in Europe characterized as 'Centre Left' in their ideological orientation. This trend may be responding to a fundamental shift in social perceptions where collaboration and interdependence is seen as preferable to the competitive individualism stressed by Margaret Thatcher ('there is no such thing as society'). Such feelings, in part, lay behind Tony Blair's Third Way and Gerhard Schroeder's *Neue Mitte*. Their political challenge is to achieve both market competitiveness and social cohesion at the same time. Whether or not they achieve such an ambitious goal is debatable. In neither case have the policies pursued since gaining office been radically different from those pursued by their conservative predecessors. Their view that government has a role to play, not so much in the direct provision of services, but in facilitating the involvement of other parties in providing those services has 'partnership' overtones that echo those predecessors.

In essence the 1980s and 1990s have been a period of mutual learning by partners and potential partners in the political, legal and management challenges posed by the use of public–private partnerships. Expectations, while largely positive, have been cautious and rightly so on all sides, at least outside of the USA. There are signs that this caution is being replaced by greater enthusiasm, to a more rapid embrace of the use of partnerships as a valuable policy instrument. One of the aims of The Public–Private Partnerships Programme Ltd, established by UK local authorities, for example, was to provide a source of advice for authorities uncertain of the challenges associated with partnerships. Another aim was to use it to lobby central government to remove perceived barriers to the greater use of PFI for creating partnerships (Department of the Environment 1997). Both were signs that very active and successful policy learning was taking place, leading to revisions to the PFI and the clarification of the legal power of local authorities and the National Health Service to enter into public–private partnerships (Department of the Environment 1997).

The situation in the USA is markedly different, as described by several authors, with generally greater enthusiasm for public–private partnerships, especially on the side of local and state authorities. What has characterized expectations there, has been a reinvigoration of positive expectations that had existed since at least the nineteenth century, at first in the 1970s following President Carter's UBDG program, followed by President Reagan's termination of that program and greater emphasis upon the use of the private sector. This experience has not gone unnoticed, for both British and German governments have based their policies in regard to partnerships, in part, on US examples (Friederichs 1998; Chandler 1998). In turn, the more cautious approach used, for example, in the UK in the shape of the PFI, has been viewed with increasing interest by a wide variety of other countries (Anonymous 1998).

What is clear is that the field of public–private partnerships is growing rapidly in importance, that our knowledge and understanding of those partnerships is limited and that there is a greater need for further, systematic research. It is particularly important that research focus on the management issues involved as well as the costs and benefits of partnerships, for we have little detailed appreciation of many of the issues. Without such an appreciation our ability to train and educate the future managers of public–private partnerships will be limited.

References

Allen, J., Chi, K., Devlin, K., Fall, M., Hartry, H. and Masterman, W. (1989) *The Private Sector in State Service Delivery: Examples of Innovative Practices'*, Washington, D.C.: The Council of State Governments and The Urban Institute Press.

Andersen, S., Eliassen, K. (eds) (1993) *Making Policy in Europe: The Europeification of National Policy-making*, London: Sage.

Anonymous (1998) 'British initiatives arouses international interest', *The Banker*, 148(871): 26.

Bell, S. and Head, B. (1994) 'Australia's political economy: critical themes and issues', in S. Bell and B. Head (eds) *State, Economy and Public Policy in Australia*, Melbourne: Oxford University Press.

Butlin, N. (1983) 'Trends in public-private relations 1901–75', in B. W. Head (ed.) *State and Economy in Australia*, Melbourne: Oxford University Press.

Canadian Council for Public–Private Partnerships (1999) 'About the Council for Public–Private Partnerships' Online at http://Home.InfoRamp.Net/-partners/aboutppp.html

Capling, M. and Galligan, B. (1992) *Beyond the Protective State: The Political Economy of Australia's Manufacturing Industry Policy*, Melbourne: Cambridge University Press.

Carroll, P. (1993) 'Regulatory reform', in B. Stevens, and J. Wanna (eds) *The Goss Government: Promise and Performance of Labor in Queensland*, Melbourne: Macmillan.

—— (1995) 'The Railway Department 1863–1914', in Cohen R. and Wiltshire J. (eds) *People, Places and Policies*, Brisbane: University of Queensland Press.

Castles, F. (1985) *The Working Class and Welfare*, Sydney: Allen and Unwin.

—— (1988) *Australian Public Policy and Economic Vulnerability*, Sydney: Allen and Unwin.

Chandler, J., (1998) 'Regenerating South Yorkshire: How the public sector dominates business partnerships in Britain', in N. Walzer and B. Jacobs (eds) *Public Private Partnerships for Local Economic Development*, Westport, CT: Praeger.

Clarke, S. (1998) 'Economic development roles in American cities: A contextual analysis of shifting partnership arrangements', in N. Walzer and B. Jacobs (eds) *'Public–Private Partnerships for Local Economic Development'*, Westport, CT: Praeger.

Colman, W. (1989) *State and Local Government and Public–Private Partnerships: A Policy-issues Handbook*, Westport: Greenwood Press Inc.

Department for Education and Employment (1997) 'Competitiveness through Partnership'. Online at the Office of the Cabinet, Better Regulation Unit Website at http://www.open.gov.uk/bru/bruhome.htm

Department of the Environment (1997) 'Local Government (Contracts) Bill. Online at the Office of the Cabinet, Better Regulation Unit Web site at http://www.open.gov.uk/bru/bruhome.htm.

Department of Industry, Science and Technology (1995) 'Lindsay launches partnerships publication', Media Release 143/95.

DiMaggio, P. and Powell, W. (1983) 'The iron cage revisited: Institutional isomorphisms and collective rationality in organizational fields', *American Sociological Review* 48: 147–60.

Fischer, F. (1980) *Politics, Values, and Public Policy: The Problem of Methodology*, Colorado: Westview Press.

Friederichs, J. (1998) 'Urban revitalization strategies and public–private partnerships in German cities', in N. Walzer and B. Jacobs (eds) *Public–Private Partnerships for Local Economic Development*, Westport, CT: Praeger.

Glezer, L. (1982) *Tariff Politics*, Melbourne: Melbourne University Press.

Goetz, E. and Clarke, S., (eds) (1993) *The New Localism: Comparative Urban Politics in a Global Era*, Newbury Park, CA: Sage.

Hall, J. (1998) 'Private opportunity, public benefit?', *Fiscal Studies*, 19(2): 121–40.

Halligan, J. and Power, J. (1992) *Political Management in the 1990s*, Melbourne: Oxford University Press.

Hansmann, H. (1980) 'The role of non profit enterprises', *Yale Law Journal*, 89(5): 835–98.

Harding, A., Dawson, J., Evans, R. and Parkinson, M. (eds) (1994) *European Cities Towards 2000: Profiles, Policies and Prospects*, Manchester, UK: Manchester University Press.

House of Commons Library (1998) 'Regional Development Agencies Bill', Research Paper 98/7, 9 January.

Industry Commission (IC) (1995) 'Charitable Organisations in Australia', Report No. 45, 16 June, AGPS, Melbourne.

Hudson, M. (1995) *Managing Without Profit: The Art of Managing Third-Sector Organizations*, London: Penguin.

Jacobs, B. (1998) 'Bureaupolitics and public/private partnerships in economic development in the British West Midlands', in N. Walzer and B. Jacobs (eds) *Public–Private Partnerships for Local Economic Development*, Westport, CT: Praeger.

Jeavons, T. (1992) 'When management is the message: Relating values to management practice in nonprofit organizations', *Nonprofit Management and Leadership* 2: 403–17.

Kamensky, J. (1999) 'National partnership for reinventing government: A brief history'. Online at Web site http://www.npr.gov

Kinnock, N. (1995) 'The private sector's role in development of TENS', speech to the European Investment Bank Conference, Amsterdam, 18 May.

Kucera, D. (1998) 'Are public–private partnerships really partnerships?'. Online at http://news.publicworks.com/daniel/kucera4.html

Leonardi, R. (1995) *Convergence, Cohesion and Integration in the European Union*, New York: St Martin's Press.

McEachern, D. (1986) 'Corporatism and business responses to the Hawke Government', *Politics*, 21(1): 19–26.

Mason, D. (1996) *Leading and Managing the Expressive Dimension: Harnessing the Hidden Power Source of the Nonprofit Sector*, San Francisco: Jossey Bass.

Matthews, T. (1994) 'Employers associations, corporatism and the accord', in S. Bell and B. Head (eds) *Australia's Political Economy: Critical Themes and Issues*, Melbourne: Oxford University Press.

Mawson, J. and Spencer, K. (1997) 'The government offices for the regions: Towards Regional Governance?' *Policy and Politics*, 25(1): 71–84.

Middlemas, K., Crowe, C., Peucker, F., Algieri, L., Badiello, R., Ballester, R. and Griffiths, R. (1995) *Orchestrating Europe: The Informal Politics of the European Union 1973–95*, London: Fontana Press.

Mulgan, G. (1998) *Ethics, Business and Politics in a Connected World*, Sydney: St James Ethics Centre Annual Lecture.

National Audit Office (1998) 'Annual Report 1997', National Audit Office, London.

National Council for Public–Private Partnerships (1999) 'Mission'. Online at Web site http://www.ncppp.org

Newchurch and Company Ltd (1997) *Local Partnerships: A Research Review of Local Authorities' Statutory Duties to Consult with Business*, Rotherham: Department of Environment, Transport and the Regions, Publications Sales Centre.

Nygren, D., Ukeritis, M., McClelland, D. and Hickman, J. (1994) 'Outstanding leadership in nonprofit organizations: Leadership competencies in Roman Catholic religious orders' *Nonprofit Management and Leadership*, 4(4): 375–91.

OECD (1993) *Partnerships: The Key to Job Creation*, Paris: OECD.

O'Faircheallaigh, C., Wanna, J. and Weller, P. (1999) *Public Sector Management in Australia: New Challenges, New Directions*, 2nd edn, Melbourne: Macmillan.

Oster, S. (1995) *Strategic Management for Nonprofit Organizations*, Oxford: Oxford University Press.

Paton, R. (1996) 'How are values handled in voluntary agencies?', in D. Billis and M. Harris (eds) *Voluntary Agencies*, London: Macmillan.

Plowman, D. (1987) 'Economic forces and the New Right: Employer matters in 1986', *Journal of Industrial Relations* 29: 84–91.

Pusey, M. (1988) 'State and polity', in J. M. Najman and J. S. Western (eds) *A Sociology of Australian Society*, St Lucia: University of Queensland Press.

Rose-Ackerman, S. (1996) 'Altruism, nonprofits, and economic theory', *Journal of Economic Literature*, 34 (June): 701–28.

Sudarskis, M. and Edwards, M. (eds) (1993) *Urban Regeneration in European Cities: Its Physical, Social, and Economic Dimensions*, The Hague: International Union Development Association (INTA).

UNDP (1997) *Public–Private Partnership for the Urban Environment*, New York: United Nations Development Program.

Walzer, N. and Jacobs, B. (eds) (1998) *Public–Private Partnerships for Local Economic Development*, Westport, CT: Praeger Publishers.

Walzer, N. and York, L. (1998) 'Public–private partnerships in US cities', in N. Walzer and B. Jacobs (eds) *Public–Private Partnerships for Local Economic Development*, Westport, CT: Praeger.

3 Public–private partnerships

Rethinking the boundary between public and private law

Gavin Drewry

3.1 Introduction

Public–private partnerships have been developed in many countries around the world in the context of radical programmes of 'new public management' (NPM) reform.[1] Some commentators have argued that the NPM phenomenon adds up to a 'new global paradigm', while others have been much more sceptical.[2] Certainly these reform programmes have taken very different forms in the countries that have embraced them, but common elements in many such programmes have included a movement towards 'marketizing' the state sector by way of privatization, decentralization of functions and responsibilities, contracting out services and creating 'internal markets' (separating responsibility for the provision of public services from the responsibility for purchasing those services on behalf of the consumer) and, of course, central to the purpose of this study – the promotion of partnerships of one kind or another between the state sector and the private and voluntary sectors.

Such developments have had major impacts on the working arrangements and cultures of public institutions in the countries concerned. It has had particularly significant implications for the accountability – including the legal accountability, as discussed in Section 3.5 below – of public functionaries and for the relationships between politicians and bureaucrats/managers.

Public administration has been influenced, perhaps in some systems even substantially displaced, by an NPM ethos, which places a much greater emphasis on measurement and optimization of performance outcomes. Top-down reform of public-service institutions and processes has, in some countries, been accompanied by moves – such as the promulgation of 'citizens' charters' to 'empower' the consumers of public services and encourage the exercise of informed choice.

An important by-product of all this has been a blurring of the boundaries between the traditional public and private sectors, and the growth of a large 'grey area' between the two, in which state and non-state institutions sometimes collaborate, and sometimes compete, in the operation and delivery of public services. Public–private partnerships, in various guises – the UK Private Finance Initiative is just one example – are a clear manifestation of this tendency. There is nothing very novel in principle in the creation of such grey areas of quasi-government, but they have taken new forms and grown markedly in their extent.

A lot has been written – much of it by public lawyers, as well as by political scientists – about the opportunities and threats posed by the emergence of a more 'managerial' style of government.[3] This chapter does not seek to revisit well-trodden and continuing debates about the history and rationale of such developments, or to seek to come to any general conclusion about their merits. Its theme is mainly a *legal* one. The writer's contention is that, alongside the economic and political implications of public-sector reform, the legal implications also merit the close attention of analysts and commentators – and indeed of reformers themselves. One specific issue to be addressed is that the blurring of the traditional public–private divide must also blur the traditional distinction between public and private law, and that the NPM phenomenon, whatever form it takes in any given country, needs to be accompanied by some re-thinking of the legal implications and consequences.

A British author venturing into this territory must ruefully concede at the outset that the UK, with its 'unwritten' constitution, its stunted system of administrative law and the enduring 'generalist' (and anti-legalistic) culture of its central bureaucracy, does not look to be a particularly promising starting point for a legal analysis of this kind. On the other hand, the British case does serve to illustrate some aspects of the case precisely *because* it is so peculiar. In any case Britain's increased interaction with the EU and with the more legalistic political cultures of continental Europe – not to forget the Blair Government's decision to incorporate the European Convention on Human Rights into UK domestic law – has begun to challenge some of the residual resistance to thinking about public administration and public management in legal and constitutional terms.

3.2 The legal and constitutional basis of the modern state – an overview

The state itself is quintessentially a *legal* construction. Law is a defining ingredient in the classical Weberian conception of states as entities having a monopoly of the legitimate use of force. The literature, both ancient and modern, on theories of government and the state is replete with legal concepts and terminologies – such as rights, justice, legitimacy and (of course) the seminal conception of state formation by way of social contract. Contract in a less abstract sense – though not always with the lawyer's strict connotation of a binding agreement, enforceable in the courts – has become an important mechanism for organizing the delivery of public services in the NPM era. Law is an instrument of social regulation and control; it is also one of the most visible products of state activity. In many countries politicians and political parties compete to offer ever more ambitious legislative programmes. They often do this in the same breath that they court popular support by decrying the growth of state regulation.

Many of the institutional arrangements and normative aspirations of states are set out in constitutions, which are products of collaboration between statesmen and politicians on the one hand and jurists and lawyers on the other,[4] and which may then fall to be applied and interpreted by constitutional courts. The concept of constitutionalism – fuelled by a perception that 'a State powerful enough to maintain order may also be strong enough to suppress liberty', and that the machinery of government needs to be equipped 'with brakes as well as a motor'[5] – has been the source of much scholarly debate in the West, particularly in the USA. So too (especially in the UK, which does not have a written constitution, but has inherited instead the writings of Professor A. V. Dicey) has the related concept of the rule of law[6] – in particular, the notion that governors as well as governed must be *equally* subject to the law of the land.

The governing apparatus and personnel of developed states are subject to bodies of *public* law, whose distinction from *private* law is based on the special characteristics and requirements of the state, as contrasted with those of individual citizens and of the private–commercial economic sector.

Public law is traditionally divided into two subcategories, constitutional law and administrative law. The boundary between the two is in practice not clear-cut, but its location is captured in a memorable passage in a classical British treatise on jurisprudence, first published more than a century ago:

> The various organs of the sovereign power are described by constitutional law as at rest; but it is also necessary that they should be considered as in motion, and that the manner of their activity should be prescribed in detail. The branch of the law that does this is called Administrative law, 'Verwaltungsrecht' in the widest sense of the term. In this sense Administration has been defined as 'the exercise of political powers within the limits of the constitution' ...[7]

The peculiarly British view (inspired towards the end of the nineteenth century by Professor Dicey) that separate systems of administrative law in some way subvert the rule of law by placing state functionaries in a privileged legal position has long gone out of fashion, increasingly recognized as being as inapplicable to the complexities of large-scale interventionist government. As Wolfgang Friedmann observed, nearly 40 years ago:

> The deeper fallacy of Dicey's assumptions lies in his contention that the rule of law demands full equality in every respect between government and subject or citizens. But it is inherent in the very nature of government that it cannot in all respects be equal to the governed, because it has to govern. In a multitude of ways, government must be left to interfere, without legal sanctions, in the lives and interests of citizens, where private persons could not be allowed to do so with impunity.[8]

Public law is qualitatively different from private law because public functions and obligations are – in so many respects – different from private ones (though it is a central tenet of this chapter that this does not require all those functions necessarily to be exercised by public institutions). Hence the fact that governments are often subject to the jurisdiction of constitutional courts; and state bureaucracies are usually subject to regimes of administrative law, of which there are numerous variations, applied in many cases by specialized administrative courts, tribunals and ombudsman systems. And, increasingly, globalization has resulted in a growth in the impact of *international* law, which has both public and private aspects: in the sphere of public international law, the international human-rights agenda and the impact of the European Court of Justice on the domestic law and politics of EU member states, are obvious instances.

But the distinction between public and private law has never been completely watertight. Public bodies and state functionaries may, in the course of exercising public functions, be liable to private law actions in contract or tort (and/or to criminal prosecutions – e.g. for corruption). The line between public and private conduct may be difficult to draw. The distinctions have become more problematical as variants of NPM have created new contractual and quasi-contractual modes of delivery of public services and hybrid relationships, often partnerships of one kind or another, between public and private bodies.

Like 'contract', the word 'partnership' itself – at the heart of the present study – is a familiar part of the day-to-day vocabulary of lawyers, though in practice its usage in NPM public-service contexts is often sharply divergent from that understood by business lawyers. The standard legal understanding of partnership is that it is:

> The relation which subsists between persons carrying on a business, including every trade, occupation or profession, in common with a view of profit ... The individuals who constitute the partnership are collectively called the 'firm' and they trade under the firm name ... Partnership is constituted by agreement, usually in writing. It is presumed based on trust and confidence, and the utmost good faith is required in the relations of partners ...[9]

Public–private partnerships of the kind discussed here are more like bilateral (though as already noted, not necessarily legally binding) contracts between public and private bodies than the kinds of intra-organizational 'partnerships' described in the previous paragraphs, but there are resonances in common. The private companies that enter into arrangements like this with the public sector are certainly in it for profit: very large sums of money are often at stake, and there will usually be a legal–contractual bottom line, ultimately enforceable in the courts. Yet there is also that interesting reference to 'trust and confidence' and 'good faith' – reminding us of the important complementarity of contract-based and trust-based relationships in day-to-day life, within organizations, in the relationships between government and citizen, and throughout the public services.[10]

This chapter views public–private partnerships as illustrative of a more general phenomenon – the blurring of the boundaries between public and private law (and indeed between law and non-law) consequent upon NPM developments. Its starting point is the UK experience – though in the belief that there are some cross-national lessons to be learned. However, in trying to examine cross-nationally the legal implications of public-sector change we quickly encounter problems, to do in part with the varied nature of the reform process from one country to another – compounded by the wide variety in the legal systems and traditions of the countries concerned.

3.3 Problems of comparison

The perennial problems involved in undertaking cross-national comparisons of political systems hardly need to be laboured here. They lie at the very heart of political science, and its struggle to justify its 'scientific' credentials. Suffice it to say that many aspects of such problems show up when we start to 'internationalize' the vocabulary. Problems of translating words and phrases from one language to another are often compounded by deeper structural conceptual problems of comparing the things and phenomena for which translations are sought. Even at a domestic level, as already noted, words like 'contract' and 'partnership' mean different things to different actors in different contexts.

The problem of how to classify states has been a major preoccupation of political scientists and political philosophers since Aristotle. Classifying legal systems has similarly been a continuing concern of legal theorists and of course, given the intrinsically legal basis of states, already noted, these preoccupations are closely interrelated. Many examples of such legal taxonomy could be cited.[11]

When we turn more specifically to public-law classification and comparison we quickly find ourselves facing issues that reflect the diversities of governance and the varieties of forms of the state itself. To take one obvious instance, the Western Liberal–Democratic tradition of government being subject to judicial review (in a constitutional law and/or an administrative law sense) by an independent judiciary, simply does not apply in a one-party or military dictatorship in which the interests of the ruling regime are regarded as synonymous with the public interest and the judges are expected to put such collective interests above the redress of individual grievances.

3.4 Law and the dynamics of public management reform[12]

Much of the recent NPM movement, driven by a belief that markets are inherently superior to public bureaucracies when it comes to delivering efficient and user-friendly public services, has been based on free-market economic arguments that have important legal ingredients. This can clearly be seen in relation to the British experience.

We have already made passing reference to the negative contribution of A. V. Dicey (particularly his influential *Introduction to the Study of the Law of the Constitution*, first published in 1885) to the development of administrative law in the modern British state. Dicey was resistant to any notion that, even given the rapid growth of government intervention and of the administrative apparatus of the state from the second half of the nineteenth century onwards, the English common law, applicable to government and governed alike, might be displaced by the development of a separate system of administrative law, along the lines of the French *droit administratif*. He condemned the prospect of the latter as a threat to the rule of law.

In 1929 the Lord Chief Justice of England, Lord Hewart, like many lawyers of that generation a loyal follower of Dicey, launched a fierce attack on 'The New Despotism'. Denouncing the increasing 'pretensions and encroachments of bureaucracy',[13] he asserted: 'that there is in existence, and in certain quarters in the ascendant, a genuine belief that Parliamentary institutions and the Rule of Law have been tried and found wanting, and that the time has come for the departmental despot who shall be at once scientific and benevolent, but above all a law unto himself, needs no demonstration'.[14]

Leaving aside Hewart's intemperate language, his concern about the growth of unaccountable bureaucracy, and the decline of parliamentary control, undoubtedly hit a popular chord – in some respects anticipating the 'New Right' ideas that were to come into political fashion many years later, in the 1980s. Much of this New Right thinking derives its inspiration from free-market economic theory, some aspects of which can be traced back to the eighteenth-century Scottish economist, Adam Smith, now recast in the mould of American public choice theory – notably the works of writers like Buchanan, Tullock, Niskanen and Olson.[15] Even more immediately influential, particularly in a UK-Thatcherite context, was the work of two major economists in the classical liberal free-market tradition – Friedrich von Hayek[16] and Milton Friedman[17] – both of whose writings helped to shape the ideas of many leading politicians in Britain and elsewhere, including Mrs Thatcher herself and some of her closest ministerial colleagues.

Hayek, who won the Nobel Prize for Economics in 1974, and is widely regarded as the founding father of the New Right, strongly opposed economic planning, and throughout his extensive writings on political economy was a consistent advocate of free-market principles. He argued strongly against redistributive legislation:

> formal equality before the law is in conflict, and in fact incompatible, with any activity of the government deliberately aiming at material or substantive equality of different people, and ... any policy aimed at a substantive ideal of redistributive justice must lead to the destruction of the Rule of Law.[18]

It is striking to note the interplay in this context between legal and economic thought. Laws are major products of State activity and this in itself makes them natural targets of free-market radicals, who believe in a minimal State sector. They tend to be suspicious, in particular, of redistributive legislation and State welfare, which are seen as encouraging welfare dependency and discouraging self-help; and they condemn excessive commercial regulation, which is seen as an impediment to commercial freedom and as stifling economic enterprise. It has been suggested that the 'stock' of laws in existence at any given time effectively binds governments to honour many open-ended entitlements to social benefits and obliges them to carry out a multiplicity of inherited spending programmes: 'in an era of big government, laws may be seen as having a positive inertia, carrying forward binding commitment of government to provide costly programme benefits to citizens, whether or not the government of the day would have initially chosen to do so.'[19]

Yet there is an element of ambivalence in the 'free market' suspicions of law. Some aspects of law and regulation may be seen as undesirable by-products of an over-large and overactive state, but the task of rolling back the State by privatizing, contracting out and deregulating often requires a substantial amount of legislative action. As law is one of the building blocks of the State, reconstruction of the State – or demolition of some of its functions – must have significant legal consequences. It is a paradox that the very process of deregulation can generate more regulations rather than fewer, particularly in the short term. Certainly the British experience has been that the Thatcher–Major years (1979–97) – the golden years of NPM Reform – saw no perceptible diminution in the volume of laws enacted.

In all countries a major public-sector reform process itself generates a lot of legislation, both primary and secondary. In the UK many items of legislation have been concerned with the changing status, powers and obligations of public authorities. In the first 10 years of Mrs Thatcher's premiership (1979–89) some sixty-six Acts of Parliament dealt specifically with local-government structure, finance and functions.[20] Other aspects of NPM Reform – notably the restructuring of the National Health Service and the introduction of an 'internal market' (subsequently abolished by the Blair Government), and the privatization of most of the nationalized industries – also required major primary legislation. But interestingly – and this is a by-product of the UK's monarchical inheritance and of the unique absence of an entrenched written constitution – much of the reform of the central civil service was effected administratively, by ministerial exercise of the royal prerogative, without much recourse to legislation. Those who look in the British statute book for a legislative record of, for instance, the introduction and development of Next Steps executive agencies – perhaps the most important single reform of the civil service in the last 100 years – will find few examples. Similarly, the introduction of the Citizen's Charter in 1991[21] has resulted in some, but not much, legislation, and it has been made clear from the outset that the Charter itself is not intended to be a legally enforceable instrument.

The Major Government resisted the idea of enacting a general Civil Service Act, specifically on the grounds that such an Act would impede ministers' attempts to reform the management of the civil service, though the Blair Administration has promised to introduce such an Act.

When we come to consider constitutional constraints that can constrain public-sector change, the UK system has no illustrative examples to offer – though recent decisions by the European Court of Justice have underlined the quasi-constitutional status of national obligations under the EU Treaties, and EU law does have important implications for public-management reforms.[22]   But throughout continental Europe many governments are accustomed to operating within strong constitutional constraints. And in France the constraining role of the Constitutional Council has acquired increasing significance since 1982, when it issued a landmark ruling in the context of President Mitterand's nationalization programme.

Certainly, most of the 'reforming' countries (including ones in Eastern Europe) of which this writer has knowledge and experience make the reform of the constitution and of public-sector law the starting point of the whole process. The legal draftsman, working in partnership with politicians, is a key actor, and sometimes seems to drive the reform process. There is a lot to be said for such an approach insofar as it is obviously essential to get the legal basis of the proposed reform absolutely right, and arguing over a draft text often brings important substantive issues to light that might not otherwise emerge until too late. But there are some dangers – not least the risk of overestimating the capacity of law to bring about acceptable change without there first being a capacity and an appetite for change in the political and bureaucratic culture.

3.5 Law and accountability in the 'new' public sector

At the heart of any discussion about administrative or management systems lie difficult issues of accountability and responsibility. These include matters to do with the interrelationships between central and decentralized institutions; between officials and politicians; between executive and legislative bodies (including variations on the theme of ministerial responsibility); and, in Liberal–Democratic systems, between politicians and the electorate. The matrix of accountabilities in any system is always a complex one, with internal and external aspects, and with political, legal and constitutional dimensions. Such complexities have in many respects been exacerbated by the NPM reforms. The following remarks are concerned mainly with the legal dimensions.

Here a major issue – noted earlier – is where the line is to be drawn between private law and public law in circumstances where the boundary between public and private-sector institutions and functions has become increasingly blurred. A leading treatise on UK judicial review summarizes the most important aspects of recent public service reform and concludes that:

> The legal relationships that arise out of these new forms of service provision are neither wholly 'public' nor 'private'. They involve a complex mixture of regulatory activity on the traditional 'command and control' model, inter-twined with regulation based upon contractual-type arrangements between the direct provider of services and the ultimate purchaser, consumer or customer.[23]

In countries that have undergone variants of NPM reform, patterns of judicial review (and other mechanisms of accountability) have reflected a continuing struggle to keep abreast of the changing machinery of State functions and services, and to establish a workable line of demarcation between public law per se, and private law (including the law of contract and tort) as it applies in the context of public functions and State power.

In the UK, a major restructuring of the machinery of judicial review (in its narrower, administrative law sense) in 1977, almost coincided with the election of a new Conservative Government, committed to reducing the size of the public sector via privatization and the contracting out of public services. Some of the most interesting judicial review cases in recent years have been ones that have explored where the boundary lies in a society where many public functions and services have been entrusted, either deliberately or by default, to non-government and quasi-government bodies. The question, 'who is subject to judicial review?', has been discussed by, among others, the public lawyer, David Pannick,[24] with particular reference to the principles set in a case called Datafin,[25] in which the Court of Appeal decided that the City Panel on Take-overs and Mergers (a self-regulatory body) was susceptible to judicial review. Pannick notes that, since *Datafin*, the British courts have held that 'judicial review applies to the decisions of the Advertising Standards Authority, and the Code of Practice Committee of the British Pharmaceutical Association, but not to the decisions of the Jockey Club, the Chief Rabbi, or the Football Association.'

This line of cases is also discussed by Murray Hunt who concludes that the blurring of the public and private has had the unwelcome side-effect of setting back the recent development by the courts of a distinctive, post-Diceyan, body of administrative law:

> The great irony is that, just as English courts are on the verge of articulating for themselves a version of constitutionalism which gives them a legitimate role in the protection of constitutional values in the administrative state, that state, as it has traditionally been conceived, is starting to disappear, as the political branches promote the private over the public.[26]

Of course, the 'constitutionalist' contention that the power of the state should be constrained by judicial review is not uncontested. There are both pros and cons, constitutional and practical, in encouraging judicial activism in public-law disputes and raising the profile of the courts as arenas for resolving disputes between citizen and State. In Britain the growth of judicial review has been noted with some mixed feelings. Senior judges have sometimes complained about the overloading of an under-resourced judicial system. In the mid-1980s the Thatcher Government became alarmed by the number of judicial cases that it was losing – invariably to the accompaniment of gleeful media publicity. A Cabinet Committee was set up to look into the subject, and came up with various proposals intended to heighten the awareness of administrative civil servants that their actions might become subject to judicial review. One visible product of this was the preparation of a booklet called *The Judge Over Your Shoulder*, giving officials very basic information about judicial review, and advice on how to keep on the right side of the law.

Perhaps it is only when governments begin to get worried about judicial review that we can really begin to feel that the procedure is beginning to work? However, there are of course some fundamental, and non-partisan objections to extending its scope. One objection is based on the widely held view that the administrative process must not be allowed to become a series of 'justiciable controversies' because, if it does, then government will simply grind to a halt. There are constitutional and democratic objections to the courts 'second guessing' the actions of expert administrators who are subject to instructions from political ministers, the latter in turn being, in Liberal–Democratic systems, answerable ultimately to the electorate; objectors who subscribe to this position often point to the non-accountability of the judges themselves. Judges may themselves be wary of the threat to their perceived impartiality that may result from their being drawn into political controversies.

Then there are arguments to do with the nature of the judges and the judicial process itself: the judges are not specialists, and seldom have any direct knowledge of the administrative process; court proceedings are adversarial, geared to the resolution of 'bipolar' disputes, but not to comprehending the broader picture. An American academic, Donald Horowitz, wrote some years ago of the hazards of overreliance on the courts as guardians of the public interest. He noted that:

> Judges may be performing new roles in administrative-agency litigation, but they continue to act very much within the framework of an old process, a process that evolved, not to devise new programs or to oversee administration, but to decide controversies. The constraints of that process operate to limit the range of what can reasonably be expected from courts.[27]

And the British scholar, Peter Cane, included the following passage in the first edition of his widely used textbook:

> Because judicial proceedings are essentially bipolar, they are designed to resolve disputes in terms of the interests of only two parties or groups represented by those parties. And, because judicial proceedings are adversarial, disputes are to be decided only on the basis of material which the parties choose to put before the courts. If the problem is one which is felt to require, for its proper resolution, the consideration of interests of parties not before the court and not in formal dispute with one another, of persons who will be affected consequentially or incidentally by any resolution of the dispute between the parties, then a court is not the ideal body to resolve that dispute.[28]

As I have argued elsewhere,[29] we must recognize the inherent limitations in any system of judicial review, and be wary of naive and overenthusiastic promotion of the cause of increased judicial activism.

Finally, it should be remarked that the same reformist pressures that have led to the growth of the grey area between the public sector and the private sector, and to a similar greyness in the distinction between public and private law, have also led to the development of new 'hybrid' mechanisms for securing public accountability and redress of grievances. These include specialized administrative tribunals, operating alongside the ordinary courts, and various kinds of ombudsman, often working at the interface between executive and legislature, and concerned mainly with 'maladministration' (variously defined) rather than with 'illegality'.[30]

3.6 Conclusion

This chapter has sought to address two issues. First, it has tried to flag up some of the generic consequences of public management reform from a legal standpoint. It has done so mainly from a UK perspective which, even in Western terms, is highly peculiar. We have noted the perennial problem of comparing and classifying both political and legal systems. Many of the political and legal principles – to do, e.g. with constitutionalism, the rule of law and accountability – which are such important features of Western Liberal–Democratic states, do not apply, or apply in highly modified forms, in other parts of the world. The public-management reforms referred to in this chapter have followed very different paths in different countries.

Second, it has explored the specific issues of the legal implications of the current trend toward public–private partnerships. It has emphasized that legal ambiguities lurk at the interface between 'public' and 'private', and that such partnerships exist in the no man's land between the state and the market and which is itself occupied increasingly by hybrid modes of service delivery that are contractual at least in form. The kinds of partnership discussed here are, when all is said and done, contractual relationships. Sometimes (as in commercial business partnerships) such contracts may be of the legal kind, enforceable in the courts; but sometimes, as with many of the kinds of partnership referred to here, the glue that binds the partners together usually has more to do with political or commercial expediency or with moral obligation – or with 'trust' – than with any implicit threat of litigation. But insofar as legal relationships do come into the picture the traditional distinctions between public law (judicial review) and private law (including the law of contract) break down.

Paradoxically, the British case – taken as illustrative here – may be less problematical than that of many countries with much stronger public-law traditions. It is interesting to note a persuasive line of argument (curiously reminiscent of Dicey, though coming from a different direction) that disavows the desirability of drawing a sharp dividing line between regimes of public and private law and favours a 'private law model of public law.'[31] This is very 'English' but also quite 'un-European'.

This chapter has sought to highlight some broad issues to do with the legal basis of the modern state in an era when the role of states, and the manner in which they function, is widely under review. The blurring of the demarcation line between public and private law is an inevitable by-product of developments that are occurring (almost) throughout the world. The questions addressed here are global ones but the possibility of finding global solutions is defeated at the outset by the sheer diversity of political, administrative and legal systems and by the inherently slippery nature of a legally resonant concept like 'partnership', particularly when used in non-legal contexts.

Notes

1 OECD, *Survey of Public Management Reforms*, 1990; ditto, 1993; update, 1994; PUMA-OECD, *Issues and Developments in Public Management: Survey 1996–97*, Country Reports. Online at http:///www.oecd.fr/puma/gvrnance/surveys/toc.htm

2 The arguments are reviewed (from a 'sceptical' standpoint) by Christopher Hood (1995) 'Contemporary public management: A new global paradigm?', *Public Policy and Administration*, 10(2): 104–17. See also his book, *The Art of the State*, Clarendon Press, 1998, chapter 9.

3 For some legal perspectives see, for instances, the essays in Michael Taggart (ed.) (1997) *The Province of Administrative Law*, Oxford: Hart Publishing; Ian Harden (1992) *The Contracting State*, Buckingham: Open University Press; Carol Harlow and Richard Rawlings (1997) *Law and Administration*, 2nd edn, London: Butterworth; also, a review by Nicholas Bamforth of Taggart's collection (1999) *Modern Law Review* 62(3): 476–83.

4 Though of course the categories are not mutually exclusive; the historic convergence of legal and political careers is a well-recognized phenomenon worldwide.

5 William G. Andrews (1968) *Constitutions and Constitutionalism*, 3rd edn, Princeton, NJ: Van Nostrand, p. 9. See also D. Greenberg *et al.* (eds) (1993) *Constitutionalism and Democracy: Transitions in the Contemporary World*, New York: Oxford University Press.

6 See Jeffrey Jowell (1994) 'The rule of law today', in Jeffrey Jowell and Dawn Oliver (eds) *The Changing Constitution*, 3rd edn, Oxford: Clarendon Press, chapter 3.

7 T. E. Holland (1880(1916)) *The Elements of Jurisprudence*, 12th edn, Oxford: Clarendon Press, p. 374.

8 Wolfgang Friedmann (1959(1972)) *Law in a Changing Society*, 2nd edn, Penguin, Harmondsworth, p. 380.

9 David M. Walker (ed.) *The Oxford Companion to Law*, Oxford: Oxford University Press, p. 932.

10 See Andrew Coulson (ed.) (1998) *Trust and Contracts*, Bristol: Policy Press.

11 This writer has a particular liking for the schema based on 'families of law', developed by the German scholars, Konrad Zweight and Hein Kötz (1998) *An Introduction to Comparative Law*, trans. Tony Weir, 3rd edn, Oxford: Oxford University Press.

12 Parts of this section are adapted from chapter 2 of Dawn Oliver and Gavin Drewry, (1996) *Public Service Reforms: Issues of Accountability and Public Law*, London: Pinter.

13 Lord Hewart of Bury (1929) *The New Despotism*, Ernest Benn, London, p. v.

14 *Ibid.*, p. 14.

15 See in particular: James Buchanan and Gordon Tullock (1962) *The Calculus of Consent*, University of Michigan Press; Gordon Tullock (1965) *The Politics of Bureaucracy*, Public Affairs Press; Mancur Olson (1965) *The Logic of Collective Action*, Harvard University Press; Mancur Olson (1982) *The Rise and Decline of Nations*, Yale University Press; William Niskanen (1971) *Bureaucracy and Representative Government*, Aldine-Atherton; William Niskanen (1973) *Bureaucracy: Servant or Master?*, London: Institute of Economic Affairs.

16 Friedrich von Hayek (1944) *The Road to Serfdom*, London: Routledge; (1960) *The Constitution of Liberty*, London: Routledge; (1973–79) *Law, Legislation and Liberty*, 3 vols, London: Routledge.

17 For instance: Milton Friedman (1962) *Capitalism and Freedom*, Chicago: University of Chicago Press; (1975) *Unemployment or Inflation?*, Institute of Economic Affairs.

18 *The Road to Serfdom, op. cit.*, p. 59 (see Note 16).

19 Richard Rose (1986) 'Law as a resource of public policy', *Parliamentary Affairs*, 39(3): 297–314, at p. 306.

20 They are conveniently listed and summarized in Appendix 1 of S. P. Savage and L. Robins (eds) (1990) *Public Policy Under Thatcher*, Macmillan.

21 Relaunched by the Blair Government in June 1998 as 'Service First'.

22 One of the best-known instances is the EU's Acquired Rights Directive (1977) which protects employees' terms of employment in the event of, for example, their public-sector employers being privatized or their jobs being contracted out.

23 Lord Woolf and Jeffrey Jowell (1995) *Judicial Review of Administrative Action*, 5th edn, Sweet and Maxwell, London, p. 165.

24 'Who is subject to judicial review and in respect of what?' *Public Law*, pp. 1–4. See also Peter Cane (1992) *An Introduction to Administrative Law*, 2nd edn, Oxford: Clarendon Press, chapter 2.

25 *R v Panel on Take-overs and Mergers, ex p. Datafin* [1987] Q.B. 815.

26 Murray Hunt, 'Constitutionalism and the contractualisation of government in the United Kingdom', in M. Taggart, *op. cit.*, chapter 2, at p. 26 (see Note 3).

27 Donald L. Horowitz (1977) 'The courts as guardians of the public interest', *Public Administration Review*, 37: 148–54, at p. 151. See also Horowitz (1982) 'Judiciary: Umpire or Empire', *Law and Human Behaviour*, 6: 129–43.

28 Peter Cane (1986) *An Introduction to Administrative Law*, Oxford: Clarendon Press, p. 33.

29 Gavin Drewry (1990) 'Judicial review – quite enough of a fairly good thing?', *Public Policy and Administration*, 5: 19–31.

30 See Gavin Drewry (1977) 'The ombudsman: Parochial stopgap or global panacea', in Peter Leyland and Terry Woods (eds) *Administrative Law Facing the Future*, Blackstone Press, London, chapter 4.

31 Harlow and Rawlings, *op. cit.*, p. 42 (see Note 3). See also a review article by Michael Taggart (1999) *Public Law*, Spring: 124–38.

4 Understanding the process of public–private partnerships

Stephen P. Osborne and Vic Murray

This chapter explores the stages of the partnership process and offers a model with which to understand them. It is based upon work carried out by its authors, both at a conceptual level (Murray 1998) and at an empirical level (Osborne and Murray 1998), about government–non-profit relationships in Canada. It commences by offering a model of the stages of collaboration involved in a partnership. It then uses this model to explore a partnership between four non-profit organizations in Canada as part of their evolving relationship with the provincial government. In this case, the public–private partnership is the broader context for the non-profit partnership that this case example focuses on. However, the micro-case discussed here provides an excellent example of how an understanding of the stages of partnership is essential to both the analysis and management of public–private partnerships.

4.1 Background

In common with governments across the world, the Canadian Government has experienced a period of great transformation over the last decade. Fuelled by a mixture of concerns over the spiralling costs of government and growing distrust of 'big government' (e.g. Waterfall 1995), this transformation has involved a combination of 'downsizing' government departments and responsibilities and developing alternative, plural models for the provision of services formerly provided by the state.

Much of the literature which has exhorted the introduction of plural models of public service provision (e.g. Pirie 1988; Osborne and Gaebler 1992), has emphasized the importance of competition as a central component of such pluralism, bringing benefits of increased efficiency and responsiveness to the end-user of public services. Recently though this orthodoxy has been questioned, both in the macroeconomic literature where the concept of the 'new competition' has emphasized the importance of collaboration in economic success (Best 1990) and in the organization-theory literature which has emphasized the cost disincentives of competition compared with collaboration (Ring and Van de Ven 1992; Alter and Hage 1993).

Within this context, the chapter explores non-profit collaboration in the provision of local public services in Canada – in this case, community-based services for disadvantaged children and their families in one city in British Columbia. Its purpose is to present and test the utility of a conceptual approach to understanding the structure and process of collaboration between voluntary and non-profit organizations (VNPOs) in public–private partnerships. This is the model of *collaboration as a multi-phase process* (Murray 1998).

It is important to emphasize that this is not the only conceptual model within which such collaboration could be examined. The public governance literature (Kickert 1997; Kickert *et al.* 1997), for example, has developed models which use game theory as the starting point for its analysis of collaboration (Klijn *et al.* 1995; Klijn and Teisman 1997), whilst Bovaird and Sharifi (1998) have used the concept of 'self organization' (Waldrop 1994) as a means through which to explore partnership and collaboration. These are important conceptual approaches to collaboration. The model presented here, however, has been chosen because of its potential to highlight the *structure* of organizational collaboration, and its impact upon its management, both in terms of the relationships between different levels of organizational goals and in terms of the impact of the process upon collaboration.

4.2 A conceptual model of collaboration: collaboration as a multi-phase process

Murray (1998; see also Osborne, 1996) draws upon significant work in the organization theory domain (including Ring and Van de Ven 1992 and Alter and Hage 1993) in order to develop an understanding of the collaborative process as a multi-phased series of stages. Each phase of the process has to be successfully negotiated in order to achieve sustainable collaboration. Failure at any stage will not only end a specific collaboration, but also militate against the success of any future collaborative efforts.

Murray argues for a five-stage model of such a collaborative process: *the pre-contact phase*, the *preliminary contact phase*, the *negotiating phase*, the *implementation phase* and the *evaluation phase*. Finally Murray isolates four sets of factors which affect the probability of this multi-phase process of collaboration being successfully negotiated. These are factors concerned with:

- the type of collaboration sought,
- the characteristics of the organizations entering into the collaboration,
- the process of developing and implementing the collaborative process, and
- the environmental and contextual factors which impinge on the collaboration.

4.3 Research methodology

This paper is based upon an exploratory cross-sectional case study of VNPO–Provincial Government collaboration in the provision of social services for children and families in 'Columbia', a major urban area of approximately 400,000 population in the province of British Columbia in Canada. Fictitious names have been used throughout this paper to preserve the confidentiality of those involved in the research. It involved a series of interviews with the senior managers of four VNPOs involved in a joint collaboration in the field of child-care services, as well as with senior managers of both the provincial Ministry for Children and Families and the local branch of the United Way (an independent North American federated fund-raising and grant-giving organization). These interviews explored the process and progress of the collaboration from the perspective of each organization and considered how its success was to be evaluated.

The interviews were conducted on a semi-structured basis, covering a number of key themes but allowing the respondents to reflect the complexity of their own organizational situation. The interviews covered:

- the context and history of each organization,
- its role in the provision of child-care services in Columbia,
- the relationships both between the four VNPOs, and with the provincial government, and their management, and
- the key issues that each agency was facing over the next decade.

All interviews were conducted over an intensive 4-week period in the summer of 1997. The focus of the study was upon senior managers because of their grasp of the strategic issues facing their organizations (Haulrich 1981). The use of multiple respondents was felt to be important for this study not only because of the dynamic perspectives that they offered on the collaboration but also because of the data triangulation and validation that they offered to the study overall (Yin 1989). The key characteristics of the VNPOs involved in this study are presented in Table 4.1. As can be seen, they were diverse in size and funding patterns, though all had at least 20 per cent funding from the Provincial Government.

4.4   The collaboration described

The focus of this case study is a collaboration between four VNPOs in Columbia as part of their ongoing involvement in a public–private partnership with the provincial government of the state. It is concerned with developing an integrated strategic approach to their role in providing child-care services. At the time of the study, all four agencies were experiencing pressure from their external funders to demonstrate both their effectiveness and their distinctive (as opposed to overlapping) contribution to service provision. Two of the chief funders of the agencies studied, the Provincial Government and the United Way, were experiencing financial stringencies.

At the Government level, financial and ideological pressures had begun the privatization of social services in British Columbia in 1982, and this trend acceler-

Table 4.1 Organizational characteristics

Agency	Structure	Nature of services	Annual budget (1996/97)*
A	Over 100 paid staff, plus over 200 volunteers	Range of programmes around four themes: child-care support, health and well-being, young people at risk, sport for young people	$2,000,000 (24%) [10%]
B	15 paid staff plus a fluctuating number of volunteers	Detached youth work	$386,880 (50%) [10%]
C	60 paid staff	Youth support services on behalf of the Provincial Government: alternatives to custody; school counselling; employment programmes, etc.	$496,331 (99%) [0%]
D	5 paid staff plus over 200 volunteers	Befriending service for deprived children	$250,640 (20%) [40%]

* Percentage of this received from Provincial Government in parentheses, and percentage received from the United Way in brackets.

ated in the early 1990s. In the earlier wave of privatizations, the Government had been content to take a 'residualist' and minimalist role in the overall management and coordination of the resultant plural service provision (Prince 1996). However, in the 1990s the political context changed and the Provincial Government determined to be more proactive in their coordination of service delivery (Ruff 1996).

The United Way was also facing pressures to rationalize its own funding procedures and demonstrate greater effectiveness in its funding of non-profit organizations (United Way 1995). As a consequence, both agencies were concerned with ensuring that their resources were being allocated as efficiently as possible. This resulted in a pressure on the four non-profit organizations discussed here to reduce the perceived potential for overlap and (wasteful) duplication in plural service provision. Interestingly, in this study, the response of the key managers in both the Provincial Government and the United Way to these pressures was the attempt to develop a more corporate approach to service delivery, rather than to increase competition. They expressed the belief that competition among agencies to provide the same service would lead not to cost efficiency but rather to a wasteful duplication of effort. As two of the respondents noted:

> We haven't enough money to give to all our agencies any more so we need to do it in a different way. We are having to cut back. We did it last year, but not in a rational way, so we're looking for a better process … We also need to guard against duplication, it's wasteful. Where there is duplication, we want pooling. It's not efficient otherwise. We would prefer the agencies

themselves to target different needs, to be honest, rather than to compete for the same services.

(CEO of Columbia United Way)

We need to review how we work with non-profit agencies. At the moment we have twelve thousand contracts, with six thousand agencies across the province! Can you believe that? It's just not efficient. We want to reduce the number and enter into more long-term relationships with our agencies, where we can concentrate on helping them have the greatest effect on the community.

(Senior Manager of the Provincial Ministry for Children)

The mechanism that both the United Way and the Ministry chose was the model of 'outcome funding' (Williams and Webb 1992; United Way 1995; Plantz *et al.* 1997). This is where the contracting process and the service evaluation are focused on the achievements of a programme rather than upon the levels of inputs and outputs. Two important themes emerged here. The first, from the United Way, was the perception that the non-profit agencies that they funded might be providing duplicate services. As will be seen below this was a perception not shared by the agencies themselves and one which they sought to change. The second, from the provincial Ministry, was the desire to move away from short-term competitive contractual processes and towards longer term 'relational contracting' (Ring and Van de Ven 1992). This change was believed to offer both explicit savings on the transaction costs (Williamson 1988) of the contractual process and the development of longer term relationships through which to encourage innovation in service delivery (Osborne 1998).

For the four VNPOs involved, their perception of the context, not surprisingly perhaps, was somewhat different. Whilst they understood the financial pressures and the need to demonstrate effective use of resources, they believed that there was little actual duplication of services between their agencies. Each organization asserted that it was distinctive, in two ways. The first was in the loci and foci of their work, in terms of serving different geographic communities and/or different client groups. When they met to discuss collaborative activities, therefore, they constructed a matrix within which to put their service delivery. One dimension was concerned with the different kinds of service that were being provided in the community (on a prevention–integration–rehabilitation continuum). The other dimension was concerned with the target group that each was aiming to help (such as children under 10 and their families or homeless people living on the streets). They felt this approach demonstrated graphically that there was only minimal overlap between their services across those two dimensions, even where the services might have apparently similar names. The second way in which the agencies studied believed themselves to be distinctive was in terms of their different organizational values and the impact of these on how they delivered services. As one chief executive explained:

You have to understand that our approach is different from (Organization B). They are more structured – rigid would be my value judgement! But it is important to have these different philosophies working together so we can reach different kids and different needs. This provides a more integrative service overall to the community. So it's some of the same kids we are serving yes, but in different ways and so we're meeting different needs.

(CEO of Organization A)

Predictably, this value difference and its import was rather more difficult to convey to the funders of these agencies. As a result, they proposed a collaborative solution to the problem of convincing the funders of their uniqueness. When the annual funding review for the United Way came around, therefore, they requested an initial joint presentation, rather than separate ones. This joint presentation mapped their services against the matrix developed above and led to a discussion of their distinctive service philosophies.

The strategy was a success. Funding from both the United Way and the provincial Ministry was maintained for all four agencies at their existing levels, when they might otherwise have been expecting it to be cut. The matrix produced for the presentation also became the basis for further joint work between the agencies. This was predicated on their discovered need to take control of the *outcome funding* model. It became apparent that their funders had only vague ideas of the types of outcomes that they wanted to encourage – or, indeed, what an 'outcome' actually was! By developing a range of impact measures for the different service scenarios that they had identified, these four VNPOs hoped to gain a greater say in the service-management process. This further collaboration is ongoing.

4.5 Analysing the collaboration

The goals of the collaboration

It could be argued that this collaboration was simply an example of oligopolistic behaviour by the four VNPOs determined to use their collective weight to influence two major funders and in order to maintain hegemony in their organizational field. There was undoubtedly an element of this. However, as Table 4.2 demonstrates, it was not this desire for survival by itself which assured the success of the collaboration. In fact, although there were similar meta-level and micro-level pressures on all four chief executives and their agencies, quite different macro-level pressures were driving their desire for collaboration. For the collaboration to succeed, it was not necessary that these pressures be similar, but rather that they motivated these four agencies to collaborate and to behave in a mutually beneficial way.

Thus, for Organization A (the largest of the four), the motivation to collaborate was a broad desire to increase its negotiating stance with its funders.

Table 4.2 Typology of organizational goals

Goal level	Organization A	Organization B	Organization C	Organization D
Meta	To provide a continuum of preventative and rehabilitative services to facilitate the integration of young people into the community			
Macro (specific)	To enhance negotiating stance with funding agencies	To expand its influence over other non-profit agencies by joint work	To gain leverage with provincial government by linking with other service providers	To gain legitimacy with its stakeholders from linking with larger organizations
Micro	To enhance personal reputations with their Board of Trustees			

Organization B, although relatively small, believed its services and philosophy were outstanding and saw the collaboration as a way to expand its influence with the other VNPOs. Organization C was highly dependent upon provincial government for funding. By collaborating with the other agencies, it saw a route to greater leverage with the provincial government. Finally, Organization D, the smallest of the four, saw distinct advantages in many areas – with funders, with its general community profile and with the children and youth area of the non-profit sector by linking with the other larger agencies. This dynamic was well described by the Chief Executive of Organization C:

> We have a certain level of trust that we won't be cut-throat. We have co-operated in the committees of the United Way in the past and this [work] took us forward ... The need for close collaboration has never been greater than now. Now we understand that working together will get you further than competition. Of course, that's not to say that we all want the same things – we don't. For example, our main relationship is with the [provincial] government and our main concern is to influence what they think. But I know that [Organization B] sees this collaboration as a way to increase its influence with other local non-profits. So what? We're different and I guess we want different things but we co-operate. There is something in it for everyone and that is what keeps us going.

It is important to stress one point here. Collaboration within partnerships does not have to involve equitable power relationships – indeed it probably hardly ever does. Yet if there were power inequalities, each partner to the collaboration had something to contribute. For example, in this collaboration, Organization A had far greater resource power because of its larger size and resource base, thus giving it a far greater capacity for independent action. Organization B, with its relatively smaller size and resource base, was in a much less powerful position and indeed was ultimately dependent upon the success of the collaboration for its survival. Despite this power inequality, the involvement of Organization B was essential to the success of the collaboration because of the experience and expertise in outcome evaluation that it brought with it. All parties to the collaboration were not equal partners, therefore, but all had a significant contribution to make. To explore such issues in more detail, it is useful to apply the typology of collaboration outlined above.

The process of collaboration

As described above, the model of Murray has five stages. We do not have data on how the organizations perceived one another before they first came in contact (the *pre-contact stage*). However, it was discovered that there was a significant *preliminary contact stage*. The four agencies had all worked with each other within the committee structure of the United Way. On these occasions each came to perceive the other as competent and non-threatening. This provided a grounding of trust which made coming together for specific collaborative activities in the future more easy.

> We had a certain level of trust from our past relationships inside the United Way and that certainly helped here. Now this work has taken this relationship further for the future ... Now we know we can work together on organizational issues as well – and that this gets you further than competition. We can build upon this.
>
> (CEO of Organization C)

Just as this collaboration was legitimated by the previous working relationships, so the current effort gave impetus to further, and possibly even more cooperative, collaboration for the future. Each incident of successful collaboration thus creates the potential for further, more sophisticated if risky, collaborative effort.

Because of the initial level of trust established during earlier contacts, the *negotiating stage* of this specific collaboration was less difficult. The direct stimulus to this collaboration had been the need to present a joint approach to the United Way and to the provincial Ministry of Children and Families in their funding reviews. This scenario presented the potential for the four agencies to be pitted against each other in the funding process and the actuality of vastly increased transaction costs for each agency as the funding process moved from a three-year to an annual cycle. Thus the collaboration both increased the negotiating stance of each VNPO in the funding process and decreased their transaction costs.

Out of this specific context arose the need to develop expertise in the management of 'outcome evaluation'. Given that this form of evaluation was the direction in which many major funders were moving in Columbia, it was felt that gaining early expertise in its management would put the four agencies in a superior position when negotiating, individually or collectively, with their funders. The negotiating phase initially involved the four agencies in exploring the extent to which they could actually trust each other inside the specific context of the collaboration being considered. This was not without its tensions. There was no inevitability about the success of the collaboration and its failure could have led to acrimony and greater competition between the four agencies.

> How did we cope? Well of course there were tensions between collaboration and competition. We had to be open about this and up front. We all knew competition would be our undoing, but it wasn't always easy. We used jokes a lot to bring things into the open and to diffuse them. Like, the CEO of (Organization B) is very ambitious so we used to joke that this was the first step to his kingdom! It enabled us to deal with this without falling out. So we don't have illusions about each other, but know that the way forward for the service and for our agencies is by collaboration ... It doesn't mean that we are close friends of course, but we are good colleagues.
>
> (CEO of Organization A)

The *implementation stage* of the collaboration concerned the preparation and timing of their first presentation to the United Way. This body was further forward in its funding review than was the provincial Ministry. The four CEOs of these VNPOs believed, rightly as it turned out, that influencing the funding review of the United Way would have a significant impact on the thinking of the Provincial Government. This presentation was facilitated by several 'away days' for the four agencies to prepare the joint presentation.

A crucial aspect here was the attention paid to the issues of defining the boundaries of the collaboration while respecting the integrity of the four agencies as independent organizations. The collaboration did not involve a pooling of funding, but rather a joint framework for individual bids. Thus, once the four agencies had made their joint presentation to the United Way, to establish the framework, they made their individual presentations in relation to their own funding needs. This maintenance of the integrity of organizational boundaries was as essential to the success of this collaboration as was the spanning of these boundaries in developing their collaborative framework.

The final stage of collaboration is that of *evaluation and continuity*. All four agencies were pleased with the outcomes of the collaboration and were committed to further work, especially in developing their expertise in outcome evaluation.

> So we all came together for the joint presentation to the United Way in the first instance, and then the provincial government, so that it could understand the big picture. And it worked. So now we are carrying on meeting, to develop our relationship further.
>
> (CEO of Organization B)

The second part of this analysis of collaboration involves looking at the collaborative process in terms of the four sets of factors identified by Murray as affecting the probability of the success of a collaboration. The first factor is the *type of collaboration* sought. In this case it was what Murray calls 'Type 2' collaboration – involving joint planning and advocacy but not implying any significant reduction in the autonomy of the agencies involved. Such 'Type 2' collaboration is often an essential starting point for more profound, and risky, types of collaboration which involve the sharing of organizational autonomy and resources. For at least two of the organizations concerned (A and C), such organizational sharing was a clear aspiration for the future and was believed to have been facilitated by the success of this initial, less risky, collaboration.

The second set of factors are *organizational*, particularly organizational culture, leadership and structure. Here the four VNPOs shared common values about children and youth which facilitated their coming together. Although they had distinctive cultures and structures, these shared values allowed such differences to be negotiated. It is by no means clear, for example, that future collaboration to develop outcome evaluation methods which would have to involve partners from the Provincial Government, as well as other agencies in the children and families area of non-profit sector, would be as successful. This kind of collaboration would be between evaluators and evaluatees and, as Tassie *et al.* (1998) have shown this is particularly difficult to achieve.

The third set of factors are the *processual ones* themselves. Here the collaboration was aided immeasurably by the level of prior contact between the four agencies, by the commitment and direct involvement of the four CEOs in the collaboration and by the initial level of trust which precluded an overemphasis on 'legal safeguards' with the collaboration. These facilitated its success.

The final set of factors are the *environmental ones*. Again, the embeddedness of these four organizations in a pre-existing informal network of VNPOs facilitated the easy initiation of this collaboration, as did the common external pressure of the changing expectations of their funders. Significantly, this pressure was 'moderate' rather than 'extreme' – that is, the United Way was at the beginning of a funding review process concerned with rationalization rather than drastic cuts. As Plant (1987) has argued, 'moderate' anxiety (which this review produced) increases individual and organizational willingness to change, whilst 'extreme anxiety' (which a more drastic approach would have induced) can breed panic and a closed mentality which precludes a willingness to change. This willingness to change allowed these four organizations to consider new options for organizational collaboration as a response to their changing environment.

4.6 Conclusions

This chapter has examined the genesis and management of a collaboration between four VNPOs involved in a partnership with the BC Provincial

Government to provide social services in that province of Canada. We would highlight two issues coming out of this analysis.

Understanding public–private partnerships in a plural world

As the plural model of the delivery of local public, and particularly social, services by multiple VNPOs is developed further by governments seeking to withdraw from direct service delivery, the necessity for such collaboration is likely to increase. This chapter has outlined a conceptual model which we believe will help our understanding of the factors governing the success, or otherwise, of such collaborative provision. From the point of view of the VNPOs concerned, such collaboration can provide legitimacy and leverage in developing relationships with their key external stakeholders. DiMaggio and Powell (1988; see also Singh *et al.* 1991 and Tucker *et al.* 1992) have demonstrated how the requirements of these key stakeholders can lead to isomorphism and the loss of organizational distinctiveness. In this case, the collaboration of the four agencies studied enabled them to maintain, and indeed to promote, both their common *and* distinctive values in the face of such institutional pressure. It also provided them with the potential for greater influence and leverage upon their institutional environment through their pooled influence.

The point of view of the key external stakeholders, in this case the Provincial Government and the United Way, such collaboration was also desirable. There was a concern to rationalize a funding system which involved a myriad of agencies in providing public services, with the potential both for significant trans-action costs for funders and recipients alike and for the fragmentation of the social-service system from the perspective of its end-users.

Such collaboration, such as this one, helps to lay the foundation for future col-laboration at a more significant service level, involving the joint planning and provision of services. As Ring and Van de Ven (1992) have noted, the trust required for such significant collaboration will not automatically exist but has to be built up over a period. Collaborations such as the one discussed here are an essential starting point for this building process.

This said, however, a note of caution must be introduced to this analysis. The success of future collaborative efforts will not be the product of past successes, or failures, alone. Whilst this past history is an essential precursor to a collaborative venture, each episode will be embedded also in its own context and process and will continue to be influenced by the four sets of processual factors identified by Murray above. For example, this study was based around a need for a collabora-tive effort which all four VNPOs could view positively. However, if the pressure from their external stakeholders had been more divisive, such as by pushing for unlooked-for mergers or pooling of resources, then it would have been far more difficult to initiate collaboration or to build on positive experience from the past. No matter how much goodwill and trust is developed through prior collaboration, each new venture continues to be embedded within its own context and the pressures engendered by that context are significant in its development. Rather than being a simple causal relationship between prehistory and context what needs to be understood is the dynamic interaction of these two forces. Similarly, Huxham and Vangen (1996) have suggested, the complexity of public–private partnerships, and their management, increases geometrically, not arithmetically, as more partners are introduced.

Key management issues in public–private partnerships

We believe that this model of partnership processes has important lessons for strategic managers of organizations involved in such partnerships. We would highlight five issues in particular. These are the need:

- to build upon existing relationships whenever possible – if this is not possible, then to allow more time to develop the necessary relationships before launching into the actual negotiations and the initial stages of collaboration;
- to build from limited collaborations, which involve limited challenges to organizational autonomy, and toward more significant (and risky) ones;
- to be explicit about organizational and personal goals within a collaboration and to look for congruence between them whilst not trying to force them, or expect them, to be the same;
- to accept that competitive tensions will continue to be a legitimate part of collaborative ventures and which need to be recognized and managed, not ignored; and
- to be aware of the impact of external factors upon the success of collaborative ventures – they do not exist in a vacuum, but are embedded in a context.

References

Alter, C. and Hage, J. (1993) *Organizations Working Together*, Newbury Park, CA: Sage.

Best, M. (1990) *The New Competition*, Cambridge: Policy Press.

Bovaird, T. and Sharifi, S. (1998) 'Partnerships and networks as self organising systems: An antidote to principal-agent theory', in A. Halachmi and P. Boorsman (eds) *Inter and Intra Government Arrangements for Productivity*, Boston: Kluwer; pp. 31–44.

DiMaggio, P. and Powell, W. (1988) 'The iron cage revisited', in C. Milofsky (ed.) *Community Organizations*, New York: Oxford University Press, pp. 77–99.

Haulrich, D. (1981) 'Strategic awareness within top management teams', *Strategic Management Journal*, 263–79.

Huxham, C. (1991) 'Facilitating collaboration', *Journal of Operational Research Society* 41(12): 1,037–46.

Huxham, C. (1993) 'Collaborative capability', *Public Money and Management* 13(3): 21–8.

Huxham, C and Vangen, S. (1996) 'Managing inter-organizational relationships', in S. Osborne (ed.) *Managing the Voluntary Sector*, London: International Thompson Business Press, pp. 202–16.

Kickert, W. (1997) 'Public governance in the Netherlands: An alternative to Anglo-American "managerialism" ', *Public Administration* 75(4): 731–52.

Kickert, W., Klijn, E-H. and Koppenjan, J. (eds) (1997) *Managing Complex Networks. Strategies for the Public Sector*, London: Sage.

Klijn, E-H., Koppenjan, J. and Termeer, K. (1995) 'Managing networks in the public sector: A theoretical study of management strategies in policy networks', *Public Administration* 73: 437–54.

Klijn, E-H. and Teisman, G. (1997) 'Strategies and games in networks', in W. Kickert, E-H. Klijn and J. Koppenjan (eds) *Managing Complex Networks. Strategies for the Public Sector*, London: Sage, pp. 98–136.

Murray, V. (1998) 'Interorganizational collaboration in the non profit sector', in *International Encyclopaedia of Public Policy and Administration*, Vol. 2, Boulder: Westview Press, pp. 1,192–6.

Osborne, D. and Gaebler, D. (1992) *Reinventing Government*, New York: Plenum Press.

Osborne, S. (1996) 'The hitch-hikers guide to innovation? Managing innovation – and other organizational processes – in an inter-agency context', *International Journal of Public Sector Management* 9(7): 72–81.

Osborne, S. and Murray, V. (1998) *Voluntary and Non-profit Organizations and the Development of Public Services for Local Communities in Canada. An exploratory case study*, PSMRC Working Paper, Birmingham: Aston University.

Osborne, S. (1998) 'The innovative capacity of voluntary organizations: Managerial challenges for local government', *Local Government Studies* 24(1): 19–40.

Pirie, M. (1988) *Privatisation*, Aldershot: Wildwood House.

Plant, R. (1987) *Managing Change and Making it Stick*, London: Fontana.

Plantz, M., Greenway, M. and Hendricks, M. (1997) 'Outcome measurement: Showing results in the non-profit sector', in K. Newcomer (ed.) *Using Performance Measurement to Improve Public and Non Profit Programs*, San Francisco: Jossey Bass.

Prince, M. (1996) 'At the edge of Canada's welfare state: Social policy making in British Columbia', in R. Carty (ed.) *Politics, Policy and Government in British Columbia*, Vancouver: UBC Press, pp. 236–71.

Ring, S. and Van de Ven, A. (1992) 'Structuring co-operative relations between organizations', *Strategic Management Journal* 13: 483–98.

Ruff, N. (1996) 'Provincial governance and the public service: Bureaucratic transitions and change', in R. Carty (ed.) *Politics, Policy and Government in British Columbia*, Vancouver: UBC Press, pp. 163–73.

Singh, J., Tucker, D. and Meinhard, A. (1991) 'Institutional change and ecological dynamics', in W. Powell and P. DiMaggio (eds) *The New Institutionalism in Organizational Analysis*, Chicago: University of Chicago Press, pp. 390–422.

Tassie, W., Murray, V. and Cutt, J. (1998) 'Evaluating social services agencies: Fuzzy pictures of effectiveness' *Voluntas* 9(1): 59–79.

Tucker, D., Baum, J. and Singh, J. (1992) 'The institutional ecology of human service organizations', in Y. Hasenfeld (ed.) *Human Services as Complex Organizations*, Newbury Park, CA: Sage, pp. 47–72.

United Way (1995) *Current United Way Approaches to Measuring Program Outcomes and Community Change*, Alexandria: OEIE.

Waldrop, M. (1994) *Complexity: the Emerging Science at the Edge of Order and Chaos*, London: Penguin.

Waterfall, D. (1995) *Dismantling Leviathan*, Toronto: Dundurn.

Williams, H. and Webb, A. (1992) *Outcome Funding*, New York: Renselaerville Institute.

Williamson, O. (1998) *Economic Organization*, Brighton: Wheatsheaf Books.

Yin, R. (1989) *Case Study Research*, London: Sage.

5 Governing public–private partnerships

Analysing and managing the processes and institutional characteristics of public–private partnerships

Erik-Hans Klijn and Geert R. Teisman

5.1 Introduction: public–private partnerships as a governance strategy

Governments all over Europe are looking for new institutional arrangements to provide services for their citizens and to meet public interest. The term 'third way' is used by some politicians to indicate the direction in which these new arrangements are being explored. The word 'third' usually refers to finding a new way between two that already exist. In this instance, the two traditional ways are market production and government production. Production or provision of services financed entirely by government, common in the 1970s and 1980s, led to rising costs and even economic crisis. For that reason much more emphasis is now being placed on reducing budget deficits and governments controlling their budgets. At the same time there is social pressure to maintain an adequate, and sometimes even above adequate, level of public services. For this reason private involvement has increased, although a purely private production arrangement does not appear to satisfy social needs either. The third way, if we ignore the rhetoric and try to define it positively, can be understood as an attempt to combine the added value of governmental interference with the qualities of market-oriented parties. Public–private partnerships can be seen as the organizational manifestation of this idea.

Contracting out versus partnerships

Public–private partnerships can be defined in various ways. Here we want to make a distinction between partnership as a combination of market parties and governments, and privatization, defined as a shift from public to private-sector production. This distinction is often not made. Privatization and partnership arrangements were both introduced in the 1980s, when the rearrangement discussion was dominated by financial arguments. Governments tried to privatize sections of public services and did so more rigorously in some countries (e.g. the UK and New Zealand) than in others (Germany, the Nordic Countries, the Netherlands) (Kickert *et al.* 1997;

Pollitt *et al.* 1998; Pollitt and Brouckaert 1999). Privatization was organized in a variety of ways, ranging from newly separated agencies within the domain of public administration (such as the Next Step agencies in Britain) to contracting out production to the private sector (with public agencies retaining responsibility for the final product) to new private-market organizations.

Several contracting-out arrangements have been labelled as partnerships. There is, however, an essential difference that will be emphasized here. Contracting out implies that the public principal is able to specify the service that should be delivered by private enterprises and also to define the desired output. Most of the contracting-out arrangements have been established in the realm of service provision (health care, welfare services, social security and many other kinds of services) although even here the principals often have difficulty specifying the product and the performance indicators (Pollitt 1990).

Contracting out becomes an obsolete arrangement in situations in which neither products nor performance indicators are clear. The number of situations is growing in which the governments involved do not have a clear image of the specifications of the policy, product or project that they want to produce. In such a situation cooperation between the public and private sector can still be fruitful. This is the area in which partnership arrangements should be established. It is our prediction that this area will expand in the next decade and will become a significant part of public service production.

Several decision-making processes concerning infrastructure projects, for instance, can be characterized by a high degree of uncertainty and ambiguity concerning the nature of the product and the way it should be produced. The production requires a lot of specialized knowledge owned by different organizations. At the same time this knowledge is rapidly changing. In this sense the public sector faces the same problems as the private sector. Because of the high development costs of new products and their often short life cycles, firms have to create strategic alliances to spread risk and to have access to different kinds of expertise in order to develop new products (Miles and Snow 1986; Alter and Hage 1993; Faulkner 1995). So it is not surprising that public agencies use partnerships as well as contracting-out arrangements to achieve public goals. Partnerships differ clearly from situations in which public agencies are engaged in contracting out. If we define public–private partnerships roughly as 'a commitment between public and private actors of some durability, in which partners develop products together and share risks, costs and revenues which are associated with these products' the differences between contracting out and partnership arrangements become apparent (Table 5.1).

Contracting out is characterized by a principal–agent relationship in which the public actor defines the problem and provides the specifications of the solution. Contracting out often aims to increase the efficiency of the production process. For this, contractual transparency is needed. Partnership, on the other hand, is based on joint decision making and production in order to achieve effectiveness for both partners. Relational transparency, or in other words trust, is crucial in a

Table 5.1 A comparison between contracting-out arrangements and partnership

Contracting out	Partnership
Government and company (or consortium) are involved in principal–agent relationship	Government and company (consortium) are involved in joint decision making and production
Government defines the problem, specifies the solution and selects a private company that can produce results in a cost-efficient way	Both parties are involved in joint processes early on in order to develop joint products that contribute to both their interests
Benefits of contracting out arrangements especially concern efficiency (quicker and cheaper)	Benefits of partnership arrangements especially concern increasing effectiveness (synergy and enrichment of output)
Keys to success are unambiguous definitions of goals, projects, rules of tendering, rules of selection and rules of delivery	Keys to success are an interweaving of goals, establishing rules for ongoing interaction, developing rules and tailor-made assignments concerning joint effort and production commitments
Based on the principles of project management because there is a clear principle, clear goals and well-defined project specifications	Based on the principles of process management because the joint goals, the art of financing, realization and utilization remain subject to joint decision making
Contractual transparency regarding rules of tendering, selection and delivery and rules of inspection are crucial for a good relationship	Mutual trust is crucial for lasting relationships between partners who maintain their own interests, ways of working, accountability and financing principles

Adapted from Teisman (1998).

partnership. Added value can only be created in interaction. We will deal with this in Section 5.3. Keys to success for contracting out are clear goals and clear rules for tendering, selection and delivery. In contrast, the key to successful partnerships lies in the ability to interweave goals and in creating tailor-made arrangements. We will discuss these issues in Section 5.4.

The question of governance: outline of the chapter

Public–private partnership is an ambitious governance arrangement. Synergy can only be achieved if partners are able to manage the open and unspecified nature of the decision-making process. Tensions that arise from the interdependency and competing self-interests of the partners have to be solved adequately: they will not disappear by themselves.

We explore the governance problems that occur within public–private partnerships and we elaborate some management strategies to tackle these problems.

First, we argue that the trend toward the 'network society' is an important impetus behind partnership arrangements since partnerships are assumed to be a more suitable way of organizing public initiatives in network-oriented societies. Successful partnerships, however, are not easy to achieve. We discuss the problems partnership arrangements encounter. We focus on the problem of creating synergy, which requires partners to trust each other. Trust is more than just a feeling. It can be generated and secured through governance strategies. We will deal with three types of strategies that can be combined to make partnerships work: process management, project management and network constitution. At the end we wrap things up in a conclusion.

5.2 The context for public–private partnerships: the network society

The network society has been heralded by several authors (Castells 1996). In such a society the public and private sector are intertwined. This principle of intertwining can be illustrated with a case from the field of urban development.

Leidsche Rijn is a large city in the centre of the Netherlands currently under construction. It has been designated by the National Department of Housing, Planning and Environmental Affairs (VROM) as a suitable place to concentrate a large share of the country's building activities. About 30,000 housing units are expected to be built there before 2015. In contrast to the 1980s, private project developers are now expected to finance and realize between 70 and 80 per cent of the investment projects. For this reason, public actors (VROM and two local governments) face a more intense interdependency. This is even more the case because private parties already have acquired a large number of the plots in the area.

Control of planning procedures, however, is still dominated by the public actors. Private firms are more or less forced to hand over their property rights to the planning authority in order to receive building permits. Both parties tend to give priority to their own considerations, which has led to a classical principal–agent problem. The principal is defining the products and the performance indicators, but does so from its own point of view. The question then is to what extent will private developers actually implement these terms since they were not involved in the planning process and probably do not feel responsible for carrying out the Government's master plan.

In practice, this means that the local governmental authorities are developing increasingly concrete and detailed plans for every part of the area and then contracting out for production. In the meantime, however, the agents have been developing their own decision-making processes, which include their own goals. This leads to tension. For example, collective facilities such as public transport require a certain number of users but potential homeowners do not want this degree of density. Second, while the most profitable items in the total master plan can be easily realized, crucial ones such as public parks perhaps never will be. Furthermore, diversity in types of housing units may be attractive in terms of public interest, but private parties tend to create more homogenous areas.

This use of a principal–agent arrangement leads to a dilemma: the planning process is being organized in great detail by public actors, reducing the private actors to simple implementers. But at the same time the public actors are not free to choose the agents and have to do business with a few private parties. Not being involved in the overall planning these parties tend to narrow their focus to their own plots. They tend to try to maximize their profits, but this can lead to mutual disaster. Private parties could benefit from a high-quality master plan in terms of added value for their plots, especially for plots that will be developed in the period after 2005. Public actors, on the other hand, could benefit from developing common goals with private investors and so secure a better final product. In the principal–agent arrangement public and private sectors, however, act separately. This case illustrates a transition phase to a network society in which interdependency exists but there is an ongoing use of traditional arrangements. A distinction between market and hierarchy, between public and private sectors, is cherished but appears to be less than useful. Partnership is feared, but is possibly the only workable way out.

Beyond markets and hierarchy

Traditionally, the market and hierarchy have been seen as distinct and opposing mechanisms. Markets are forms of coordination in which individual, autonomous parties achieve equilibrium through pricing mechanisms. Hierarchy gives the appearance of coordination in which command, control and legislation are important. In the private sector coordination takes place spontaneously, while hierarchy is usually associated with government agencies that coordinate through bureaucratic procedures. The distinction is also linked to specific products: the market supplies private products and government agencies supply collective ones. In this way, two separate worlds coexist.

This classification has been critiqued from different theoretical perspectives. The transaction-costs approach (e.g. Coase 1937; Williamson 1975, 1979; Hendrikse 1993) highlights the contingency of the two coordination mechanisms. The choice depends on the characteristics of transactions. Williamson (1979) identifies three key characteristics: uncertainty, the frequency of transactions and the extent to which durable transaction-specific investments are required. The extent to which transactions require more transaction-specific investments, the more frequently they occur, and the more uncertain they are, the more suitable is hierarchy as a coordination mechanism.

But also individual firms are becoming increasingly dependent on each other for their functioning and survival in markets. The number of strategic alliances between firms has increased significantly (Faulkner 1995). More and more firms operate within 'industrial networks' in which they are dependent on a range of other firms for the manufacturing and selling of their products. A growing body of literature tries to explain these developing relations between firms and addresses the question of how these industrial networks function and what advantages they have to offer (Miles and Snow 1986; Hakansson and Johansson 1993; Lundvall 1993; Alter and Hage 1993). Noteworthy is the attention that is addressed in some of this literature to the importance of trust in replacing costly and time-consuming processes of contracting (Lundvall 1993; Alter and Hage 1993).

At the same time, theoretical development in the field of public administration stresses the dependency of governmental agencies on a whole set of private and third-sector actors through the formation and implementation of networks. This network perspective of public policy focuses on the existence and relevance of networks of public and private actors for policy making and addresses the implications of these networks for governance (Hanf and Scharpf 1978; Rhodes 1988; Hufen and Ringeling 1990; Klijn *et al.* 1995; Kickert *et al.* 1997).

The conclusion that can be drawn, therefore, is that the traditional distinction between market and hierarchy has become less strict (Alter and Hage 1993). Markets increasingly resemble networks in which companies function as a result of a good relationship with other organizations. Governmental agencies, on the other hand, for their own efficiency and effectiveness depend more and more on the networks of organizations in which they function or acquire a less clear-cut hierarchical structure. The boundary between the private and public sectors as an expression of the distinction between market and hierarchy also seems to be fading. Local conditions for the establishment of new businesses, of major importance for economic activity, are determined largely by the actions (and lack of action) of governmental agencies, while the actual decision about location is made by individual companies. The mutual adjustment of public and private strategies becomes a fundamental prerequisite for the success of numerous economic and infrastructure initiatives.

Characteristics of the network society

Characteristic of the network society is the blurring of the borders between the public and private sector but also the *interdependency* of various organizations (Guehenno 1994; Castells 1996). Both are very apparent in the case presented above. As we can see, a satisfactory achievement of the goals of each of the individual actors requires activities of the other actors. This occurs because knowledge and resources, which are necessary for reaching these outcomes and which can vary in their nature and importance, are distributed among different actors. The importance of the resources that actors possess gives them more or less power in the network (Scharpf 1978, 1997). But even less powerful actors often have some veto power, which means the power to block decisions (Klijn and Koppenjan 1999). The potential veto power that all these actors possess, because of their control of various resources, creates a 'world in which nobody is in charge' (Bryson and Crosby 1992: vi). This interdependency and the veto power that accompanies it means that interesting (policy) proposals, projects and outcomes cannot be reached without a certain cooperation of various actors. This interdependency leads to *complexity*.

Complexity is a result of the interaction and negotiation processes between different actors whose resources are indispensable for a joint undertaking. This complexity is enhanced by the fact that these actors have their own perceptions and strategies which can conflict with each other (Klijn *et al.* 1995). Powerful public–private partnership can only be established if the partners are able to deal with complexity. If complexity is seen as a threat, partnership will probably soon be transformed into a traditional contracting-out arrangement. This means that not only does the project have to create a fruitful partnership among the different perceptions, interests and goals of the various actors, but it also has to achieve a way of coordinating the different activities of the actors so that actual results are achieved. Or to put it another way: the network society with its interdependencies and dispersion of resources, information and (political) legitimacy creates a management problem of how to bring both knowledge and resources together in public–private partnerships.

Institutional barriers to public–private partnerships

Given the above, it is understandable why public and private cooperation has attracted considerable attention for quite some time. For this cooperation to be achieved adequate arrangements to direct the coordination between public and private actors is required. Development of these arrangements, however, seems to be blocked by various institutional barriers, which are related to the classical separation of the public and private sectors.

An illustration of this is that while many pay lip service to the need for more private financing and public–private cooperation, at the same time opposing trends are at work, as seen in parts of The Project on Market Functioning, Deregulation and Legislation in the Netherlands in which the report of the Cohen Committee in particular contains proposals for disassociating Government and industry. EU legislation concerning tendering procedures also does not encourage alliance formation.

Theoretically, these examples are important. The two Government positions mentioned above are based on the long-standing idea of a vast difference between Government and industry or, to put it another way, between hierarchy and market, between the general interest and self-interest. Furthermore, each of these worlds is believed to require its own institutional framework with special rules (private law is based on fairness and reasonability; public-law provisions are only those explicitly stated). The only arrangements that are binding concern forms of outsourcing. The underlying principle involves a transfer from one sector to the other, clearly regulated with a contract. This arrangement has been fully tested in the United States (Kettl 1988). As mentioned before, however, this arrangement works well in situations in which the project and/or goals can be well specified. Contracting out is less suitable in situations characterized by interdependence and where it is felt that there is a need to generate new, creative solutions.

Ultimately, private financing of projects fully elaborated in the public sector appears to be too expensive for the Government. Furthermore, private knowledge about design, building and management is difficult to utilize if contributed only after public input has fully run its course, as the above example of Leidsche Rijn shows. Much has already been set by then. The network society needs alternative arrangements to contracting out, and public–private partnership could be one of the answers. Summing up:

- actors find themselves in networks of interdependency in which resources and information are divided among different actors,
- it is within these interdependent networks that public–private partnerships are situated and have to flourish, which also means that the classical division between public and private sector, or market and hierarchy, does not tell us much about the context in which public–private partnerships operate, although institutional barriers between these sectors (like European rules for tendering and anti-trust regulations) can create problems,
- to reach satisfactory results in public–private partnerships these interdependencies have to be recognized and managed.

5.3 The creation of quality and the problem of trust

The essence of public–private partnership thus is the creation of extra value because of the cooperation of public and private partners (Borys and Jemison 1989; Teisman and in 't Veld 1992). This can be realized because costs are shared, economies of scale are achieved, etc. A well-known example is that decision making on infrastructure projects can be speeded up by cooperation between public and private partners. In this situation partners are not adding something new to the partnership but simply achieve better performance in the fields they are already expert in. Thus in the example of Leidsche Rijn, building permits are being arranged faster and can be more tailor-made to the projects. In this situation extra benefits resulting from partnership have to outweigh the extra costs of coordinating the interactions between actors. Or to formulate it differently, the extra value has to be greater than the extra transaction costs that result from the more intense form of coordination of partnerships compared with, for instance, contracting out (which of course also includes transaction costs).

But even better is if the partnership results in outcomes and/or products that could not have been achieved without the partnership. In the example of Leidsche Rijn this synergy effect – i.e. extra value as a result of new ideas and better products/outcomes – can for instance be found in the way partners formulate and implement the master plan so that the individual projects gain extra value. Among other things this requires that individual plans within the total project be connected to each other.

Trust as the thing to manage

Synergy requires partners willing to look for new solutions for joint ambitions. This requires exchange of information and ideas. Or in other words: achieving synergy demands a true partnership in which the partners are willing to discuss their perceptions and goals in a search for new solutions. But this raises the problem of trust, not by accident a theme that is dealt with extensively in the literature on strategic alliances and public–private partnerships (see Borys and Jemison 1989; Kouwenhoven 1991; Lundvall 1993; Faulkner 1995).

In the first place, partners are not likely to cooperate in a search for new solutions if they do not have assurance that the outcomes will not hurt them (Scharpf 1997; de Bruijn *et al.* 1998). In this way the creation of extra value is connected to its distribution. The search for creative solutions, therefore, is vulnerable to misrepresentation, asymmetric information and opportunism (Scharpf, 1997). This threat often leads to a situation in which partners stick to their own interests and refuse to search for new solutions out of fear of being exploited by the other actors.

But even if guarantees are given that the interests of partners will not be hurt, the partnership remains vulnerable to opportunistic behaviour. In essence, partners find themselves in the classical negotiators' dilemma. The successful search for new solutions that create extra value requires that actors be open-minded and that a certain minimum level of trust between the partners exists, while success in the distributive 'game' requires opportunistic behaviour which includes all the usual tactics of misinformation and strategic communication (see Scharpf 1997). So the conclusion can be that partnerships that work need processes of interactive learning, which in their turn require trust between the partners (Lundvall 1993). This is precisely what networks can provide under certain circumstances.

Trust and networks

Because of interdependencies in networks actors may be tied to each other for long periods. This generates all kinds of rules and organizational arrangements over time (Klijn 1996a). In networks a kind of weak trust can evolve (Scharpf 1997: 137). This is the expectation that communication about each other's options and preferences is needed and that commitment to others will be honoured. Trust relations mainly will be based on rules, many of which will have a rather informal character. Trust, therefore, is vulnerable to opportunism. Actors can choose to break the rules.

Mechanisms to maintain trust and the rules that support these mechanisms have to be developed. In network societies this is possible. The endurance of network relations creates a 'longer shadow of the future' (Axelrod 1984); that is, a stream of future benefits which increases the chances that partners will remain working together.

Fear as an important reason to avoid partnership: the case of corridor development

In the Netherlands, as is the case in many other countries, there is a conflict between the aim of improving the quality of cities and the aim of facilitating the mobility of citizens and companies. One governmental agency is responsible for the improvement of cities, another for facilitating mobility and a third for improvement of the economy and employment. In fact these three agencies represent three important elements of what citizens would define as the public interest.

The three agencies, however, each tend to behave as if their share of the public interest is superior to that of others. The Minister of City Planning and Housing, for instance, defines the development of transport corridors and new adjoining industrial terrains as enemies of urban development and therefore fights against the policies of the Minister of Transport and Economic Affairs. As a consequence there is no partnership. They are not able to develop a joint strategy. New solutions which possibly could combine their three aspirations are not developed. The situation is defined as a zero-sum game. This strategy, however, results in a collective tragedy, because the absence of a joint policy allows all kinds of undesirable developments like low-quality building along the highways. The moral of this story is that sticking to one's own narrow interests can lead to very meagre results.

Network relations also reduce transaction costs. In partnerships, contracts are problematic arrangements because it is not clear what has to be contracted. To define all possible outcomes in contractual terms would be too costly. Transaction costs in networks are reduced because partners can rely on that specific long-term trust (see Borys and Jemison 1989; Lundvall 1993; Scharpf 1997). Scharpf (1997: 138) rightly observes that the maintaining of trust relations, however, is also costly. He expects that strong trust relations can only be maintained with a limited number of organizations. This means that networks will often consist of all kinds of different trust relations, some of them weak, some of them strong. Governance of public–private partnerships should not only recognize these differences but can also use them in managing partnerships. It is, for instance, possible to use strong trust relations to activate relations that are weak and not built on trust and mutual appreciation.

5.4 Three types of management for public–private partnerships

The challenge of managing public–private partnerships is thus to create extra value by using the knowledge and resources of the partners while at the same time fostering a minimum level of trust in the relationship and achieving concrete outcomes, which are the actual realization of the extra value. To accomplish this a fine tuning of three different types of management strategies is needed: process management to develop interesting projects, project management to realize concrete projects and network constitution to create and maintain a base line of trust. Of course, this is an analytical distinction. In practice all three types of management strategies are being employed at the same time.

Project management: preoccupation with producing projects

There is a tendency to approach public–private partnerships with project management strategies. These strategies are based on the classical requirements for executing projects and include specifying goals, organizing resources, setting up financing, developing contractual relations, etc. Within this framework a lot of attention is given to the scope of the project and the organizational cooperation that it demands (Mulford and Rogers 1982). Traditionally, much attention has gone to financial risks and the way contracting out has to be organized. Although good project management is important, too much focus on it tends to narrow the scope of public–private partnerships and ignores the dynamics that partnerships have to cope with. The development of the Rotterdam Harbour illustrates this, with a shift from a process dominated by *project* management to a process dominated by *process* management.

Development of the Rotterdam Harbour

The doctrine of project management assumes stability in goals, solutions and decision making. But this is often not the way things are in real-life situations. Rotterdam is the most important harbour in Europe. In order to maintain its position new investment is needed, especially since a shortage of industrial terrain is expected. In the early 1990s the Harbour Authority presented a trend report in which this shortage was pointed out (clear problem definition) and a solution was chosen (creation of a new artificial island in the mouth of the river, resembling the island that was created in the 1960s). From that point on the Harbour Authority stuck to its guns: the problem was a shortage of industrial terrain, especially for container trans-shipments and for the chemical industry.

The Authority set up a Project Organization to implement the chosen solution and contacted the Ministry of Transport for financial support. In 1995 the project became entangled with other social issues and developments. The goals and the solution were questioned. The response of the Harbour Authority was predictable from its project-management perspective: there cannot be any question about the urgency of the problem or about the correctness of the solution. But unlike in the earlier post-war period, the harbour authority now faced an audience that no longer accepted the dominance of its views.

Questions about the actuality of the shortage, the kind of shortage, if there were possibilities to solve the problem in other regions and about the added value and environmental costs of investments in new industrial areas compared with investments in, for instance, telematics could not be answered by the Harbour Authority or the Project Organizsation because these were beyond their scope. The Project Organisation could not deal with this new and hostile environment. Confusion and frustration were the results.

The national Government took over decision making. In order to regain support a national debate about the benefit and necessity of the harbour investments was organized. During that time the Project Organization continued its work. The debate, however, generated new directions for solutions. The output of the debate was presented to the Government. In contrast to what the Harbour Authority had expected, the Government was not convinced about the necessity of a new island. A new round of decision making began in which the search for solutions was broadened. The idea of a new island would now be compared with the proposal to intensify the use of existing areas in Rotterdam and with the development of new industrial areas in the south-west of the Netherlands. In addition, the need for environmental safeguards was incorporated into the decision-making process.

So the principles of process management have been adopted. The set of relevant actors has been increased from five to more than thirty. The set of solutions has been increased from one to three directions as well as several combinations. Investment in the environment and ecology now are part of decision making. And last but not least, it is now accepted that the process of decision making has become dynamic, ambiguous and much more extensive. Process management is needed to answer questions about added value, for benchmarking the three solutions and to connect the process concerning harbour investment to a whole range of related processes. This variety can help public and private investors to develop mutually interesting package deals.

Process management: achieving creative solutions

Partnership is based on the idea that projects evolve from long-term interaction. During the period of partnership (and for urban development this can take several decades) the subject of cooperation can change shape over and over again. Perhaps the most important aim for process management is to preserve flexibility and openness in the cooperative effort, without losing the ability to make progress in terms of actual investments. The case of the development of the Rotterdam Harbour illustrates the need for process management.

Process management, which can roughly be described as influencing and facilitating interaction processes (de Bruijn *et al.* 1998), must be introduced in addition to project management in order to carry out processes of interaction between a variety of actors (Teisman 1998). In order to make effective arrangements in networks it will be necessary to take four elements into account again and again:

- What is the context in which any actor is taking action (dynamics, actors, means and related processes)? A partnership must include all stakeholders whose contributions are necessary for achieving the partnership's goals. It is risky to exclude parties that have to contribute resources or have veto power in the interaction process, and not sensible to include parties that are not significantly affected by the (expected) activities of the partnership. The demarcation between stakeholders and outsiders is vague and develops during the evolution of a partnership. This also means that activating actors requires a strategy that does not pertain to only the start of the process but has to be worked on throughout the partnership.

- What kinds of interactions are needed from one's own perspective and what can be expected from others? Achievement of interdependency is more a state of mind than an actual fact of life. A partnership with limited objectives is easier to develop. The arrangements are more manageable and likely to require fewer partners and fewer resources. Nevertheless, it is interesting to consider the opposite hypothesis: 'In order to create successful partnerships a broadening of scope, ambition and involvement is needed.' There are two important arguments that support this statement. The first is that an orientation toward partnerships with a limited objective often will lead to a situation in which an organization is involved in a huge number of partnerships. Adequate strategic steering of these partnerships becomes problematic and a fragmentation of focus is the result. Top managers are involved in so many steering groups and committees that it becomes difficult to invest in all these groups. The second argument is that limitation also implies a more narrow perspective. Partnerships are established in order to deal with broader complexes of problems and solutions in a context of interdependency. If this is true, it probably will be wise to introduce broad objectives and goals. Within a partnership it will be possible to create consortia responsible for limited solutions. This refers to the necessity to combine openness and closeness in the network society. Openness is needed toward goals and actors; closeness is needed to establish an effective and efficient search for interesting solutions. As far as management strategies are concerned, this problem requires exploring different perceptions of the partners and connecting them to each other.

Table 5.2 Process-management strategies for public–private partnerships

Strategy	Aim
Activation of actors	Assemble a set of actors that have the resources, power and ability to achieve significant outcomes
Intertwining perceptions and goals	Promote a creative setting for analysing existing goals and searching for new goals
Mediating interactions	Bring about continuous interaction between partners and coordination of different (strategic) actions
Creating arrangements and starting points	Get the partnership off the ground and create stable organizational arrangements for interaction which do not result in high transaction costs

- How can actors be joined together and what are the conditions for creating ongoing interaction? In order to create an enduring and effective partnership a great degree of mutual dependency is needed. If the degree of dependency is light it is better to also create a lightweight arrangement. If the dependency is one-sided it is better to create a one-sided arrangement, like contracting out and tendering.[1] Who can or should bring parties together, can propose a certain process architecture and can play a mediation role? So this question raises the point: Which management strategies can be used for guiding inter-action and, above all, guarantee that interactions between partners will continue?
- What form and content can a 'kick-off moment' take (document, meeting, contract, covenant, gentlemen's agreement, etc.) and on what should the choice for a certain form and content be based (contingency (cost–benefit analysis) or considerations and preferences of actors involved)?

Network constitution: creating and sustaining trust

Trust is important in partnerships. Trust, however, not only depends on the specific process itself, but also on the stability of the network in which partner-ships are developed and the type of rules that are at work. If a network is dominated by the rule that autonomy is important, it will be difficult to develop partnerships. The actors will not be inclined to exchange information and ideas and will tend to focus on their own ambitions and goals (Klijn 1996b). If this rule exists a network reconstitution is needed. Reconstitution

---

1 In practice it has become clear that many contracting-out arrangements lead as much to mutual dependency as partnerships do.

aims to change the rules and structure of a network and by so doing changes the context for partnerships. The three strategies of reconstitution can be distinguished: (1) changing positions of actors, (2) reframing perceptions of actors and (3) changing the rules (Klijn *et al.* 1995). In order to get networks ready for partnership three sets of questions have to be answered:

- What is the structure of the network in which partnerships have to be developed? A network consists of actors, means and connections. Every network will be limited in certain ways. Some actors, along with their capabilities and expertise, will not be available. In order to create a more fertile ground for partnership development some actors, especially governments, can introduce or invite new actors into networks (e.g. a board of end-users).
- What preconceptions are operating in the network in which partnerships have to be developed? In some networks the agenda and the opinion about what quality is can be rather dated and narrow. This will leave out sets of interesting partnerships. In order to encourage creativity, it can be useful to bring new concepts about quality into the network.
- What are the rules in the network, and what are conflicting rules if the partners are participating in different networks? Partners can decide on rules to regulate possible conflict; for instance, by appointing a negotiator or setting standard procedures for dealing with conflicts. If, however, these contrast with already-developed rules conflicts may occur. It also is important to set rules for evaluation and dividing up added value achieved in partnerships. But if opportunistic behaviour, for instance, is a tendency in one of the networks, creative learning processes will be frustrated. Finally, the positions of actors are important. It will be difficult to establish a partnership between two parties if they occupy asymmetric positions in networks.

Table 5.3 Network constitution strategies for public–private partnerships

Strategy	*Aim*
Add new actors/change distribution of means over different actors	Break the closed character of networks in order to generate a wider field for formation of partnerships
Reframe the themes and beliefs in a network by introducing alternatives	Establish new ideas and transform inflexible thinking in order to facilitate the search for quality
Change rules of behaviour towards: – Conflict regulation – Evaluation/benefits – Positions	Establish rules that facilitate partnering and also generate a common approach concerning how to behave in partnerships

5.5 Conclusion: the need for administrative process redesign

Partnership became popular in the 1980s, together with privatization and contracting out. Theoretically partnership differs considerably from contracting out. While contracting out is an attempt to hand over activities to the private sector in order to improve efficiency (cost reduction), partnership is in essence a joint venture aimed at innovation and improvement of quality. Partnership fits within the concept of the network society very well, especially because it can contribute to efforts to increase the quality of life, a central issue in network societies.

Partnerships, however, can only be successful as long as trust between the partners can be established and maintained. In partnerships trust cannot merely be generated by project management, as in the case of contracting out. In order to create added value and quality, two specific categories of management are needed: process management and network constitution.

The introduction of these two types of management probably means that governments will have to redesign their internal organizational structure and procedures in order to respond adequately to external interdependency. An analogy can be drawn with the private sector where the establishment of embedded firms (Graeber 1993) coincided with internal business process redesign. Partnerships have to be maintained in a turbulent context. Not only the private company, but also other governments, semi-public organizations and citizens are part of the partnership arrangement. In order to generate cogent partnerships within this inherent complexity all partners, including governmental partners, have to increase their efficiency.

Even though it may sound contradictory, Government has to establish a kind of project organization in order to deal with the challenges of process management. Process managers will be appointed by the partners and held responsible for generating quality projects and achieving detailed sets of solutions, including the commitment of the partners.

References

Alter, C. and Hage, J. (1993) *Organizations Working Together*, Newbury Park, CA: Sage.

Axelrod, R. (1984) *The Evolution of Cooperation*, New York: Basic Books.

Berenschot, A. (1998) *Procesarchitectuur: Voorbereidings- en besluitvormingsprocessen*, Utrecht: PPS.

Borys, B. and Jemison, D. B. (1989) 'Hybrid arrangements as strategic alliances: Theoretical issues in organizational combinations', *Academy of Management Review*, 14(2).

Bryson, J. M. and Cosby, B. C. (1992) *Leadership for the Common Good; Tackling Public Problems in a Shared-power World*, San Francisco: Jossey-Bass.

Castells, M. (1996) *The Rise of the Network Society: Economy, Society and Culture*, Cambridge: Blackwell.

Coase, R. H. (1937) 'The nature of the firm', *Economica* N.S. 4: 386–405.

de Bruijn, H., Ten Heuvelhof, E. F. and in 't Veld, R. J. (1998) *Procesmanagement; over procesontwerpen en besluitvorming* [*Process Management, About Designing Processes and Decision Making*], Schoonhoven, 1998.

de Jong, M.(1997) *Prioriteitstelling van transportinfrastuctuur. Een vergelijking van institutionele systemen in zes Westerse landen*, Delft University.

—— (forthcoming) 'Institutional transplantation', proefschrift (thesis), Delft University.

Eggertsson, T. (1990) *Economic Behavior and Institutions*, Cambridge: Cambridge University Press.

Faulkner, D. (1995) *International Strategic Alliances*, McGraw-Hill.

Graeber, G. (1993) *The Embedded Firm; Understanding Networks: Actors, Resources and Processes in Interfirm Cooperation*, London: Routledge.

Guehenno, J. M. (1994) *Het einde van de democratie*, Tielt: Lannoo.

Hakansson, H. and Johansson, J. (1993) 'The network as a governance structure; interfirm cooperation beyond markets and hierarchies', in Graeber G. (ed.) 1993.

Hanf, K. and Scharpf, F. W. (eds) (1978) *Interorganizational Policy Making; Limits to Coordination and Central Control*, London: Sage.

Hendrikse, G. W. J. (1993) *Coordineren en motiveren; een overzicht van de economische organisatietheorie*, Schoonhoven: Academic Service.

Hesse, J. J. and Benz, A. (1990) *Die Modernisierung der Staatsorganisation, Institutionspolitik im internationalen Vergleich: USA, Grossbritannien, Frankreich, Bundesrepublik Deutschland*, Baden-Baden: Nomos Verlag.

Hofstede, G. (1997) *Cultures and Organizations; Software of the Mind*, New York: McGraw-Hill.

Hufen, J. A. M. and Ringeling, A. B. (1990) *Beleidsnetwerken; overheids- semioverheids- en particuliere organisaties in wisselwerking*, Vuga: 's-Gravenhage.

Jacons, J. (1992) *Systems of Survival, A Dialogue on Moral Foundations of Commerce and Politics*, Random House.

Kaufman, F. X., Majone, G. and Ostrom, V. (eds) (1986) *Guidance, Control and Evaluation in the Public Sector; The Bielefeld Interdisciplinary Project*, Berlin/New York: De Gruyter.

Kettl, D. F. (1988) *Government by Proxi: (Mis)managing federal Programs*, Washington D.C.: C. Q. Press.

Kickert, W. J. M., Klijn, E. H. and Koppenjan, J. F. M. (eds) (1997) *Managing Complex Networks; Strategies for the Public Sector*, London: Sage.

Klijn, E. H., (1996a) 'Analyzing and managing policy processes in complex networks; a theoretical examination of the concept policy networks and its problems', *Administration and Society*, 28(1): 90–119.

Klijn, E. H. (1996b) *Regels en sturing in netwerken; de invloed van netwerkregels op de herstructurering van naoorlogse wijken* [*Rules and Governance in Networks; The Influence of Network Rules on the Restructuring of Post War Housing*] Delft: Eburon.

Klijn, E. H., Koppenjan, J. F. M. and Termeer, C. J. A. M. (1995) 'Managing networks in the public sector', *Public Administration*, 73(3): 437–54.

Kouwenhoven, V. P. (1991) *Publiek-private samenwerking: mode of model?*, Delft.

Lehmbruch, G. and Schmitter, P. C. (eds) (1982) *Patterns of Corporatist Policy-making*, London: Sage.

Lemstra, W. (1997) 'Publiek-private samenwerking. Een fenomeen tussen twee werelden', Oratie (thesis), Universiteit Twente.

Lundvall, B. A. (1993) 'Explaining interfirm cooperation; limits of the transaction-cost approach', in Graeber, G. (ed.), 1993.

Lijphart, A. (1968 (1992)) *Verzuiling, pacificatie en kentering in de Nederlandse Politiek*, Haarlem: Becht.

Miles, R. E. and Snow, C. C. (1986) 'Organization: New concepts for new forms', *California Management Review*, 28(3).

Ministry of Finance, Projectbureau PPS (n.d.) 'Meer Waarde door samen Werken', Tussenrapportage ['More value through cooperation', interim report].

Ministry of Finance, Projectbureau PPS (1998) Eindrapport 'Meer Waarde door samen Werken' [Final report on 'More value through cooperation'], The Hague.

Mulford, C. L. and Rogers, D. L. (1982) 'Definitions and models' in D. L. Rogers and D. A. Whetten (eds), *Interorganizational Coordinaton: Theory, Research and Implementation*, Iowa: Iowa State University Press.

Ministry of Finance (1998) Final report of the MDW Working Party on Market and Government, The Hague.

Nalebuff, O. and Brandenburger, C. (1996) *Spelen met de concurrent: speltheorie als strategisch wapen*, Amsterdam: Contact.

Ostrom, E. (ed.) (1982) *Strategies of Political Inquiry*, Beverly Hills.

—— (1986), 'A method for institutional analysis', in F. X. Kaufman, G. Majone and V. Ostrom (eds), *Guidance, Control and Evaluation in the Public Sector; The Bielefeld Interdisciplinary Project*, Berlin/New York: De Gruyter.

—— (1990) *Governing the Commons: The Evolution of Institutions for Collective Action*, Cambridge: Cambridge University Press.

Pollitt, C. (1990) *Managerialism in the Public Sector: the Anglo-American Experience*, Oxford: Blackwell.

Ragin (1987) *The Comparative Method: Moving Beyond Qualitative and Quantitative Strategies*, Berkeley: University of California.

Rhodes, R. A. W. (1988) *Beyond Westminster and Whitehall; the Subsectoral Governments of Britain*, London: Unwin Hyman.

Rogers, D. L. and Whetten, D. A. (1982) *Interorganizational Coordination: Theory, Research and Implementation*, Iowa: Iowa State University Press.

Rosenthal (1992) *Effective Product Design and Development*, Chicago: Irwin.

Scharpf, F. W. (1978) 'Interorganizational policy studies: Issues, concepts and perspectives', in K. Hanf and F. W. Scharpf (eds) (1978), *Interorganizational Policy-making*, London: Sage.

—— (1997) *Games Real Actors Play; Actor-centred Institutionalism in Policy Research*, Boulder CO: Westview Press.

Scott, W. R. (1995) *Institutions and Organizations*, Thousand Oaks: Sage.

Teisman, G. R. (1992/1995) *Complexe besluitvorming; een pluricentrisch perspectief op besluitvorming over infrastructuren* [*Complex Decision Making; A Pluricentric Vision on Decision Making on Infrastructural Investments*] Den Haag: Vuga.

—— (1997) *Sturen via creatieve concurrentie* [*Governance by Creative Competition*], Nijmegen: Katholieke Universiteit Nijmegen.

—— (1998) 'Procesmanagement: de basis voor partnerschap' [Process management: the basis for partnership'], *ESB*, 83e(4170): 21–26.

Teisman, G. R. and in 't Veld, R. J. (1992) Innovatief investeren in infrastructuur (studie verricht in opdracht van het GWWO).

in 't Veld, R. J. (1995) *Spelen met vuur. Over hybride organisaties*, Den Haag: Vuga.

Waddock, S. A. (1991) 'A typology of social partnership organizations', *Administration and Society*, 22(4): 480–508.

Watson, A. (1993) *Legal Transplants. An Approach to Comparative Law*, Athens and London.

Weimar, D. L. (ed.) (1995) *Institutional design*, Boston, Dordrecht, London.

Williamson, O. E. (1975) *Markets and hierarchies*, New York.

Williamson, O. E. (1979) 'Transactional costs economics: The governance of contractual relations', *Journal of Law and Economics*, (2): 233–261.

—— (1998) 'Transaction cost economics: How it works; where it is headed', *De economist* 146: 23–58.

Wheelwright, S. C. and Clark, K. B. (1992) *Revolutionizing Product Development*, New York: The Free Press.

Zweigert, K. and Kotz, H. (1992) *An Introduction to Comparative Law*, 2nd edn, Oxford: Clarendon Paperbacks.

Part II

Comparative public policy contexts for public–private partnerships

6 Public–private partnerships in the United States

Historical patterns and current trends

Lynne Moulton and Helmut K. Anheier

6.1 Introduction

In the United States, the non-profit sector has consistently relied on federal, state, and local governments for a significant proportion of its funds and clients since the 1960s. Smith and Lipsky (1993) report that government financing often accounts for over half the income of non-profit social-service agencies and that there are hundreds of contractual arrangements between public and private non-profit entities in any given state of the Union. These arrangements reflect the unique type of welfare state operating through the political economy of the United States.

Voluntary free association among citizens preceded the development of the government apparatus and the corporation as means for pursuing collective action in the United States (Salamon 1998; Smith and Lipsky 1993). Throughout the history of this country, registered and unregistered non-profit organizations assumed a variety of roles addressing public needs defined outside the scope of either the State or private enterprise. Along with their fundamental role as service providers, non-profits offer a complement to the formal political system as the organizational sphere through which citizens can participate in the democratic process. For example, non-profit organizations account for half of the country's hospitals, colleges and universities; 60 per cent of the social-service agencies; and most of the civic organizations (Salamon 1998). In addition, every social movement and effort to defend citizens' rights can trace its roots back to the non-profit sector (Melendez 1998).

The growth and development of the non-profit sector in its service and civil society capacities could not have taken the course it did by relying solely on private voluntary contributions. Need consistently outweighs levels of private donations to non-profit organizations. In other industrialized countries, this situation often inspired the development of expansive public social-service apparatuses. The United States, however, has been historically loathe – from both liberal and conservative perspectives – to rely solely on centralized government structures for the provision of public goods and turned instead to the private non-profit sector.

Direct government support of non-profit organizations comes in the form of direct payments, tax exemption, preferential regulatory treatment and deductibility of donations. Non-profits also benefit indirectly from payments through subsidies to individual clients. (The public–private partnerships, which result from this array of support mechanisms and allow the non-profit sector to assume the roles at the scale described above, are the focus of this chapter.)

(Public–private partnerships generally take the form of purchase-of-services contracts, where government entities buy services from non-profit contracting agencies.)Programmes that rely on contracting often require contractors to be non-profit entities. These contracts are characterized by relatively short funding cycles where the government funder enjoys varying control over admission criteria, service delivery and discharge decisions for clients of the contracted services. Smith and Lipsky (1993) refer to this partnership configuration as a 'contracting regime' in which public and private agencies are involved in a mutually dependent but not equal relationship. These contractual arrangements typically subordinate non-profit agencies to a hegemonic state that often serves as more of a sponsor than a partner to their non-profit contractors (Smith and Lipsky 1993: 44–5).

American culture, like those of other countries, contains certain classic polarities, 'inner tensions' and contradictions. In the United States, one such tension involves the deeply seated notions of American individualism and self-reliance on the one hand, and commitments to community, formal equality, justice and civic virtues on the other (Bellah *et al.* 1985). Within this cultural context, American political economy takes place. It is, first of all, a political economy capable of enacting policies that have become landmarks of modern legislative history that reach over much of the twentieth century – from the New Deal programmes of the 1930s, the GI Bill in the late 1940s, the civil-rights legislation and the Great Society programs over the next two decades, to affirmative action policies, and the welfare reform of the Clinton Administration in the 1990s.

All these policies represent bold moves to address what are perceived as pressing social, economic and political problems and issues: the unemployed, the soldiers returning home, the war widows left without sufficient income, the elderly, African Americans, and the ongoing policy debate about the deserving and the undeserving poor. They are demand-driven policies (Skocpol 1992; Amenta and Carruther 1988) that neither represent nor amount to a systematic and comprehensive approach to address social problems. Particular groups with specific agendas can yield considerable influence in American policies, if political constellations accommodate them, and that their demands meet the political needs of other stakeholders (Laumann and Knoke 1987). The war widows of World Wars I and II pressed for social security and found a government both sympathetic and politically conflicted, and hence open to bold initiatives. The civil-rights movement pressed for affirmative action and equal opportunities, and met a government willing to take on their demands, at least in part.

The result of demand-driven policies is, as many observers of the US welfare state have noted (Amenta and Carruther 1988), a patchwork approach to social policy, and an approach altogether distinct in style and aspiration from the European model. This contrast applies not only to social democracy and

Christian democratic ideas of policy making, but also to large-scale programmes like the National Health Service in Britain. None of these approaches fit the American style of policy making.

What, then, is the US model? We have already noted the demand-driven aspect of it, and the patchwork character of the overall result. These characteristics are made possible by an electorate that can be seen as reconciling three value streams (Lipset 1996):

- individual freedom, formal equality before the law, and due process;
- high levels of tolerance for significant disparities in material wealth and well-being combined with a belief in individual advancement and responsibility (the 'American Dream'), and
- a 'taken-for-grantedness' of the US Government as best blueprint for the political constitution of society and system of government that requires only 'fine-tuning', never major 'overhauls' to maintain and perfect it.

The overall result is a small government at local, state and federal levels by international standards. What is more, it is both a strong and a weak form of government. It is strong because of its secure moorings in an over 200-year-old democratic tradition and process, and the deeply embedded democratic ideals in the population. By contrast, the government is weak because it can actually do very little on its own without involving third parties as partners. Limited financial resources and lack of popular support help prevent all levels of government, and particularly the federal level, to assume any exclusive role of service provider in many fields that are the prominent domain of the State in most other countries: culture, education, health, social services, community development, environmental protection, international development, to mention a few. Frequently, government is only in a position to finance some of the major parts of policy implementation. Rarely, however, can federal and state governments actually offer the services themselves by building up a network of institutions dedicated for such purposes. The result is a system of what Salamon (1987) called *third-party government* – an emerging model whereby governments at all levels involve private organizations in delivering public services. Typically, these partner organizations are non-profit entities, and, as we will see below, increasingly business corporations.

Thus, the US Government works closely with the non-profit sector to address a variety of social problems (Salamon 1995). Whereas common notions of welfare states assume that welfare provision corresponds to the size of the public social-service apparatus (Quadagno 1987), the American version of the welfare state consists of a public sector that makes policy, generates tax revenue and hires private non-profit agencies to manage and deliver goods and services.

Within the US non-profit sector, there are few large 'pure' non-profit service providers that rely solely on private donations. 'Contrary to the common view, non-profits are far from independent of private enterprise and government. They compete and collaborate with these other organizations in countless ways in their efforts to finance themselves, to find workers, managers, and other resources to produce their outputs, and to develop markets for those outputs' (Weisbrod 1998: 4). This partnership arrangement reflects the rugged individual-versus-community-member dichotomy of American culture, the pluralistic tenets of the political structure and 'represents a pragmatic, piecemeal adaptation to prevailing realities that emerged in ad hoc fashion in different fields' (Salamon and Anheier 1998: 158). In summary, public–private partnerships are a basic characteristic of American politics and social-welfare system – not by design but by happenstance. Public–private partnership is also the *modus vivendi* of America's contemporary non-profit sector.

6.2 Theoretical background

Many theories of the non-profit sector argue that public collaboration with non-profit agencies also represents a division of labour in the provision of collective goods, coordinating the relative strengths and weaknesses of each sector. These theories describe the relationship between government and the non-profit sector as complementary and symbiotic. The third-party government theory (Salamon 1987), for example, conceives of the non-profit sector as the preferred mechanism for the provision of public goods. From this perspective, solving new and expanding social and economic problems is most appropriately and effectively accomplished on a voluntary bottom-up basis (Lipsky and Smith 1989–90). Government is the secondary institution that steps in when the voluntary sector 'fails'. Reliance on the non-profit sector for performance of various government functions, in turn, allows the US Government to promote general welfare without expanding its administrative apparatus (Salamon 1987).

The public-goods theory, on the other hand, flips the logic of the third-party government theory. From this perspective, the government, whose responsibility it is to produce public goods, fails to provide goods and services that meet the needs of the entire population, particularly in heterogeneous societies with a diversity of needs. The non-profit sector exists to satisfy demands for collective products and services left unfulfilled by the government (Weisbrod 1988). While the logic of the third-party government theory and the public-goods theory make different assumptions about how government and non-profits come to be mutually dependent, both see such coordination as optimal within modern industrialized economies.

The assumption among many scholars of the non-profit sector is that non-profit organizations offer the State a flexible, localized way to respond to emerging or entrenched social and economic problems. These organizations are more able than government bureaucracies to be both responsive to shifting public needs and to establish long-term service relationships with clients. Government agencies can rely on existing, often community-based, organizations to manage and deliver specialized goods and services that would be costly for them to establish and maintain. In doing so, the government also shifts the financial and political risks of collective good provision to the non-profit sector. In turn, non-profits receive reliable streams of funding and clients, tax exemption and preferential regulatory treatment from public sources.

Much recent research on the mutual dependence between the public and private non-profit spheres shows that this partnering is not always straightforward and uncomplicated (see Lipsky and Smith 1989–90; Smith and Lipsky 1993). The prevailing concern in recent work is how government funding impacts the scope and direction of its non-profit recipients. Non-profit experts ask if government support impacts non-profit management decisions in ways that pull non-profit organizations away from their missions (Weisbrod 1998; Lipsky and Smith 1989–90). Some scholars wonder if the comparative benefits of non-profit service provision over for-profit provision warrants continued government political and financial protection (Bloche 1998; Schlesinger *et al.* 1996). Still others worry about the impact on the sector of the recent and simultaneous trends of government retrenchment on social-welfare spending, for-profit encroachment into traditionally non-profit industries and the subsequent commercialization of the non-profit sector (Ryan 1999; Salamon 1999; Weisbrod 1998). In the balance of this chapter, we will explore these and other issues related to the coupling of the public and non-profit sector in the United States political economy.

6.3 Extent of the public–private partnership

The mutual dependence between the public and private sectors was established in large part during the Great Society days of the 1960s and 1970s with much of the sector's growth happened during that period and has held ground since then. Non-profit organizations received over 50 per cent of federal social-service expenditures in 1989, up from almost nothing in 1960 (Lipsky and Smith 1989–90). 'In a sense, government became the principal philanthropist of the nonprofit sector, significantly boosting nonprofit revenues in a wide variety of fields and freeing the sector of its total dependence on the far less-reliable base of private charitable support' (Salamon 1999: 168). While government contributions to non-profit organizations varies within and among public-service industries, government funding remains the second most important source of income for the sector behind fee income. Salamon (1999) reports that overall government support accounts for 36 per cent of non-profit service organizations income.

Some small organizations rely on government funds for their entire budgets (Lipsky and Smith 1989–90). In fact, public money is so important to the ongoing financial stability of non-profit social-service agencies, that non-profit coalitions, advocacy groups, and 'affinity groups' now exist, whose partial or sole mission is to lobby the government for increased government spending for a variety of their social and economic welfare causes from youth services to elder care (Oliver 1999).

While government support of the non-profit sector continues to grow – albeit at a slower pace and mostly in the health-care industry – recent policy-making trends have begun to alter the long-standing public–private partnership arrangement. Beginning with the presidency of Ronald Reagan in 1980, the Federal Government has pursued an ongoing campaign to both 'reduce big government' and 'reinvent government', which are catchphrases for retrenching social-program spending and streamlining government bureaucracy.

In keeping with this dual agenda, devolution of responsibility for a wide variety of health and welfare issues has simultaneously changed the structure and reduced the level of government funding for non-profit activities across the board. Over the last two decades, fifty-seven federal grant categories were consolidated into nine block grants that carried lighter funding for state programmes (Coble 1999). Also as part of this process, funding structures to social-service agencies shifted from the reimbursement plans of conventional contracting to performance contracts that emphasize efficiency and capacity (Behn and Kant 1999; Ryan 1999).

With this new focus on accountability and performance came a newfound recognition of qualities that for-profit firms could bring to the service-provision table. Throughout the past decade, public funders at all levels of government began relaxing their historical resistance to contracting with for-profit organizations to manage and deliver social-welfare services. The consequences of this trend for the non-profit sector is an increasing level of competition for government contracts and the encroachment of for-profit firms in social-service industries that had been traditionally non-profit domains. As government spending shrinks and competition from for-profit providers increases, non-profit organizations must find alternative funding sources. Increasingly, the non-profit sector has come to rely more heavily on commercial income, which accounted for over half of the sector's revenue growth from 1977–1996 (Salamon 1999: 70–1).

6.4 Consequences of public support

According to the non-profit literature, the consequences arising from the mutual dependence of the public and private sector are twofold. One set of consequences involves non-profit-sector changes – potential and actual – because of reliance on public funds in general. For example, some scholars argue that fundamental differences in priorities between the public and private sectors creates myriad opportunities for conflict, the underlying assumption being that non-profits will tend to adjust their behaviours to satisfy the agendas of their public funders. To whatever extent government agendas differ from those of the non-profit organizations seeking funding, non-profits are at risk of having to stray from their intended missions to attract and keep public funding. In fact, Lipsky and Smith caution that 'government contracting may alter nonprofit agencies' approaches to services and clients, even if their goals *are entirely compatible* with those of government. In essence, they may be forced to conform to standards imposed by

contracting policy at the expense of their homegrown notions of what constitutes effective service delivery' (Lipsky and Smith 1989–90: 638, emphasis
ours). In particular, non-profit scholars worry that non-profit organizations
will become too bureaucratized, over-professionalized and politicized as a
result of governmental influence. Non-profits might also lose their autonomy
and flexibility regarding a number of organizational goals and succumb to
'vendorism', where the organizational mission is distorted in the pursuit for
government support (Salamon 1987).

Another set of consequences of public–private partnerships concerns the impact
of for-profit encroachment into non-profit fields of operation and the accompanying emphasis on efficiency and capacity within government contracting. To both
compete and compensate for shrinking federal dollars, non-profit firms are
becoming increasingly commercialized with moves into sales and investment.
The extent of this commercialism within the non-profit sector varies considerably
by industry (see Weisbrod 1998: table 1.2, 17). Nonetheless, non-profits in a
variety of industries are engaged in selling theme licence plates, opening health
clubs and off-site museum stores, leasing mailing lists, sponsoring conferences,
publishing journals, loaning their logos, licensing and patenting discoveries,
among many other fee-generating income strategies (Anheier and Toepler 1999;
Cain and Merritt Jr 1998; Powell and Owen-Smith 1998; Weisbrod 1999;
Young 1998). In addition to commercial outputs, non-profits are commercializ-
ing in terms of the labour market as well. As Ayres-Williams writes, 'the sector
can now afford to be an employer of choice. Gone is the image of do-gooders
working inefficiently and at pittance wages for the sheer pleasure of helping
others. The reality of operating with multimillion dollar budgets has led most
nonprofits to adopt a more focused business approach' (Ayres-Williams 1998:
110). With commercial activity representing the largest proportion of income
growth for non-profits across the board, the question remains whether and to
what extent non-profit commercialism affects both public–private partnerships
and the character of the non-profit sector as a whole.

Business-like non-profits

As non-profits increasingly embark on commercial activities and as government funders place more weight on performance and capacity measures in
contracting relationships, the argument that non-profit organizations are
the most effective mechanisms for managing and delivering public goods
is called into question. The prevailing concern is that non-profit response
to increasing competition will be to adopt more businesslike management
strategies that compromise the social benefits non-profit organizations contribute in a variety of industries. The health-care field, for example, has seen
dramatic growth in commercialization, mergers and conversions to
for-profit status among non-profit hospitals and other non-profit health-
care organizations. The aftermath of these transformations provides an

opportunity to evaluate the continuing role of the non-profit sector in health-care provision.

One concern is how these transformations affect hospital pricing. Most economic models of non-profit hospital pricing assume that non-profit hospitals depart from profit-maximizing production choices because they tend to spend their profit in ways that meet objectives that meet their organizational mission to provide care, education and improve quality. Melnick *et al.* (1999) argue, however, that non-profits are nearly as likely as for-profit hospitals to meet their organizational objectives by raising prices, especially in a concentrated health-care market increasingly dominated by managed care. In their econometric model of hospital pricing, they also found that expected price increases depended on ownership and market share of merging hospitals. Although merging for-profit hospitals are more likely than merging non-profit hospitals to use their increased market share to raise prices, merging non-profit hospitals are likely to raise prices after mergers, just at a slightly smaller rate than among for-profit hospitals. Such findings indicate that non-profit behaviour is not unchanged by increasing competition with for-profit firms. The extent to which ownership status and commercialization affect public–private partnerships is an empirical question that warrants exploration as conversion and commercialization trends increase in the health-care field and beyond.

Some scholars now speculate about the justification of continued preferential treatment of non-profit organizations from the government. Again from the health-care field, Bloche (1998) argues that the 'putative social advantages' of the non-profit form over for-profit ownership status in health-care financing are uncertain and do not compensate for the costs of government protection. He claims that non-profit health-care facilities are no more likely to provide free care to the poor than for-profits and vary in their production of other social benefits, such as research and health-care promotion. Therefore, according to Bloche, these spotty social benefits do not mitigate direct and indirect economic costs to the government enough to warrant continued protection of the non-profit category of health-care organizations. This perspective contends that the government should pull even further away from non-profit sector and allow a more free-market approach to social-service delivery.

Another perspective on government support of non-profits holds more to the notion that the public–non-profit relationship has been and should remain mutually dependent. Melnick *et al.* (1999), for example, suggest that changing organizational behaviour within the non-profit sector actually warrants closer attention to the sector in terms of regulation. They argue that non-profit organizations respond to regulatory pressures better than for-profit firms. So by retaining their close relationships with the non-profit sector, government funders are still in a good position to control the output of collective goods from the non-profit sector (Lipsky and Smith 1989–90). This leverage may be especially distinct within periods of constricted government spending where there is increased competition for less funding.

Schlesinger *et al.* (1996) extend this argument by suggesting a regulatory division of labour within the government for the non-profit sector. They maintain that the Internal Revenue Service should define the parameters of the potential community benefit of the non-profit sector and define these benefits broadly enough to capture all possible dimensions of non-profit contributions. According to their scheme, other policy makers should then be left to prioritize these benefits because they have 'a better understanding of trade-offs among competing goals for public action and who are more responsive to contemporary public concerns' (Schlesinger *et al.* 1996: 738). This perspective recognizes the political nature of service provision and government contracting, arguing that the government needs to do more than provide funding to assure that collective goods provision meets demand.

Still other scholars find that non-profit organizations do still behave in traditionally beneficial ways, justifying continued government support of the non-profit form. Ryan (1999) argues that non-profits generally spend surplus on mission-related activities, promote civic virtues and advocate for the publics they serve. Weisbrod writes that these other findings of 'differential organization behaviour suggest, but do not necessarily prove, that when financial constraints allow, nonprofits do behave in a fundamentally different manner from for-profit organizations' (Weisbrod 1999: 12). This argument maintains that these behavioural differences between non-profit and for-profit organizations should give the non-profit form a comparative advantage in the competition for public funds.

Ryan (1999) cautions that the community benefits non-profits do offer are threatened by for-profit encroachment. When competition drives prices down, non-profits are likely to be left with less surplus revenue to spend on mission-related activities. In addition, competition with for-profits for government contracts may divide the client pools. For-profits will likely seek those clients who are easiest to serve, leaving harder, more expensive cases to non-profit providers. This perspective suggests that continued or even increased government support of the non-profit sector is crucial to preserve the collective benefits that non-profit organizations provide.

6.5 New contracting patterns

There is not much doubt about whether or not non-profits can survive in this new competitive climate because non-profit commercial activities tend to be innovative and profitable. In fact, non-profit response to external pressures from the for-profit sector increasingly involve some degree of coordination and collaboration among the public, non-profit and for-profit sectors. The danger surrounding this issue, however, is that non-profit organizations might succumb to 'institutional cusp pressures' and become more for-profit-like as boundaries between the non-profit sector and the for-profit sector continue to blur (Alexander 1998: 275). Non-profit scholars and advocates worry that non-profit entities will take the 'if you can't beat them, join them' response too much to heart, at the expense of their intended missions.

Government funds still play an important role in the financial stability of non-profit organizations across industries, but this role has changed to accommodate for-profit entrance into traditionally non-profit service areas and the resulting collaboration between sectors. More and more, public money becomes a lynchpin for non-profit partnerships with for-profit entities. Non-profit organizations increasingly find that they must team up with for-profit firms to compete for larger, consolidated funding streams. This trend is partially the result of push factors from the government. Social-spending retrenchment, emphasis on accountability in contracting relationships, devolution of social-welfare responsibility to states and local governments and the dismantling of many New Deal/Great Society welfare programmes have disrupted longstanding partnerships between government agencies and non-profit social-service providers.

For example, YWCA of Greater Milwaukee recently faced a 40 per cent revenue reduction as the Wisconsin legislature consolidated existing social-service programmes to develop an aggressive welfare-reform package. On their own, YWCA did not have the resources to make a competitive bid for the new $40 million welfare-to-work contract. Their response was to seek out a partnership with two for-profit firms to build the scale and managerial capacity to win the contract. The newly formed YW Works now provides almost every service that welfare recipients need in finding a job (Ryan 1999).

Other cases of non-profit partnerships with for-profit firms demonstrate how public money can help give non-profit organizations leverage with local business leaders, inspiring a variety of collaborative efforts in service delivery. For example, seven states have developed trust funds for affordable housing, ranging from $10–50 million. These funds are awarded to local-community developers to build and manage low and moderate-income housing. The Rio Tower project, a housing facility for elderly poor, in the Little Havana district of Miami was built with Florida's trust-fund money. The non-profit East Havana Community Development Corporation built and now manages the facility. Non-profit housing coalitions in various states have been able to use the local infusion of trust-fund money to leverage additional revenue from local realtors and home-builders in the form of real-estate transfer fees (Wayne 1998).

The US credit industry offers another example of how new welfare-policy initiatives, government funds and regulation create an environment that fosters public partnerships with non-profit and for-profit organizations in a variety of combinations. In the process of dismantling several public-assistance programmes, lawmakers have adopted 'hand up, not hand out' rallying slogans in support of new programmes that promote self-sufficiency. Some of the most politically popular self-sufficiency-type initiatives are micro-finance programmes. Borrowed from similar initiatives implemented throughout the developing world, these programmes are designed to provide credit and financial training to low-income entrepreneurs and homebuyers (Edgcomb et al. 1996). Various for-profit and non-profit micro-finance institutions receive public funds for lending to targeted low-income individuals for their credit needs and to groups for specific projects such as affordable housing development, neighbourhood-renewal projects and commercial revitalization projects.

Lawmakers have an interest in providing funds for such initiatives so they can fulfil social-welfare objectives that begin to compensate for retrenchment of other public-assistance programmes. However, in keeping with the trend of reducing government, they do not want to administer these lending programmes. They rely heavily on for-profit and non-profit partnerships to develop and manage these initiatives. In turn, for-profits, particularly banks, have an interest in participating in these micro-finance initiatives to boost their public image, meet certain regulatory demands for local investment and tap federal funding streams. Non-profit organizations also have an interest in taking advantage of these federal dollars so they can continue to provide investment capital in their service areas in spite of cuts in other federal programmes. Because non-profit micro-lending programmes are rarely self-sufficient, however, they often need to coordinate with local banks and businesses for additional funding, technical assistance provision and client referrals. These non-profit lenders also maintain relationships with local banks so they may refer clients back to the banks when the clients' needs grow beyond micro-finance lending caps.

Through these micro-finance initiatives, millions of federal dollars filter from the US Department of Housing and Urban Development (HUD) and the Small Business Administration (SBA) down through variable structures of local governments, for-profit and non-profit organizations to individual borrowers. These sectors partner up in various ways to disburse these funds and pool financial and technical resources. For example, the SBA and HUD Program for Investments in Microentrepreneurs (PRIME) funnels federal dollars to private for-profit venture capital and other investment companies for investment in local small-business initiatives (White House Fact Sheet 5 February 1999; US SBA Press Release 15 January 1999). These investment coalitions often coordinate with local banks for additional funds and technical expertise and with non-profit agencies for their existing network access to the targeted areas and populations and for their service expertise.

A new kind of mutual dependency?

A simultaneous and important trend in public–private-sector relationships is the government's reversal of its historically hostile stance toward for-profit firms. For-profit firms have been bidding for and getting government contracts to manage social-welfare programmes since 1996 in the wake of massive welfare-reform initiatives. While the move of for-profit firms into this traditionally non-profit turf was initially dismissed as 'poverty profiteering', for-profit firms are now managing dozens of new multi-million dollar welfare-to-work programmes nationwide (Ryan 1999). Outsourcing to for-profit firms has been an answer to lawmakers' desire to unload management responsibilities of large-scale social-welfare programmes. Driving the increasing reliance on for-profit firms is the assumption that for-profits are more experienced at managing complex systems than non-profit organizations. Not only do for-profit firms generally have better management-information systems, but they also have more collateral to guard against contract failure than most non-profits. So, for-profit firms are the logical outsourcing choice for lawmakers intent on reducing governmental bureaucracy.

Instead of shutting non-profit service providers out of the market, though, for-profit encroachment has actually inspired a new kind of mutual dependency among for-profit firms and non-profit organizations. In this new scheme, the government contracts out with for-profit firms for management of social programmes and for-profits then contract with non-profit organizations for service provision. For-profit firms may have the technical expertise and organizational capacity to manage large-scale delivery systems, but they often lack local access and specialized service-provision expertise. So, for-profit firms come to rely on non-profit organizations to help them fulfil their contracts at the provision end of the delivery system. For-profits become the middleman entity between government purchasers and non-profit providers.

6.6 Conclusion

This chapter looked at public–private partnerships in the United States. Cooperation between government and the non-profit sector has a long history in this country, and is, as we have seen, deeply rooted in its ideological and cultural make-up. This system of third-party government, however, has over time neither been stable nor comprehensive in its coverage. Pushed along by major policy initiatives that periodically seemingly revolutionized the substance and practice of government–non-profit relations, public–private partnerships remained a flexible and open system, unaffected by standardization any more comprehensive policy would bring about.

At the turn of the century, it seems as if we are witnessing the beginnings of an emerging trend that could lead to major changes in public–private partnerships. As we have seen, blurring sectoral boundaries have become more frequent, and the role of for-profit firms has become more pronounced. While it is difficult to gauge what the end result of these developments might be, it is safe to assume that more complex forms of partnerships will evolve. Future policy scenarios will increasingly include various combinations among government, business and non-profit providers. What is more, the three-way partnerships of the future will involve organizations no longer strictly bound by their legal form or sector membership. Organizational form may become more project-specific rather than a constant as was the case in the past.

What is more, project-specific rather than policy-specific partnership will allow more flexibility in developing contract regimes sensitive to local circumstances and challenges. At the same time, such developments make it necessary for local governments in particular not only to improve governance and accountability requirements but to put in place new ones that may be more in line with the complex partnership arrangements of the future. Standard public-administration programmes and tools will most certainly not measure up to the new contract regimes.

Of course, these policy developments also have theoretical implications. In a sense, they introduce a new twist to the government failure and voluntary-failure theories: Are for-profit providers the 'missing links' that helps governments overcome policy inertia in dealing with non-profit organizations, and non-profit organizations overcome commercialization pressures that may threaten their basic *raison d'être*? In theoretical terms at least, we are moving from partnerships to quasi-markets, or at least to 'staged scenarios' where each form brings in its own competitive advantage that supposedly compensates for the disadvantages of others. The outcome of this development is far from clear: Will such staged markets sort out the 'good' and 'bad' for-profit firms? Will non-profit organizations be overwhelmed by the temptations of profit motive and compromise their social agendas? and Will governments – like the sorcerer's apprentice – be able to master the forces they unleashed?

References

Alexander, V. D. (1998) 'Environmental constraints and organizational strategies: Complexity, conflict, and coping in the nonprofit sector', in W. W. Powell and E. S. Clemens (eds) *Private Action and the Public Good*, New Haven, CT: Yale University Press.

Amenta, E. and Carruther, B. G. (1988) 'The formative years of US social spending policies: Theories of the welfare state and the American states during the Great Depression', *American Sociological Review* 53(5): 661–78.

Anheier, H. K. and Toepler, S. (1999) 'Commerce and the muse: Are art museums becoming commercial?' in B. A. Weisbrod (ed.) *To Profit or Not to Profit: The Commercial Transformation of the Nonprofit Sector*, New York: Cambridge University Press.

Ayres-Williams, R. (1998) 'Changing the face of nonprofits', *Black Enterprise* 28(10): 110–14.

Behn, R. D. and Kant, P. A. (1999) 'Strategies for avoiding the pitfalls of performance contracting', *Public Productivity and Management Review* 22(4): 470–89.

Bellah, R., Madsen, R., Sullivan, W. M., Swidler, A. and Tipton, S. M. (1985) *Habits of the Heart*, Berkeley: University of California Press.

Bloche, M. G. (1998) 'Should government intervene to protect nonprofits?', *Health Affairs* 17(5): 7–25.

Cain, L. and Meritt Jr. D. (1999) 'Zoos and aquariums', in B. A. Weisbrod (ed.) *To Profit or Not to Profit: The Commercial Transformation of the Nonprofit Sector*, New York: Cambridge University Press.

Coble, R. (1999) 'The nonprofit sector and state governments: Public policy issues facing nonprofits in North Carolina and other states', *Nonprofit Management and Leadership* 9(3): 293–313.

Edgcomb, E., Klein, J. and Clark. P. (1996) *The Practice of Microenterprise in the U.S.: Strategies, Costs, and Effectiveness*, Washington, D.C.: Aspen Institute.

Laumann, E. and Knoke, D. (1987) *The Organizational State: Social Choice in National Policy Domains*, Madison: University of Wisconsin Press.

Lipset, S. M. (1996) *American Exceptionalism: A Double-edged Sword*, New York: W. W. Norton.

Lipsky, M. and Smith, S. R. (1989–90) 'Nonprofit organizations, government, and the welfare state', *Political Science Quarterly* 104(4): 625–48.

Melendez, S. E. (1998) 'The nonprofit sector: The cornerstone of civil society', *Issues of Democracy* (USIA Electronic Journal) 3(1).

Melnick, G., Keeler, E. and Zwanziger, J. (1999) 'Market power and hospital pricing: Are nonprofits different?', *Health Affairs* 18(3): 167–173.

National Low Income Housing Coalition. Online at http://www.nlihc.org/advocates

Oliver, D. T. (1999) 'Nonprofits rake in billions in government funds.' *Human Events* 55(36): 9–18.

Powell, W. W. and Owen-Smith, J. (1998) 'Universities as creators and retailers of intellectual property: Life-sciences research and commercial development.' in B. A. Weisbrod (ed.) *To Profit or Not to Profit: The Commercial Transformation of the Nonprofit Sector*, New York: Cambridge University Press.

Quadagno, J. (1987) 'Theories of the welfare state', *Annual Review of Sociology* 13: 109–28.

Ryan, W. P. (1999) 'The new landscape for nonprofits.' *Harvard Business Review*, 77(1): 127–36.

Salamon, L. M. (1987) 'Partners in public service: The scope and theory of government–nonprofit relations', in W. W. Powell (ed.) *The Nonprofit Sector: A Research Handbook*, New Haven: Yale University Press.

—— (1998) 'Nonprofit organizations: America's invisible sector', *Issues of Democracy* (USIA Electronic Journal) 3(1).

—— (1999) *America's Nonprofit Sector: A Primer*, New York: The Foundation Center.

Salamon, L. M. and Anheier, H. K. (1998) 'The third route: government–nonprofit collaboration in Germany and the United States', in W. W. Powell and E. S. Clemens (eds) *Private Action and the Public Good*, New Haven, CT: Yale University Press.

Skocpol, T. (1992) *Protecting Soldiers and Mothers: The Political Origins of Social Policy in the United States*, Cambridge, MA: Belknap Press of Harvard University Press.

Schlesinger, M., Gray, B. and Bradley, E. (1996) 'Charity and community: The role of nonprofit ownership in a managed health care system', *Journal of Health Politics* 21(4): 697–51.

Smith, S. R. and Lipsky, M. (1993) *Nonprofits for Hire: The Welfare State in the Age of Contracting*, Cambridge, MA: Harvard University Press.

U.S. Small Business Administration Press Release (15 January 1999) 'President Clinton, SBA Offer New Markets Investment Initiatives to Fuel Business and Job Creation in Rural, Inner City Areas.' New York, NY: PR Newswire.

Wayne, J. (1998) 'Affordable housing', *Commonweal* 125(14): 8–9.

Weisbrod, B. A. (1988) *The Nonprofit Economy*, Cambridge, MA: Harvard University Press.

—— (1999) 'The nonprofit mission and its financing: Growing links between nonprofits and the rest of the economy', in B. A. Weisbrod (ed.) *To Profit or Not to Profit: The Commercial Transformation of the Nonprofit Sector*, New York: Cambridge University Press.

White House Fact Sheet (5 February 1998) 'Creating Opportunity by Supporting Microenterprise.' White House Press Office: U.S. Newswire.

Young, D. R. (1998) 'Commercialism in nonprofit social service associations: Its character, significance, and rationale', in B. A. Weisbrod (ed.) *To Profit or Not to Profit: The Commercial Transformation of the Nonprofit Sector*, New York: Cambridge University Press.

7

UNIVERSITY OF
LIVERPOOL | Centre for Genomic Research

Peter Carroll Pusey

state - society relationship

7.1

As a[n] ... ate
partn[er] ... [b]een
Cons ... ng
and t ... on
of public–private partnership under the Conservative Government was the Private Finance Initiative (PFI), introduced in 1992 (see Terry 1996; Falconer and Ross 1998; Broadbent and Laughlin 1999). The Conservative approach to public–private partnership, as enshrined within the PFI, was principally ideological, fuelled by a belief in the primacy of the private sector over the public sector.

The perspective that drove the PFI was the same as that which had driven the overall Conservative public sector reform agenda since the early 1980s: that improvements in public sector performance would result from the public sector's exposure to private sector methods and management techniques, and to the disciplines of the market. This attempt to fuse the public sector with the rigours and alleged benefits of private sector disciplines had begun in the early 1980s, with the introduction of private sector management approaches in public sector organizations. It continued with the expansion of compulsory competitive tendering, through which private companies were able to compete for contracts under which public services were delivered. In 1992, with the establishment of the PFI, the role of the private sector was developed further, from that of involvement in the provision of public services to one of designing, building, operating and owning public sector facilities, such as schools and hospitals.

Throughout the 1980s and 1990s, the Labour Party in opposition had fiercely contested the Conservative view on the primacy of the private sector and the policy agenda which had been taken forward to reform the public sector. However, since taking office in May 1997, the Labour Government, under the leadership of Tony Blair, has largely reversed the position of Labour in opposition, and pursued a public-policy portfolio that is premised on a strong allegiance to the concept of public–private partnership. In so doing, the Labour Government has taken forward an important element of the 'new public management' reform

agenda, with its increasing focus on public service provision through the establishment of partnership relationships between the agencies of government, both
central and local, the private sector and the voluntary (the 'third') sector. In the
early years of the Blair Government, partnership has become a favourite word
in the lexicon of 'New Labour', giving rise to a wide range of public–private
partnership initiatives, some representing a continuation and development of
Conservative policies, and some representing new Labour approaches to public
policy. The use of public–private arrangements serve a number of important
objectives: the need to provide alternative sources of capital funding for the
public sector, as in the case of the Private Finance Initiative (Falconer and Ross
1998); the need to 'reinvent' government and establish legitimacy with local communities in the implementation of local economic development policies
(Osborne and Ross 1998); and the need to address the challenge posed by the
increasing involvement and participation in the policy process of civil society
organizations (Scott 1998).

As it moves through its first term in office, the Labour Government has been
increasingly attracted to the benefits which, it believes, accrue from partnership-
based policies, especially in regard to the overarching commitment to
'modernize' government. This chapter examines the developing partnership
ethos of the Labour Government in Britain, and considers the way in which
public–private partnerships are increasingly being advocated as the foundation
for the pursuit of public policy. As a case study illustration, the chapter gives
attention to the development of policy in the area of early years education, in
order to demonstrate the role and importance of partnership within the Labour
public policy agenda, and to make the important distinction between the
Labour approach to public–private partnership and that of its Conservative
predecessors.[1]

7.2 'New Labour' and partnership

Falconer and Ross (1998) make the point that the Labour Government's
commitment to public–private sector partnership is, in many ways, understandable:

> It was Labour local authorities that first advocated the notion of improving
> public sector provision through partnership and cooperation with the
> private sector. Moreover, Labour leader Tony Blair is intellectually sympa-
> thetic to a move away from the heavy reliance on the state as a central
> feature of Labour thinking, and, as leader of the Party, has argued consis-
> tently from a communitarian, cooperative standpoint which has advocated

1 The case-study analysis which follows is developed from research presented at the Fourth
International Conference on Public–Private Sector Partnerships, University of Liubljana, 1998
(see Falconer and Ross 1998).

strongly the value of partnership between the public sector and private enterprise.

(Falconer and Ross 1998: 133)

Moreover, O'Brien (1997) reminds us that:

> The origins of partnership are to be found under the last Labour administration. Business and the voluntary sector were working together with state and city. Peter Shore, then environment secretary, visited the US in 1978, and saw how government intervened to regenerate depressed communities. He decided to see if such novel groupings could be stimulated in Britain, but after the 1979 election it fell to the Conservatives to take the concept forward. It was thus both accidental and enormously significant that partnership was born as a cross-party concept.

(O'Brien 1997: 32)

This new approach to government for Labour in 1997 was underpinned further by the revised Clause IV of the Party's Constitution, promoting as it does:

> A dynamic economy, serving the public interest, in which *the enterprise of the market and the rigour of competition are joined with the forces of partnership and cooperation ... with a thriving private sector and high quality public services*, where those undertakings essential to the common good are either owned by the public or accountable to them.

(Labour Party 1995; emphasis added)

The development of partnership as a guiding principle of 'New Labour' is derived from changing attitudes toward the business sector. A clear distinguishing feature of 'New Labour', as opposed to 'Old Labour', is the nature of its posture toward the private sector. A political party which once held firmly to the view that the State should play a leading role in the workings of the nation's economy now promotes the belief that very little can be achieved in government without the active support of business. The Labour Government, under Blair's leadership, holds to the belief that one of its principal economic responsibilities is to provide the framework whereby the private sector can make profits, create employment and become involved in the delivery of public services in partnership with the public sector.

An example of Labour's developing relationship with business is the way in which the private sector is represented within 'New Labour's' quangocracy. The Labour Government has hardly moved on policy without establishing a task force or a stakeholding panel. In the various and numerous bodies established by Labour since taking office, a significant number of non-government members (at least half) have been drawn from the private sector. Labour Party officials and local councillors are conspicuous by their absence. Trade Unions are better represented, but not nearly as much as private-sector employers. This is not to say that such an approach is undesirable. Since many of the task forces are concerned with business-related matters, it seems reasonable that business expertise should be utilized. For example, there would be little point in establishing task forces on 'encouraging business investment' or 'Welfare to Work' without bringing employers on board. However, the prevailing view that efficient and effective management of public sector affairs requires the involvement of business represents a defining characteristic of the 'newness' of Labour.

The partnership principle is further bolstered by Labour's belief in a 'stakeholder' society (see Blair 1996: 291–321). In this sense, the public sector is viewed as consisting of a large number of stakeholder groups, each of which have a 'stake' in the way in which public services are financed and delivered. When the term 'stakeholder' first found its way into 'New Labour' rhetoric in 1996, it represented something of a bridge, linking Labour's desire to forge for itself a modern, electable, political vision with the needs and objectives of business. This link paved the way for a partnership ethos. The language of stakeholding, embracing notions of inclusiveness, community, corporate governance and partnership is 'cast in terms of acceptance of responsibilities as well as assertion of rights and changing culture' (Hutton 1997: 65). The role of government in this respect is, to quote Kelly and Gamble (1997: 38–9), clear:

> The state should ensure resources are tailored to each individual's needs, and then be wilfully promiscuous in utilising public, private and voluntary sectors to deliver them as appropriate. The terms of the contract between citizen and state will be flexible, however, often meaning that the more individuals put into the bargain the more they will get back in return ... Stakeholding has also been applied to the governance of organisations, especially companies. Inclusive forms of governance are recommended to balance the interests of various groups (such as shareholders, employees, and suppliers) who constitute the organisation. Overall, the debate which stakeholding has sparked on corporate governance has been useful. Progressive business ideas have been aired, contributing to a gathering momentum for change.

For Labour, partnership is central to the success of public service delivery. It is through partnership between the public sector, the private sector and the increasing number of voluntary sector organizations, that both the infrastructure of the public sector and the quality of public services are maintained and improved.

A cursory glance at Labour public policy rhetoric illustrates the way in which the language of partnership has permeated across the wide spectrum of public sector activity, at national, local and regional level, between public, private and voluntary organizations, and between service providers, communities and citizens. Based upon a strongly communitarian emphasis, Labour has promoted the idea of partnership arrangements as the key to efficient and responsive public services, and to value for money for citizens in public-service provision. There is no presumption on the part of Government, as there was on the part of its predecessor, that one sector provides the best route to the achievement of public sector objectives. Moreover, it is clear that, under Labour, no one model of partnership is favoured. Rather, the Government displays a highly pragmatic view, acknowledging the need for a flexible system of public sector funding and service provision which makes the best use of what the public, private and voluntary sectors have to offer, through the establishment of a wide variety of partnership arrangements.

Of course, Labour's allegiance to the language of partnership is not without its criticisms. In certain policy areas, such as that of the PFI, there are clear tensions between the Government's policy approach and the political perspectives of Labour's more 'traditional' supporters, amongst whom the new alliances with the private sector do not sit well. The fact that Labour has taken this strong ideologically based Conservative policy, and acted to strengthen and develop its implementation has placed the Labour leadership in the position of having to counter significant opposition from within the Labour Party. Falconer and Ross (1998: 137) consider Labour's adoption of PFI, arguing that 'one of the first indications that the new Labour Government intended to be a "New Labour" Government was its approach to PFI'. However, the difference for Labour was that the PFI was not being pursued on ideological grounds:

> The real task for Labour was to move the PFI forward in substantive terms, particularly since what had begun for the Conservatives as an ideologically acceptable method of enhancing public sector capital spending had, for Labour, become something of a necessity. For the new government, the PFI represented an essential means of avoiding what would otherwise be inadequate levels of investment in the public sector.
>
> (Falconer and Ross 1998: 137)

More general criticisms of Labour's allegiance to partnership focus on the ever-increasing scope of its usage which, it is argued, raises the danger of its value as a term 'being worn down to meaninglessness by endless repetition' (Deakin 1997: 35), and being eradicated through a lack of specific content in its precise meaning. Beckett (1998: xxiv) refers to partnership as little more than a jargonistic buzzword,

> . . . used, not for its intrinsic meaning, but as a hurrah-word. In Blair's Britain, words like new, community, innovative and partnership are used to convey a feeling of comfort rather than an exact meaning.

Using the example of education, Beckett continues:

> So everything you touch in education these days is a partnership. Universities, schools and colleges have partnerships with companies,

sponsors, parents, governments, students, other educational institutions and anyone with whom their business brings them into contact. I suspect that if a school needs its drains cleared, it enters into a partnership with a local plumber.

Nevertheless, despite this sort of criticism, Labour's commitment to partnership as the way forward for public service delivery and management is clear. For example, in the foreword to the policy document *Better Quality Services*, published in July 1998, the then Chancellor of the Duchy of Lancaster David Clark stated:

> The Government is re-inventing Britain. We want all Government services to be of the very highest quality, efficient, responsive and customer-focused. We are working with the private sector through competition to achieve this. What matters to the citizen, and therefore to the Government, is quality for the customer at the most reasonable cost to the taxpayer. If these are right, the distinctions between public and private are not so important. We want to encourage business to play a fuller role in providing public services. That is why we stress Public–Private Partnerships.
>
> (Cabinet Office 1998: 3; see also Falconer 1999)

Further, in November 1998, Transport Minister John Reid, emphasized the importance of partnerships, in true 'New Labour' fashion, to the development of transport policy:

> There will be no going back to the old days, with the state running everything, heedless of the results and the service delivery to the public and the consumer. The Government's proposals for public–private partnerships demonstrate that we will not let dogma stand in the way of the right solution, the right balance of public and private sector responsibility. Achieving a sustainable transport system must be a joint responsibility.
>
> (Department of the Environment, Transport and the Regions 1998)

In July 1999, the Secretary of State for Health Frank Dobson stressed the value of the Labour approach to the PFI, announcing the growth of the hospital-building programme launched by Labour under the PFI:

> Before we took office, local people up and down the country had been promised hospitals time after time, but not a single one had been built. £30 million had been spent on consultants' fees without a single brick being laid for a new hospital. We have changed all that. These latest hospitals are proof that when we make promises, we keep them. That's great news for local people in the areas getting the new hospitals. But it's good news for jobs in and around the new hospitals as well.
>
> (Department of Health 1999)

Arching over all these individual policy areas is the *Modernising Government* agenda, launched in March 1999. Founded upon the primary objective of improving governmental performance, *Modernising Government* embodies three stated goals:

- Ensuring that policy making is more joined up and strategic.
- Ensuring that public service users, not providers, are the principal focus.
- Demonstrating efficiency and a high level of quality in public service provision (CM 4310 1999).

Within this modernizing agenda, the role of partnership is clear:

> Distinctions between services delivered by the public and private sector are breaking down in many areas, opening the way to new ideas, partnerships and opportunities for devising and delivering what the public wants.
>
> (CM 4310 1999: 9)

> We will build on the many strengths in the public sector to equip it with a culture of improvement, innovation and collaborative purpose.
>
> (CM 4310 1999: 10)

> Some parts of the public service are as efficient, dynamic and effective as anything in the private sector. But others are not. There are numerous reasons for this, and … to help counter some of these difficulties, the Government is working in partnership – partnership with the new, devolved ways of government, and partnership with local authorities, other organisations and other countries.
>
> (CM 4310 1999: 11)

Partnership thus occupies a central place in both the rhetoric and practice of the Labour Government's public policy agenda. An examination of partnership within the context of a particular policy – that of early years' education policy – will further illustrate its role.

7.3 Partnership and 'early education' policy

Pre-school education has until recently been a neglected area of policy in Britain, with the nation's poor record in stimulating provision and uptake of nursery education relative to its European counterparts a source of frequent concern and critical comment (Moss and Penn 1996). This trend has reversed over the last four years and the sector has experienced an unprecedented rate of change inspired by the competing ideologies of Conservative and New Labour Governments. During this period Early Education has become something of a political football and subject to sea changes of public policy. Two models of public–private partnership have dominated this period of change: one market based – the Nursery Voucher Initiative developed by the previous Conservative Government; the other rooted in a rejection of the market-based approach to partnership and based on a model of community governance with the discourse of partnership encompassing the manner in which policy is to be developed at a local level, and as a pre-scribed context for the continued commitment to plural-service provision.

New Labour's early-education partnership policy has developed against a background of dissent against the inherited Nursery Voucher Initiative. The Voucher Initiative was rooted in classic market-based partnership thinking where parents were issued with a voucher to purchase suitable education for the pre-school year from accredited public, private and voluntary providers (Department of Education and Employment 1996a). Parental choice was to be the driving force behind expansion of provision in this area with local authority budgets top-sliced to fund the project and experienced local authority providers required to compete thereafter to regenerate lost income. Crucially, the voucher initiative did not commit itself to providing a place for every four-year-old in the pre-school year. Rather it offered a voucher to all parents, arguing that in the longer term the injection of funding through vouchers would lead to an increase in suppliers, particularly from the private sector, willing to make capital invest-ments as a result of increased demand for services from governmental pump-priming. In addition the initiative was noted for being devoid of any substantive policy framework for early education, other than to signal probable expansion of the sector through a combination of government pump-priming, private sector investment and parental top-up contribution.

Then in opposition, the Labour Party orchestrated a detailed campaign against the voucher concept and the market-based model of plural service provision which it espoused (Labour Party 1996). They pointed to a host of critical reviews including official evaluations of the pilot projects pioneering the policy (Department of Education and Employment 1996b; Stephen 1997) as well as highlighting the force-related nature of the legislation underpinning the policy itself (Conner 1996), and the cumbersome and bureaucratic nature of the voucher machinery. They contended that as vouchers did not guarantee places they were worthless to many parents living in areas with undersupply of places, and that this was further compounded by funding revenue costs and not investing similarly in capital-expansion projects to provide 'real' places. The fact that the Conservative Minister designated to take forward the initiative, Gillian Shephard, was known to be unconvinced about the workability of the initiative added power to the organized voice of dissent and the argument that vouchers failed to offer a suitable policy framework for expansion of early-education services.

The Labour Party in opposition became the mouthpiece in uniting a disparate-issue network of organizations in the public and voluntary sector, which lobbied fiercely against the Nursery Voucher Initiative, both during its legislative passage and in the lead-up to the 1997 general election. Their principal argument was for a more substantive policy framework to underpin the expansion of the sector. The case for an alternative and immediate replacement of nursery vouchers became a key electoral issue, creating a series of expectations for the incoming Labour Government in developing its alternative policy. Co-opting the views and interests of this broad-issue network into the new policy environment was an immediate task for the new government, as was the delivery of an expansion of services in the policy field. One of the key policy challenges facing the Labour Government lay in policy differentiation, and in positioning a new policy product within the minds of the public in a way that would appear distinct from the previous policy while still remaining capable of offering benefits to all stakeholders across the public, private and voluntary sectors. It is this context within which Labour has developed critical elements of its partnership thinking, to give a voice and role to all providers within the sector, but also to enhance the involvement of local communities in planning the development of provision and types of service offered. The partnership rubric is therefore used to incorporate increasingly articulate and diverse provider/interest groups into mainstream policy making, and to balance this provider-campaigning voice with involvement of the community in general and service users in particular in the policy decision-making process.

The Labour Government's emergent Early Years policy provides an interesting example of a 'top-down', centrally led policy of public–private partnerships, to be implemented at the local level with close attention paid to the challenge of building legitimacy into the mechanics of public–private partnerships as part of the policy process itself. The policy is therefore concerned with the principles of effective partnering relationships as a key element of delivering an expansion of a range of education and childcare services. Tony Blair is frequently quoted as saying 'what matters is what works', in an attempt to exhume inertia from public administration.

In reality, as we examine the development of policy in this area, it becomes evident that 'what matters is what counts', and that partnerships in this area count as a political vehicle for aligning interest-group voices with the modernizing intentions of the current government. Partnerships are espoused out of pragmatic necessity, and fulfil a highly useful function in shaping a growth sector against the backdrop of tools and techniques espoused to promote community governance in the development of a substantive policy framework for early education.

During its early months in office, the Labour Government responded to the 'policy void' in early-years education, through the development of a policy framework built on partnership between private, public and voluntary sectors. The ultimate objective was the establishment of an integrated Early Years policy and, to this end, the Government have stipulated a number of strategic principles to guide policy making:

> The key element is that early years services should be placed in each local authority area. The plans should be drawn up with a body which represents all the relevant interests in the local authority area, and should show how

the target of securing an early education place for all eligible four-year-olds can be achieved by September 1998 ... The Plans should also show how other services for young children, such as day care and after school care, can be provided; and be related to other relevant plans drawn up by the local authority.

(Department of Education and Employment 1997: 1)

The integrated framework for early-years education is, for Labour, an essential prerequisite for tackling the problems in standards of educational achievement in Britain. Moreover, offering pre-school and after-school facilities enables parents who so desire to enter the labour market. In this way, the Early Years policy is linked to Labour's wider 'welfare to work' strategy and its principles for welfare reform. This is important in terms of government policy toward issues of poverty, unemployment and social security. The emergent Early Years policy thus represents the centrepiece of a range of economic and social policy concerns to promote joined-up policy thinking to tackle endemic social and economic problems. Interestingly too, service provision in the Early Years policy field serves to defy classic policy boundaries between 'education' and 'care', the long-term objective of public–private partnerships being to drive forward the delivery of joined-up service provision, in order to make available an integrated education/care package to meet the needs of parents and the local labour market.

Funding decisions to underpin the expansion of the sector and the implementation of the public–private partnering policy itself have been piecemeal. As an initial step the Labour Government committed all resources previously allocated to the Conservatives' voucher scheme to the new Early Years policy, together with additional financial resources carried forward from unclaimed vouchers under the Conservative scheme. More recently the Government's outline of the new Working Families Tax Credit earmarks a further £250 million a year for the sector from 1999 onwards. In addition the ring-fencing of National Lottery funding to develop aftercare provision indicates a plural-funding base for expansion in the sector. Nevertheless, even with these additional sources of funding, it is clear that alternative sources of income will be necessary in order to meet current and future expansion of local provision, consistent with local needs. For example, in regard to the approach to the policy in Scotland, the Scottish office has noted that:

Although much can be achieved within the existing funding envelope, some elements of quality improvement do imply additional resource demands ... The overall context of funding is extremely constrained. Although Government will seek to do what they can, as resources permit, no commitment or guarantees can be given. Against this overall context, the aims of the funding mechanisms are ambitious, and will not be easy to satisfy.

(Scottish Office 1997: 16)

The Scottish Office's consultation exercise makes a crucial distinction between government provision of 'free education' and 'parental contribution' to the child care element provided as part of the overall educational package. As such, the thorny issue of 'top-up fees' for pre-school education is revisited. This issue has been an important issue of contention during debates over the voucher scheme, under which local-authority providers were not permitted to charge top-up fees for additional services, whereas private providers were entitled to use top-up fees to expand access to the service. The critical factor here is the way in which part-nerships are used as a chameleon concept to address the practical problems facing government of expanding services within the constraint of limited budgets. The partnership rhetoric extends beyond parental voice and choice in the development of local services, into a business relationship between providers and local customers who are now encouraged to buy into top-up services to suit their needs.

While the present concerns of policy makers are focused upon delivering the immediate objective of free educational provision for 4-year-olds, the wider policy goal of developing an integrated early-years service will, as noted above, intensify the need to search for alternative income sources. The Department of Education and Employment (Department of Education and Employment 1998a) has indicated that, while local authorities may not charge parents for pre-school education itself, they may impose charges for before- and after-school services, where applicable. Nevertheless, the central point remains: the realization of an integrated Early Years policy within the existing resource envelope will compel the development and expansion of public–private partnership in the search for solutions to resource difficulties. Furthermore the plural funding base underpinning expansion of services within the policy area will provide a challen-ging set of incentives to service providers to respond to the wide range of stake-holders who stand to benefit from the development of services in the area.

The nature of evolving public–private partnership arrangements will impact critically on the Government's ability to deliver on its pledge to expand the service. In this regard, it is impossible to ignore the policy legacy inherited by Labour from the previous Conservative regime. The new Government's early-years strategy is developing within the legislative framework established by the Conservative Government for their Nursery Vouchers scheme. Although Labour's approach gives evidence of a shift in policy emphasis, the point remains that the Conservatives' statutory framework for pre-school education remains intact. In terms of policy emphasis, the Nursery Vouchers scheme threatened to marginalize the role of local authorities in the provision of educational services for pre-school children. The current policy reinstates the central role of local gov-ernment as lead agents in the development and expansion of the service. Moreover, where a local authority's Early Years development plan fails to take account of the importance of partnership, the provision exists for funding to be withheld.

The new role for local authorities as lead agents requires local government to operate on 'enabling' principles similar to those espoused under the Nursery

Voucher Initiative. While the local authority receives a grant for the provision of services directly from Central Government, it will inevitably require to subcontract with the private and voluntary sectors, in order to provide the level of places consistent with the Government's longer term commitment to a free educational place for all three-year-olds as well as four-year-olds. Contracts and market mechanisms will ultimately govern the nature of the relationship between the local authority and its constituent partners. As lead agents implementing a national policy of public–private partnering, local authorities face a range of issues in reconciling funding conditionality and evidence of partnership, with the attractions of expanding directly provided services in the growth area of early education and the broader funded policy domain of childcare provision.

The local authority will also be required to consult widely with parental and community groups on the type of service provided, and the articulation between the education and care components of the service, as well as on the issue of charges and top-up fees for this 'integrated package'. The recent Green Paper consulting on a National Childcare Strategy (Department of Education and Employment 1998b) promotes the concept of 'local childcare partnerships', which will play a pivotal role in tempering the producer interests of local authorities as well as co-opting a wide range of provider and stakeholder groups into the local policy decision-making process. It is envisaged that childcare partnerships will be involved in a range of activities, including local audits of supply and demand, and developing local childcare plans. Membership of these partnerships will include local authorities, parents, private and voluntary providers, employers, local enterprise companies, colleges and schools, health boards and trusts. While responsibility for convening and supporting these partnerships lies with the local authority, it is important that partnerships are not seen as local-authority bodies, thus reinforcing the enabling model of plural-service provision within localities and the central requirements of inclusive policy making at a local level.

The concept of partnership within which the expansion of early education is rooted helps to illustrate the manner in which partnership thinking per se has been elevated to a core political principle within the Labour Government (Ross and Osborne 1999). Within this policy area, we see partnership espoused as a means of navigating the complex and dynamic environment comprising the actions and interactions of provider interests, user voice and community needs, as per the stakeholder model. These dynamic interactions between Government and non-government organizations, including both voluntary and private sector providers, are intended to encourage creative responses to the provision of appropriate, valued, quality public services (Ross 1999).

7.4 Conclusions

The Labour Government's commitment to the principle and value of partnership is clear, both in terms of rhetoric and public policy practice. As this chapter has illustrated, the Labour allegiance to public–private partnership demonstrates both change and continuity in the development of partnership as a modus operandi in British government thinking. There is continuity, in the sense that the Labour Government has carried forward a policy agenda established and developed by its Conservative predecessors. On the other hand, there is change, in the sense that the Labour approach to public–private partnership is distinctive in two important respects. First, while the Conservative allegiance to partnership was strongly ideological, driven by a belief in the primacy of the private sector and the need for the public sector to be subjected increasingly to private sector influences, the Labour approach is pragmatic, grounded as it is in perceived realities deriving from economic constraints on public finance. Second, while the Conservative policy agenda was developed from a strong allegiance to market principles, the Labour philosophy of partnership is grounded within a stakeholder model, and founded on an adherence to the principles of community and com-munitarianism. As Labour's public–private partnership initiatives continue to develop, it is apparent that they are taking on an increasingly distinctive guise which serves to locate them firmly within the context of what has become known in Britain as 'New Labour'.

References

Beckett, F. (1998) 'A key article, with quality delivery', New Statesman Lifelong Learning Supplement, *New Statesman*, 13 November.

Blair, T. (1996) *New Britain: My Vision of a Young Country*, London: Fourth Estate.

Broadbent, J. and Laughlin, R. (1999)'The private finance initiative: Clarification of a future research agenda', *Financial Accountability and Management* 15(2): 95–114.

Cabinet Office (1998) *Better Quality Services: A Handbook on Creating Public/Private Partnerships Through Market Testing and Contracting Out*, London: Cabinet Office.

CM 4310 (1999) *Modernising Government*, London: Stationery Office.

Conner, M. (1996) 'The Implementation of Nursery Vouchers: the Scottish Experience', unpublished report, Department of Law and Public Administration, Glasgow Caledonian University.

Deakin, N. (1997) 'True partnership: A word urgently needs clearer definition', *New Statesman*, 20 June.

Department of Education and Employment (1996a) *Nursery Education Scheme; the Next Steps*, London: Department of Education and Employment.

Department of Education and Employment (1996b) *Nursery Education Scheme: Report on Phase 1*, London: Department of Education and Employment.

Department of Education and Employment (1997) *Early Years Development Partnership*, London: Department of Education and Employment.

Department of Education and Employment (1998a) *Early Years Update: Information on New Plans for Early Years Education*, Issue 1, London: Department of Education and Employment.

Department of Education and Employment (1998b) *Meeting the Childcare Challenge: A Framework and Consultation Document*, CM 3959, London: Department of Education and Employment.

Department of the Environment, Transport and the Regions (1998) 'Press Release 1998/931', London: Department of Environment, Transport and the Regions, 3 November.

Department of Health (1999) 'Press Release 1999/0421', London: Department of Health.

Falconer, P. (1999) 'Better quality services: Enhancing public service quality through partnership in the UK', in L. Montanheiro *et al.* (eds) *Public–Private Sector Partnerships: Furthering Development*, Sheffield: Sheffield Hallam University Press, pp. 175–87.

Falconer, P. and Ross, K. (1998) 'Public–private partnership and the new public management in Britain', in L. Montanheiro *et al.* (eds) *Public–Private Sector Partnerships: Fostering Enterprise*, Sheffield: Sheffield Hallam University Press, pp. 133–48.

Hutton, W. (1997) *The State to Come*, London: Vantage.

Kelly, G. and Gamble, A. (1997) 'A helping hand to autonomy', *New Statesman*, 21 March.

Labour Party (1995) *The Constitution of the Labour Party*, London: Labour Party.

Labour Party (1996) *The Politics of the Nursery Voucher – Why Nursery Vouchers Are Not the Answer for Our Children*, London: Labour Party.

Moss, P. and Penn, H. (1996) *Transforming Nursery Education*, London: Paul Chapman.

O'Brien, S. (1997) 'London's Team Spirit', *New Statesman*, 13 June.

Osborne, S. P. and Ross, K. (1998) *Local development agencies and public private partnerships in local communities: The policy practice interface*, paper given at the 20th Anniversary Conference of Third Sector Organisations, London School of Economics.

Ross, K. and Osborne, S. P. (1999) 'Making a reality of community governance: Structuring Government–voluntary sector relationships at the local level', *Public Policy and Administration*, 14(3): 49–61.

Ross, K. (1999) 'Collaborative marketing and early years partnerships in Scottish local authorities', paper given at the Third International Research Symposium on Public Management, Aston University.

Scott, J. (1998) 'Law, legitimacy and EC governance: Prospects for partnership', *Journal of Common Market Studies* 36(2): 175–92.

Scottish Office (1997) *Education in Early Childhood: The Pre-School Years – A Consultation Paper*, Edinburgh: Scottish Office Education and Industry Department, January.

Stephen, C. (1997) *Pre-School Education Voucher Initiative: National Evaluation of the Pilot Year*, Final Report, Part 1, Stirling: Stirling University.

Terry, F. (1996) 'The private finance initiative – overdue reform or policy breakthrough', *Public Policy and Management*, January–March: 9–16.

8 The East Asia region

Do public–private partnerships make sense?

Richard Common

8.1 Introduction

At first glance, public–private partnerships appear to be conceptually hard to apply in a region that does not lend itself readily to a Western analytical perspective. The diffusion of policy ideas and innovations assumes receptive environments. Therefore this chapter seeks to provide an understanding of the context of social policy within the region, a context which has profound implications for the development of public–private partnerships. Although it is difficult to generalize about the region, the central argument here is that the concept of public–private partnerships has developed within the context of fundamental structural changes to the welfare state in Western liberal democracies. In the West, there has been a growing consensus about the legitimacy of encouraging the private and the non-profit sectors to provide public services. Lowndes and Skelcher (1998) ascribe the development of partnerships in the UK to growing restraints on public resources, the organizational fragmentation brought about by the New Public Management, persistent social problems that demanded a partnership approach and strategies to democratize grass-roots decision making. As this chapter seeks to demonstrate, the absence or fragility of these determinants in East Asia means that we cannot assume that is inevitable that public–private partnership will become an automatic feature of governance. After an assessment of the prospects for partnerships in relation to the impact of economic globalization, the demands of the state and the influence of culture, the chapter will evaluate the uneven scope for public–private partnerships by reviewing policy change in the countries that constitute the region. For the purposes of this chapter, East Asia refers to the People's Republic of China (PRC), the Hong Kong Special Administrative Region (SAR) of the PRC (formerly Hong Kong), the Republic of China on Taiwan (Taiwan), South Korea and Japan. If we expand the categorization to that of 'Confucianist' Asia, Singapore is also included (Tu 1996). Singapore also shares many socio-economic features with the rest of East Asia.

8.2 The changing context of social and public policy in East Asia

Economic globalization and the emergence of partnerships

Arguably, the emergence of partnerships has also been precipitated by structural changes to the welfare state brought about by an increasingly globalized economic environment. Under the yoke of economic globalization, 'all governments are obliged to bear down upon public spending' (Castles and Pierson 1996: 234). However, the impact of economic globalization has had more fundamental consequences. The welfare state can no longer regard itself as having a purely domestic role 'in an increasingly internationalised world' where 'it is being forced to act more and more like a market player' (Cerny 1990: 230). Thus, the net result of competition in global markets is the appearance of the 'competition state' (Cerny 1997: 263) which is replacing the welfare state in Western liberal democracies. Cerny (1997: 264) argues that in such a state, the 'institutions and practices of the state itself are increasingly marketized or "commodified"', and the state becomes the spearhead of structural transformation to market norms both at home and abroad'. It appears that public–private partnerships are manifestations of the Competition State, along with the 'reinventing government' movement. The developmental states of East Asia may be regarded as nascent competition states, which are being transformed by further integration into the global economy but remain characterized by strong technocratic control.

Furthermore, globalization forces economic and business integration with the consequence that 'conventional wisdom has it that a more integrated world will be a more homogeneous one' (Micklethwait and Wooldridge 1996: 243). The homogenizing effects of globalization thus result in 'institutional isomorphism' (DiMaggio and Powell 1991). Therefore, despite the contextual differences, whether based in London or Beijing, organizations start to behave in a similar fashion. Therefore, the link between the development of partnerships and the economic interdependence that underpins 'strong' versions of globalization appears to be an attractive one. This often leads to dramatic assumptions being made that public and social policy is 'global' and national 'domains' of culture and politics are often subsumed. Therefore, to accept Cerny's argument that the consequence of greater integration into the global economy is the emergence of the Competition State, then we might also expect the development of public–private partnerships in diverse localities.

If we take the narrow view of economic globalization to mean the development of international trade and integration with the world economy, then countries in East Asia are highly globalized. The recent economic success of the region comes 'in part through its links to world commerce and to the free-trade blocs of North America and Europe' (Means 1998: 108). Moreover, this success, at least until recently, was attributed to the region's capacity (particularly in the Asian 'Tigers': Hong Kong, Singapore, South Korea and Taiwan, plus Japan) in attracting foreign direct investment and an openness to international trade that brought modern jobs and goods to the region. Market reforms in China meant it too could enter the world market. Although by the end of 1997, this growth began to look like it had peaked and had reversed into a 'development crisis' (Wade and Veneroso 1998), it is the impetus towards economic development that shapes public and social policy in the region. Recent waves of innovation and reform in public policy are regarded as being triggered by 'the newly recognized need to compete effectively in the international market' (Ingraham 1996: 250). Such innovations include the development of partnerships.

The State in East Asia: prospects for partnerships

States in the region are generally described as 'developmental states' (McCargo 1998: 126). Leftwich (1994: 9) defines developmental states 'as those states whose politics have concentrated sufficient power, autonomy and capacity at the centre to shape, pursue and encourage the achievement of explicit developmental objectives'. Government activity is chiefly directed to the pursuit of economic success, using varying degrees of authoritarian methods. Although the developmental state is not confined to the East Asia region, it is often associated with it (Leftwich 1994: 14). Ro (1993: 94) argues that development in East Asia, in contrast to the West, 'is a centralized impulse that spreads ever outward and downward through bureaucracy and the organizational forms of industrialization'. In general, the role of government in East Asia is that of national planning and development, although there are variations between the countries in their approach to development. As centralization is implicit in the developmental state, then it can be assumed that decentralization and managerial discretion, which underpin much social policy development in the West, are unlikely to be welcomed in the drive to modernize and develop.

The association of the welfare state with liberal democracies is also problematic in the East Asian context. Liberal democracy, 'which assumes the neutrality, anonymity and impartiality of the administrative apparatus and its accountability to elected politicians, is either absent or fragile in most Asian ... countries' (Haque 1996: 319). Therefore, it is difficult to describe states in the region as liberal democracies in the Western sense. Commentators prefer to refer to 'Asian style democracy' (Neher 1994) or 'semidemocracy' (Islam and Chowdhury 1997) with regime types varying considerably within the region from the quasi-democracies of South Korea, Singapore and Taiwan to the one-party state of China. Only the Japanese political system can be compared with that of a liberal democracy yet it scores low in terms of citizen and interest-group participation (Moon and Ingraham 1998: 81). Japan also has a single dominant party, the Liberal Democratic Party, which despite recent setbacks, has dominated since the 1950s. Hong Kong's political parties compete for a third of seats in the SAR Government's legislature, yet the bureaucracy wields executive power. Although within the region we can observe a mix of liberal-democratic components (regular elections with universal franchises, interest group activity, etc.) there remains varying degrees of state authoritarianism. Unlike Western liberal democracies, 'modern nations in Asia have emerged out of a lineage of authoritarian states' (Chun 1996: 70).

The cultural variable in East Asia

As 'culture' may be regarded as a major determinant of social attitudes, and that partnerships are largely an Anglo-American invention, we might expect them to be incompatible with local cultural values. Hofstede (1980: 25) defines culture as 'the interactive aggregate of common characteristics that influence a human group's response to its environment'. Culture can be used as an explanatory variable in comparative studies as it can cause differences and affect the 'transferability of management and organizational practices' as well as determining organizational behaviour (Lachman *et al.* 1994: 40).

In any analysis of working methods in Asia, Confucianism is often regarded as an important cultural variable. In particular, economic development in East Asian countries has been ascribed to Confucian principles. Stella Quah (1995: 287) argues that another significant feature of these countries, which may be as important as Confucianism, is pragmatic acculturation. This is a process related to economic development and involves 'the adoption by individuals or groups of aspects of a culture that is not their native one'. This process gained momentum across Asia following World War II as countries across the region industrialized. Thus, there are contradictions where methods and techniques introduced from elsewhere clash with more deeply embedded socio-cultural practices.

Root (1996: 2) dismisses Confucianism as an independent variable and regards it as a cliché. Islam and Chowdhury (1997: 131) concur by arguing that 'once core "Asian"/Confucian values are diluted' to a 'level of generality, they lose their distinctiveness and become part of universal human values'. However, others regard the Confucian tradition as a major force that guides societies where Chinese influence is strong (Huque 1996: 14). Undoubtedly, national cultures can have a powerful influence on the way public policy is delivered, and Confucian culture is not homogenous across the region. Sikorski (1996: 830) observes that 'a Confucian culture implies respect for authority, individual cultivation and merit, and community welfare'. However, the value placed on hierarchy and top-down decision making, which is also central to Confucian philosophy, would appear to suggest that partnerships, with their emphasis on collaboration and networks are likely to be shunned by organizations influenced by Confucian culture. Therefore, Lachman *et al.* (1994: 53) argue that 'imported' practices may fail, or be ineffectively implemented, if they are inconsistent with the core values of local settings.

Pressures for indigenization include the reinforcement of culture. According to Henderson (1995: 17): 'indigenization is thought of as native patterns which are neither imposed nor copied from the West'. The assumption here is that partnerships are indigenous to the West and Western cultural values. When combined with indigenization, culture may powerfully affect the transferability of social-welfare models. Therefore, in an effort to affirm Asian values there may be a tendency in the region to resist programmes and principles promulgated in the West. Majstorovic (1997: 149) notes how Kishore Mahbubani, a senior Singaporean politician, 'contends that Asian interests and methods are different and must be decoupled from the West'. In particular, Islam and Chowdhury (1997: 131) argue that some sections of East Asian society regard social problems in the United States with such horror that these problems 'have tarnished – perhaps for ever – the USA as an exemplar worthy of emulation'. Sikorski (1996: 819) argues nearly all East Asian nations, including Japan, 'have lately been sending consistent messages to America – expressions of doubt about the applicability in Asia of Western values and processes'.

Furthermore, the core value of individualism in the West conflicts with the notion of collective responsibility found in much of East Asia. Hickson and Pugh (1995) examine Asian management culture and much of it conflicts directly with Western management theory. In particular, the stress on 'managing relationships in a harmonious manner' and 'managing authority firmly from the top' means that notions of devolved management, 'freedom to manage' and 'brainstorming sessions' are viewed as alien. The kind of restructuring of public organizations required by partnerships demands participation by lower level staff, which often runs against the grain of deeply entrenched communication and authority systems. Also, the notion of social egalitarianism, which is implicit in the Western partnership concept, may clash with cultural values in East Asia. Although rapid economic development in the Asia–Pacific region has brought about more egalitarian social conditions, and some degree of welfarism, egalitarianism is not compatible with East Asian Confucian societies if inequality can be properly legitimated (Shils 1996: 59). The implications for partnerships, where they exist, are likely to be in the form of vertical, hierarchical arrangements rather than voluntary collaboration.

In sum, the context for public–private partnerships appears unpromising in East Asia. The centralized control wielded by developmental states wedded to semi-authoritarian political systems would appear to discourage collaboration between public and private providers, especially if it is to address a policy problem unrelated to economic objectives. Furthermore, such collaboration is likely to be inhibited if the non-statutory partner was perceived to be political and critical of state policies. Culturally, the Confucian tradition, which stresses the notion of community harmony, influences governance in East Asia. Although opinion is divided on the importance that should be placed on the influence of Confucianism culturally, the notion of partnerships as an egalitarian approach to governance appears to be inappropriate in the East Asian context.

8.3 The scope for public–private partnerships in East Asia

Partnerships have appeared in part as a result of the fragmentation of the welfare state. However, in East Asia, the development of a welfare state was never among the priorities of the governments in the region, neither was there any popular demand for social investment. As White *et al.* (1998: 213) observe:

> The notion of state-provided or guaranteed welfare as a social right of citizens is still not well established. Rather, non-state agencies – community, firm and family – have been expected to play a major welfare role in an ideological context wherein self/mutual help is encouraged and dependence on the state is discouraged or indeed stigmatized.

Rather, emphasis was given to 'community building', which was 'about restoring the family to its role as bulwark of society and rendering the neighbourhood the functional equivalent of a traditional village' (Jones 1990: 453). Priority was given to education, followed by health and housing as the main social services provided by governments. The easy explanations for the absence of a voluntary sector in East Asia are Chinese cultural values that emphasize familial and community duties that exclude strangers.

This unpromising environment for the development of partnerships in the region demands a review of social policy developments. Beginning with the People's Republic of China (PRC), it appears to be so exceptional that it defies generalizations and comparisons. China began its shift from a command economy to market socialism in the late 1970s as a result of changing elite values. Economic change began when it became obvious to the leadership that in order to maintain its legitimacy it had to abandon its revolutionary ideology in favour of economic well-being (Wang 1995). A document released by the Chinese Government in late 1993 distinguished between three types of market economies (Lam 1995: 127). These 'models' were:

- the Anglo-Saxon or American model, which stressed individual effort;
- a Northern Europe model which stressed social welfare and worker participation; and
- an East Asiatic or Asia Pacific model, which argues for a collectivist approach to the market place.

Naturally, the Chinese leadership was keen to stress the third model in their approach to market reforms in order to create a 'socialist market economy'.

In terms of welfare, China has never had a welfare state, in the Western liberal-democratic sense. Hutchings (1997) cites Szreter who likens the social policy situation in China to that of Victorian England when rapid economic growth in a relatively free market context directly caused a number of social problems. Before 1949, it was families that mainly provided 'social security'. After the communist revolution, it was the centralized wage system that took care of redistribution. How the different enterprises and municipalities took care of meeting people's needs varied considerably across the country. Labour insurance systems were introduced that involved pensions, sickness and invalidity benefits which covered State-owned enterprises (SOEs) and collective enterprises employing more than 100 people. By the time of the Cultural Revolution, the system had become damaged and retirement discouraged. It was only after the economic reforms of 1978 that Western-style formal contributory systems were established. These systems were the responsibility of each work unit and consisted of pensions, maternity and sickness benefits and some health care. Also, minimum retirement ages and basic pensions were specified by regulations. However, enterprises were not encouraged to pool or coordinate their resources (Pudney 1995: 233–4).

Although Britain developed a welfare state to cope with the problems of economic growth, in China it was the SOEs that provided welfare services directly. Therefore, social provision in China is highly atomized and fragmented as it is based largely on individual State firms. Therefore, welfare is synonymous with employment in both urban and rural China. Given that unemployment is incompatible with communism, guaranteed employment in turn guaranteed the welfare benefits supplied by the work units or communes. Lee (1999) describes how the work units (*danwei*) 'constituted a mini welfare state, providing not only jobs and earnings but also a wide array of goods and services for employees and their families, ranging from housing, medical care, educational provisions, childcare to pensions and crematorial service'. The recent thrust to 'privatize' SOEs does not involve the transfer of systems of welfare delivery to private companies, especially as much commercial activity is undertaken by 'collectively owned' businesses. Therefore, 'social policy' in China is largely a consequence of the impact of 'privatization' and marketization of the SOEs. The 'iron rice bowl' that guaranteed welfare benefits for state-enterprise employees is no longer reliable.

Social welfare systems to absorb workers made redundant as a consequence of the economic reforms are only being developed at the local level. There is no national unified plan although there are social services, social insurance and security systems at provincial and municipal levels. For instance, Heibei province has established welfare service networks for the disabled, disaster and poverty relief, and services for the dependants of soldiers and the elderly, as well as wedding and funeral arrangements (BBC Monitoring Service 1998). As Pudney (1995: 233) observes, social welfare 'was (and remains) an extremely fragmented, ill-defined system operated by a variety of bodies'. There are signs at the national level that a social-welfare net is being considered. A pension-reform plan has been drawn up by the State Council, which includes a basic subsistence pension for every Chinese citizen combined with separate, transferable schemes paid for by workers and employers (Hillis 1997). However, the danger is that social security will continue to miss small enterprises, the self-employed, temporary workers and people living in the rural counties of China's cities (Pudney 1995: 233).

The scope for partnership exists in China, but much of its development depends upon continuing economic growth. Wong (1995: 56) argues that the guiding concept for welfare reforms in China is the 'socialization of social welfare', or in other words, people should avoid dependence on the State and that participation in social welfare should be widened to include volunteers and other non-State actors. Municipal civil affairs departments have been encouraged to boost revenue and this has resulted in a number of joint ventures with foreign companies and commercial activities (Wong 1995: 64). The *shetuan* offers the closest approximation to Western-style NGOs (non-government organisations) in that they are voluntary social organizations, but their advocacy role is heavily circumscribed and they are subservient to the government agency which acts as a parent organization (Ye 1995: 95). Although rapid economic growth has encouraged the *shetuan* system, China is a huge country and so considerable disparities remain between both urban and rural areas and coastal and inland provinces.

Hong Kong and Singapore are two countries in the region that are former British colonies. The colonial imprint therefore provides an important factor in determining the social policy context in these two countries. In Hong Kong, colonialism provided a rationale for the lack of government involvement in social welfare by a 'convenient conjunction of cultural sensitivity' (Brewer and MacPherson 1997: 73). The stress on economic priorities has historically meant social welfare has not been the chief concern of the State, but on the other hand, spectacular economic growth has led to a considerable number of 'philanthropic organizations'. In particular, there is a significant non-profit sector that provides a range of welfare services to the people. In terms of social security, the first direct government provision was the Comprehensive Social Security Assistance Scheme (CSSA), introduced in 1971, but this provides only very basic help, usually to the elderly. Otherwise, Hong Kong relies on a network of NGOs to deliver various social services, many of which have roots in the colony's history as the successors to early missions and social services. However, some receive up to 100 per cent government funding and are not strictly autonomous under a fiscal subvention policy.

The notion of a partnership between the Hong Kong Government and the NGO sector was underlined in a 1991 White Paper on Social Welfare (Pearson 1997: 100). The consultants Coopers and Lybrand were invited to review the subvention system in 1995 following unease with the existing system, especially among the NGOs. The consultants suggested moving the subvention scheme on to a contractual basis with the Social Welfare Department. Concern was also raised about the impact of new funding arrangements on NGOs. The Director of the Social Welfare Department reportedly said the new arrangements would constitute 'a much more clearly defined partnership' between the Government as fund providers and the NGOs as service providers (Forestier 1997). In fact, it appears that the partnership has been dissolved in favour of a more arm's-length relationship between Government and the NGOs. The proposals mark the introduction of a market-like relationship as the potential is increased for competition between NGOs providing similar services based on cost and quality, although the Coopers and Lybrand report rejects market-related options.

In contrast to Hong Kong, Singapore's intervention in welfare has a longer history. The Central Provident Fund (CPF) was established in 1955 under the Colonial Government, but originally it was 'essentially a pension fund managed by the government' (White *et al.* 1998: 202). The CPF model is unique to Singapore as a high-income country. The CPF is the dominant social security institution in Singapore with a wide range of schemes under it including home ownership, investment and various types of group insurance. Membership of the CPF is compulsory for Singapore citizens. The CPF can be regarded as a social investment, originally regarded as a luxury for developing nations. Singapore's attitude towards welfare vacillates between viewing it as a 'consumption good' and an 'investment good'. The dominant party, the People's Action Party (PAP) originally took the latter view but Japanese-style 'company welfarism' proved to be attractive in the mid-1980s, especially during the 1985–86 recession. Therefore, welfare services such as health care were 'viewed as a commodity to be marketed for profit, and subsidies are consequently disapproved' (Lim 1989: 177).

The voluntary sector in Singapore is inhibited by a highly centralized government, and NGOs face legal challenges when they are established, particularly as only charities have special tax status. Also, the Government insists that individuals can only express their political views through officially sanctioned political parties. A distinction is made between 'state NGOs', as they were initiated and established by the Government, and 'autonomous' NGOs, which tend to resemble interest groups (Chan 1995: 222). The prospect of public–private partnerships that are likely to diminish state control over social policy looks extremely remote for Singapore at present. Also, Singapore's continued rejection of the welfare state and the central role of the CPF mean that the notion of partnerships for public-service delivery is highly unlikely in the foreseeable future.

Along with Singapore, Japan appears to have the most developed welfare sector in the region, but it is often described as a welfare society rather than a welfare state. The Japanese authorities claimed to have a welfare society based on a 'unique welfare mix' of family, employers, the voluntary and the private sectors (Gould 1993: 6). However, Osborne (1998: 129) argues that this uniqueness is due to welfare provision being more reliant on Government than elsewhere in the region. Moreover, the role of NGOs is more developed in Japan than elsewhere in South-East Asia, with the exception of Hong Kong. The shift in emphasis from a welfare state, albeit a minimalist one, to a welfare society had occurred back in the early 1970s when the notion of a Western-style welfare state came under increasing attack from Conservatives. Reducing reliance on government provision was balanced by an increasing reliance on private-sector programmes (Shinkawa and Pempel 1996: 310).

In particular, the Kobe Earthquake in 1995 apparently gave a strong impetus to the notion of partnership in Japan (Takahashi 1997: 199 and Osborne 1998, 126) by revealing the inadequacies of the existing public sector arrangements for coordinating public and voluntary-sector services. The pluralist 'welfare mix' which characterizes Japanese social policy appears to provide a more promising context for the development of public–private partnerships when compared with elsewhere in East Asia. However, public–private partnerships means a 'more hierarchical relationship in Japan with the government controlling the agenda and the private sector merely implementing government instructions' (Yamamoto and Hubbard 1995: 54). Furthermore, as in Singapore, a legal framework that restricts the legal incorporation of NGOs and denies them tax-exempt status inhibits the establishment of the non-profit sector. Continued dominance by the bureaucracy of governance in Japan appears to be a further constraint in the development of genuine public–private partnerships.

Like Hong Kong and Singapore, both Taiwan and South Korea witnessed sharp economic growth from the 1970s. In Taiwan, the notion of social welfare is regarded as being an underlying principle of the country's Constitution and in South Korea, social welfare was enshrined in the Republic's Constitution (Jones 1990: 452). However, during the 1970s, the development of links between business and the dominant party, the *Kuomintang* (KMT), served to arrest growth in social welfare spending (Haggard 1998: 85). With 'the onset of democratization' in 1987 and political competition from the main opposition party, the Democratic Progress Party, so the political momentum for welfare reform began (White *et al.* 1998: 205). The end of authoritarian rule also marked the appearance of interest groups concerned with public and social policy issues, and the corporate sector established charitable foundations, which also function as a way of connecting politicians with the business sector. The ruling KMT enshrined the 'mixed economy of welfare' as a 'guiding principle' of social-welfare policy in 1994, although the potential to realize this principle is uncertain (Ku 1997: 249). However, Hsiao (1995: 239) describes Taiwan as a 'demanding' civil society as evidenced by a number of social movements that have spawned new NGOs or energized existing ones.

Social policies in both Taiwan and South Korea are underpinned by a reliance on systems of minimal social insurance. In South Korea, social insurance provides income maintenance for the elderly and disabled as well as basic health care for the entire population and thus its social-security system has been described as 'relatively advanced' (Ramesh 1995: 237). However, Kwon (1999: 135) argues that social welfare programmes in Korea were introduced as 'short-term political measures' to avoid long-term financial commitments by the Government. Therefore, the role of the State has been one of regulation rather than provision where the majority of the programmes are funded by employees and employers and is usually managed by non-governmental agencies. Furthermore, as in the case of Taiwan, the end of authoritarian rule in 1987 in Korea marked growing interest in the role of NGOs as alternative providers of public services (Lee 1995: 164).

In narrow social welfare terms, South Korea, Taiwan, Japan and Singapore have witnessed the 'deepening involvement of the market economy' in the financing of social security (Asher 1993: 161). However, East Asian governments are relatively low spenders on social welfare when compared with those of the West, although 'the state in these countries is, to varying degrees, a regulator which enforces welfare programmes without providing direct finance' (White *et al.* 1998: 212–13). The greatest similarity in the pattern of welfare development in the region is between Japan, South Korea and Taiwan, with the latter two having emulated Japan. White *et al.* (1998: 214) argue that it is better to call them developmental welfare systems as welfare was not introduced as a direct response to political demands. Hong Kong and Singapore, as the two most comparable small city states, still display considerable divergences. Hong Kong lacks a comparable CPF system, relying instead on the system of subvented NGOs to deliver social welfare. Finally, China is struggling with the social impact of the marketization of SOEs but the picture is far from being complete.

8.4 Conclusions

Much stands in the way in the development of partnerships in East Asia. Political systems and culture act as considerable obstacles despite the apparent impact of the homogenization of public and social policy implicit in economic globalization. As stated earlier, the priority for governments in the region is economic development, and thus the notion of partnership with the private sector has been developed to meet economic rather than social goals. Therefore, the welfare state has largely been bypassed in East Asia in favour of economic development objectives. The Singapore Government explicitly tries to behave like a 'model' private sector company and elsewhere in East Asia, the public sector has traditionally led the way for private sector development. In Singapore, for example, the weak development of a local private sector meant that foreign transnational enterprises were more favoured than local companies (Khong 1995: 119). Economic development does not automatically mean social-policy development. If a shift towards 'partnership' in social policy in East Asia has occurred, it has come in the form of increasing private-sector involvement through provident and pension funds.

Furthermore, the organizational fragmentation, exacerbated by the New Public Management, which has encouraged the partnership approach elsewhere, has not taken hold in East Asia. Although many countries purport to engage in New Public Management reforms in East Asia, the marketization of public services in line with the demands of the Competition State is largely absent. Moreover, the application of public management reforms tends to avoid major structural changes to administrative systems. 'Strong' bureaucracy remains a feature of East Asian states.

However, economic development has generated social problems for East Asia which governments will be forced to respond to. The problem remains that the NGOs and voluntary organizations are regarded with suspicion by governments in the region, who may regard them as vehicles for special and particularistic interests. Therefore, governments will try and exercise control over their activities, particularly by using finance as a lever. As Yamamoto and Hubbard explain:

> Public–private partnerships present an important challenge in broadening the supply side of the civil society ... (NGOs and voluntary organizations) cannot make effective contributions to society in the manner they are

expected to do, if they will come under strong government control due to financial dependency.

(Yamamoto and Hubbard 1995: 53)

The appearance of a 'civil society' in much of East Asia is a result of the link between economic development and the emergence of a middle class. This is often cited as a rationale for the development of a non-profit or non-governmental sector. The evidence in East Asia appears to be compelling, particularly in the newly industrialized economies and Japan (Yamamoto 1995: 10). Consequently, the need for a civil society has moved up the political agenda, even in China. In Japan, where the Government has failed to address social issues, voluntary and community organizations have grown up in response. Wider democratization will encourage the development of partnerships but examples of 'community empowerment' are still rare. On the other hand, constraints on public resources are unlikely to be a motivation for the development of partnerships. Although the irony is that the welfare state in East Asia can be best described as 'minimal', the present economic crisis where governments are anxious to check growth, may act as a spur to partnership activity.

References

Asher, M. (1993) 'Planning for the future: The welfare system in a new phase of development', in G. Rodan (ed.) *Singapore Changes Guard*, Melbourne: Longman Cheshire.

BBC Monitoring Service (1998) 'Hebei announces welfare reforms', BBC Monitoring Service (Asia–Pacific), 7 January.

Brewer, B. and MacPherson, S. (1997) 'Poverty and social security', in P. Wilding, A. S. Huque and J. Tao (eds) *Social Policy in Hong Kong*, Cheltenham: Edward Elgar.

Castles, F. and Pierson, C. (1996) 'A new convergence?', *Policy and Politics*, 24(3): 233–45.

Cerny, P. (1990) *The Changing Architecture of Politics*, London: Sage.

—— (1997) 'Paradoxes of the Competition State: The dynamics of political globalization', *Governance and Opposition* 32(2) 251–74.

Chan, T. C. (1995) 'Nongovernmental organizations in Singapore', in T. Yamamoto (ed.) *Emerging Civil Society in the Asia Pacific Community*, Singapore: Institute of Southeast Asian Studies and Tokyo: Japan Center for International Exchange.

Chun, A. (1996) 'Discourses of identity in the changing spaces of public culture in Taiwan, Hong Kong and Singapore', *Theory, Culture and Society* 13(1): 51–75.

DiMaggio, P. and Powell, W. (1991) 'The iron cage revisited: institutional isomorphism and collective rationality in organizational fields', in W. Powell and P. DiMaggio (eds) *The New Institutionalism in Organizational Analysis*, Chicago: University of Chicago Press.

Forestier, K. (1997) 'A case of all's not well', *Sunday Morning Post*, 16 November, p. 11.

Gould, A. (1993) *Capitalist Welfare Systems: A Comparison of Japan, Britain and Sweden*, London: Longman.

Haggard, S. (1998) 'Business, politics and policy in East and Southeast Asia', in H. Rowen (ed.) *Behind East Asian Growth*, London: Routledge.

Haque, M. S. (1996) 'The contextless nature of public administration in Third World countries', *International Review of Administrative Sciences* 62(3): 315–29.

Henderson, K. (1995) 'Reinventing comparative public administration: Indigenous models of study and application', *International Journal of Public Sector Management* 8(4): 17–25.

Hickson, D. and Pugh, D. (1995) *Management Worldwide: The Impact of Societal Culture on Organizations around the Globe*, London: Penguin.

Hillis, S. (1997) 'China privatisation – China stitches a welfare net', *Reuters News Service*, 8 December.

Hofstede, G. (1980) *Culture's Consequences*, Beverly Hills, CA: Sage.

Hsiao, M. (1995) 'The growing Asia Pacific concern among Taiwan's NGOs', in T. Yamamoto (ed.) *Emerging Civil Society in the Asia Pacific Community*, Singapore: Institute of Southeast Asian Studies and Tokyo: Japan Center for International Exchange.

Huque, A. S. (1996) 'Administering the dragons: Challenges and issues', in A. S. Huque, J. Lee and J. Lam (eds) *Public Administration in the NICs: Challenges and Accomplishments*, Basingstoke: Macmillan.

Hutchings, G. (1997) 'China's Great Leap Forward poses a threat to health', *Daily Telegraph*, 18 October, p. 13.

Ingraham, P. (1996) 'The reform agenda for national civil service systems: External stress and internal strains', in H. Bekke, J. Perry and T. Toonen (eds) *Civil Service Systems in Comparative Perspective*, Bloomington, IN: Indiana University Press.

Islam, I. and Chowdhury, A. (1997) *Asia-Pacific Economies: A Survey*, London: Routledge.

Jones, C. (1990) 'Hong Kong, Singapore, South Korea and Taiwan: Oikonomic welfare states', *Government and Opposition* 25(4): 446–62.

Khong, C-O. (1995) 'Singapore: Political legitimacy through managing conformity', in M. Alagappa (ed.) *Political Legitimacy in Southeast Asia*, Stanford, CA: Stanford University Press.

Ku, Y-w. (1997) *Welfare Capitalism in Taiwan*, Basingstoke: Macmillan.

Kwon, H-j. (1999) *The Welfare State in Korea: The Politics of Legitimation*, Basingstoke: Macmillan.

Lachman, R., Nedd, A. and Hinings, B. (1994) 'Analyzing cross-national management and organizations: A theoretical framework', *Management Science* 40(1): 40–55.

Lam, W. (1995) *China after Deng Xiaoping*, Hong Kong: PA Professional Consultants.

Lee, G. O. M. (1999) 'Labor market re-emerging: Development and constraints', in N. Flynn and L. Wong (eds) *Privatizing Social Welfare in China*, (forthcoming).

Lee, H-K. (1995) 'NGOs in Korea', in T. Yamamoto (ed.) *Emerging Civil Society in the Asia Pacific Community*, Singapore: Institute of Southeast Asian Studies and Tokyo: Japan Center for International Exchange.

Leftwich, A. (1994) *The Developmental State*, York: University of York, Department of Politics Working Papers No. 6.

Lim, L. (1989) 'Social welfare', in K. Sandhu and P. Wheatley (eds) *The Management of Success: The Moulding of Modern Singapore*, Singapore: Institute of Southeast Asian Studies.

Lowndes, V. and Skelcher, C. (1998) 'The Dynamics of multi-organizational partnerships: An analysis of changing modes of governance', *Public Administration* 76(2): 313–33.

McCargo, D. (1998) 'Elite governance: Business, bureaucrats and the military', in R. Maidment, D. Goldblatt and R. Mitchell (eds) *Governance in the Asia-Pacific*, London: Routledge, pp. 126–49.

Majstorovic, S. (1997) 'The politics of ethnicity and post-Cold War Malaysia: The dynamics of an ethnic state', in M. Berger and D. Borer (eds) *The Rise of East Asia*, London: Routledge.

Means, G. (1998) 'Soft authoritarianism in Malaysia and Singapore', in L. Diamond and M. Plattner (eds) *Democracy in East Asia*, Baltimore, MD: The Johns Hopkins University Press.

Menju, T. and Aoki, T. (1999) 'The evolution of Japanese NGOs in the Asia Pacific context', in T. Yamamoto (ed.) *Emerging Civil Society in the Asia Pacific Community*, Singapore: Institute of Southeast Asian Studies and Tokyo: Japan Center for International Exchange.

Micklethwait, J. and Wooldridge, A. (1996) *The Witch Doctors*, London: Heinemann.

Moon, M-J. and Ingraham, P. (1998) 'Shaping administrative reform and governance: An examination of the political nexus triads in three asian countries', *Governance* 11(1): 77–100.

Neher, C. (1994) 'Asian style democracy', *Asian Survey* 34(11): 949–61.

Osborne, S. (1998) 'The voluntary and non-profit sector in contemporary Japan: An emerging response to a changing society', *Public Administration and Policy* 7(2): 125–38.

Pearson, V. (1997) 'Social care', in P. Wilding, A. S. Huque and J. Tao (eds) *Social Policy in Hong Kong*, Cheltenham: Edward Elgar.

Pudney, S. (1995) 'Social security reform in urban China: The case of Shanghai', in H-J. Chang and P. Nolan (eds) *The Transformation of the Communist Economies*, Basingstoke: Macmillan.

Quah, S. (1995) 'Socio-cultural factors and productivity: The case of Singapore', in K-K. Hwang (ed.) *Easternization: Socio-cultural Impact on Productivity*, Tokyo: Asian Productivity Organization.

Ramesh, M. (1995) 'Social security in South Korea and Singapore: Explaining the differences', *Social Policy and Administration* 29(3): 228–40.

Ro, C-h. (1993) *Public Administration and the Korean Transformation*, West Hartford, CT: Kumarian Press.

Root, H. (1996) *Small Countries, Big Lessons: Governance and the Rise of East Asia*, Hong Kong: Oxford University Press (China).

Scalapino, R. (1998) 'A tale of three systems', in L. Diamond and M. Plattner (eds) *Democracy in East Asia*, Baltimore, MD: The Johns Hopkins University Press.

Shils, E. (1996) 'Reflections on civil society and civility in the Chinese intellectual tradition', in W-M. Tu (ed.) *Confucian Traditions in East Asian Modernity*, Cambridge, MA: Harvard University Press.

Shinkawa, T. and Pempel, T. (1996) 'Occupational welfare in the social policy nexus', in M. Shalev (ed.) *The Privatization of Social Policy?*, Basingstoke: Macmillan.

Sikorski, D. (1996) 'Effective government in Singapore: Perspective of a Concerned American', *Asian Survey* 36(8): 818–32.

Takahashi, M. (1997) *The Emergence of Welfare Society in Japan*, Aldershot: Avebury.

Tu, W-M. (1996) 'Introduction', in W-M. Tu (ed.) *Confucian Traditions in East Asian Modernity*, Cambridge, MA: Harvard University Press.

Wade, R. and Veneroso, F. (1998) 'The Asian crisis: The high debt model versus the Wall Street–Treasury–IMF complex', *New Left Review* 228: 3–23, March/April.

Wang, J. (1995) *Contemporary Chinese Politics*, 5th edn, Englewood Cliffs, NJ: Prentice-Hall.

White, G., Goodman, R. and Kwon, H-j. (1998) 'The politics of welfare in East Asia', in R. Maidment, D. Goldblatt and J. Mitchell (eds) *Governance in the Asia-Pacific*, London: Routledge.

Wong, L. (1995) 'Reforming welfare and relief – socializing the state's burden', in L. Wong and S. MacPherson (eds) *Social Change and Social Policy in Contemporary China*, Aldershot: Avebury.

Yamamoto, T. (1995) 'Integrative report', in T. Yamamoto (ed.) *Emerging Civil Society in the Asia Pacific Community*, Singapore: Institute of Southeast Asian Studies and Tokyo: Japan Center for International Exchange.

Yamamoto, T. and Hubbard, S. (1995) 'Conference report', in T. Yamamoto (ed.) *Emerging Civil Society in the Asia Pacific Community*, Singapore: Institute of Southeast Asian Studies and Tokyo: Japan Center for International Exchange.

Ye, Z. (1995) 'Chinese NGOs: A survey report', in T. Yamamoto (ed.) *Emerging Civil Society in the Asia Pacific Community*, Singapore: Institute of Southeast Asian Studies and Tokyo: Japan Center for International Exchange.

9 The decline of Leviathan

State, market and civil society in South-East Asia 1986–1998

Gerard Clarke

9.1 Introduction

In the 13 years from 1986 to 1998, the character of the South-East Asian state changed significantly. Prior to 1986, the ten governments that ruled over the region's 500m population were almost exclusively authoritarian, from the civilian-led but nevertheless semi-democratic regimes of Malaysia, Singapore and Brunei, to the military-led or -dominated regimes of Thailand, the Philippines, and Indonesia, from the communist states of Vietnam, Cambodia and Laos to an eclectic socialist dictatorship in Burma. In each case, markets were subject to political interference or control and civil society carefully circumscribed or outrightly repressed. The pattern differed enormously from country to country, yet everywhere the State was a great leviathan, powerful, overbearing and repressive and the institutions of a free market and civil society weak and ineffective.

In the 10 years that followed, however, Leviathan all but died. In the Philippines and Cambodia, competitive, multi-party democracy was restored. In Indonesia, Thailand, and Malaysia, some of the region's most dynamic economies, the State became more democratic and military and bureaucratic power was significantly reduced. In Vietnam, Laos and Burma, governments dabbled in pro-market reforms that strengthened the private sector and encouraged foreign investment. Even in Singapore, the region's most successful capitalist economy, the State sought new relations with business and community organizations. Despite enormous regional variation, a common pattern emerged. As the state weakened in the face of economic, political and social pressure, new models of public–private partnership emerged, many of them suggesting far-reaching change in the nature and character of public policy across one of the most dynamic regions in the developing world.

This chapter focuses on three countries in South-East Asia – Thailand, Indonesia and the Philippines – and in the case of each looks at these pressures and at the new partnerships to which they led. In examining the political economy of reform in South-East Asia, it highlights the broad economic, social and political context to the emergence of new public–private partnerships in the 1980s and 1990s. The chapter also highlights some of the new challenges that managers face in adapting to these new partnerships.

9.2 South-East Asia: the generation of the Great Leviathan

'This is the Generation of that great Leviathan', Thomas Hobbes wrote in 1651, referring to the centralized states that emerged from the embers of religious conflict in mid-seventeenth-century Europe (Hobbes 1991: 120). The English Civil War ended in 1651, restoring the son of Charles I to the throne in 1660, the Peace of Westphalia in 1648 ended the Thirty Years War in Germany, and in France, royal control was effectively re-established by 1655. In the aftermath of such chaos, Hobbes argued, no middle ground existed between absolute government and complete anarchy. Governments now existed to preserve peace and order and derived legitimacy solely from their ability to maintain it. Individuals, in turn, owed their complete loyalty to the State and no distinction between State and society could be contemplated.

The period from World War II to the mid-1980s was effectively the generation of the Great Leviathan in South-East Asia. With the exception of Thailand, each state acquired its independence over a three-decade spell from the end of World War II, leading to the emergence of centralized governments and bureaucratic machines controlled by relatively cohesive national elites. These states, with notable exceptions, promoted economic growth and served as the mainstay of the post-independence nation-building process, but they were often corrupt, clientelistic, authoritarian (even totalitarian), and in certain cases, klepto- or megalomanic. Whereas Hobbes used the aftermath of primarily religious conflict to justify his notion of the absolutist state, South-East Asian leaders used ethnic, social and religious conflict, and the threat of it, to justify their suppression of institutions organized independently of the state.[1]

During the post-war decades, a number of South-East Asian countries achieved an enviable economic record growth, not just for economic growth but for poverty reduction and declining income inequality, and achieved status as Newly Industrializing Countries (NICs), High Performing Asian Economies (HPAEs) or as 'Tigers' or 'Tiger Cubs' (see Table 9.1).[2] This economic growth was underpinned to a large extent by capitalism but it was overseen by a state that existed *for* capitalists rather than a state run *by* capitalists.[3] In Thailand, for instance, a 'bureaucratic polity' emerged in response to the Revolution of 1932 and the end of the absolute monarchy, characterized by rule by a military-bureaucratic elite (Riggs 1966). This dominance is illustrated by the fact that: three military strongmen dominated Thailand as prime ministers for 32 years between 1932 and 1973 while only 2 out of 228 people who held cabinet office between 1932 and 1944 and only 7 of the 97 who served between 1959 and 1973 were not drawn from the bureaucracy (Anek 1994: 196).

From the mid-1930s, this elite sought to challenge colonial economic influence in Thailand, and 'foreign', Chinese, domination over trading and manufacturing activity. Chinese businesses were confiscated, Chinese immigration limited and new state-owned enterprises established in an attempt to create 'a Thai economy for the Thai people'. The Government also brought the urban economy under a large degree of state control, including the rice trade and the distribution

Table 9.1 Economic growth in South-East Asia: 1965–1993

	GNP growth per capita 1965–1980	GNP growth per capita 1980–1993	Real per capita GNP 1993 (US$)
Brunei	–	–	–
Cambodia	0.6	–	–
Indonesia	5.2	4.2	740
Laos	0.6	–	280
Malaysia	4.7	3.5	3,140
Myanmar	1.6	–	–
Philippines	3.2	−0.6	850
Singapore	8.3	6.1	19,850
Thailand	4.4	6.4	2,110
Vietnam	0.6	–	170

Source: Jonathan Rigg (1997).

networks governing the flow of goods from city to village, using the accumulated surpluses to invest in public utilities and in import-substitution manufacturing, and using the economic disruptions of the war as partial justification (Pasuk and Baker 1995: 118–20). By the mid-1950s, all major Chinese–Thai business groups had been forced to establish alliances with the military-bureaucratic elite, effectively treated as 'pariah entrepreneurs' by a wary and distrustful state (ibid.: 125).[4]

By the late 1950s, the 'bureaucratic polity' in Thailand had reached its zenith and the economy languished in a state of semi-modernization from which it seemed unable to escape. The omnipotent bureaucracy was interested mainly in defending its own powers and prerogatives. Businessmen and entrepreneurs had no influence on government policy and the bureaucracy had relatively little interest in promoting overall economic development, and for this reason had little interest in establishing ties with business leaders. Under the leadership of General Sarit Thanarat, however, economic nationalism was effectively abandoned, state agencies responsible for economic management were vigorously streamlined and state antipathy to the Chinese replaced by efforts to encourage their integration into Thai society (Anek 1994: 199).

The strategy proved effective and by the mid-1960s Thailand had entered a period of sustained economic growth (see Table 9.1) that increased the power of non-bureaucratic forces. One such group, students, were instrumental in toppling the military from power briefly in 1973 but by 1976 military rule was re-established. The genie was by now long out of the bottle, however, and General Prem Tinsulanond, the military strongman who ruled from 1980 to 1988, was forced to share power with elected politicians. By the late 1980s, the 'bureaucratic polity' had been seriously weakened.

In Indonesia, the decades immediately following independence in 1949 were also characterized by the rise of a 'bureaucratic polity' that marginalized non-state institutions from the policy-making process. From 1957, President Sukarno embarked on a crusade known as the 'Guided Democracy' or 'Guided Economy', to transform Indonesia and to establish the hegemony of the State over civil society and the economy. The assets of Dutch companies were nationalized and handed to state-owned enterprises, mostly led by members of the armed forces, barriers to foreign investment were erected and a system of licences instituted to develop a class of indigenous businessmen beholden to the state. With the collapse of parliamentary democracy, decision making became centred on individual patron–client ties between businessmen and bureaucrats or army officers and a period of chaotic state-led import-substitution industrialization (ISI) drove Indonesia to the edge of disaster and beyond.

Anywhere from 200,000 to a million people died in the bloodletting that followed the collapse of the Sukarno Government in October 1965. In the preceding months, Indonesia was gripped by an economic and social crisis. Inflation reached 500 per cent, 900 per cent for rice, the nation's staple food, and the state budget deficit climbed to 300%. Food and clothes were in short supply, workers and students had taken to the streets and the Communist Party was growing in power and influence. Amid a suspected Communist Party coup attempt on 1 October, army elements led by Major General Suharto, Commander of the Army Strategic Reserve, assumed control. In subsequent days and weeks, soldiers and civilians alike triggered a pogrom in Central and Eastern Java, killing known and suspected Communists along with Chinese traders and moneylenders.

From July 1966, when the Consultative Assembly confirmed him as Indonesia's new President, Suharto presided over a dramatic shift in economic policy and a parallel transformation of the Indonesian State. Primary product and other exports were encouraged, and donor support secured, helping to restore macroeconomic stability. Expenditure on state-owned enterprises was cut back, barriers to exports and foreign investment pulled down and disincentives to agricultural production reduced. By the dawn of the 1970s, social order had been restored and the economy stabilized. The Indonesian State was by now a Great Leviathan in the Hobbesian mould, a State that had restored peace and order in the wake of social chaos and to which Indonesians were expected to commit their unquestioning loyalty in return. The name that Suharto ascribed to his new regime, New Order, bore testament to this fact.

Liberalization of the economy in the late 1960s aided economic and social stabilization but from the early 1970s Indonesia embarked once more on a strategy of state expansion and intervention. In 1971, the Government created the *Korps Karyawan Pegawi Republic Indonesia* (KOPRI), the Corps of Civil Servants of the Republic of Indonesia, a single all-embracing organization of bureaucrats and functionaries wedded to the ruling political party GOLKAR (an acronym from the Indonesian for 'Functional Groups'). Within GOLKAR, KOPRI was the biggest functional group of all, as employment in the civil service increased from 608,000 in 1963 to 1.6 m in 1974 and 2.7 m in 1984, a fourfold increase in less than 20 years (Bresnan 1993: 105). Suharto also strengthened military participation in the process of Government and from 41 per cent in 1964–65, the number of military officials heading civilian departments of Government increased to 44 per cent in 1967 and to 47 per cent by 1982 (ibid.: 109).

Ultimately, the New Order regime over which Suharto presided until May 1998 achieved significant economic success. Per-capita economic growth (GNP) averaged 5.2 per cent from 1965 to 1980 and 4.2 per cent from 1980 to 1993 (see Table 9.1) and the proportion of people living in poverty reduced from 58 per cent in 1960 to 17 per cent in 1990 (World Bank 1993: 4). According to the World Bank, Indonesia was not only the third-fastest growing economy in the world between 1965 and 1985, but also made the greatest progress in reducing poverty, especially in rural areas (ibid.: 3 and 33). Critical, above all else, in the achievement of this success was the exponential increase in revenue from oil exports, especially in the aftermath of the 1973–74 oil crisis. By late 1974, oil revenues accounted for over 50 per cent of government income from domestic sources and for the next 13 years they doubled the domestic resources otherwise available to the Government, facilitating a dramatic expansion of government investment in agricultural and industrial development.

The flip-side of the economic success story, however, was the consolidation of the clientelistic nature of decision-making and resource-allocation policies. Businessmen succeeded to the extent that they forged ties with the Suharto family, senior politicians or military officials. Chinese–Indonesian businessmen in particular were forced to provide seats in the boards of prominent companies to military officers and a circle of friends and relations around the President enriched themselves through graft and corruption. Political scientists gave various names to the economic system that resulted: crony capitalism, rentier capitalism, bureaucrat capitalism. Whatever the title, it was evident that the system could not be maintained.

In the Philippines, in contrast to Thailand or Indonesia, the development process until the early 1970s was characterized by relatively democratic forms of politics and relatively little state intervention in the economy. Throughout the 1960s, however, the state began to expand dramatically; between 1960 and 1972 the number of state employees grew from 361,000 to 500,000 while the government budget doubled (Wurfel 1988: 13). With the benefit of this enhanced capacity, President Ferdinand Marcos declared martial law in September 1972 amid growing Muslim and Communist insurgency. Initially the business community embraced martial law, believing that military rule would prove conducive to economic growth (Thompson 1995: 9)[5] but by the late 1970s support had waned considerably amid growing corruption and cronyism. Throughout the 1970s, Marcos dramatically increased state intervention in the economy, marginalizing the private sector. Businesses associated with opposition politicians were confiscated or nationalized and new state-owned enterprises were established. Control of the key economic sector, including airlines, banks, telephone companies and electricity generators, and of markets for key agricultural commodities such as sugar and coconuts, were granted to friends, relatives and business associates of the President and his wife. By 1983, however, this system of crony capitalism was under pressure and political opposition to the Marcos dictatorship was about to increase dramatically. In the Philippines, as in Thailand and Indonesia, the stage was set for a reversal of fortunes for Leviathan, the omnipotent South-East Asian state.

9.3 The decline of Leviathan in South-East Asia 1986–1995

Ultimately, Thomas Hobbes was proved wrong in his prescriptions for political change in late seventeenth-century Europe, for the generation of the Great Leviathan proved short lived. The modern, largely monarchical, states that developed from the beginning of the sixteenth to the middle of the seventeenth centuries were characterized by the strong centralized authority admired by Hobbes but such authority was quickly counterbalanced by the emergence of a civil society of strong institutions organized independently of the State. Central to the rise of such institutions was the development of capitalism, the economic growth to which it gave rise and the concomitant social change, especially the emergence of a distinct urban-based 'middle class' or *bourgeoisie*, between the gentry and peasantry.

The generation of the Great Leviathan proved equally short lived in South-East Asia. As in Europe, the development of capitalism and the economic growth to which it gave rise undermined the economic and social basis of Leviathan. In South-East Asia, however, it was very different, not least because a process that took over 200 years in Europe was concertina-ed into a period of barely five decades from the end of World War II. In another significant difference, the decline of Leviathan was accelerated in unexpected ways by one critical event, the global economic recession of the mid-1980s.

In 1988, the Japanese economist Yoshihara Kunio famously argued that South-East Asian capitalism was 'ersatz', an imperfect and inferior imitation of the capitalism that developed in late eighteenth and nineteenth-century Europe (Yoshihara 1988). Among other factors, Yoshihara noted the significant degree of state intervention in manufacturing activity and the prevalence of 'rent-seeking' where businessmen profited from concessions, licences and monopoly rights rather than efficiency, productivity or innovation. Ultimately, Yoshihara suggested, such a capitalism could not play the same developmental role as in Europe. If capitalism was to sustain the momentum of economic growth in South-East Asia, Yoshihara thus implied, it had to be reformed. Yoshihara's warning proved prescient, for over the coming decade, economic and political change dramatically altered the character of the state and of capitalism in South-East Asia, cementing a new relationship between the State, the private sector and civil society.

In the first harbinger of change, the dictatorship of Ferdinand Marcos collapsed in the Philippines in February 1986 to be replaced by the democratically elected regime of President Corazón Aquino. Under Aquino, a new constitution was promulgated, the civil service reorganized and the elaborate system of 'crony capitalism', based on concessions and monopoly rights, dismantled. Multi-party elections to a new Senate and House of Representatives were held in 1987, a redistributive land-reform programme launched the same year, and in 1991 a radical programme of local government was enacted, decentralizing power from the capital, Manila. The reforms in many ways restored to power the traditional landed elite marginalized by the Marcos regime. This elite, from a base in the new Senate and House of Representatives, undermined or halted many of the reforms instituted by the Government but in other respects they were powerless in opposing significant economic and political change.

From 1986, relations between Government and the business community were transformed in the Philippines. State-owned enterprises were privatized, key sectors of the economy deregulated and barriers to foreign investment and trade dismantled. Businessmen and women were brought into the Cabinet, and new institutional arrangements established to facilitate consultation with the business community; for instance, in the preparation of 5-year plans. In many eyes, clientelism remained a key feature of economic policy making, with preferential treatment of European *mestizo* businessmen in contrast to Chinese–Filipinos during the regime of President Aquino (1986–1992). From 1986, the Government also established important ties with non-governmental organizations (NGOs). By the late 1980s, the Philippines had the third-largest NGO community in the developing world, and one of its best organized. NGO leaders were appointed to cabinet positions, NGOs were consulted on important policy areas and government departments involved NGO in the implementation and in some cases the design of donor-funded projects. In 1993, for instance, the Government of President Fidel Ramos launched the Social Reform Agenda and appointed business and NGO representatives to the Social Reform Council tasked with implementing it (Clarke 1998). Since its election in May 1998, the Government of Joseph Estrada has continued this partnership through the new National Poverty Alleviation Council.

In Thailand, the decline of Leviathan gained momentum during the Prem years (1980–1988) when business associations proliferated (from 124 in 1979 to 177 by 1987) and interacted with Government through new institutional arrangements such as the Joint Public and Private Sector Consultative Committees (JPPCCs) (Anek 1994: 203). In 1988, the momentum speeded up when Chatichai Choonavan became the first elected prime minister in 12 years. An ex-army general, Chatichai brought businessmen into cabinet positions to an extent that was historically unprecedented and strengthened the participation of regional, as distinct from Bangkok-based, business interests in the process of government. Chatichai had two key reasons for involving businessmen in the process of government, one strategic and the other economic. First, Thailand's geostrategic interests obliged it to play a central role in stimulating economic development throughout mainland South-East Asia. Indochinese politics involves competition between Thailand and Vietnam for supremacy. Vietnam wielded military supremacy over the region as its invasion of Cambodia in 1978 and its war with China in 1979 testified. Economic crisis in Vietnam, however, and the prospect of Vietnam's withdrawal from Cambodia threatened to leave a vacuum in the region that China might have filled. Therefore, the Thai Government had to move quickly to prevent China establishing a strategic foothold in the region. As a result the Government encouraged investment in Burma, Cambodia, Laos and Vietnam, and depended on prominent Bangkok and regional businessmen to spearhead the drive.

The clientelistic dealings and corruption to which these changes gave rise, however, especially among political parties in parliament, provoked public disquiet. This prompted a military coup in February 1991 and the installation of a military-dominated National Peace Keeping Council. On the surface, the NPKC heralded the resurrection of Leviathan, an overwhelming power (in this case, military-technocratic) intervening in the face of anarchy to restore and preserve order. In March 1992, the NPKC held parliamentary elections to install a new 'government' party in power and to institutionalize military domination of parliament, based on an alliance with Bangkok-based big business.

From April, however, mass demonstrations and hunger strikes by prominent activists rocked the regime. By 17 May, daily demonstrations attracted up to 200,000 people, and from 20 to 24 May, the demonstrations degenerated into violence as the military moved to break them up. On 24 May, after the death of fifty people officially and 'hundreds' unofficially, the NPKC regime collapsed and a civilian interim prime minister was appointed by the King. Elections held in September 1992 restored parliamentary democracy and intermittent parliamentary elections since then have maintained it. 'Liberal Corporatism', according to Anek, born under the regimes of Prem and Chatichai and briefly interrupted by the NPKC regime is now well established and stable with the active participation of the business community and other civil-society organizations in the process of government at national and regional level.

In Indonesia, economic challenges in the 1980s similarly led to the decline of Leviathan. In 1981–82, the price of oil fell dramatically on world markets and growth rates of 7 per cent per annum since 1973 were suddenly undermined as oil revenues fell. To make up the shortfall, the Government turned to the private sector and in its 5-year plan for 1984 to 1989, asked it to generate 50 per cent of total investment over the 5-year period. Inevitably, the Indonesian–Chinese were called upon to make the greatest contribution since they dominated the private sector.

In addition, government intervention in the economy was reduced. During the 1974 to 1981 period, oil revenues enabled the Government to concentrate on 'high politics', the goals of income redistribution, agricultural development and population-control pressures on which social order depended. From 1981, however, the Government was forced to focus on 'low politics', and the maintenance of macroeconomic order in the face of plummeting oil revenues. To improve public finances and maintain existing rates of growth, the Government was forced to reduce and abolish monopoly rights, price distortions and other forms of rent-seeking activity.

From 1983, a series of laws were introduced to reduce controls and to encourage private investment. Equally, business associations were given new powers of representation. One of the most important, however, came in 1989 when the 'approved traders' system was abolished and manufacturers were allowed to import raw materials themselves.

As in Thailand, the Government had also switched to export-oriented industrialization. The effect of reforms in the 1980s was to increase private investment especially in manufacturing and services, and to move the Indonesian economy away from its dependence on oil. As a result manufacturing grew by 12 per cent between 1981 and 1990. In turn this led to the growth in the size of the middle class. The Government responded to this by allowing a greater voice to business associations and other interest groups. In Indonesia, however, the process has been problematic. One problem, for instance, is that Chinese companies in particular have turned to the stock exchange to raise capital. Chinese companies previously were private and family run, so Indonesians had little idea of their real power or wealth. By seeking a public listing, however, Chinese companies had to make detailed financial declarations. Many Indonesians were shocked to hear how wealthy many Chinese businessmen were. One Chinese businessman alone, for instance, Liem Sioe Liong was revealed to have assets of over US$2b, making him one of the fifty richest people in the world. His companies in 1990 had a turnover of $8b, equivalent to 5 per cent of Indonesian GDP.

Another problem has been slow progress in privatization. The growth in government revenues from oil exports from 1974 onwards led to dramatic government investment in industry. By 1985, for instance, there were over 500 large or medium-sized companies controlled by national or local-government agencies or involved in joint ventures with the private sector, and their total sales accounted for 30 per cent of GDP, compared with 20 per cent in 1979. The state sector had encroached on the private sector. Throughout the late 1980s, however, pressure to denationalize these companies was resisted, and the effect was to discourage private investment, both from Indonesia and abroad.

Most problematic of all, however, was the sheer extent and magnitude of the system of crony capitalism in which the relatives and friends of General Suharto were granted key economic concessions and in which banks lent money on the basis of political rather than strictly economic or financial criteria. The result was to distort the market, to undermine the banking system and to alienate the business sector, especially the Chinese. As a result, Indonesia was more severely affected than any other South-East Asian nation by the financial and economic crisis that swept the region from July 1997. From September 1997, the Indonesian rupiah came under sustained attack and by February 1998 had lost 80 per cent of its value against the US dollar. The consequences were cataclysmic. Banks collapsed and the financial sector was seriously weakened. Companies closed or retrenched, laying off tens of thousands of workers. Chinese businessmen began fleeing the country, often with suitcases stashed with dollars and other foreign currencies. Prices for food and other basic commodities rose steeply, provoking social unrest. As an IMF team sought to agree a stabilization programme with the Government, demonstrators rallied around key government buildings in the south of Jakarta and in many key cities, rioters (with the support in many cases of the police and military) attacked (and in many cases killed) Chinese businessmen and women, blaming them for the price rises and accusing them of hoarding supplies. In May 1998, after 8 months of instability, the government of General Suharto finally collapsed and B. J. Habibe appointed as interim President, tasked with overseeing democratic elections in 1999.

9.4 Conclusion

The generation of Leviathan in South-East Asia, the period of state omnipotence and of distorted markets and weak civil societies, is rapidly eroding. Throughout the region, political and economic reform since the late 1980s has led to reduced state intervention and interference in the economy, to the strengthening of markets and to the emergence and proliferation of a range of civil-society actors. In turn, the decline of Leviathan has created an environment in which new forms of public–private partnerships have emerged and consolidated: between Government, business associations, and non-governmental organizations. Post-Leviathan, Government, businesses and NGOs alike acknowledge that public–private partnerships are essential in embedding fragile democracies, in sustaining high rates of economic growth and in reducing poverty. One important consequence, however, is that the typical South-East Asian state is now run *by* capital rather than *for* capital as was previously the case. In this light, it is significant that trade unions have been largely excluded *from*, and in some respects *by*, these new partnerships.

A significant explanation for the erosion of Leviathan in South-East Asia is the end of the Cold War. First, the policies of the Gorbachev Government in the Soviet Union, notably the reduction of economic assistance to client states in the region, prompted governments in Vietnam and Laos to introduce economic measures designed to reduce or remove subsidies to state enterprises, to attract foreign investment and to strengthen the role of the private sector. Second, the end of the Cold War weakened right-wing authoritarian governments, especially in Thailand, the Philippines and Indonesia which have traditionally derived legitimacy from their efforts to suppress socialist or communist agitation.

An equally important explanation for the decline of Leviathan, however, has been the cycle of economic growth and recession in South-East Asia. Economic growth has strengthened and diversified the economies of most South-East Asian states, enabling them to reduce their dependence on agriculture and to develop dynamic manufacturing and service sectors. This has enabled states to increase export earnings, to attract foreign investment and to create skilled jobs. Economic growth has also triggered important processes of social change by stimulating the emergence of a middle class or *bourgeoisie*. Recession, however, has also proved vital to the decline of Leviathan. Until the mid-1980s, governments intervened significantly in the region's economies and the middle class and business sector tolerated it because of the high growth rates that intervention induced. From the mid-1980s, however, many South-East Asian governments built up significant budget and balance of payments deficits. To secure financial support from the IMF and World Bank, the governments of Thailand, the Philippines and Indonesia were all forced to sign up to structural adjustment programmes (SAPs) which obliged them to cut government expenditure, to reduce the number of state-owned enterprises and to liberalize or deregulate their economies to encourage exports, foreign investment and the growth of the private sector.[6] In Malaysia, and to a lesser extent in Singapore, governments also introduced SAP-like policies to revive economic growth. The consequence of such policies was to reduce state intervention in the economy, to undermine the clientelistic nature of government–business partnerships and to institutionalize and strengthen government relations with business associations, foreign donors and non-governmental organizations alike.

These policies proved effective in many respects and the new partnerships to which they led revived economic growth rates. Throughout the early and mid-1990s, South-East Asia's four High Performing Asian Economies (HPAEs) continued to grow rapidly and by the mid-1990s, the Philippines, Vietnam and Burma/Myanmar have also begun to achieve sustained rates of economic growth. Such growth, however, came to an abrupt end in July 1997 following the devaluation of the Thai Baht, as contagion spread rapidly to Malaysia, Indonesia and the Philippines (see FEER 1998). The lessons from the 1980s suggest that the recent East Asian crisis will have both negative and positive consequences for regional economies and for the relations between Government, business and civil society. In Thailand, Indonesia and the Philippines, the crisis has reversed or reduced economic growth rates and increased unemployment and poverty rates. It will take a number of years before these effects are reversed. The crisis, however, should also trigger further economic and political reform. This is already evident in Indonesia, where the combined impact of IMF-supervised structural-adjustment measures and the more democratic regime heralded by the Government of President B. J. Habibe is eroding the system of crony capitalism leading to a strengthening of both the market and of civil society. In Thailand the crisis should also lead to reforms in the banking system and liberalization to allow greater foreign participation in the economy. Although such reforms will not compensate for the human suffering brought about by the crisis, they will nevertheless hasten the further decline of Leviathan in South-East Asia.

In turn, business will have to adapt to the new conditions heralded by these reforms. Businesses will have to establish partnerships at three main levels. First, to maintain and increase their competitiveness amid growing competition from foreign investors and from liberalization and structural reforms, big companies need to establish new partnerships among themselves and with government. In place of individual businessmen currying political favour, businesses will have to lobby governments through representative business or trade associations and establish mechanisms that enable them to do so. Second, in more democratic environments, companies have to become more open and transparent and to improve their public images. Businesses will have to subject themselves to greater media, parliamentary and stock-market oversight and will need to develop appropriate partnerships or relationships. Third, in the absence of welfare states and in the social turmoil of the post-July 1997 crisis, many businesses will have to work with civic and non-governmental organizations. In many respects, companies will have to go beyond their traditional philanthropic approach to work with organizations seeking more far-reaching change, often through coalitions rather than direct bilateral relationships. Businesses face a far more complicated and diverse institutional landscape amid the decline of Leviathan and the establishment of new public–private partnerships will be an important means through which they adapt.

References

Anek, L. (1994) 'From clientelism to partnership: Business–Government relations in Thailand', in A. MacIntyre (ed.) *Business and Government in Industrialising Asia*, St Leonards: Allen and Unwin.

Bresnan, J. (1993) *Managing Indonesia: The Modern Political Economy*, New York: Columbia University Press.

Clarke, G. (1998) *The Politics of NGOs in South-East Asia: Participation and Protest in the Philippines*, London: Routledge.

—— (Forthcoming) 'Ethnic minorities, indigenous peoples and development in South-East Asia', in A. Rew, G. Clarke, and R. Montgomery (eds) *Ethnic Minorities, Indigenous Peoples and the Impact of Development*, London: Routledge.

FEER (1998) *Crash of '97: How the Financial Crisis is Reshaping Asia*, Hong Kong: Far Eastern Economic Review.

Hobbes, T. (1991) *Leviathan*, edited R. Tuck, Cambridge: Cambridge University Press.

Mosley, P., Harrigan, J. and Toye, J. (eds) (1991) *Aid and Power: The World Bank and Policy-Based Lending*, Vol. 2: *Case Studies*, London: Routledge.

Pasuk, P. and Baker, C. (1995) *Thailand: Economy and Politics*, Oxford: Oxford University Press.

Rigg, J. (1997) *Southeast Asia: The Human Landscape of Modernization and Development*, London: Routledge.

Riggs, F. (1966) *Thailand: The Modernization of a Bureaucratic Policy*, Honolulu: East-West Centre.

Thompson, M. (1995) *The Anti-Marcos Struggle: Personalistic Rule and Democratic Transition in the Philippines*, New Haven: Yale University Press.

World Bank (1993) *The East Asian Miracle: Economic Growth and Public Policy*, Oxford: The World Bank and Oxford University Press.

Wurfel, D. (1988) *Filipino Politics: Development and Decay*, Ithaca: Cornell University Press.

Yoshihara, K. (1988) *The Rise of Ersatz Capitalism in South-East Asia*, Oxford: Oxford University Press.

Notes

1   For a discussion of such conflicts and the repression to which it led, see Clarke (forthcoming).

2   The World Bank, for instance, identified Singapore, Malaysia, Thailand and Indonesia in 1993 as High Performing Asian Economies and lauded each for combining economic growth with delining income inequality (World Bank 1993).
3   Anek's argument with respect to Thailand can be equally applied to other South-East Asian countries.
4   The term 'pariah entrepreneurs' comes from Riggs (1966).
5   International business and the World Bank also supported the declaration of martial law (see Wurfel 1988: chapter 7).
6   For case studies of the SAPs in each country, see Mosley *et al.* (1991).

Part III

Public–private partnerships in international perspective

Practice and management

10 Public–private partnerships in the European Union

Officially suspect, embraced in daily practice

Geert R. Teisman and Erik-Hans Klijn

10.1 Introduction: dominant orientations and new trends in EU procurement

Although public–private partnerships have grown in number and importance among the member states of the European Union (EU) and although the topic has received the attention of the EU, there is still a lot of confusion about how to actually deal with this phenomena. Until recently EU policies were strongly focused on the promotion of competition in European markets including separating production from policy, a practice we have called *untwining*. Public–private partnerships, which are in fact a result of the strategy to entwine private-production companies and public-policy agencies, do not fit very well under this predominant policy.

This chapter explores the tension between EU policies and the development of public–private partnerships in the member states. We look at EU policy in the transport sector (Section 10.4). This is followed by an exploration of some of the major trends found in public–private partnerships in France, Sweden, the Netherlands and Germany (Section 10.5). The chapter ends with a number of observations about dilemmas that must be faced at the EU policy level. But to start, we discuss some of the general trends in European policy that are important for public–private partnerships.

10.2 Concerns regarding legislation on procurement

In the EU much attention has been paid to the possibilities of privatization and to the creation of a free and open market. The close cooperation that historically existed between companies and governments was seen more as a threat to the establishment of a European common market than as a foundation on which to build. For a long time the creation of a common market mainly was seen as a way to improve competition, especially among individual organizations. For this reason many types of systems that were more or less closed, such as public monopolies and closed tendering systems, came under attack.

The process of European unification to a large extent aimed at breaking down inward-looking national policies based on an old-fashioned striving for self-protection. This included the policy to dismantle many of the existing state monopolies in the area of transport, energy, etc. In the last decade parts of these sectors have in fact been rearranged. Monopolies have been broken down into several distinctive parts and some of these have been transferred to the private sector.

In the legislation on procurement we see characteristics of the market orientation that was prevalent in European policies. Rules mainly focused on transparency and the openness of contracting-out procedures.[1] Governments were forced to put out much of their work to tender, allowing at least three companies to make a bid and opening substantial projects to everyone.

Privatization policy was based on the predominant idea in the 1980s that governments performed poorly when it came to the production of goods and services. The dangers of cooperation mainly had to do with the potential for corruption and the misuse of public money for private goals. This fear is realistic. Examples of misuse are plentiful, especially in the construction industry where close cooperation between the public principal and the private real-estate developer often was tainted with the smell of abuse.

It is in this light that the Directive of the European Union with strict rules on contracting out must be understood. And it is for this reason that almost all forms of public–private partnerships are governed by fundamental principles established by the Treaty of Rome and developed by the European Court of Justice. Essential values at stake here are the principles of non-discrimination, equality of treatment, transparency, mutual recognition and proportionality (Clark and Norris, 1999: 42). The European Court of Justice has said that the principle of equality of treatment is a fundamental aspect of Community law. All forms of discrimination are forbidden. In public–private relations this implies that procurement processes must be conducted objectively and transparently, and they must comply with the procedural rules and basic requirements originally set out.

10.3 New trends in European Union public policy

The procurement framework of the EU has been critiqued a great deal, especially its formal character and lack of practicality. In practice many governments had long-term relationships with private companies and were often used to contracting-out arrangements based on these. The new Directive now forced them to open up their tendering procedures. Governments had to reorganize their terms of relations with private companies. Private partners involved in the policy process at an early stage no longer could be confident that they would be selected during the tendering procedure, even if they had supported and improved the feasibility of policy proposals. To some extent this led to a rather contradictory development. In order to open up tendering procedures, the policy process preceding the tender tended to become more public, but it also became more fixed in terms of the goals to be achieved and the means to achieve them. This did not improve the quality of this part of the process since a crucial exchange of information between the process of (public) policy development and the (private) production process was lost.

For this reason it is understandable that, despite this procurement policy, public–private partnerships in the member states grew in number and importance (Cowie 1996; Matuschewski 1996; Budaus and Eichhorn 1997; Collin 1998; Teisman 1999). While the European policies were tending toward untwining, social developments were tending toward cooperation and partnerships, in the private as well as public–private domain. The question how to deal with these opposing tendencies is now on the European policy agenda. It is recognized that in all spheres of society there is a call to improve competitive advantage through better organization of interactions, based on high skills, high trust and high quality.[2] This demands new organizational arrangements[3] between the public and private sectors in many areas of society, whether dealing with employment and work, social security, private enterprises, urban planning or mobility and transport, or whether dealing with local government,[4] national policy domains or international questions (e.g. Green Paper 1997: 5, Note 2). To conclude the introduction we present a comparison (Table 10.1) of the characteristics of the existing European policy on competition and of a possibly emerging policy on partnerships.

It is clear that tensions exist between the procurement policies of the European Union and the recent interest in public–private partnerships. We will explore this further in Section 10.4 in which we look at European policies toward the transport sector. Before this we sketch some of the general background that is now influencing development toward public–private partnerships.

Embeddedness, flexibility and the search for quality as key concepts to explain partnerships

The private sector has taken the lead with respect to all kinds of internal and inter-organizational rearranging. Business-process redesign was already a hot issue in the 1980s, and the traditional organization of work has been open to question (Wheelwright and Clark 1992; Braganza and Myers 1997).

Concentration on core competence, quality circles, just-in-time delivery, concurrent engineering, teamwork, etc. are concrete forms of a fundamental change that concern the shift from fixed and relatively closed organizations of production to a flexible, open-ended process of ongoing organizational development and adhocracy (Green Paper 1997, Note 2; Morgan 1986). In business administration this new concept of an internal process of continuous change is known as the flexible firm.

This is, however, strongly linked to another development, the embedded firm. By this is meant that firms increasingly function within loosely linked networks which act as a chain to produce products and/or services. No one firm is responsible for the final product or service but that product is the result of a whole chain of organizations which each contribute something special. The quality of

Table 10.1 European policies with respect to public–private relationships

Dominant orientation in the European Union during the last decades	New trends arising looking for governmental response
Breaking down state monopolies and separating the public and private sectors as much as possible	Breaking down national domestic barriers and allowing foreign companies to participate on an equal basis in procurement procedures
Transferring parts of governmental production to the private sector, as much as possible	Accepting the need for ad-hoc arrangements, even beyond the scope of public and private sectors
Improving and reinforcing competitiveness of private companies	Accepting the dynamics of project development, such as the possibility that qualifications will change during the development process, as well as the increased complexity of project-development processes and the embeddedness of project development in an ecology of processes
Opening up public procurement procedures by:	Accepting that the search for quality can be facilitated by private finance as well as private involvement
Explicitly defining the procedures	Looking for new rules for public–private partnership
Detailed listing of evaluation criteria in advance Requiring governments to choose the cheapest offer that meets the qualifications	Recognizing that a kind of policy competition has developed between regions on many levels which stimulates public and private partners within regions to join together.

the products depends on a well-organized coordination of the 'chain' (Miles and Snow 1986; Grabner 1993).

These concepts are two sides of the same coin. Flexible firms can be created if there is a considerable ability to act on all layers of the organization. Firms in which flexibility and change are imposed mainly by top officials will not be seen as flexible by others. This is important because flexibility also implies the ability to adapt to other working cultures and processes. In this way the firm can operate more effectively in the chain.

Flexibility in fact means that there is no one model of the flexible organization, designated by clear tasks, clear responsibilities, etc., but that the flexible firm is characterized by a variety of models, which are regularly being adapted to the circumstances of the individual firm and its units. The embedded firm, on the other hand, refers to an increased dependency on other firms with respect to one's own market position. It is widely accepted that the quality of the production chain and of the configuration of interacting enterprises has become an increasingly determining factor concerning the chances for survival and growth.

In the 1990s the question has been raised: To what extent does the public sector have to adapt to the trend toward flexibility? This contrasts to the 1980s when the main issues in the public sector were privatization and deregulation: government should become smaller and less meddlesome, and tasks were transferred from the public to the private domain. Furthermore, governments introduced internal-management principles from the private sector, a trend which has become known as 'new public management' (Kickert *et al.* 1997). Flexibility and embeddedness, however, were not important features of this. To some extent the new public-management movement even increased the internal orientation of public managers to their own production defined by limited performance indicators. Furthermore, privatization and deregulation did not make public actors less dependent on other actors. So long as public actors are held responsible for societal problems and are driven to tackle these problems they will have to cooperate with other actors. Privatization can even be said to have increased the network-like setting of public policies in this situation: interdependencies remain but the autonomy of various organizations (or former parts of the public sector) has grown (Kickert *et al.* 1997; Lowndes and Skelcher, 1998; Painter and Clarence 1999).

So the trend toward flexibility and embeddedness refers to an external orientation, to the ability to create joint decision-making processes and to achieve arrangements that create interesting outcomes for the participating actors. This trend is becoming apparent now. It is, however, a trend that will also have impact on the internal organizational processes of (public) organizations. We assume that decision-making process redesign will become a hot issue at the start of the twenty-first century.

10.4 From government and privatization to governance and partnership: the case of the transport sector

We have discussed the procurement policy of the EU and the trends toward embeddedness and interdependency among organizations. In this section we will elaborate on some developments in the transport sector to illustrate these points. On the one hand, the transport sector is tending toward market principles and competition and breaking down monopolies, but at the same time it is looking for public–private governance arrangements. This search has to do with the externalities of transport, but also with the fact that free markets cannot be established. While public authorities try to create competition the market parties tend toward upscaling and takeovers. In several parts of the transport market, such as air transport, container trans-shipment and rail transport, only a few private enterprises have a market share of more than 50 per cent and sometimes as much as 90 per cent. In these cases the hidden hand of the free market has to be replaced by collective arrangements and government intervention.

In the 1980s several national governments in Europe privatized parts of the transport system. This trend was actively encouraged by European policies. The popularity of privatization, however, can only partly be explained in terms of a new faith in the perfect functioning of market organizations. Privatization, in combination with deregulation, also became attractive for governmental officials as a way to reduce public deficits and diminish financial support to the (public) transport sector. The growth of subsidies to this sector had been one of the reasons for the increasing budget deficits of national governments. It therefore seemed reasonable to reduce public support, not least because public transport was not performing well despite the subsidies.

After the first call for privatization, plans were made for a more market-oriented, more flexible and cheaper public-transport system. Privatization and deregulation were, however, not easy to implement. In the Netherlands, for instance, a plan was adopted for privatization of the Dutch Railway Company. It was reorganized into three separate departments, one for passenger transport, one for freight transport and one for maintenance of the railway system. This functional division of the company generated a new question: How to allocate the limited transport capacity to the two service providers (which may in the future include more)? The allocation issue is currently dealt with in terms of capacity management. It has been proposed to set up a more or less independent entity to decide about the allocation of scarce railway infrastructure capacity. So far, however, it is not clear what the selection criteria should be for the allocation. In a market perspective the price can be used as the invisible hand resulting in an optimum allocation. This mechanism would probably lead to profitable public-transport enterprises. However, it will be unable to meet the public goals of public transport; it would reduce the railway system to only a few lines of track with adequate services, and the concept of public transport as an alternative to the private car would then be lost.

To answer the question why it seems so hard to implement market mechanisms and to generate private financial means in public transport we have to look at the way public transport is organized and the functions that have to be performed. In the next section we deal with organization, and in the section after that we discuss attempts to generate private financing for public transport.

The complexity of public transport

It is interesting to look at the various attempts to introduce elements of competition into the organization of public transport. In order to decide which parts of the transport system could be privatized a distinction is made between three different functional activities:

1   Services required by passenger and freight transport.
2   The organization of transport by railway.
3   Management and maintenance of the railway system.

1 Services required by passenger and freight transport

Typical of railway transport are (1) the need for an intermodality chain and (2) the need for scheduled transport because far more system management is required than with road transport. The need for scheduling requires sharp planning by the passenger or shipper. The need for additional transport to and from the train terminal and station makes transport by train expensive and difficult to organize. In concrete terms this means that freight transport by rail over a distance of less than 150 to 200 km will probably never be profitable.

Long-distance transport through Europe may be profitable under the condition that freight streams are concentrated in a few corridors. This, however, will limit the range of rail transport. Recent experience with shuttle trains from Rotterdam Harbour to Milan showed that final destinations were all situated within 70 km of Milan. Freight transport by railway in Europe, therefore, will be profitable only for the main connections to the hinterland, that is, from the main ports of Europe to certain centres such as the Rohr region in Germany or Milan in Italy. Moreover, railway transport in Europe is profitable only if long distances are involved and only to and from commodity-oriented centres of economic activity.

These characteristics of railway-freight transport have a considerable impact on demand. If public transport is ever to compete with road transport, protection and support regulations such as road pricing must be instituted as well. It is clear that government has an important role to play here.

2 The organization of transport by railway

When a train uses the railway system it prohibits other trains from using the line for a relatively long time and for a relatively long stretch of track. This makes the organization of transport by railway complicated. We can look at this from two opposing perspectives. First, that the door-to-door transport chain has to be as quick, reliable and cheap as possible. This orientation will lead to minimization of transfer times, cost and coordination between the types of transport that are needed to bring the passenger or commodity from door to door. This chain-integrated approach is in contrast to the second perspective, in which railway transport in organized in such a way that use of the railway system involves an efficient, continuous flow of trains over the system and over time. This integrated system approach is to some extent even more complicated because Europe has a fragmented system of operation in which each country has its own operating organization. This causes delays in international freight transport by rail. Furthermore, the national operators are often conglomerates that combine maintenance, operations and the delivery of persons and freight all at the same time. Often this means that the most powerful player in the national railway system, generally the passenger-train provider, will claim and get priority.

The logic of the integrated-transport-chain approach conflicts with the logic of the integrated-system approach. This will keep the passenger and freight-transport market from ever really competing with road transport. At any rate, this was the general picture at the end of the twentieth century: fragmentation of the operating system, far too little competition between the different providers of rail services, and significant imbalances in both the capacity of the system and companies' ability to access various parts of the European railway network.

3 Management and maintenance of the railway system

The railway system needs especially intensive management and maintenance. The interdependencies between the different parts of the system are high. It is important, therefore, to have good railway-operating procedures, which can and should not be based only on profit considerations. Security, for instance, will be an important additional criterion. For this reason, management and maintenance planning in the public-transport sector will always be characterized by public involvement.

In the day-to-day reality of the European member states the railway system is and will remain a joint responsibility of different governments and agencies. Responsibility for the maintenance and management of parts of the infrastructure will be in the hands of various institutions, ranging from public to private via various intermediate schemes such as semi-public or public–private ones. In terms of the traditional privatization debate in Europe the discussion around the railway system focuses on themes concerned with 'untwining': who is responsible for what, how can input and output figures be measured and used in the negotiations between the agent and principal, how much money is needed for the maintenance and management of infrastructure facilities and how much should governments subsidise?

In recent discussions, however, the issue often is how to entwine the different functions and organizations in such a way that private aims like cost reduction and profitability can be combined with public goals like good, reliable and accessible public transport. More specifically, this issue can be illustrated by the discussion on rail-capacity management described before. There are two mechanisms a capacity manager can install in order to distribute scarce rail capacity. Pricing mechanisms would benefit the economically most powerful activity (which will in fact result in the highest added value). Another possibility is by entrance-call mechanisms based on the use of fixed prices. Distribution takes place according to the principle of 'first-call, first-use'. This can be compared with the reservation systems of hotels.

But what should be done if there are two providers of passenger services and two providers of freight trains? Suppose that one of the two providers for passengers and for freight wants a contract for the full day and the whole year at a low price. The other only wants to provide a few services during rush hours and with a flexible time schedule, but is willing to pay a much higher price. How should the capacity manager decide? What are the most important criteria: the profit of the capacity manager or the collective results in terms of an integrated European network of intermodal transport chains? If the latter criterion is the most important, the capacity manager should be a strategic part of the department of transport. If, however, the first criterion gets priority then the capacity manager may be given a reasonable amount of autonomy. And what should be done if each of the criteria is sometimes more and sometimes less important?

The saliency of these questions can be illustrated by the case of the capacity manager at the Airport Authority of Amsterdam Airport. This authority distributes scarce landing capacity to the most profitable airline companies. For that reason there was no capacity left for a variety of ad-hoc flights. So, for example, when an Italian airline company requested permission for several extra flights, for football supporters who wanted to attend a cup final played in the Netherlands, this was denied. From a market perspective the decision seems logical, but not from the perspective of tourism or the Dutch Football Association, which challenged the decision. The Government then overruled the capacity manager and admitted extra flights, even though this was against previous agreements with respect to reduction of noise and emissions. This simple case illustrates the complexity of decision making in the area of transport and the need for interaction between production decisions and policy decisions.

Even if public transport systems are split up into different functional elements it is impossible to make a proper, transparent and workable division of tasks and responsibilities. A complex relationship between the public and private sector will continue to exist.

The search for private financing of the transport infrastructure

Many publications that deal with the question how to involve private parties in transport policies mainly focus on the financial contribution the private sector can make to infrastructure projects. The Christophersen Report represents such an approach. It recommends optimizing financial involvement in priority projects (Office for Official Publications of the European Community 1995: 19). The report gives four reasons why private financing should be preferred to public financing (Table 10.2, left column). Without questioning the potential advantages of private financing, the question must also be considered: To what extent can these reasons be challenged? In the right column of Table 10.2 we present five complementary arguments which limit the attractiveness of private financing. The scheme reproduces the well-known discussion about market and non-market failures (see e.g. Wolf 1993).

This survey presents an ambivalent view of the abilities of private financing. There are good reasons for public–private co-financing, and at the same time there are good reasons to stay away from it. Private interference means private control of the building process and operational management of the project. This is rather difficult if the project is part of an interdependent network. Transaction costs will probably be increased. In such a case the private financier often demands guarantees from the public sector which, if accepted, means the

Table 10.2 Arguments in favour of private financing and the corresponding arguments against it

Arguments in favour of private financing	Arguments against private financing
Private financing reduces pressure on public budgets and on public debt levels as a result of the reduction of public investment expenditures and risk sharing with the private sector	Private financing only reduces pressure on public budgets for a short period. Recent experiences with private financing have shown that the costs are higher than in the case of public financing. Private financing will have no effect whatsoever on the need to reorganize the welfare state
Private financing contributes to the increase and speeding up of the supply of new infrastructures or to the upgrading of existing facilities	There is evidence that a lack of money is not the main reason for delays in decision making about new infrastructures. Particularly unclear or negative expectations about economic, social and political risks of a project cause delays, which will not be overcome by private financing
Increases efficiency in both construction and operation	Contracting out only leads to efficient construction and operation activities if there are enough competitors in the market. Practice shows that this is often not the case (public and private oligarchy)
Stimulates competition, both between the public and private sectors and between groups	Competition is an important incentive to produce quality. It should therefore be introduced in decision making in the transport sector as a part of decision-making schemes
Improves market awareness and responsiveness to user needs	The concept of 'user' is ambivalent. Citizens play the role of both traveller and inhabitant. The challenge will be to combine these two. It is doubtful whether the private sector can deal with both roles.

solution will probably turn out to be far more expensive than in the case of full public financing.

The Christophersen Group gives additional reasons why the private financing of projects in the transport sector is so difficult. Infrastructure projects are capital intensive, since the fixed-asset costs far exceed the variable and operational costs. The length of the construction period constitutes an added burden (capitalized interest charges and delays in revenue collection). Infrastructure projects can provide an extended utility-type revenue flow, but at the planning stage the amount of these revenues is largely uncertain. Furthermore, infrastructure projects generate high external benefits and costs. The direct revenues reflect only a fraction of the benefits and costs of the project for society. The long payback periods often greatly exceed the usual repayment terms for bank loans or bond issues.

Concluding this section we may say that private financing is sometimes useful. However, it will not lead to full privatization. Two characteristics impede full privatisation:

1   Infrastructure can earn immediate profit, but is mainly effective in terms of the added value to social and economic activities in European societies. Focusing on the internal rate of return will not lead to optimal choices. The external effects of a certain project on, for instance, the operators of the system, the users of the system, the quality of life for citizens living near a transport corridor, and contractors and construction companies will have to be taken into account. For this reason infrastructure often requires complex development and construction plans. When plans are complex it is difficult to get a clear picture of the relationship between input and financial output.
2   Before a full-blown financial plan can be drawn up, a project should be properly structured and phased according to economic needs. This is a crucial and time-consuming stage of project development. It is crucial because at this stage decisions are made that have a considerable influence on profitability and possible cost savings. Partnership schemes should then be maintained for a long period. This is difficult for private financial institutes and is also contrary to recent European legislation on open bidding processes.

Public–private cooperation as a result of intertwined activity

Public–private partnerships in the transport sector, therefore, cannot be organized in the same way as joint ventures in the private sector. During a decision-making process the relationship between the public and private sectors is likely to be based on informal rules. Only in very specific situations will formal schemes be required. Often these schemes will be traditional ones: the private sector only provides the money and receives income from user fees, often with a guaranteed minimum amount from the Government. Schemes of this type, however, are not very profitable for the public sector. It is often easier and cheaper for the Government to lend money on the capital market without having any direct relationship with an infrastructure project. And if this is the case, it seems even more profitable for the public sector to finance infrastructure projects itself.

This does not mean, however, that governments cannot learn anything from the private sector. In our society there is a basic belief that competition, which is characteristic of the private sector, is an important incentive to produce goods in an efficient way. If it is possible to introduce this concept of competition into decision making the quality of the outcome may be improved. However, the introduction of competition is not the same thing as inviting private organizations into the policy arena. In an oligarchy it is difficult to establish competitive tendering procedures. Private organizations will then act the same way as public-sector organizations. In the European countries there are only a handful of competitors in the market of high-scale infrastructure projects. Taking into consideration that the establishment of consortia is necessary, we must assume there will not be a free market. Even the current attempts to open up national markets to foreign companies will probably lead to an oligarchy on a European level within a decade.

If this prediction is correct, the science of public management as well as the practitioners in this field will have to deal with a new and challenging question: How can we create new forms of competition in a society where both the public and the private sectors are characterized by a high level of interdependency? Interdependency means that networks will be established. Cooperation will be needed. At the same time this can lead to closed shops. Organized competition will be needed, too. Groups of actors will be embedded in a network that will be based on a combination of cooperation and competition. The term 'co-opetition' has already been introduced to highlight this need for a combination (Brandenburger and Nalebuff, 1996). The complex chains of activities in such networks are indicated in Table 10.3, specific to the transport sector.

The need to look for entwining arrangements is fully recognized by the European Commission. The former member of the European Commission responsible for transport, Neil Kinnock, convened a high-level group of member-state representatives and leading people from private sector finance and industry to analyse the potential and the practicalities of public–private partnership. He embraced the group's report, presented in 1997. First of all, Kinnock (1998) proclaimed that public–private partnerships are essential in order to meet transport policy needs: 'It is clear that public–private partnerships not only mobilise complementary financing sources but also improve project design. There should, however, be no illusion on two points: first, private sector finance is only available for profitable projects. Second, public–private partnerships can help to achieve better projects, and reduce public subsidies, but in many cases significant public subsidies will continue to be justified by the broader benefits to society, in terms of competitiveness, jobs and reduced congestion and environmental problems'. The report contains five major conclusions, accepted by Kinnock:

1   Partnership should start as early as possible.
2   The public sector should, as early as possible, define its aims, but at the same time remain as flexible as possible in terms of designing a solution. Or to put it in other terms, clear signs of commitment are needed while at the same time early fixation of the product as such must be avoided.
3   Creation of ad-hoc companies with the sole purpose of implementing a project is considered to be the best framework for developing a project, particularly if it is to cross national boundaries. These companies need to have

Table 10.3 Intertwined sets of activities performed by three groups of actors in transport issues

Tasks	Government responsibility in the transport sector	Private sector interference in the transport sector	Interference by citizens
Expansion of the transport system	Making plans for missing links Feasibility studies Regulation of decision making with respect to third-party interests Financing in terms of: Investment grants Equity contributions Interest subsidies Long-term loans Risk guarantees Organize bidding and construction procedures	Proposing and developing new technical systems Providing risk-bearing capital Proposing new methods for the financial development of projects Developing new technical methods in order to meet social demands	Formulating preferences on which transport policy should be based Involvement in the process of project enrichment (generating social creativity) Control of the implementation process in terms of a proper correspondence to the existing socio-economic system
Maintenance of the transport system	Financing Setting quality criteria Supervising maintenance activities	Efficient production of maintenance activities Developing more efficient maintenance techniques	Quality boards in order to keep maintenance on the political agenda
Providing services to the developed and maintained system	Grants for internalizing social goals Organizing bidding and management procedures Capacity management	Providing services to meet the demands of private enterprises and citizens in terms of transport chains	
Generate transportation chains	Rules for chains with low negative external effects	Deciding how production processes can be organized in the most efficient way	Deciding about sets of individual activities and use of modalities
Transportation demand	Decision making about the extent to which demand will lead to supply	Important autonomous generators of transport demand	Important, relatively autonomous generators of transport demand

the autonomy to manage projects efficiently and to be accountable for their performance.

4   Public–private partnership should be envisaged for a number of the transport top-ten priority projects and for smaller infrastructure developments. Partnerships have merit in themselves and could liberate public-sector resources for infrastructure activities that really need subsidies.

5   Public and private sectors should bear the risks depending on which of the two is best able to manage and has the most interest in managing.

This set of recommendations illustrates the state of mind at the end of the twentieth century. The fundamental trend toward embeddedness and cooperation in order to compete in an international market as well as the trend toward flexibility can be clearly recognized. At the same time the report contains more traditional orientations, such as the creation of a single organization to be in charge (Conclusion 3) and the assumption that a clear distinction between responsibilities and risks can be made (Conclusion 5). Finally, it seems that financial considerations are still dominant in the European discussion on partnerships. Considerations with regard to improvement of the quality of infrastructure projects have been insufficient. Finishing up this section about partnership in the transport sector, the following conclusions can be drawn about the relationship between public and private parties.

Public–private relations in the transport sector have been seen mainly in terms of privatization of organizations and private funding. This fits in with the restructuring of welfare states in the 1980s. During this period (which for some countries has not yet come to an end) there was a lack of public funds. For this reason the private financing of major projects seemed to be a solution.

Recently, however, there seems to be a shift in the discussion. Much more attention is paid now to partnerships and co-financing. In fact this is a search for new governance arrangements. In the nineteenth century the private sector was the leading provider. In the twentieth century the public sector took over this role. In the twenty-first century public–private partnerships could become the central provider of infrastructure in Europe (in agreement with the conclusions of Cowie 1996).

Nevertheless, there still is a lot of confusion about what should be the proper relationship between the public and private sectors. The preferred single organization for developing a project, for instance, is mainly based on the idea of separation and autonomy. This contradicts the trend toward embeddedness and flexibility.

We will continue our exploration of public–private relations and partnership in the European Union with an analysis of developments in some countries.

10.5   Public–private partnership: trends and policy in European Union member countries. The case of Germany, the Netherlands, Sweden and France

In this section we will review some recent developments in four European countries: Germany, the Netherlands, Sweden and France. We will look at the rise and the nature of partnership in these countries, at the policy and motives for partnership, and at the discussion in these countries concerning financial orientation versus quality orientation of public–private partnerships. Empirical research on partnerships in European countries still is scarce, and comparative empirical studies are not available at all. Because of the fact that our analyses are based upon various materials which often were incomplete and – more importantly – often based more on wishful thinking than on extensive evidence, the following is explorative and definitely not the last word on public–private partnerships in the EU.

The rise and nature of public–private partnership projects

At first sight, France is the country on the Continent with the real bulk of functioning public–private partnerships. Since the seventeenth century many canals and bridges have been built by granting concessions (Cowie 1996: 23). A concession can be granted before all the details are known. Tenders are decided on the basis of the concept and the track record of the bidders. The French approach is based on trust. 'The success ... depends on the harmony which prevails between the partners for as long as they are together and which ensures their well-being' (ibid.: 24). A closer analysis of the French system, however, leads to the conclusion that even in France real public–private partnerships hardly exist. Let us look at the case of the concession system for highways. In the mid-1950s the toll operation of highway projects was introduced and four concessionaires were created. However, these were not consortia from the private sector, but more or less public–private ventures under the ownership of local authorities. Furthermore, the French Government set the level of tolls. As a result of the energy crisis in the 1970s three of the four concessionaires did not survive, again an example of the difficulties in creating competitive markets. The other three were renationalized. The state then provided a guarantee to the remaining concessionaire that should it run into financial problems, government would take responsibility. It seems to us that this so-called pragmatic approach of the French Government can in fact hardly be defined as partnership.

It was only recently, in the middle of the 1980s, that public–private partnership was reconsidered on the continent. At the start of the twenty-first century several so-called public–private partnership projects are now under way and some have already been completed. Well known are the large interstate projects like the Channel Tunnel between Great Britain and France, the Oresund connection between Sweden and Denmark, and transnational high-speed railroad tracks and stations. These projects attract the attention of the media, scientists and practitioners. They are, however, relatively few in number. On the local level there are a larger number of smaller public–private projects being developed but these have been less intensely analysed than projects such as the Channel Tunnel (see e.g. Holiday *et al.* 1991; Gibb 1994; European Commission 1996).

Table 10.4 Nature of public–private partnership projects on the Continent

Area	Share in total number of projects	Characteristics	Involved actors (central and peripheral)
Urban development	Very high	Mostly local projects in city centres In the 1980s mainly in the large cities, later also in other cities	Central: local governments, private developers and/or financiers, housing associations Peripheral: civil groups Some of these projects are supported by Central Government (if they are of major importance)
Transport	High	Mostly large projects	Central: governments (central, regional and local), transport agencies (railways) Peripheral: environmental groups
Environmental/ Green projects	Growing, but tending toward contracting out	Arrangements for environmental protection and revitalization	Governments, Not-for profit organizations
Technology/ Knowledge	Growing, but tending toward expertise networks	Projects for technological innovation and sharing knowledge	Private companies, knowledge institutes, consultants and governments

In the Netherlands almost every large and medium-sized city has at least one or two partnership projects. In Sweden, Collin used a sample of 64 municipalities (out of 280) and found an average of 1.85 public–private partnerships per city. Most of the selected municipalities had at least one public–private partnership (Collin 1998). In Germany also many municipalities have at least one or more public–private partnership project (Budäus and Eichhorn, 1997).

Many public–private partnerships on the local level are urban development and transport projects. Some of the public–private partnerships deal with environmental issues, technology innovation and knowledge development. Many of these activities, however, are not analysed in terms of complex networks. Table 10.4 presents an overview of some areas of public–private partnerships, the share of partnerships in the total number of projects in that field, and the actors involved.[5]

Generally speaking one can observe that many of the public–private partnership projects in the field of transport are mainly focused on private financing of transport projects (Teisman 1999; Matuschewski 1996). Public authorities, often central governments, remain dominant actors. The development and construction processes are often strongly determined by legislative requirements. Examples in the Netherlands are high-speed railroads (HSL) and investments in the main port of Rotterdam. Even though private financing and private construction are involved, national government is still the major actor.

In urban development public–private partnerships have experienced strong growth. In Sweden negotiated planning practices, where private actors are involved in planning processes through negotiating rounds, have become common in urban-development projects. Matuschewski (1996) concludes in a study on urban-development by public-private partnerships in Sweden that such a mixed cooperative approach in one form or another dominates urban development (Matuschewski 1996: 177–8). Especially in the 1990s, real partnerships, not only private financing arrangements which could often be found in the 1980s, have come into being. As an example she describes urban renewal in Stockholm. Several other local partnerships in urban development are seen as successful, such as the development of Lille, Bilbao and Barcelona. In the Netherlands large projects in city centres have been developed through interaction between public and private partners. It is, however, our basic contention that most planning and development activities are still carried out by government as an institute (such as in the Netherlands) or by public leaders, such as the Mayor of Lille.

Policy and motives in membership states

An important underlying development that must be mentioned is the internationalization of the economy, which led to an increase in competition between countries but also to an increase in competition between local and regional governments (Nashold 1997; Heinz 1998). As a result governments in Western Europe, including the Netherlands, Sweden and Germany, favoured more deregulation and privatization, which enhances the chances for private involvement.

Nevertheless, the restructuring of the welfare state and the use of instruments from 'new public management' thinking on the Continent were far less drastic than in countries like England, New Zealand and the United States (Kickert *et al.* 1997). In Western Europe the leading role of public actors was not fundamentally discussed. This goes for Sweden, the Netherlands and France as well as Germany. Of course, there are specific differences; for example, in Germany where development was influenced by the unification of West and East Germany. A huge effort was needed to renew and improve old-fashioned East German industry. A special organization called *Treuhand* was created to oversee the transformation processes. Many of the new partnership arrangements especially in the field of urban development were designed in and for the new Länder in the former Eastern German Republic (Matuschewski 1996). Interesting is the so-called developer model, used to organize a public competition among private partners in which the winners are granted property rights at the cost of only 30–40 per cent of the market value of the location. This is followed by the creation of a joint development organization in which the private partners combine their properties. The development organization then draws up an urban-development programme. The different private companies become co-producers and can profit from good results of the joint venture.

This arrangement resembles the negotiating planning process in Sweden (Matuschewski 1996). In both countries competitive tendering (if the initiative is public) is used in selecting private partners who become involved in making the plans for urban development. After negotiations and the development of plans, implementation is arranged by mutual contracting. Negotiation is deliberately used as an instrument to achieve permanent coordination between public and private partners from the outset. An important motive behind the development of this form of planning was dissatisfaction with the cumbersome traditional planning procedures in which public actors played a very large role (Matuschewski 1996).

Financial orientation versus quality orientation

Public–private partnerships in Sweden started in the larger urban areas and later spread to medium-sized cities. The findings of Collin (1998; see also Chapter 12) confirm the widespread use of public–private-partnership arrangements on the local level. She also concludes that the first partnerships mainly had a strong financial basis and were primarily secured by financial means or with the profit of private investors. These projects took place during a building boom in Sweden. There was, however, criticism that these projects were not tailored to the needs of local communities (Matuschewski 1996: 173–7).

The same criticism was levelled at some of the large public–private-partnership projects in the Netherlands in the 1980s. There are several examples of city coun-cillors and their political parties losing elections, or being subject to heavy criticism because of fierce debates around large inner-city projects. In all these cases (in large cities such as Utrecht and Amersfoort and medium-sized cities such as Haarlem) the electorate questioned the benefits to the local community. The projects were seen as too large, damaging to the appearance and nature of the inner city and only profiting private investors. The transport projects that were carried out by private financing were criticized even more. The financial arrangements between the Government and private-investment banks turned out to be more costly for the Government than pure public financing would have been (Teisman 1998).

These disappointing results seem to have led to changes in Dutch public–private-partnership arrangements in the 1990s. In the first place the role of local govern-ments and civil and environmental groups as well as citizens has been strengthened. Second, the partnership arrangement is now less used for financial reasons and more for reasons of quality improvement of the investment projects as such. Although it is too early to draw final conclusions early results are promising. The new and rather complex arrangements for project development have increased both the quality of projects and support for them (although controversies do still exist) (Teisman 1997; Klijn 1998; Klijn and Koppenjan 1999). Recent policy of the Central Government on public–private partnerships emphasizes the need for a well-designed and well-functioning cooperative arrangement in which decisions and responsibilities are shared (Ministerie van Financieen 1998).

To a large extent, public–private partnership is still more rhetoric than reality in the different countries on the Continent. Several projects are presented as partnerships, but in many cases a closer look shows the centrality of government and the lack of creative interaction. If the twenty-first century really is to become the century of public–private partnership, as some predict, then much experimentation has to take place and much still has to be learned.

10.6   Conclusions. Unsolved dilemmas with respect to public–private partnerships in Europe

In the European Union the discussion about public–private partnerships has in fact just started. The action plan entitled Procurement in the European Union indicates the state of affairs. This report (European Union 1998) deals with the treatment of public–private partnerships under the rules of procurement. The European Commission recognizes its duty to devise a legal framework that allows the development of partnerships, which account for nearly 11 per cent of the European Union's gross domestic product and are expected to become even more important in the future. But partnerships must be in compliance with EC competition rules and the fundamental principles of the Treaty of Rome (see e.g. Clark and Norris 1999: 42). In the report the Commission indicates that it intends to introduce greater legal certainty by clarifying and simplifying the conditions in which public–private partnerships operate. The Commission recognizes on the one hand that a stable legal framework is needed for a smooth functioning of the market for public works and, on the other hand, that the existing legal framework is too complex and the procedures too rigid. Rules, policies and implementation should be adjusted to reality, not the other way around (European Union 1998: 3).

Simplification, the remedy for complexity, is to be carried out in a two-step process that first attempts to demystify the existing guidelines. Only when the guidelines cannot be clarified will adjustments be considered. This reflects the reticence of the Commission with respect to deregulation in the field of public–private partnerships and probably has to do with several dilemmas that must first be dealt with in order to create fruitful ground for public–private partnerships in Europe. These dilemmas require distinguishing between:

- Shared responsibility as a necessary element of partnership versus a blurring of responsibility between government and business that can lead to misuse of public money (OECD 1997: 13).

- Transparency for third parties not involved in the partnership, on the one hand, and misuse and free-rider behaviour by third parties if the results of partnerships are accessible to all.
- Flexibility in order to reach new levels of quality and creative solutions versus fixation in order to get production started and increase earnings.
- The building up of long-term public–private relations based on mutual knowledge and trust which can lead to reduced transaction costs versus the principle of equality of treatment that assumes that everyone should be able to know the rules in advance and that the rules will be applied to everyone in the same way, regardless of the degree of mutual trust and the effect on transaction costs.

Because these dilemmas have not been well explored, the Commission is still reluctant when it comes to developing new guidelines that should facilitate public–private partnerships. In February 1999, DG XV produced an interpretative draft. Mario Monti, the Commissioner then responsible for the internal market and, more particularly, for public procurement policy, stated that 'cooperation between the public and the private sectors is growing in all member states, . . . It is essential, however, to provide a framework for public–private partnerships . . . that is transparent and open to competition'. This remark is in line with the trend outlined at the beginning of this chapter. New arrangements are accepted as unavoidable, but at the same time transparency (read: division of tasks and responsibility between public and private sectors) and intensified competition are still driving forces in EU decision making. A reconciliation of reality and the legal framework has to be found.

References

Brandenburger, A. M. and Nalebuff, B. J. (1996) *Co-opetition*, New York: Doubleday.

Braganza, A. and Myers, A. (eds) (1997) *Business Process Redesign, a View from the Inside*, London: ITBP.

Budäus, D. and Eichhorn, P. (eds) (1997) *Public Private Partnership; neue Formen öffentlicher Aufgabenerfullung*, Baden-Baden: Nomos Verlagsgesellschaft.

Cavallier, G. (1998) *Challenges for Urban Governance in the European Union*, Dublin: European Foundation for the Improvement of Living and Working Conditions.

Clark, B. and Norris, S. (1999) 'Euro Procurement', *Supply Management* April: 42.

Collin, S. O. (1998) 'In the twilight zone; a survey of public private partnerships in Sweden', *Public Productivity and Management Review* 21(3): 272–83.

Cowie, H. (1996) *Private Partnerships and Public Networks in Europe*, London: Federal Trust.

European Commission (1996) 'The regional impact of the Channel tunnel throughout the community', Luxembourg: European Commission.

European Union (1998) 'Public procurement in the European Union', Announcement of the Commission, Brussels: European Union, p. 3.

Gibb, R. (ed.) (1994) *The Channel Tunnel: A Geographic Perspective*, Chichester: John Wiley and Sons.

Grabner, G. (1993) *The embedded firm; understanding networks: actors, resources and processes in interfirm cooperation*, London: Routledge.

Heinz, W. (1998) 'Public-private partnership', *Archiv für Kommunalwissen-schaften*, Berlin, 37(2): 210–329.

Holiday, I., Marcou, G. and Vickerman, R. (1991) *The Channel Tunnel: Public Policy, Regional Development and European Integration*, London: Belhaven Press.

Kickert, W. J. M., Klijn, E. H. and Koppenjan, J. F. M. (1997) *Managing Complex Networks; Strategies for the Public Sector*, London: Sage.

Kinnock, N. (1998) 'Transport policy needs at the turn of the century', *European Business Journal* 10(3): 122–9.

Klijn, E. H. (1998) *Ruilm voor beslissen [Space for Decision]*, Delft: Eburon.

Lowndes, V. and Skelcher, C. (1998) 'The dynamics of multi-organisational partnerships: An analysis of changing modes of governance', *Public Administration*, 76(3): 437–54.

Matuschewski, A. (1996) *Stadentwicklung durch Public-Private-Partnership in Schweden; Kooperationsansatze der achtziger und neunziger Jahre im Vergleich*, Kiel: Geographischen Instituut der Universität Kiel.

Miles, R. E. and Snow, C. C. (1986) 'Organizations: New concepts and new forms', *California Management Review*, 28(3).

Ministerie van Financieen (1998) *Meer waarde door samenwerken (eidrapportage)*, Den Haag: Uitgave Ministerie van Financieen (Projectbureau Publiek-Private Samenwerking).

Morgan, G. (1986) *Images of Organisations*, London: Sage.

Nashold, T. (1997) 'Public private partnerships in den internationalen modernisierungs Strategien des Staates', in D. Budäus and P. Eichorn (eds).

OECD (1997) 'Public/private alternatives to traditional regulations', Working Paper No. 28, Paris: OECD.

Office for Official Publications of the European Community (1995) 'Trans-European Networks', Report to the Essen European Council (Report of the Christophersen Group), Luxembourg: European Commission.

Teisman, G. R. (1997) *Sturen via creatieve concurrenti [Governance by Creative Competition]*, Nijmegen, Netherlands: Katholieke Universiteit.

—— (1999) 'New arrangements and management principles for public private partnerships; a search for product of high quality in a network society', paper given at the Third International Research Symposium on Public Management, 25 and 26 March 1999, Birmingham.

Wheelwright, S. C. and Clark, K. B. (1992) *Revolutionizing Product Development*, New York: The Free Press, 1992.

Wolf, C. (1993) *Markets or Governments; Choosing between Imperfect Alternatives*, London: The MIT Press.

Notes

1   For example, Directives 93/36/EEG, 93/37/EEG and 92/50/EEG concerning public orders for deliveries, works and services, the so-called classical guidelines.

2   See, for instance, the Green Paper of the European Union entitled 'Partnership for a new organisation of work', published in 1997. The first sentence is: 'This Green Paper is about the scope for improving employment and competitiveness through

a better organisation of work at the workplace, based on high skills, high trust and high quality'.

3 'A whole range of institutional arrangements are obviously needed if this partnership is to be adapted on a case-by-case basis to very different situations involving very different partners' (Cavallier 1998: 17).

4 See, for instance, George Cavallier (1998) In this report, infrastructure and institutions are pinpointed as the cornerstones of productivity and high-quality urban life. In addition, the term governance is used deliberately in contrast to government. Governance refers to interorganizational cooperation in the urban domain between several public as well as private actors. 'Private actors have become essential partners in local urban policies.' (ibid.: 48). 'The new balance and the new compromises to be found between market-based and political approaches consequently need to be thought about, given that the relationships between the public and private sector are organised in very different ways in different countries just as there are different national practices in the areas of housing, urban development, property transactions, public transport or commercial services' (ibid.: 48).

5 This is based on available literature (see Matuschewski 1996; Budäus and Eichhorn 1997; Ministerie van Financieen 1998). No exact figures are available.

11 Transforming the state into a partner in cooperative development

An evaluation of NGO–government partnership in the Philippines

Teresa S. Encarnación Tadem

11.1 Introduction[1]

In the 1970s, non-governmental organizations (NGOs)[2] grew rapidly in the Philippines because of the inability of the martial-law regime to adequately provide for the basic needs of the marginalized sectors of society. Because of the authoritarian nature of the Marcos Government, NGOs worked independent of this government. The latter, on the other hand, looked at the NGOs with suspicion. They were, for example, viewed as a conduit of funds for the communist insurgency. Such a relationship, however, changed after the February 1986 People Power Revolution which overthrew that regime. The establishment of an 'elite democracy', as opposed to an authoritarian regime, made it possible for NGOs to engage the state in partnerships for development. Such a situation is seen, for example, in the development of cooperatives, where NGOs began to involve themselves specially under the Aquino Administration.[3]

This was quite unusual because, unlike most countries in the developed world, cooperative development in the Philippines has generally been a state initiative. However, NGOs in this work still realized the importance of government support in such an endeavour and they have therefore looked into various forms of public–private partnership whereby they could transform the state into a viable partner in cooperative development. This chapter charts some of the successes – and failures – of such attempts to develop a cooperative partnership for community development and support in the Philippines.

This chapter will therefore evaluate the experience of the Cooperative Foundation of the Philippines Inc. (CFPI), an NGO, in its attempt to engage the state in partnership to create a more favourable environment for the growth of cooperatives. It will highlight both the successes as well as limitations of such government–community partnerships. *It focuses in particular on the micro-level of individual relationships between government officials and community organizations.* Often partnerships between the state and local communities in the Philippines arise slowly and through such personal interaction between key participants, because of the lack of pre-existing legitimate organizational channels for partner-ship between the state and local communities. Such partnerships also contribute to the potential for sustainable economic and social development in the Philippines.

11.2 Creating a national environment for cooperative development

The CFPI is part of a growing breed of cooperative players who see the importance of engaging the state in partnership in development efforts. It was originally established as a quasi-government agency but in 1986; it was transformed into an NGO under the leadership of Horacio 'Boy' Morales, former head of the National Democratic Front (NDF), the underground united-front movement of the Communist Party of the Philippines (CPP). One of its initial aims was to pressure the state to come out with a favourable environment for cooperatives through legislation.

Together with other cooperatives, NGOs, institutions and individuals in the cooperative movement, they lobbied for the promulgation of a new cooperative code. It was in this area that they were able to forge a partnership with the State. This was seen in the appointment of Morales by the Aquino Administration in 1986 as the head of a newly established task force, after the 1986 Philippine People Power Revolution, to assess the role which cooperatives can play under the new political dispensation.

CFPI's efforts, together with those of the other cooperative movement's members, gave birth on 10 March 1990 to two important cooperative bills, Republic Act (R.A.) 6938, known as the Cooperative Code of the Philippines, creating an organic law for cooperatives and R.A. 6939 establishing the Cooperative Development Authority (CDA) as the government agency to implement the Cooperative Code. This new cooperative code replaced the Presidential Decree (P.D.) 175 of the previous government, or the Cooperative Law. For the CFPI, the need to come out with a new cooperative code to replace P.D. 175 was important in order to spell out the relationship of the cooperatives with the Government.

Despite the implementation of a new cooperative code, there was still much to be desired in the role the Government could play in such a partnership with the local community. The key issues to be managed were those of financing and access to capital for cooperatives, infrastructural support, the creation of a favourable marketing environment for the organization of the cooperative movement (Gaffud: 1990). NGOs like the CFPI have also to fill in the gaps left by state agencies in cooperative training.

If the State is to be a potent partner in such an endeavour, the CFPI saw the need to have government officials who could play a role in strengthening the cooperative movement. Thus, during the May 1995 national and local elections, it campaigned for particular candidates who were deemed to be both 'pro-people' and 'pro-cooperative'. Moreover, in the 1998 national elections, a number of cooperative coalitions, including the CFPI, ran under the party-list system which chose the country's sectoral representatives in the Philippine Congress.

The top sectoral party was also a coalition of electric cooperatives. This is significant because it reveals that cooperative players like NGOs no longer had to rely solely on others to represent them in government because they (the NGOs) themselves could be state officials. Some view this as a potent strategy in consolidating NGO and state partnership endeavours.

NGO–government partnership at the national level, however, is only one dimension of cooperative organizing. Of further importance is consolidating such a partnership at the local level. This was particularly true in local-government support for agricultural cooperatives, which accounted for 60 per cent to 69 per cent of the estimated total of 32,000 cooperatives in 1995. For the CFPI, therefore, the implementation of the government's Comprehensive Agrarian Reform Program (CARP) is a key to the sustainability of a favourable environment for the growth of cooperatives. Moreover, the distribution of land is only a first step to cooperative development. As important is the government's rural development support services. Failure of the government to provide for these has made Agrarian Reform beneficiaries vulnerable to the massive land conversions going on in the countryside. Public–private partnerships for local-community development offered one route to resolving this cluster of problems in the Philippines.

11.3 Engaging the state in agrarian reform and in cooperative organizing

The task of engaging the state to play a key role in public–private partnerships, however, continues to be a challenge for NGOs in the Philippines. This was seen in the experience of the Masagana Multi-Purpose Cooperative Inc. (MPCI). The Masagana MPCI, which was organized in June 1995, was mainly concerned with organizing a cooperative in order to supplement the income of its members. In June 1995, the group was officially registered with nineteen members. All the farmers lived in *Barangays*[4] Frances, Calumpit and Bulacan. The majority of its members had been beneficiaries of the martial-law regime's Agrarian Reform programme. Their average farm size was only 1.9 ha and, because of the fertile land in Calumpit, the farmers were able to harvest 100 cavans per hectare. To pay for their land, the Agrarian Reform beneficiaries had been stipulated to give around 29 cavans (1 cavan = 2.13 bushels) per year to the landowner, whilst the tenant farmers and the landowner divided the costs of production equally between themselves.

The CFPI basically assisted in the organization of the Masagana MPCI and in the start of its capital build-up. The cooperative initially stipulated a membership fee of P500 (US$13)[5]. Each member donated P100 (US$2.60) during their monthly meetings, with a P50 (US$1.25) penalty for anyone who was late or was not able to attend the meeting. Aside from this, the members gave an additional P500 (US$13) every year in March, the month whereby they started their capital build-up. By this process the MPCI was able to raise initially P8,500 (US$224) in capital and in 4 months' time, this had increased to P12,000 (US$316). This amount is a substantial one by Philippine standards – a small farmer's average income amounts to only P98 (US$2.60) a day (Romero 1995a: 6).

The Masagana MPCI seemed to have embarked on a good start until July 1995 when two of its members were charged in court by the community's former landowner, Lucrecia Tumbaga. Tumbaga wanted to get back her land which she inherited from her mother, the *barangay's* previous landowner. Manlapat had willed 39.7687 ha of rice and sugar lands in Frances, Calumpit and Bulacan to Tumbaga and her husband and children. Six years after Presidential Decree (P.D.) 27 was enacted in 1972, the Tumbagas filed exemption from the Marcos Government's Operation Land Transfer (OLT) arguing that 'the share of each heir/petitioner is less than seven hectares and, therefore, not within the purview of P.D. 27, as amended by Letter of Instruction (LOI) 474' (DAR, 1989).

The Tumbaga family followed this up with another petition, 3 years later, on 2 December 1981 'seeking cancellation of the Certification of Land Transfer'.[6] (CLT) issued to the tenant-tillers of the subject landholdings (DAR, 1989). The Department of Agrarian Reform's (DAR) Conflicts and Resolution Unit (CRU) Team Office of Pulilan, Bulacan looked into the matter. Although it found that the petitioner's children did not own more than the 7 ha of land which is the right of the landowner's heirs, it noted that the Tumbagas had transformed some of their lands into commercial and residential lots and were even operating two movie houses. Thus, the DAR recommended that the Tumbagas should not be exempted and, on 17 January 1989, it dismissed the landowners' petition. Such a decision had the approval of the Aquino Administration's Agrarian Reform Secretary Philip Juico who signed the court decision on 17 January 1989. In such a situation therefore the State has rightfully upheld the interests of the farmers and supported the development of the cooperative.

Unfortunately, the state was impotent in preventing these powerful landowners from intimidating the Agrarian Reform beneficiaries. The Tumbagas, for example, have continued to harass the latter by filing a case against five of them in an attempt to get back their lands. All of those charged reside in *Barangay* Frances, and of these five, two are members of the Masagana MPCI. The fear of the farmers is that if the landowners succeed in their case against these five, they may continue to file cases against the rest. There have been other similar cases against other farmers filed by other landowners in the area.

The CFPI took on the role of informing the Masagana MPCI members of their rights as Agrarian Reform beneficiaries, and more importantly, of organizing them in their struggle against their previous landowners who wanted to get back their lands. Thus, the NGO organized a series of meetings with the farmers; the CFPI also linked the cooperative with the Partnership for Agrarian Reform and Rural Development Services Inc. (PARRDS). PARRDS is a coalition of various organizations and one of its major objectives is to strengthen the role of people's organizations (POs), non-governmental organizations (NGOs) and non-political formations in implementing agrarian reform and rural development.

Because Agrarian Reform is an issue which affects the other members of the community, the cooperative became a vehicle for rallying other non-farmer members who are Agrarian Reform beneficiaries. In the process, an alliance was formed with two other organizations in the area. This led to the formation of an umbrella coalition which they called the United Farmers of Calumpit or UFC. Its immediate tasks were to seek a dismissal of the landowner's court case against the five farmers, to look into the delay in the issuance of the farmers' CLTs and to ask for an accounting of their land-amortization payments to their landowner.

Getting the support of governmental Agrarian Reform officials

In addition to developing community opposition to such landowners, the CFPI was also determined to pressure the Government on developing its supportive partnership with the UFC farmers. Thus, it brought forth their problems to the responsible Agrarian Reform officials. One way it did this was to bring the issue of *Barangay* Frances to the Provincial Agrarian Reform Officer (PARO) during PARRDS Leader Forum held in Malolos, Bulacan on 8 August 1995 (the Forum in general seeks to pinpoint difficulties in the Government's Agrarian Reform programme, and more importantly, to take consolidated action on these issues). During this meeting, the PARO promised to follow up the CLTs of the UFC's Agrarian Reform beneficiaries by checking and verifying their records with the DAR.

The PARO was sympathetic to the plight of the farmers. She immediately said that the court should dismiss the landowner's petition. She, however, admitted that her office could not afford the services of a lawyer for the Agrarian Reform beneficiaries. The most it could do was to hire paralegals, of which there are only twelve for the whole of Bulacan. Six of them are assigned to the provincial Agrarian Reform office.[7]

Because the CFPI was determined to involve all responsible Agrarian Reform officials into the case, it arranged a meeting with the Municipal Agrarian Reform Officer (MARO) who directly deals with the Agrarian Reform beneficiaries. The farmers generally perceived the MARO as having been largely responsible for their present problems. The CFPI's goal, therefore, was to transform the MARO into *a partner for the farmers*. With this in mind, the NGO, together with its partner organizations in PARRDS, assisted the UFC in strategizing for this meeting. The PO–NGO organizers specifically told the UFC leadership to prioritize the issues they will raise during the Forum.

The Forum was also looked on as an opportunity to bring out the complaints of the farmers concerning DAR personnel who, instead of supporting the Agrarian Reform beneficiaries, abuse them. This included the DAR 'lawyer' (actually only a paralegal), who charges an exhorbitant P500 per court hearing from the farmers, and the municipal Agrarian Reform personnel who would charge them for following up their papers. This would amount to P200 (US$5) for the documents for each hectare of the farmers' land. This P200 (US$5) is supposed to take care of the MARO personnel's 'snacks' while he is following up the farmers' papers. Thus, there a situation whereby the farmers view the DAR officers as 'enemies' rather than 'partners' in implementing the Agrarian Reform programme.

The meeting therefore with the MARO and his DAR Development Facilitator was hoped to correct such a situation. During the Forum the two Agrarian Reform officers were informed by the farmers that the land-reform process has been slowed down as a result of the landowner's resistance. When he was asked why the case had to be brought to the court, the MARO answered that it was the right of any private citizen to resort to this. He, however, assured the farmers that the landowner's case against them was weak. When pressed further by a farmer on when they could get their CLTs, the MARO was non-committal. All he said was that he would do his best pending the circumstances they were in.

The MARO, nevertheless, advised the group to start paying their land amortization. On his part, he told them that he would issue out a certificate informing the Land Bank of the Philippines (LBP) that these farmers were CLT holders and they could already start paying their land amortization even if they could only remit a small amount. Thus, the first issue resolved by the group was concerning this. With regard to the issue of previous payments, the MARO said that the receipts were with him together with other pertinent data on the farmers' land. These were all contained in each of the Agrarian Reform beneficiaries' claim folder in his office. The MARO was urged to give the farmers their CLTs which they could use as proof that they are the Agrarian Reform beneficiaries of the land they were tilling. And as for the landowner's case against the five UFC farmers, the MARO was requested to tell the DAR attorney to dismiss the case.

On 17 August 1995, the farmers were able to get all the papers they needed which the MARO supplied to them – even their CLT numbers were given. The landowners, however, made a counter-offer to the farmers. That is, they would drop their court case against the five farmers if they (the farmers) would only get 50 per cent of their land. Moreover, an LBP officer told the farmers that they should take pity on the landowner since the LBP valuation of the land was only P5,568 (US$147). He further added that the previous amortization which the farmers have already been paying to the landowner would be deducted from this amount. The farmers, therefore, found themselves in a situation whereby the LBP, their major creditor, sympathized with the landowner instead of the Agrarian Reform beneficiaries!

The LBP officer's position reinforced the attitude of some of the UFC members, particularly those who had court cases, to consider succumbing to the landowners' wishes because they feared that if they lost the court case, they would be left with no land at all. However, they changed their minds when one of the PARRDS' organizers told them that the landowners were now willing to settle for only 50 per cent of the land because they (the landowners) realized that they were losing the battle. Furthermore, to debunk the view of the LBP officer, the PARRDS' organizer argued that there was no reason to 'pity' the landowner because, as former tenants, they themselves had been exploited enough already. He proved this by calculating how much they had already been paying the landowner through all these years which amounted to over 'a million pesos' – adding that this did not even take into account the 'blood, sweat and tears' of the farmer's parents and grandparents which went into tilling the land. The UFC members, therefore, all agreed that they did not want to give half of their land to the land-owners.

In December 1995, the *Barangay* Frances Agrarian Reform beneficiaries finally received their CLTs. The struggle, however, has not yet ended as the landowners have pursued legal means to prevent these CLTs from being transformed into Emancipation Patents (EPs).[8] Their case is now pending in the Office of the Philippine President. In the meantime, the UFC farmers have not given up their fight. They are now part of a bigger coalition of NGOs, POs and cooperatives, which is fighting for agrarian reform and rural development in the province.

Obstacles to NGO and state partnership in Agrarian Reform

The Masagana MPCI experience, therefore, reveals that there is still much left to be desired in NGO–government partnership in creating a more favourable en-vironment for cooperative development particularly in the implementation of Agrarian Reform. The experience of the CFPI, on the one hand, has shown that there are open-minded government officials who are able to assist the farmers in their demand. This was seen in their meeting with the PARO during the PARRDS Forum. The PARO herself, however, admitted that her office has its limitations – such as the extent to which it can provide an effective legal services to the farmers. The CFPI therefore agreed to find a lawyer to replace the DAR paralegal.

On the other hand, there are also government officials who do not see partner-ships with the local community as their role, such as in the case of the MARO who the CFPI and the farmers had to pressure to do his task of implementing Agrarian Reform at the municipal level. Unlike the PARO, the MARO seems to be an example of an agrarian official who does not really care about the local community and the farmers; that is, he only reacts when he is told to do something about their situation. Thus, a big limitation in public – private partner-ships between local communities and the state for cooperative development in the Philippines is the *personal perspective* of the government officials themselves. As noted by the Ramos Administration's DAR Secretary Ernesto Garilao, only 15 to 20 per cent of his personnel are committed to the Government's Comprehensive Agrarian Reform Program (CARP). The strategy thus for the CFPI is to work at the local level by selecting Agrarian Officials who are sympa-thetic to the plight of the farmers as partners in cooperative development. As for those who are not, their strategy is to pressure and to even coerce them into per-forming their roles.

11.4 Land conversion: the impact of state indifference

Another reality for Filipino farmers is that owning the land is only half the battle, the other half is keeping it. The CFPI realizes this and it is for this reason that it believes that the establishment of agricultural cooperatives among Agrarian

Reform beneficiaries can help in arresting such a situation, by providing mutual support. An example was the Santa Rosa Multi-Purpose Cooperative (MPCI) situated in Pandi, Bulacan. With the consent of its community, the CFPI started organizing the cooperative in this *barangay* on 10 June 1991. Because the landownership in the area did not exceed 7 ha, the landowners were exempted from the Government's Agrarian Reform programme. What is granted, however, to the tenant-tiller is a share of the crop with the absentee landlord.

Members who joined the cooperative had to pay an initial membership fee of P500 (US$13). The Cooperative's initial paid-up capital was P2,000 (US$53) and it began with 16 members. Two years later, the membership expanded to twenty, while the capital increased to P23,000 (US$605) or by 1,150 per cent, after 1 year, and to P34,600 (US$911) or by 1,730 per cent, after 2 years. In 1995, they had a total of P86,000 (US$ 2,263.00). Every month, each member contributes P30 (US$0.80). Every 23rd of the month, they hold a monthly general assembly. There is a P20 fine for those who fail to attend the meeting. The rapid increase in capital build-up in the cooperative from these arrangements was quite significant, especially considering that the Santa Rosa MPCI members are some of the poorest in the country.

The Cooperative's money is lent to its members for production purposes as well as for emergency situations. This is loaned at two per cent interest a month, which is much lower than that of the usurers, who lend at 6 per cent interest every month or 72 per cent for 12 months. The members are given 6 months to pay, but consideration is given when they are unable to meet this requirement as a result of emergency. In these cases, the group gives these members a 1-year leeway before paying. The maximum amount a person can borrow is P4,000 (US$105).

The organization also increased its capital by borrowing from the Land Bank of the Philippines (LBP). CFPI assisted them in this process during the first month, and afterwards, they were able to do this on their own. The first time the group borrowed from the LBP, they were given P81,000 (US$2,132). For the second and third time, the amount was P117,000.00 (US$3,079.00) for a total of 19.6 ha. Because the Santa Rosa MPCI members required around P10,000 a hectare, they borrowed the remaining amount needed from the cooperative fund.

The farmers were generally grateful to CFPI for its help. The CFPI undertook the feasibility study for the economic venture and it also assisted the members in doing the paperwork to register their organization(s) – unlike the Government's Department of Agriculture (DA). Aside from this, the CFPI also helped the cooperative with its accounting which included the preparation of financial statements and the recording of financial transactions, which, the CFPI has shown to the farmers, seemed to pale in comparison with an offer the majority of them found difficult to refuse; that is, the Santa Rosa MPCI members were being persuaded to sell their land for as much as P100 (US$2.6) per square metre or P1 million (US$26,316.00) per hectare.

As for who is buying their land, the key concern of the farmers is that it may be investors concerned with land conversion; that is, converting their land from agricultural to other usages, which could be as varied as industrialization and the creation of golf courses. What is happening in *Barangay* Santa Rosa is only a microcosm of the massive land conversions occurring throughout the rural areas in the Philippines.[9] This is another key area where NGOs have sought partnership with the government to prevent land conversions, though with rather less success than on other issues.

The farmers also complain about harassment from both the landowner and the putative buyer. They say that the landowners would get 'angry' if they did not agree to sell their land. A number of the farmers are too scared (*nahihiya*) to say 'no' to them. One farmer also complained that the landowner could easily sell the farmers' land because they hold the title deed which they pass on to the buyer. Another fear of the farmers is that if the land, which has been converted in their *barangay*, is used for commercial purposes, then their land tax might increase. Aggravating the situation is that the farmers are generally left in the dark about plans for their land. Their *barangay* captain claims that he was shown a map of Pandi which revealed parts of the town which were to be converted into industrial, commercial and residential areas. The bottom line is that the farmers also want to be consulted concerning what the plans are for their community. What worsens the situation of the tenant-farmers is their perception that people in power are behind these land conversions. Whether this is true or not, some farmers believe that big politicians, even at the provincial level, are involved. Thus, they feel more and more helpless about the situation.

Creating public–private partnerships: getting the attention of government officials

If ever the farmers have any natural government allies, it would be the Municipal Agrarian Reform Officer (MARO) of Pandi. This is because the buying and selling of land are deemed illegal unless it has the MARO's approval. The tenant-farmers, however, felt demoralized that the current MARO was not doing anything about the situation. He claimed that he could not act until a formal complaint has been lodged by the landowner or tenant. However, the former did not want to do this and the latter were invariably ignorant of the law.

The farmers tried to do something about their situation when the *barangay* council, whose officers are also members of the Cooperative, came out with a resolution in June 1993 demanding a stop to the illegal land conversions which were going on in their area. They sent this to the municipal government. This action was intended to show that the people were against the unlawful buying and selling of property in their community. The Mayor, however, criticized them for this petition and dismissed this. Thus, a common comment among the farmers was that they have no recourse but to sell their land, because of a lack of support for their cause from local politicians like this mayor.

Such an attitude worried the CFPI. The NGO believes that the farmers who have sold their land have failed to see the long-term implication of this; that is, the money they will receive will easily disappear. The CFPI has brought the issue of illegal land conversions to the PARRDS Leader Forum on 13 August 1995. During this meeting, it informed the PARO that there was massive buying of land, not only in Santa Rosa but also in its neighbouring towns of Santa Maria and Santa Cruz. The PARO promised to look into this.

The CFPI also arranged a meeting with the MARO of Pandi because the farmers wanted to interrogate him concerning their land situation. During the meeting, the MARO assured the farmers that if they were not in agreement to sell their land, then no one could force them to do so. He called this the tenants' right of redemption or security of tenure. He also advised the farmers to continue paying their 22 cavans of tax (*buwis*) and that their receipt should bear the land-owner's name. The MARO also informed the group that, before their land could be sold, it goes through a whole process of certification from various agencies such as the Department of Environment and Natural Resources (DENR) and the National Irrigation Authority (NIA). It is only when these certifications are made that a document for sale will be issued.

The MARO, however, could not hide his personal support for land conversion. He argued that the provinces which witnessed massive land conversion – particularly in the CALABARZON[10] – have experienced industrialization and economic growth. He also added that he could not blame the farmers for selling their land since the money they will earn from this far exceeds the amount they could earn by farming. Yet other reports revealed that land conversion in the CALABARZON has been a cause of rural conflict because of the massive dislocation of farmers and the steep increase in land value and in the rise in land rent (*Daily Globe* 1990) Ironically, it was also during the months in which this meeting took place that the country experienced a nationwide rice shortage. One of the major reasons blamed for this was the rapid conversion of rice lands to other uses like residential subdivisions and golf clubs[11] (Romero 1995b: 1).

To the CFPI's dismay, the farmers did not need much convincing from the MARO to sell their land. In December 1995, the Santa Rosa MPCI members voted to terminate their Cooperative giving preference to the money they will earn from selling their land as opposed to the income they earn from operating as a Cooperative. For the CFPI, such a reality further reinforced the need to engage in advocacy work if its ends were to be achieved. It needed both to pursuade farmers of their best interests and to engage government officials in cooperative partnerships, in opposition to the interests of the absentee landlords.

11.5 Forming NGO–government partnership through dialogue

In situations such as the two described above, therefore, one can find an Agrarian Reform officer, the MARO, who completely negates the CFPI's rural development thrust for cooperatives. One way in which the CFPI hopes to eliminate such a situation is to hold forums where they can have a dialogue with more open-minded Agrarian Reform officials and form partnerships with them for development. One such forum could be the Provincial Education Training (PET) seminars, which brings together the CFPI with other NGOs and POs in a forum, where they could agree a common development agenda for presentation to the provincial government for implementation. Another approach is participation in political activity concerning development projects in the agricultural sector. During the 1995 elections for the Regional Development Council (RDC) for Region III,[12] which is a government agency working closely with the private sector including NGOs and POs, CFPI Bulacan's field unit manager was elected as one of the private-sector representatives to the body. And at the national level, CFPI is part of the Philippine Campaign for Agrarian Reform and Rural Development (PhilCARRD). This joins together efforts of NGOs, POs and DAR officials and other government agencies in addressing apprehensions concerning the government's long-term development thrusts. Such NGO–government partnership is essential if a strategy for cooperative development is to be pursued at the national, as well as the local, level.

In June 1995, for example, a PhilCARRD national consultation proposed, among other things, to organize provincial consultations on agrarian reform and rural development so as to address local land problems and policy issues effectively. It also sought to establish working NGO coalition mechanisms at the provincial level that could deal with POs and the government (PhilCARRD 1995b). Such an endeavour has been welcomed by the former Secretary of the Department of Agrarian Reform who called for a national advocacy drive for the Agrarian Reform programme, and specifically for the Philippine Congress to pass more bills that will strengthen the CARP, such as a bill that fights land-reform exemptions. He also called for the strengthening of NGO–PO–TriPARRD partnerships at the provincial, municipal and regional levels (Garilao 1995). These are only some of CFPI's efforts to link up government officials with like-minded NGOs and POs to create a more suitable environment both for cooperative organizing and for public–private partnerships.

Another recent strategy, as mentioned previously, is not only to elect politicians who are supportive of cooperatives but for cooperative players themselves to assume government positions from the local to the national levels, either through elections or appointment. A most recent development was the appointment of former CFPI Executive Director Horacio 'Boy' Morales as Secretary of the Department of Agrarian Reform, the agency which CFPI has to deal with in its campaign for the implementation of agrarian reform and rural-development support services. As revealed by the Santa Rosa MPCI experience, such partnerships are essential for creating a milieu in order for cooperatives to be deemed as feasible alternatives to serfdom in the country's cash-starved rural areas.

11.6 Conclusions

The experiences of the Masagana MPCI and the Santa Rosa MPCI reveal that the creation of a favourable environment for cooperative development can only be attained through NGO–state partnership at both a national and a local level.

A key theme in this chapter is that the particular political culture of the Philippines, and other countries in the Pacific Rim region, *puts prime emphasis upon personal relationships as the central negotiating and governance mechanism for such partnerships.*

Such partnerships are, however, essential for the development and support of impoverished rural communities in the Philippines. This is because old and new societal forces – such as powerful landowners and real-estate developers respectively – have made the fate of agricultural cooperatives vulnerable. The problem, however, is that there are Agrarian Reform officials who do not only fail in their roles in implementing Agrarian Reform, but worse undermine such a programme. The CFPI therefore has to resort to pinpointing responsible and committed DAR officials with whom they could have a dialogue about counteracting such a reality. In the process, the NGO is able to bring the problems of its cooperative communities to the attention of concerned government officials. There have been successes and failures in their efforts and what remains is a resolve that cooperative organizing can only succeed with constant pressure on the state to be responsive to the needs of the farmers particularly in the area of Agrarian Reform and rural-development support. Such an engagement will hopefully pave the way for a viable NGO–state partnership in cooperative development.

References

Department of Agrarian Reform (DAR) (1989) 'Petition for exemption from operation land transfer coverage of certain landholdings situation in Calumpit, Bulacan and cancellation of certificates of land transfer issued covering the same', Manila, Philippines: Department of Agrarian Reform.

Gaffud, R. B. (1990) 'Cooperatives amidst the current national crisis', *Angkoop* 2(5) September–October: 1–15.

Garilao, E. D. (1987) 'Indigenous NGOs as strategic institutions: Managing relationships with government and resource agencies', *World Development*, 15(Supplementary): 113–20.

—— (1995) 'Presentation of CARP Assessment (1992–1995)', *Pakiramdam, Paninimbang, Panawagan: Agrarian Reform and Rural Development National Consultation*, Quezon City, Philippines: Philippine Campaign for Agrarian Reform and Rural Deveopment.

Philippine Campaign for Agrarian Reform and Rural Development (PhilCARRD) (1995a) '*CARPe Diem* (Seize the Day): Advancing the Agrarian Reform struggle beyond 2000', *Pakiramdam, Paninimbang, Panawagan: Agrarian Reform and Rural Development National Consultation*, Quezon City, Philippines: Philippine Campaign for Agrarian Reform and Rural Development, pp. 94–6.

Philippine Campaign for Agrarian Reform and Rural Development (PhilCARRD) (1995b) *Pakiramdam, Paninimbang, Panawagan: Agrarian Reform and Rural Development National Consultation*, Quezon City, Philippines: Philippine Campaign for Agrarian Reform and Rural Development.

Romero, L. F. (1995a) 'Is there a rice cartel?', *Philippine Daily Inquirer* 8 August 1995, pp. 1 and 6.
—— (1995b) 'Why consumers reel from rice shortages', *Philippine Daily Inquirer* 20 August 1995, pp. 1 and 12.
San Pascual, R. (1991) 'Prospects of Coops in a mixed economy', *Dagyao*, Official Newsletter of the NGO–Coalition for Cooperative Development. First Issue (July) pp. 2–8.
Tadeo, J. (1995) 'Reaction to DAR presentation of CARP assessment (1992–1995), *Pakiramdam, Paninimbang, Panawagan: Agrarian Reform and Rural Development National Consultation*, Quezon City, Philippines: Philippine Campaign for Agrarian Reform and Rural Development, pp. 43–6.

Notes

1   Because of the sensitive nature of this chapter, some of the names, places and organizations have been changed.
2   NGOs are here defined as private, non-profit volunteer organizations that are committed to the task of what is broadly termed 'development'. Such NGOs are usually *intermediary organizations* which serve local communities. Those NGOs, on the other hand, whose members and constituents are also its beneficiaries are called *grassroots NGOs*, or *people's organizations* (POs). For a further discussion see Garilao (1987: 115).
3   Studies reveal that NGO-assisted cooperatives increased in the Philippines from an average of four per NGO to five per NGO over the period 1989–1990 (San Pascual 1991: 3).
4   The *barangay* is the smallest political unit in the Philippines. It generally consists of fifty to one hundred households.
5   An exchange rate of P38.00 to the US dollar is used throughout (P = pesos).
6   The 'CLT' is the document which certifies that the farmer is qualified to become an Agrarian Reform beneficiary.
7   In a Government–NGO–PO (GO–NGO–PO) forum, former DAR Secretary Garilao admitted that his department does not really have enough lawyers to provide legal-support services to farmers. Their lawyers are also only paid P8,000–P15,000 per month, so that often they do not stay long with the agency (Garilao 1995: 38).
8   The distribution of EPs, or land titles, is the final stage of the Agrarian Reform process.
9   It is estimated that 118,000 ha of the total of 1.47 million hectares of irrigated lands in the country have already been converted into non-agricultural use. Ten thousand hectares of rice and corn lands, on the other hand, are about to undergo conversions to high-value crops (Tadeo 1995: 45).
10 CALABARZON is composed of the provinces of Cavite, Laguna, Batangas and Quezon and is considered a government priority area for industrialization. Thus there have been rampant land conversions in these areas (i.e. the conversion of prime agricultural land to industrial zones). It was reported that 'a conservative estimate of 160,247 hectares have been converted in various local land-use plans on top of the 118,000 hectares of irrigated ricelands that were already converted during the period of 1988–1991' (PhilCARRD 1995a: 94).
11 It is also noted that at present there are only 2.5 million hectares of land devoted to rice production, which is further diminishing because of land conversion. It is reported that 'for every hectare of irrigate riceland converted to non-agricultural

uses, the population supporting capacity is lowered by 70–100 persons on the basis of effective demand (Romero 1995a: 12).

12 Region III covers the provinces of Bataan, Bulacan, Pampanga, Nueva Ecija, Tarlac and Zambales.

12 The propensity, persistence and performance of public–private partnerships in Sweden

Sven-Olof Collin and Lennart Hansson

12.1 Why cudgel about public–private partnerships?

An arrangement between a municipality and one or more private firms, where all parties involved share risks, profit, utilities and investments (Haider 1986) through a joint ownership of an organization constitutes a public–private partnership (PPP). It is one of the several forms that the municipal production of services and products can assume (Borys and Jemison 1989; Mackintosh *et al.* 1994; Mohr and Spekman 1994). In the USA, it has been a means of gathering capital and competencies for downtown redevelopment projects (Davis 1986; Stephenson 1991), in England a way of achieving local economic redevelopment (Bennet and Krebs 1990; Field 1990) and in Germany it has served similar purposes (Jochaimsen 1990).

The significance of PPPs is low in Sweden. In a sample of 64 out of a total of 280 municipalities (see Collin 1998b for details of this survey data), we found that there were 117 acknowledged PPPs; that is, on average 1.8 PPPs in each municipality. Most PPPs were very small in capital and personnel, 50 per cent had a capital of less than 25,000 SKr (approx. 2,700 €) and 50 per cent had less than four employees. Although most municipalities have some experience about PPPs, the frequency and the importance of PPPs appear to be very low indeed. In the Swedish scientific and popular debate the phenomenon of PPP was absent until the mid-1990s when a very limited debate occurred about the incorporation of municipal operations and of PPPs. Insignificant in scope and importance, with very few interested in the phenomenon, why then cudgel about PPPs?

12.2 Partisan reasons for public–private partnerships: the case of how social problems are solved in Osby

The municipality of Osby is a small provincial municipality with only about 13,500 inhabitants. It is located in the north of Scania (Skåne), a county in Southern Sweden, and 100–200 km from the densely populated and dynamic areas of western Scania. The people in this northern region have long been known for their enterprising spirit. In the sixteenth century they were well known for their woodwork, especially for the production of clogs and baskets, and for the exploitation of their forests in their partisan wars against the invading Swedish Army (at the time Scania was part of Denmark).

Today Osby has two dominating employers, the municipality and BRIO, which is a family-company producing wooden toys. The rest of the employed people work in the extensive small-firm sector. The number of companies in Osby is no more than 700 (i.e. one company per 20 inhabitants).

Cooperation between the private sector and the public sector has been present in Osby for many years. In the 1950s, one of the strongmen in the municipality, Gösta Darlin, who started a central-heating company, initiated the construction of a compound house, which later became a central building in the main borough. Inside there were a restaurant, an assembly hall and a theatre, and the house was financed by several of the large employers, among them the municipality, BRIO and Darlin's own company.

The municipality offers many such examples of public–private partnership. Osbyhälsan AB was created as a limited company by the municipality and several private firms as its owners. The goal of the firm was to provide health care for its owners' employees. Södra Sveriges Fastbränsle AB was created during the oil crisis of the 1970s in order to exploit the peat bogs in the surroundings. It was a cooperation between a number of municipalities located in the area and some private firms, among others Södra Skogsägarna, a wood corporation, and Sydkraft, an electrical-power company.

The habit of cooperation over institutional borders between the public and private sectors in Sweden made it possible for the modern 'partisans' in Osby to easily organize cooperation between the municipality and several private firms when the municipality was besieged by economic hardships in 1991. The central borough – Osby Municipality – is a station in the national railway system. The railroad runs through the borough separating it in two halves. Thus, it is a very obvious and important part of the Municipality. In autumn 1991, the State Railway Corporation informed Osby Municipality that it had decided to discontinue goods traffic as a result of low profitability. Many corporations in the borough used the railroad as an easily available transportation means, and some large industries were dependent on the railways. With no goods traffic to the borough some of the industries would have been forced to leave and relocate their production facilities to a substitute place where such transportation means were available. The politicians in the Municipality recognized the economic importance of goods traffic, and some even thought that this was the beginning of the end for the railway in Osby as it occurred to them that without the former the closure of the railway station would be imminent.

With the maintenance of goods service as their common interest, a group of local politicians and entrepreneurs organized a trip to the city of Malmö, the provincial capital, where they negotiated with the railway authorities. They returned home with an idea of how to organize a company and how to contract for goods traffic with the State Railway Corporation.

OsbyTåg Ek. För. was established as an incorporated association. The municipality and a group of businessmen acted as its owners. Each owner was expected to invest at least 10,000 SKr (ca. €1,100) in the firm. The firm entered a contract with the State Railway Corporation in which it undertook to pay compensation of 1,500 SKr (ca. €168) for each wagon if the yearly volume of freight did not reach at least 400 wagons. The contract was, however, constructed with a degressive tariff that meant that where the freight exceeded a volume of 1,000 wagons a year no extra charges would be levied. The task of this newly founded firm was to take care of the freight when it arrived at Osby and it included shunting, loading and unloading the wagons. The firm did not have any personnel of its own and relied on the employees of its owners to conduct the work. The Municipality provided the firm with two personnel and two of the private firms that co-owned the new company, also contributed with two employees of their own. The firm did not have any formal contracts with those working for it.

The operation has so far been more successful than was first imagined. One reason is that the firm succeeded in persuading IKEA, a large furniture corporation with headquarters not far from the Municipality, to have a storeroom in Osby, and to use the railroad for the transportation of its products. The degressive tariff combined with an increase in traffic led to a dramatically good result in 1994 and this, in turn, made it possible for the firm to bring down the cost of transportation for the goods of its owners.

The workload of the new firm is not shared equally by each one of its owners nor are its benefits accrued to them in equal proportion. The Municipality itself provided the firm with two of its employees to take care of shunting and administration, a substantial investment, and its Secretary for Industrial Policy to head the firm. Although BRIO invested 50,000 SKr ca. (€5,600), it hardly utilized the railroad. AB Heinz Nilssons Plåtbearbetning, on the other hand, depends heavily on the railroad and has considerably benefited from this joint venture. Heinz stores its customers' steel rolls, and on their demand cuts these rolls and sends them to its customers. The steel rolls are sent by rail to Osby from all over Europe. Thus, without goods traffic Heinz would have to find another location for its operations. When the threat of the railway closing down was imminent, the young owner of Heinz actively engaged in the establishment of OsbyTåg Ek. För. With the operation of the firm becoming routine, he has now discontinued his engagement in it. Of course, Heinz is still dependent on the railway traffic but none of its fifteen employees are in any way involved with the operations of OsbyTåg Ek. För.

The municipality of Osby is one of the municipalities in Sweden which has the highest number of public–private partnerships per capita. It is situated in a part of Sweden whose lack of natural resources had made the enterprising spirit of the residents its most important resource. It is this abundant local entrepreneurship which has so easily made partnerships possible when the circumstances have made them necessary. These partnerships are mostly based on informal relationships without any need for formal contracts. Each partner simply provides the resources it has or can afford to hand over. Such readiness to establish partnership is not the result of any major ideological discussions about crossing the boundary between the public and private sectors. Nor has it led to any major conflicts between profit-seeking private entrepreneurs and socially aware politicians. Indeed, such a readiness is no more than the outcome of common fear of an external threat whether it is from some state corporation or an institution such as the Swedish Army. To counter this threat, both the local politicians and entrepreneurs organized 'partisan' partnerships in order to mobilize resources and coordinate actions.

12.3 Reasons for studying public–private partnerships

Osby is an extreme case in Sweden since most municipalities do not have so many public–private partnerships in proportion to their population. But the example of Osby indicates that partnerships are viable organizations for dealing with resource transfers, facilitating action between partners from different institutional environments and coping with external threats or opportunities. The present chapter, which is based on an extensive survey of Swedish public–private partnerships conducted during 1995 and 1996 (parts of this survey have already been presented in Collin (1998b) and Collin and Hansson (1998)), will specify the conditions for the establishment of partnerships in Sweden, the way they function and the performance they have achieved.

When we started this project, we had two overriding reasons for the study: a political reason, since PPPs – whilst rather unknown – represented an opportunity for financially strained municipalities to reform their operations; a theoretical reason, since a mixture of partners from different institutional environments are involved in PPPs. Politically, it was interesting to note how the municipalities and their national federation which were faced with budget constraints and diminished social legitimacy were using PPPs as a means to rationalize their operations. One strategy was to focus on the border between public and private spheres. Privatization and deregulation – whilst a viable second strategy – was viewed as representing a retreat and causing undue administrative reforms, such as contractual arrangements and corporatization, inside the municipal organization. Stretching the legal boundaries of municipalities to overlap with the private sector (i.e. forming PPPs) was not considered a third viable strategy. That is odd since one would expect that with the rather old, and still legitimate tradition of corporativism in Sweden where close cooperation between the State and the private sector is a matter of routine and in effect supersedes socialization and regulation (Lash and Urry 1987), PPPs would easily win recognition and respect as new and viable arrangements for municipal reorganization. The low utilization of PPPs in Sweden is, therefore, rather surprising and puzzling. As there were no ideological impediments to the introduction of PPPs, our attention thus turned to examining the feasibility and efficiency of PPPs in handling the worries and opportunities of the Swedish municipalities in order to unravel whether such considerations did indeed lie behind the low frequency of PPPs in Sweden.

The theoretically interesting feature of PPPs is that by definition they are composed of two partners each of which originates from a different institutional

Table 12.1 Differences between public and private spheres

	Public	Private
Principle of distribution	Democracy	Price system
Principal	Citizen	Owner
Objective	Ambiguous	Distinct
Control	Ambiguous	Distinct
Hierarchical levels	Many	Few
Incentives	Weak	Strong
Job security	High	Low
Principle of localization	Geography	Market
Principle of competency	Municipal considerations	Market
Financing	Taxes	Sales
Market structure	Monopoly	Competition

environment (i.e. the private and the public spheres). This distinction was conceptualized by Dahl and Lindblom (1953), and has since been elaborated in a typological manner by others (Brunsson 1989; Parker 1992; Perry and Rainey 1988). A summary of the distinctions between public and private spheres (Table 12.1) provides a detailed picture of how these two institutional settings differ.

The fundamental distinction between public and private spheres is how resources are distributed. In the former it is by means of democracy whilst in the latter it is through the price system (Dahl and Lindblom 1953). The principal in the public sector is the citizen, whereas in the private sector it is the owner. These principals have quite different prerequisites in governing their organizations. A public organization such as a municipality has ambiguous objectives and thus an ambiguous control system. An owner of a capitalist corporation presumably has profit as its overriding objective and this makes the issue of control system more distinct. Whereas in a municipality there are many hierarchical levels in relation to the size of the organization, in a Swedish private enterprise the levels of command are rather few. Compared with a private firm, it is less feasible for a municipality to have an incentive system essentially based on financial rewards, which is probably why job security has tended to be higher in the public sector, at least in the past. Finally, the employees of a Swedish municipality are restrained by law to act only within the defined boundaries of their locality and not to intervene in the affairs of another municipality nor should they conduct matters which are classified to be in the realm of the private domain. Furthermore, a municipality is obliged by law to treat all citizens equally. However, it is a common practice for a private firm to differentiate between its different classes of customers as it is guided by its own strategy and market prospects. Finally, a private firm is mostly destined to operate in a competitive market in which its sources of finance ultimately depend on how it satisfies the market whereas a public institution – such as a municipality – deals with a monopoly market for its services or products and it is mainly financed by taxes.

A PPP consists of partners from these two institutional environments and as an organization it is situated between the two extremes which these environments represent. Such a situation imparts on the PPP a twilight character. It is neither a genuine public organization nor is it a private enterprise, yet it contains aspects from each. The ambiguity and diversity inherent in PPPs create both opportunities and risks. It could be hypothesized that the diversity creates a fertile soil for innovation (Ancona and Caldwell 1992; Bantel and Jackson 1989; Murray 1989; Watson *et al.* 1993). On the other hand, whilst the risks associated with the inherent diversity of PPPs could create conflicts between its different partners its ambiguous character could complicate the relationships between its stakeholders. Thus, an arrangement which is inherently prone to suffer from a conflictual inside and an ambiguous outside is a recipe for failure and this may explain why there is such a low frequency of PPPs in Sweden.

To summarize, PPPs are organizations situated in the twilight zone between the private and public spheres and are made of partners who are motivated by different reasons to act. They may be viable organizations with innovative prospects yet their conflictual and ambiguous character limits their longevity. They are as yet not popular organizations in Sweden. Such considerations beg the following questions about Swedish PPP's:

- Propensity: What are the reasons for the creation of PPPs, especially since a completely public or private organization may be a simpler solution?
- Persistence: What are the processes going on in and around PPPs, especially in view of their inherently conflictual and ambiguous character?
- Performance: What are the effects of PPPs, especially considering their possible innovative prospect?

This chapter presents the results of our research about PPPs in Sweden and is organized in response to the three main issues raised earlier: the propensity, persistence and performance of these organizations. International research on this topic has only been lightly touched on here since this task is undertaken in other chapters of this volume.

12.4 Propensity to use of public–private parterships in Sweden

A number of reasons have been reported to have influenced the move towards PPPs. These include:

1   resource sharing,
2   the need to have an instrument for transforming an organization,
3   providing the image of a proper firm to a joint venture in order to appease the private partners,
4   profit, and
5   risk sharing.

(Davis 1986; Kouwenhoven 1993; Mackintosh 1992; Quince 1990; Roberts *et al.* 1995; Stephenson 1991).

In a partial account of the research on which this chapter is based, Collin (1998b), using data from a sample of 64 of the total of 280 municipalities, reported that the propensity for using PPPs was correlated with the structural features of the municipality, thus showing that resource sharing is indeed a relevant motivation. The capacity of the population of a municipality to pay taxes was negatively related with the propensity to use PPPs which could be interpreted as suggesting that the poorer a municipality the greater is the need for it to share resources. The proportion of public employees in relation to all those who are employed in a municipal area is negatively related to the propensity for using PPPs, thus indicating that there is less of a need for large municipalities to participate in joint ventures with the private sector since their own resources are already large enough to accommodate for much of their demands. A positive association was found to exist between the propensity to use PPPs and the size of the service sector in the municipality, indicating that the abundance of resources in the private sector provided the private partners with the means and the municipal partners with the incentives to venture.

The overriding motive appears to be sharing of resources. These could either be tangible resources such as financial capital or machinery, or intangible resources such as specific competencies or the commercial mental disposition assumed to be present in the private sphere. The need to consider a wider range of resources than financial ones was emphasized in a four-case study presented in Collin and Hansson (1998). The results of this study suggested that competitive strength and risk sharing were important motives both for the public bodies engaged in PPPs and the private firms participating in them. For example, a refuse-collection firm was created through a merger between the municipal waste-collection operations and part of a carrier firm. The original motive for this joint venture was to gain logistic coordination. But soon afterwards gaining competitive advantage became a second motive since the Municipality decided to put waste collection on tender. As a result of this joint venture, the position of the municipal operations was strengthened since they had now acquired better transportation resources and a boost in commercial legitimacy. The private firm in the PPP was attracted to this joint venture partly because of the closer relationship it had hoped to gain towards one of its major customers, the Municipality, and partly because of the dynamic and innovative chief executive officer (CEO) it had recruited from the municipality.

An important distinction which should be made, and one which has been overlooked in previous research, is the difference between possible motives for collaboration between private and public partners, and the reasons why such a collaboration may take the form of a PPP. Resource sharing can be accomplished without engaging in risk and profit sharing and without the need to share utilities and investments in a joint ownership of an organization. More or less complicated contractual relationships can be constructed to govern such sharing of resources. The waste-collection operations of the Municipality mentioned earlier could have contracted the lorries from the private firm and on its own organized a wholly owned corporation, thereby gaining commercial legitimacy. But instead a joint-stock company was created which the Municipality and a private firm owned. One possible advantage with this option might have been the avoidance of contractual difficulties which could have arisen had a joint-stock company not been created. Problems encountered in coordinating the use of lorries and setting appropriate incentives to ensure wholehearted involvement from both partners, now facing a competitive environment created by the tender decision of the Municipality, were some of such difficulties.

One could couch the reasons for the creation of this collaborative venture in the language of transaction-cost economics. As such one could hypothesize that contractual difficulties arising from transaction-specific investments − i.e. hold-up or specification difficulties − create the need to find an organizational form that can govern the dependency of the firm on these resources without giving way to opportunism (Williamson 1996). Pooling of resources in an organization, headed by one management and governed through the associational form of a joint-stock company, reduces contracting and monitoring costs when coordination difficulties paired with incentive problems are present.

Conflicting results have been reported when it concerns the issue of incentive problems in a PPP; that is, when it concerns how partners should be encouraged to get involved in the joint venture. Quince (1990) argues that the corporate form reduces partner involvement. In contrast, Lyall (1986) suggests that the corporate form secures the involvement of the private partners. These claims are, however, weak and lack both explicit empirical findings and strong theoretical support. Our claim on the necessity to consider the incentive issue is both theoretically secured and, more importantly, supported by our empirical cases.

Indeed, our study indicates that a host of reasons are valid causes for the creation of PPPs. Sharing of resources, be it financial or specific competencies and attitudes, as well as sharing risks and profit, or the need to have a means for transforming municipal organizations, or for legitimating the commercial inclinations of the public sector could all be necessary motives for PPPs. However, on their own none of these motives are sufficient to cause the setting up of a PPP. There have to be considerable contractual difficulties as a result of coordination and incentive problems to promote the choice of an independent organization, jointly owned by the two partners, as a way to exclude the need to elaborate a detailed contractual solution. It is only when such a necessity imposes itself on the circumstances that the motives mentioned earlier highlight the benefits of a PPP for the parties concerned.

12.5 The persistence of public–private partnerships in Sweden

The twilight character of the PPP may be suspected of putting a spell on its organization, processes and performance. In this section we wish to argue, contrary to the public belief, that the institutional dichotomy of the PPP does not necessarily lead to internal conflicts between its two opposing partners, but it does create an ambiguous character which strains its external relationships thus endangering its very survival. The Janus face of the PPP, its ability to present itself as a public institution, or as a private organization or as something in between can be an asset for it, but this could at the same time constitute a threat to its persistence.

Previous research on the processes of PPPs has considered their ambiguous character in terms of the conflict of interests between their partners (Kouwenhoven 1993; Mackintosh 1992; Stephenson 1991). In our research, we were often recommended, and even when engaged in a project commissioned by the Swedish Ministry of Finance, were almost asked to focus on possible conflicts between the partners and to use game theory in order to show the exploitive character of the relationship between them. Theoretical premises, rooted in economics, tend to put the focus on the conflictual side of a PPP. Our empirical findings, however, did not support these doctrines.

Our case studies showed that key players in a PPP could treat it both as a private corporation which is supposed to behave according to the contingencies of the market where competition and ownership values are emphasized, and as a municipal organization which is expected to act on behalf of the citizens. Thus, the twilight character of the PPP offers management a unique freedom of action.

The refuse-collection firm mentioned earlier behaved as a private corporation when it demanded freedom to act independently in sending tenders to its own parent municipality and other nearby local authorities. But it acted as a public institution when it was engaged in refuse-collection planning performed by the sanitary department of the municipality. The Municipality which aimed to purchase the refuse-collection service treated the corporation at arm's length, like other bidders, in order to appear as an independent and objective evaluator of the bids on offer. However, when buying the service was not the issue, any one of various sections of the Municipality could have had a closer relationship with the corporation. Thus, both the corporation and its major stakeholder, the Municipality, changed their views on the character of the corporation when the situation changed.

Sometimes, key players in a PPP act as if the latter were a private firm, and sometimes as if it were a public operation. Likewise, those dealing with the PPP sometimes act as if it were a public operation and sometimes as if it were a private firm. Such views create four possible outcomes. Two outcomes in which the key players in the corporation and its stakeholders have conflicting views on the character of the PPP and two outcomes in which they have similar views on its character. Thus, there is a line of character confirmation when all actors within and surrounding the PPP have a similar view of the PPP's character.

The conscious attempt to manage the views held (i.e. to make the corporate players in the PPP and its stakeholders to hold concordant views) was recognized by Collin and Hansson (1998) as managing the line of character confirmation. A failure to balance their views could produce ambiguity about what the PPP was, and what to expect from it. Indeed, it could even produce conflicts that put the persistence of the PPP in question.

In the case of the refuse-collection firm, the CEO tried to present the corporation as a public institution, but the municipal authorities handling the bids rejected that strategy. This increased the tensions between the corporation and the municipality. The conflict was eventually resolved when the privatization of the corporation clarified the position of the firm. Thus, we see that the failure of the CEO to successfully manage the line of character confirmation produced a conflict with the major stakeholder which ended the persistence of the PPP.

Thus, an empirically induced hypothesis is that a PPP tends to be an unstable organizational arrangement because of its ambiguous character which inherently produces uncertainty and conflicts between the PPP and its stakeholders. However, the persistence of a PPP is not solely determined by ambiguity in its character. We found in our case studies that the persistence of a PPP is also influenced by three additional factors; that is, the management of the ambiguity by the PPP, contractual difficulties in sharing resources and the competitive strategy enforced by the Municipality. The ambiguous character of the PPP and the three factors mentioned above influence how a PPP continues to operate and whether its fate ends in privatization or socialization. The refuse-collection firm in our study was privatized as a response to resolving the ongoing conflicts between the CEO and the municipal authorities over its character, and as a consequence of the municipal strategy for enhancing competition, which was not the outcome of all the PPPs we studied. For instance, in the case of another corporation which had a CEO who was very skilful at managing the ambiguous character of the PPP despite attacks on the municipal ownership of the corporation, the PPP continued to survive. A third planned corporation was not created because of fear of overriding contractual difficulties.

In the literature on PPPs, neither the significance of its unstable character, nor, therefore, the importance of forces stabilizing it, have been properly recognized. By sheer speculation, Borys and Jemison (1989) recognized the ambiguous character of a PPP and argued for institutional leadership to deal with it. Based on our empirically induced hypothesis we have argued here that PPPs are unstable organizations because of their ambiguous character. We have further identified management of the ambiguous character of the PPP, contractual difficulties over sharing of resources and the competitive strategy enforced by the Municipality as three factors which influence whether the fate of a PPP remains unaltered, or whether it is privatized or socialized.

12.6 The performance of public–private partnerships in Sweden

The performance of a PPP is as ambiguous as its character. As indicated in Table 12.1, the objectives of the private and public spheres are distinctly different. An organization whose status lies between these two spheres cannot escape having ambiguous objectives. Thus, it is difficult to determine a priori the efficiency of a PPP. Furthermore, it is difficult to make rules of thumb about what the efficiency of a PPP should be since there are diverse objectives behind the creation of each

PPP, and, hence, without knowing these specific objectives it is hard to evaluate how a particular PPP has been successful in meeting its aims.

The methodology employed in our case study made it possible for us to gain specific knowledge about the principals (owners) of each PPP and their vested interests. We have made a distinction between static efficiency (i.e. the perform-ance of a PPP in which the aim of the principals is to continue with the existing operations and ensure high profitability) and dynamic efficiency (i.e. the perform-ance of a PPP whose principals have primarily sought to form an organization capable of changing its operations and even creating new ones). Based on these distinctions we were able to evaluate the efficiency of the four PPPs studied.

The Refuse Collection Corporation mentioned earlier had a municipal owner whose intention was to change the municipal operations into a competitive venture. The intention of the private owners of this corporation was to foster good relations with the Municipality and to gain new waste-collection contracts. The outcome was a corporation that developed from the border of the Municipality and expanded in size and market. The joint ownership brought for the Municipality conflict-free relationships between its purchasers and the Refuse Collection Corporation as the service provider, a return on its invested capital as well as profits and a new competitor to the waste-collection market. As for the private owner, it profited from an extended operation. Thus, the waste cor-poration produced change, and even created new opportunities and as such it had a high dynamic efficiency.

In creating a PPP, the Harbour Corporation, which undertook the harbour operations of a large town, had the modest goal of retaining its operations without being restricted by legislation limiting municipal operations and enjoying greater freedom in coordinating its affairs. The Harbour Corporation was rather successful in continuing the harbour business on its own although we suspected that there could have been hidden subsidies present. But the Corporation expanded its operations vertically to include transportation to and from the harbour – an expansion which would have been legally doubtful had the Municipality wholly owned the operations. Thus, the Harbour Corporation achieved a moderate level of static efficiency and there were indications that it might have moved toward achieving some degree of dynamic efficiency.

The Road Corporation was planned to be a merger between municipal road-maintenance operations and a private firm. It was not implemented because of anticipated contractual difficulties and absence of private firms to act as its potential partners. That was indeed a failure.

The Health Care Corporation pooled resources from several municipalities, a private firm and a state agency, and created a new concept for dealing with juvenile addicts. The intention from both the private firm and the municipalities was to create this new form of health care. The corporation initially experienced some financial problems mainly because of poor marketing, but it managed to solve them and expand by running a similar scheme designed for drug-addicted mothers with infants. Thus, as a successful and expanding enterprise, the Health Care Corporation showed signs of dynamic efficiency.

These four cases suggest that a PPP has an inherent capacity towards dynamic efficiency. Of course, our sample was biased towards surviving PPPs and it did not include any PPP which had failed or ended in dissolution or bankruptcy. But it did include one PPP which was never instituted and one that ended as a privatized firm. Hence, our sample comprised a rather diverse set of possibilities for the development of PPPs. Thus, we believe that we can conclude that a PPP has an inbuilt capacity towards achieving dynamic efficiency. The contention that a mix of two institutionally different partners has the capacity to be a potential for change appears to be consistent with the opinion echoed by Mackintosh (1992: 211) when he claimed that: '... to turn the pressures of partnership to the service of a new "developmentalism" at local level and within the local state'.

Profitability was low to moderate in the three cases. Evidently, profitability of the operations was not of vital importance to the corporations and their principals. Analysing our survey, we reached the same conclusion as we did have the opportunity to test whether the ownership structure of each corporation was responsible for its level of profitability or whether it was determined by the market situation of each enterprise.

A PPP involves a merger of two partners, an event which is shaped by two different institutional settings and leads to a new institutional environment. It is assumed in various institutional theories (Veblen 1904; Williamson 1996; Zucker 1987) that institutions guide individual action. However, a question as yet poorly researched is whether an actor is strongly influenced by its institutional origin or whether the current institutional setting is stronger in influencing the actions of the individual actor. For example, if a Municipal organization recruited its managers from private firms, would the organization then change towards behaviours more akin to those observed in private firms because of the institutional origin of the managers, or would the institutional setting of the municipal organization influence the managers and make them accommodate to the new situation. Thus, we contrast a theory of institutional influence *ex ante* with a theory of institutional influence *ex post*. The *ex ante* argument is that the dominance of a partner in a PPP should influence the PPP and ultimately its performance. Assuming a private partner having profitability as its overriding motive, which is indeed too simplistic to assume, then the dominance of such a partner would enhance the performance of the PPP. The *ex post* argument, in contrast, states that the profitability of a PPP is determined by the institutional setting of the industry or the organizational form to which the PPP belongs.

The question of whether the institutional influence acts *ex ante* or *ex post* is not only of theoretical significance but has practical implications too. Should a municipality believe that an infusion of business principles into its current operations would enhance their productivity then it could have two alternatives to pursue: (1) it could employ a manager from the private sector in the belief that such a player would introduce new business principles into the operations; or (2) it could change its operations into businesslike organizations in the belief that whoever may be heading them would then have to follow the rules. The first choice is in line with the theory of institutional influence *ex ante* and the second one corresponds to the theory of institutional influence *ex post*.

The distinctive institutional differences presented in Table 12.1 can presumably affect the way key players in an organization act. A person from the public sector is accustomed to act in an organizational setting in which the principal can change every 4 years, thus promoting preventive actions on her part towards this risk. Since the objectives of a public organization are ambiguous, there is uncertainty towards its performance and how it could be evaluated. A person from the public sector is, therefore, more inclined to focus on negotiations since this is the major process through which objectives are revealed and performance is evaluated. A person from the private sector has, however, much more clearcut objectives. She knows that she should act mainly in response to market uncertainty. Evaluation, carried to its extreme, is only a matter of return on investments (ROI) and its improvement, and it promotes actions that could potentially lead to higher ROI. One could safely predict that a CEO from a private corporation is more likely to focus on achieving quantitatively measurable performance than her counterpart in the public sphere.

A PPP is governed by a board of directors whose composition does influence its performance. If it were true that the actions of the CEO of a PPP was determined by his or her institutional origin then the same claim could equally be stated about the members of the board. Thus, one would expect that directors with a municipal background would act politically; that is to say, they would focus on the utility of their actions for the municipality, however diverse that utility may be. Such directors are by definition less inclined to give priority to profit-seeking objectives and raising the financial efficiency of the operations. The institutional character of directors from the private sector dictates that they would act in a diagonally opposite manner with the emphasis on achieving measurable performance targets.

A similar reasoning could be applied to the ownership structure. Thus, an ownership structure dominated by private partners would tend to move the corporation towards more profit-oriented behaviour. We were not able to test this idea since some of the owners were foundations which in strict legal terms do not belong to either the private or public sector. As such, we could not test the institutional influence *ex post* as far as the issue of ownership was concerned.

An alternative theory focusing on the institutional setting *ex post* can also be proposed. Whereas the theory just presented predicts that the effect of institutions is *ex ante*, this alternative theory considers the effects to be *ex post*. In other words, such a theory maintains that the existing institution has a stronger impact on the actions taken by its players than the institutional origin of these actors has on their behaviour. This can readily be tested by means of two separate hypotheses. The legal form of an organization signals the behaviour appropriate to it. Thus, the joint-stock company creates an institutional environment in which actions are oriented towards profit seeking, cost awareness and customer sensitivity, whereas a foundation promotes benefaction and collective utility. Hence, one could expect that joint-stock companies are more profit oriented than foundations.

The branch of industry or service sector in which a PPP is situated can presumably influence the actions of its CEO and by her actions the behaviour of the PPP. An agency which is involved with formulating, say, industrial policy for the entire county has a distinct collective utility. An institution such as the public health care is prohibited to seek profit for its services. But a municipal operation such as refuse collection acts to a large extent in a similar manner to private corporations, and, hence, is more prone to adopting actions which are in tune with profit considerations. So, what branch of industry or service sector has the most influence on PPPs is an empirical question. In Sweden, we believe that, with the exceptions of health care and the agencies for formulating industrial policy, almost all other branches of industry and service sector could be structured to have a profit orientation.

Our data indicated a low average return on investment (ROI) (0.03) for the cases included in our survey. Such a finding supports the belief that a majority of PPPs have goals other than profit maximization. In 63 per cent of the cases, the CEOs were recruited from municipal organizations and on average the share of directors recruited from the Municipality was 42 per cent.

The model yielded low significance in the chi-square test ($p < 0.05$). It had a low explanatory capacity (adjusted $R^2 = 0.12$) partly because of poor ROI data and partly because of the ambiguous character of PPPs which made an evaluation of their performance difficult to ascertain. It indicated, however, that the institutional origin of the managers and of the board members was of no significance. But in the case of certain branches – such as the harbour – and in the case of the PPP's legal organizational form, it had a slight correlation with profitability. If anything can be concluded from this test, it is that there is a degree of correlation between the institutional setting and the performance of a PPP.

The major conclusion that our research allows us to draw about the performance of PPPs is that they appear to be capable of bringing dynamic efficiency to operations, which might be because they are used as an instrument of change by the municipal partners. If any institutional influence is present, it is more likely that the present institutional setting, such as the industry in which the PPP is located, and the legal organizational form of the corporation, influence their profit-seeking behaviour.

12.7 Summary and conclusions

A PPP is an arrangement between a public authority and a private firm, where all parties involved share risks, profit, utilities and investments through a joint ownership. We have found that the propensity to form a collaboration between a private and a public partner is influenced by factors such as the need to share resources, be it financial resources or specific competencies or attitudes, to share risk and profit, the need to have a means for transforming a public operation, and the need to legitimate market orientation of municipal agencies. The propensity to collaborate does not necessarily lead to the creation of a PPP, which is, however, influenced to a large extent by how problematic the contractual difficulties arising from coordination and incentive considerations are. Our empirical case studies led us to believe that the instability of PPPs is due to their ambiguous character and not some institutional conflicts from within. The twilight character of PPP contractual difficulties which would arise if an alternative arrangement is opted for, and the competitive strategy enforced by the Municipality are all factors which decide the fate of a PPP and determine whether its status remains unaltered or is ultimately privatized or socialized. The performance of PPPs is as ambiguous as its form but still they appear to be capable of bringing dynamic efficiency to operations, which explains why they are so widely used as instrument of change. The orientation of PPPs towards seeking profit is influenced by their institutional setting; for instance, the industry in which they are located or their legal organizational form.

So, to the extent that a PPP appears to offer dynamic efficiency, it is a viable alternative to introducing major changes in operations or launching innovations. But, their twilight character makes their management a difficult task, which explains why they are not a very common currency.

One may argue that the national culture of a country which is imbued with the sense of cooperation and consensus could well promote the propensity for creating PPPs. Sweden would indeed be a good test case since the Swedish culture of cooperation and consensus (Collin 1998a), and the Swedish tradition of corporativism (Lash and Urry 1987) could in theory stimulate the emergence of PPPs. But the low frequency of PPPs in Sweden and their limited scope in this country indicates that such a hypothesis fails to be vindicated. Of course, a thorough examination demands an international comparison between, say, Sweden and a number of suitable countries. However, that was not in the scheme of our current research. However, our results do point towards an explanation of the low frequency. We did find that cooperation was indeed a necessary but not a sufficient condition, as it is possible to have cooperation without organizing a corporation. Indeed, there are cases in Swedish business history that point towards close cooperation between separate organizations. Ericson, the large communication corporation, would probably have been less successful had it not established close cooperation with the state-owned telephone company. ASEA, now merged with ABB, would probably have been of less importance had it not been for the close cooperation it enjoyed with the state-owned Power Company. These cases indicate that cooperation is often preferred between two organizations especially in a small and culturally homogeneous society where there are less hassles to take care of contractual difficulties compared with those societies in which social-control mechanisms are weaker.

Another reason for the low frequency of PPPs in Sweden could be that the Swedish State, be it at national or municipal level, is a strong institution and as such it controls considerable amounts of resources compared with countries with weaker state organizations, such as the UK. In our research, we found that the frequency of PPPs varied negatively with the extent of municipal resources. Maybe this pattern could also be found at the national level as well, thus supporting the claim that the frequency of PPPs varies with how resourceful a state is.

The future of PPP as an organizational form in Sweden is hard to predict. Based on the reasoning mentioned above there are plausible factors both for and against the appearance of PPPs in Sweden. One factor promoting PPPs is the demand for a decrease in the tax burden. If the State yields to this pressure a drop in its resources could consequently stimulate the use of PPPs. Another factor promoting PPPs is the greater heterogeneity which Swedish society is destined to become. Such a situation would no doubt necessitate the creation of more formal organizations. One factor limiting the use of PPPs is the ideological attacks now staged on the very notion of state intervention in economy and the support which the idea of private enterprise has received at large. In sum, one could speculate that there are no strong reasons to believe that PPPs would be considered as a viable organizational form in municipal affairs. It could be that their chances of appearing would increase if there are more partisan municipalities such as Osby.

12.8 Acknowledgement

The work this paper represents was funded by Rådet för Kommunal Ekonomisk Forskning och Utbildning (KEFU) (The Council for Research and Training in Municipal Economics). Kent Springdal provided linguistic editing.

References

Ancona, D. G. and Caldwell, D. F. (1992) 'Demography and design: Predictors of new product team performance',. *Organization Science* 3: 321–41.

Bantel, K. A. and Jackson, S. E. (1989) 'Top management and innovations in banking: Does the composition of the top team make a difference?', *Strategic Management Journal* 10: 107–24.

Bennet, R. and Krebs, G. (1990) 'Towards a partnership model of local economic development initiatives in Britain and Germany', in R. J. Bennet, G. Krebs and H. Zimmermann (eds) *Local Economic Development in Britain and Germany*, London: Anglo-German Foundation, pp. 1–40.

Borys, B. and Jemison, D. B. (1989) 'Hybrid arrangements as strategic alliances: Theoretical issues in organisational combinations', *Academy of Management Review* 14: 234–49.

Brunsson, N. (1989) *The Organization of Hypocrisy*, New York: John Wiley and Sons.

Collin, S-O. (1998a) 'Why are these islands of conscious power found in the ocean of ownership? Institutional and governance hypotheses explaining the existence of business groups in Sweden', *Journal of Management Studies* 35: 719–46.

Collin, S-O. (1998b) 'In the twilight zone: A survey of public–private partnerships in Sweden', *Public Productivity and Management Review* 21: 272–83.

Collin, S-O. and Hansson, L. (1998) 'Motives for public–private partnerships and factors for their persistence – an inductive analysis of four Swedish cases', in L.

Montanheiro *et al.* (eds) *Public and Private Sector Partnerships: Fostering Enterprise*, Sheffield: Sheffield Hallam University Press, pp. 79–96.

Dahl, R. and Lindblom, C. (1953) *Politics, Economics and Welfare*, New York: Harper and Brothers.

Davis, D. (1986) 'Why partnerships? Why now?', in P. Davis (ed.) *Public–Private Partnerships: Improving Urban Life*, New York: The Academy of Political Science, Vol. 36:2, pp. 1–3.

Field, R. (1990) 'The business role in local economic regeneration: The Sheffield story', in R. J. Bennet, G. Krebs and H. Zimmermann (eds) *Local Economic Development in Britain and Germany*, London: Anglo-German Foundation, pp. 49–64.

Haider, D. (1986) 'Partnerships redefined: Chicago's new opportunities', in P. Davis, (ed.) *Public–Private Partnerships: Improving Urban Life*, New York: The Academy of Political Science, Vol. 36:2, pp. 137–49.

Jochaimsen, R. (1990) 'The Länder role in local economic development', in R. J. Bennet, G. Krebs, and H. Zimmermann (eds) *Local Economic Development in Britain and Germany*, London: Anglo-German Foundation, pp. 75–84.

Kouwenhoven, V. (1993) 'Public–private partnership: A model for the management of public–private cooperation', in J. Kooiman (ed.) *Modern Governance*. London: Sage, pp. 119–30.

Lash, S. and Urry, J. (1987) *The End of Organized Capitalism*, Cambridge: Polity Press.

Lyall, K. C. (1986) 'Public–private partnerships in the Carter years', in P. Davis (ed.) *Public–Private Partnerships: Improving Urban Life*, New York: The Academy of Political Science, Vol. 36:2, pp. 14–30.

Mackintosh, M. (1992) 'Partnership: Issues of policy and negotiation', *Local Economy* 7: 210–24.

Mackintosh, M., Jarvis, R. and Heery, E. (1994) 'On managing hybrids: Some dilemmas in higher education management', *Financial Accountability and Management* 10: 339–53.

Murray, A. I. (1989) 'Top management group heterogeneity and firm performance', *Strategic Management Journal* 10: 125–41.

Parker, D. (1992) 'Ownership, change and improved performance', paper given at the 12th Annual International Conference of the Strategic Management Society, London.

Perry, J. and Rainey, H. G. (1988) 'The public–private distinction in organization theory: A critique and research strategy', *Academy of Management Review* 13: 182–201.

Quince, R. (1990) 'Looking to the future: Overcoming problems experienced in public/private partnerships', in R. J. Bennet, G. Krebs and H. Zimmermann (eds) *Local Economic Development in Britain and Germany*, London: Anglo-German Foundation, pp. 125–34.

Roberts, V., Russell, H., Harding, A. and Parkinson, M. (1995) *Public/Private/Voluntary Partnerships in Local Government*, Luton, UK: The Local Government Board.

Stephenson, J. (1991) 'Whither the public–private partnership', *Urban Affairs Quarterly* 27: 109–27.

Veblen, T. (1904 (1978)) *The Theory of Business Enterprise*, New Brunswick, N.J.: Transaction Books.

Watson, W. E., Kumar, K. and Michaelsen, L. K. (1993) 'Cultural diversity's impact on interaction process and performance: Comparing homogeneous and diverse task groups, *Academy of Management Journal* 36: 590–602.

Williamson, O. E. (1996) *The Mechanisms of Governance*, New York: Oxford University Press.

Zucker, L. G. (1987) 'Institutional theories of organization', *Annual Review of Sociology* 13: 443–64.

13 Partnerships in Pittsburgh

The evaluation of complex local initiatives

Brian Jacobs

13.1 Introduction

This chapter reports research carried out in Pittsburgh during 1998 as part of a larger comparative study of strategy and partnership in economic development in European and North American cities and regions (Jacobs 1999). The aim here is to identify the characteristics of selected local partnerships and to discuss the analysis and evaluation of collaborative initiatives. In Pittsburgh, there are many diverse regional and local partnerships. However, this chapter concentrates on local initiatives that are difficult to evaluate because of their variety and organizational complexity. To promote a better understanding of these partnerships, a typology is presented that can be used in the evaluation of community programmes. The evaluation reveals the dynamic aspects of complex programmes and initiatives that bring together stakeholder groups with diverse agendas.

13.2 The partnership tradition

Pittsburgh is an appropriate location for the study because of the ubiquity of partnerships in local-economic development and urban regeneration. Well-established public–private-sector partnerships in the city have produced both variety and innovation in local programmes. During the 1930s, business leaders in Pittsburgh worked together to address the social and environmental problems arising from serious industrial pollution and urban dereliction. In the nineteenth century, business strongly influenced the city's growth as an industrial power-house and major contributor to the national economy. The Monongahela Valley, near Pittsburgh, was one of the most important industrial concentrations in the United States with its huge steel mills and manufacturing plants. The appalling social and environmental consequences of rapid industrialization in the Pittsburgh region led corporate leaders to take an active role in urban regeneration and community involvement. The business elite realized that the poor environment contributed to low productivity and a poor civic image in the 'smoky city'. They also identified a need for a broader regional-economic-policy focus that would safeguard the economic base of the city.

Taking up these themes, the Allegheny Conference on Community Development (ACCD) was an important private-sector-led partnership that resulted from a conference organized on post-War planning in 1943. The ACCD, formally incorporated in 1944 with an executive committee, played an important part in post-war regional economic development and urban regeneration. The 1970s and 1980s brought the profound restructuring and decline of staple industries and this confronted the ACCD with a regional economy in need of a competitive boost. By the early 1990s, the ACCD, portrayed the area as economically challenged (ACCD 1993) with Pittsburgh at the heart of a metropolitan region that increasingly had to compete globally. However, Pittsburgh was located in Allegheny County with 130 municipalities within a 731-square-mile area where government complexity and fragmentation hampered effective partnership and undermined regional competitiveness. The City of Pittsburgh cooperated with the county in economic development and planning and worked with other local-government bodies and public agencies that ran various local services, but there was a need for better coordination and regional vision.

The ACCD reported that restructuring of the regional economy during the post-World War II era produced changes in local communities and in the organization of local government. Most notably, business leaders helped to shape local regeneration efforts to revitalize the run-down communities adversely affected by the decline of the staple regional industries. The decline of the steel industry in the 1980s was a major shock, and Pittsburgh suffered from the neglect of its urban core, poor housing and deteriorating infrastructure. Post-War programmes harnessed the resources of the public, private and non-profit sectors to overcome economic decline and restore the economic fortunes of the wider region, but by the end of the 1980s continued fragmentation hindered progress. However, public–private partnerships brought groups together to deal with complex problems that organizations working by themselves could not overcome. Partnerships were appropriate mechanisms for bringing about change given the evolution of programmes that variously attuned to new conditions through organizational specialization and innovation. The partnership 'map' in the Pittsburgh region is thus complicated because of the resulting organizational interrelationships and diversification that make it hard to describe partnerships using neat categorizations, which means that it is difficult to evaluate consistently the full range of outcomes attributable to partnerships especially when cross-linkages between programmes produce fuzzy relationships and confusion about which organizations are responsible for particular impacts.

13.3 A partnership typology

To make sense of the diversity of partnerships in the Pittsburgh region it is useful to identify types of partnership structure. The typology aids analysis because it shows different partnership configurations in flux. It is also evaluative because it provides the basis for understanding change in collaborative initiatives and the processes that influence the meeting of strategic objectives. The purpose is to reveal the different kinds of structure that combine with different processes within partnerships. Therefore, the value of the partnership typology is that it accounts for the observable variety of organizational arrangements that bring together public and private-sector organizations, and it allows for the varied internal dynamics of individual partnerships. This is difficult to portray since no two partnerships are alike (Walzer and Jacobs 1998), and public and private sector organizations do not conform to organizational blueprints. Partnerships appear constantly to restructure and revise their memberships. They evolve complex functions and structures, and they display different developmental characteristics and 'corporate' cultures which make evaluation difficult. Despite this variety, it is possible to establish a typology that accommodates diversity and change. The typology here is derived from an organizational contingency model of partnerships and informal networks (Jacobs 1998) that assumes that organizations change better to 'fit' the conditions within which they work. The model presents the policy context of partnership as a changing external environment. External economic, social and political contingencies, together with factors internal to partnerships such as politics and group competition, influence the organizational characteristics of partnerships. Partners usually try better to 'configure' (Mintzberg 1996) their activities and structures to deal with the changing conditions that they confront. In urban policy, partnerships usually focus around a common objective or objectives for specific purposes, but partners often configure structures initially from local networks involving many organizations that over time adapt their internal processes to suit particular conditions. Partnerships often develop from informal networks purposely created by public and private interests, and collaboration produces complex organizational characteristics and functions as activities expand.

Two major dimensions underlie the dynamic organizational nature of partnerships portrayed in the typology. The first dimension measures degrees of political competition ranging from the 'restrained' politics of harmony and consensus to dysfunctional conflict that undermines effective collaboration (Rosenthal *et al.* 1991). Table 13.1 depicts the political relationships between groups participating in partnerships. The horizontal dimension in Table 13.1, which is a continuum that shows degrees of political competition ranging between restraint and dysfunctional conflict, suggests that partners sometimes conflict, but they frequently restrain competition by working together around an agreed consensus. Therefore, partnerships are not simply organizational spaces vaguely consisting of groups working together. Instead, they are arenas that give expression to group demands through various forms of intergroup activity.

The second important dimension, shown in the first column of Table 13.1, is the degree of organization that a partnership develops. The model shows that many different organizational arrangements are possible. It accounts for organizational ambiguity and it builds in the possibility of informal networking as well as hierarchical organization depending on the circumstances in particular partnerships. Taken together, the two dimensions shown in Table 13.1 allow for an infinite

Table 13.1 A partnership typology

Restrained competition	Competitive	Conflictual–dysfuntional
High organization	This combination of competition and organization produces b developed organization and restrained competition, which implies a potential for centralization and top-down management.	This combination signifies a highly organized partnership with competitive politics. Partners share complex tasks with a strong operating core.	Partners are likely to split the partnership. Lack of effective internal control and rivalry between partners.
Developing organization	This partnership has developing organizational structures and restrained competition.	This type of partnership can be highly political, but there is a strong possibility of a workable compromise if there is an agreement to share risks.	A developing organizational framework for the partnership, but possibly many stakeholders where conflict and competition threaten effective collaboration.
Undeveloped organization	Partnership with minimal organization, but restrained competition. One partner may dominate, or partners might share administrative tasks as the partnership develops.	There are opportunities for effective cooperation if partners strike up a workable compromise and develop effective structures.	Intense competition between partners threatens to break up the partnership and prevent organizational development and coherence.
Formal network (e.g. preceding a formal partnership)	A network with rudimentary, possibly flat organization, but where there is a general agreement to define the aims of a future partnership.	Diverse actors jostle for position in the context of a debate over proposed partnership aims and objectives.	Political disagreements lead to the early break-up of the network or informal partnership.
Informal network (e.g. preceding a formal partnership)	An informal network where actors retain their own identities but agree on general aims for the future.	Transient, unstable, and unstructured relationships between actors.	Political conflicts lead to the termination of contacts between actors.

range of combinations of political competition and kinds of organization that help to capture the variety and fluidity of partnerships.

By gauging the extent to which partners collectively develop basic organizational characteristics, it is possible to assess the degree of organizational sophistication in a partnership. According to Mintzberg (1996), the basic parts of an organization are its strategic apex, operational core, line management, technical capability, organizational culture and staff function. As partners join and activities expand, the partnership changes internally as bureaucratic structures accommodate new interorganizational relationships and extend administrative responsibilities. Operational activities – such as the development of governance processes and structures increased funding, staffing, technical assistance and programme development (The Aspen Institute 1997: 13) – all demand organizational capabilities and competencies. They also require managers to develop a strategic function to steer the partnership to achieve its objectives. In this way, a partnership becomes more like an organization as it develops the basic parts and strives to consolidate core managerial competencies. The aims of the partnership, the specific interests of stakeholders, the financial regime adopted and style of leadership are additional factors relevant in any evaluation especially as these indicate the degree of organizational development.

In practice, therefore, the typology enables managers to track partnerships as they develop and change along the organizational and competitive dimensions. Managers usually acknowledge that partnerships are not static or constrained within any single organizational configuration. The typology enables managers to characterize the direction of change within a partnership from, for example, informal networking to high organization. It also provides the basis for the envisioning of where a partnership intends to be in the future. For example, there may be a choice between informal organization combined with decentralization, or greater centralization combined with greater managerial control.

13.4 Partnership as process

All this implies that managers need to adopt a developmental perspective. The process of change affecting partnerships is important because it implies that political competition and structural change are factors that influence policy outcomes. More holistically, it is possible to view a wide range of interrelated processes that explain programme performance and the distinctiveness of local initiatives. Pawson and Tilley (1998), followed by Judge (1998), advocate what they term a 'realistic evaluation' that shows that programmes combine mechanisms with particular contexts. Pawson and Tilley (1998: 216) argue that context refers to the 'spatial and institutional locations of social situations together, crucially, with the norms, values and interrelationships found in them'. Mechanisms lead to 'regular patterns of social behaviour' (ibid.: 216) that influence outcomes according to different circumstances and the ways in which contexts and mechanisms themselves interact. For example, the contexts and mechanisms that produce desirable social and economic outcomes in large urban regeneration partnerships might differ from those in local community partnerships that have more tightly focused goals. The mechanisms for change in community programmes therefore involve diverse 'choices and capacities' (ibid.: 216) that account for 'behaviour and interrelationships' in programmes. Regarded this way, a mechanism is not a variable, rather it 'is a theory' (ibid.: 68) that 'spells out the potential of human resources and reasoning'.

The process of change is complex in local community programmes and, as Connell and Kubisch (1997) argue, this makes the evaluation of local initiatives difficult. In community initiatives, outcomes are difficult to measure especially when many different partner organizations contribute to the success of local projects. Connell and Kubisch argue that the evaluator should identify the processes that influence outcomes, and that there should be a discourse about how programmes work. This is difficult because partnerships organize at several levels, all of which influence how stakeholders work together and how communities benefit from policy interventions. For example, a partnership can bring about change at the level of the community, the individual, and at the level of the partnership's own organization. Ideally, a partnership should be operationally capable of coherently working at each level to enhance programmatic efficiency and effectiveness. Collaborative working complicates the delivery of services because partners often fail to coordinate their interventions or reconcile the operational levels. The result is a lack of a synergy within the partnership and the individual projects supported within the partnership.

In practice, lack of synergy can result from both external and internal factors. For example, in the broader environment, federal government initiatives in the USA have increasingly emphasized the need for coherence and strategy in local economic and urban regeneration initiatives. However, diverse policies have produced what many local government officials in Pittsburgh believe to be a confusing array of initiatives that lack coherence or effective coordination. There has been a distinct lack of synergy in some local initiatives and confusion about the policy intentions of federal government departments. Internally, partnerships sometimes have not worked as well as expected despite others having been successful in combining organizational capability with effective collaboration. Internal processes can be inappropriate to meeting the objectives set by managers, or intergroup competition and conflict can disrupt the ordered implementation of programmes.

13.5 Urban partnership in a changing environment: the URA

Practical attempts to evaluate performance and outcomes under changing conditions abound. It is especially important to perform meaningful evaluations since partnerships are expanding their policy horizons as they develop new interests and orientations. Evaluators are increasingly aware of the need to assess the processes that produce desired results and synergy. While policy objectives are not always clear, Vice-President Al Gore's 1997 seminar series, 'Community

2020: A New Future for the American City' identified the need for effective programmes covering sustainable development, crime reduction, educational
improvement and improved race relations. Such concerns are evidence of the
complexity and expansiveness of urban programmes particularly as policies
cater for multiple regional and local needs. An important seminar theme
described cities as regional hubs where public–private partnerships boost
economic competitiveness and expand community empowerment. Community
2020 dealt with the role of metropolitan regions in the new global high technology
economy and adopted a perspective that envisaged an urban policy spanning
outwards to the wider global and regional economies. Coordinated regional partnerships could help to overcome local community problems such as unemployment and poor housing. A Department of Housing and Urban Development
(HUD) report, 'America's New Economy' (US Department of Housing and
Urban Development 1996), showed that metropolitan regions were important in
the era of knowledge-based companies where new industrial clusters were overcoming traditional single-industry dependencies. In 'The State of the Cities'
report (US Department of Housing and Urban Develoment 1997a) the
problems of older cities remained with their urban ghettos, worn-out infrastruc-
tures and congested central business districts. For HUD, communities suffering
high unemployment, social disadvantage and communal tensions had to be
more self-sufficient through innovation and neighbourhood enterprise (Taub
1994).

All these policy aims suggest that future community initiatives are more likely
to involve different but interconnected policy issues to address a range of social
and economic problems. Their effective evaluation will be difficult given the
regional–local themes emerging in urban policy and the multi-agency nature of
local-level partnerships.

Such an example of a perspective serving both local and regional aspirations in
Pittsburgh is provided by the Urban Redevelopment Authority of Pittsburgh
(URA). The partnerships that operate within the orbit of the URA mix public
and private-sector regeneration and community organizations set within a
regional–local strategic commitment. There are strong associations between the
URA and the property development sector, and urban revitalization in
Pittsburgh involves the use of a range of economic and community-development
mechanisms that apply in different settings. The URA is a public authority
working closely with the City of Pittsburgh Mayor's Office promoting high-
profile projects around the city, and the URA operates at the interface between
property developers, public officials, community organizations and professionally
managed partnerships. The URA and its partner organizations therefore foster
harmonious relationships between different interests through restrained political
competition (see Table 13.1) in a policy process influenced by large corporate
investors and influential politicians using sophisticated organizational structures
and interventions.

The URA is a single-development authority, but its relationships with external
organizations are multifaceted and inevitably influenced by political considera-

tions. The URA strategy envisages an expanding regional role and a strong local-community focus for projects that provide what the URA describes as 'solutions for a changing market' (Urban Redevelopment Authority of Pittsburgh 1996: 5). Development priorities include land acquisition and assembly, the provision of development financing, business attraction and retention and community intervention. An important objective is to expand the use of a variety of funding sources, including state funds, and the use of tax credits. The URA provides professional services for site selection, development coordination and business financing and has responsibility for investment and business support. Such activities illustrate the degree to which the authority has developed a full range of services and established a strategic position in the city's real estate development market. It is also indicative of the range of partnership arrangements that the URA supports and the variety of networks relevant in local economic development and urban regeneration.

The URA encourages partnerships to adapt quickly to changing conditions and emphasizes the need for partnership managers constantly to assess their commitments. In the process, as a public authority, the URA is becoming more commercially aware and innovative. It is expanding its policy horizons by relating to the needs of public and private sector partners that work in fiercely competitive global markets. Under such conditions, the partnership model provides the URA and the City of Pittsburgh with a degree of organizational flexibility in achieving effective strategic interventions in urban regeneration and economic development that would otherwise be difficult to implement. This has produced a sophisticated and professional attitude to urban regeneration that has involved a concentration on core organizational competencies and the development of a variety of partnership models suited to particular local conditions.

The evaluation of the performance of the URA concentrates on the authority as a catalyst for development using different partnership configurations. The URA operates in different market settings where interventions require assessment in terms of economic, social and community benefits. The role of the authority leads policy makers to emphasize outcomes with reference to the URA contribution to the regional economy and the linking of local communities to the region through partnerships involving many groups and public agencies. It is thus important to recognize the multiple roles of the URA, the variety of partnerships that it supports and the formal and informal networking involved in implementing URA strategy. The typology in Table 13.1 predicts that a comprehensive analysis would take account of different degrees of organizational development as well as complexity in structure, spatial coverage and variety in programme goals and outcomes.

13.6 Comprehensive community initiatives

The URA presents problems of analysis relating to a large multifaceted regional and city-wide authority. The examples of specifically 'local' partnerships that follow also highlight a complex policy setting where partners seek the effective joint working of community groups with many different backgrounds and interests. As at the regional and city-wide levels in Pittsburgh, partnership structures differ widely as do attitudes to collaboration and degrees of political competition. Concern about the best way to evaluate the outcomes of complex local-level initiatives therefore has led to a reassessment of the role and methods of evaluation. The theory of change evaluation marks an important departure from traditional approaches by providing a thorough assessment of how local initiatives work and the different stakeholder perspectives on programme objectives. The approach assumes that comprehensive community initiatives (CCIs) present evaluators with special problems because of the proliferation of local programmes and groups and the uniqueness of each initiative (Connell *et al.* 1995).

Complex community initiatives are neighbourhood-based initiatives that aim to improve communities by 'working comprehensively across social, economic and physical sectors' (The Aspen Institute 1997: 1). Consequently, it is difficult for evaluators to use traditional techniques that suited single purpose or administratively 'neater' or less complex interventions. In comprehensive initiatives, the processes that produce beneficial outcomes need to be recognized by partners. The theory of change evaluation generates a discourse between stakeholders about how a community initiative can best produce desirable outcomes. Connell and Kubisch (1998: 16) define the theory of change evaluation as 'a systematic and cumulative study of the links between activities, outcomes and contexts of the initiative'. This requires a clear definition of programme outcomes, activities and the 'contextual factors that may have an effect on implementation' (Connell and Kubisch 1998: 17). They take the context of an initiative to include the wider policy environment of the programme and the legal and social factors that condition the programme.

A theory of change articulates explanations of how a programme works, who makes local decisions and the process by which the programme achieves desired outcomes. The focus is on the contexts and activities that 'sustain a process of decision making, capacity building and implementation' (The Aspen Institute 1997) in local partnerships. The theory of change evaluation thereby aids the design of the programme by building in good practice suited to the setting within which the initiative operates. This kind of evaluation is not appropriate under all circumstances, so it may not fully explain changes in regional-level initiative. However, it works well when used to analyse social and economic programmes that are of a manageable size to evaluate, and it most usefully applies to programmes with identifiable boundaries. The approach helps to surface information about the organizational, management and political processes at work within partnerships and the ways in which these influence how stakeholders deliver programmes. The assumption is that different stakeholders might have different perspectives, or theories, about how an initiative works, but it is important for partners to agree on good practice by reconciling their views through consensus. None of this denies the value of established evaluation methods that quantify outcomes and measure performance in programmes. Rather, it adds to the armoury of the evaluator by producing valuable new insights into the processes and contexts that make partnerships work.

13.7 The Pittsburgh Partnership for Neighbourhood Development

The Pittsburgh Partnership for Neighbourhood Development (PPND) is an example of a community-based partnership that has conducted a pilot exercise to assess the theory of change and its relevance to the operations of local CCIs. Ferman (1996) regards the PPND as crucially important in consolidating relationships between business and the community in Pittsburgh. The partnership shows how a large number of diverse groups can work together successfully within a framework conducive to innovation and consensus. The PPND also illustrates that there is a need for clear objectives and the active engagement of groups in the evaluation of the factors that contribute to policy success.

The PPND works with local groups and non-profit community development corporations (CDCs) active in comprehensive programmes for neighbourhood development. The CDCs improve communities through the rehabilitation and construction of affordable housing, and they and the PPND collaborate in local programmes. The CDCs run projects including day-care provisions, job schemes, and environmental improvements. Local partnerships need effectively to coordinate activities and combine the efforts of banks, corporations, foundations, government and others to 'pool their resources and expertise to effect lasting change in their communities' (Ford Foundation 1996: 1). The PPND acts as an intermediary that brings CDCs and others together working with the City of Pittsburgh, the URA, banks and foundations. This maximizes the benefits of collaboration through the sharing of business risks, and the PPND encourages neighbourhood regeneration through decentralized structures and managerial autonomy. The PPND therefore works as a decentralized networked organization with a support framework provided by its core staff. By 1996, the PPND had a board of directors with representatives from Mellon Bank, Penns Southwest Association, the URA, the City of Pittsburgh, PNC Bank, local universities and major foundations. Keystone partners included the Howard Heinz Endowment, the Pittsburgh Foundation, the Ford Foundation and the Richard King Mellon Foundation. Other partners included Dollar Bank, Landmark Savings Association and the PNC Charitable Trust. The PPND, working with these groups, applies management expertise and funds to benefit local CDCs. In this, the PPND has adopted a relatively flat but developed organization that provided high-value support to local managers. The model was flexible enough to allow for expanding local programmes with managers developing specialist services for the communities within which they worked. This spread the risks associated with programme management allowing local mangers to have responsibility to take their own initiatives. However, it also meant that the different interests in partnerships had effectively to be coordinated despite the differing 'theories of change' that they articulated. It was important that groups came to some common agreement about how they would bring about change and link their actions.

Practical lessons have informed good practice and shown how partners can work together effectively. Experience in PPND suggests that a theory of change evaluation applied broadly could reveal useful information about initiatives that combine different types of intervention through the joint actions of different groups. The important lessons from the past provide a basis for discovering what works well under particular conditions. For example, in the mid-1990s the Pittsburgh Manufacturing and Community Development Networks Initiative (Pittsburgh Partnership for Neighbourhood Development 1996) integrated PPND community and business involvement and showed that restrained competition and consensus could produce results. The CDCs in the East Liberty and Homewood-Brushton districts, with PPND, sought to expand business opportunities through community and manufacturing networks involving companies in neighbourhood projects. The manufacturing network extended to include the Lawrenceville district and the Northside, while the community network concentrated upon neighbourhood issues and employment. The networks applied community development methods by consolidating links between companies and the local workforce. Manufacturing companies learned the techniques of community development and could apply them to quality improvement and team building. The PPND supported 'the development of an interactive relationship between the manufacturing and community development networks' as important 'in reducing the boundaries between these traditionally separate community sectors' (ibid.: 2). By 1996, the initiative had enlisted the support of employers, retail firms and banks to develop local skills. There was a 'community employment response system' that connected to training agencies and educational institutions where CDCs 'could develop linkages to existing or evolving networks where members share information, resources and access' (ibid.: 3). Members of the manufacturing network discussed environmental compliance, company tax, personnel, training, benchmarking and accident prevention. The popularity of the 1995 network-training programme for supervisors brought strong support from member firms, and on-site manufacturing meetings brought the network close to local companies. Such contacts enabled members to exchange information, and companies benefited from improvements in productivity and the creation of a high-quality workforce. By the end of 1996, the manufacturing network had an impressive line-up of companies and partners including Nabisco Foods, the Pittsburgh Wool Company, and Best Feeds and Farm Supplies.

By 1998, the PPND supported comprehensive community initiatives that addressed the problem of urban poverty and encouraged greater self-sufficiency of households and workforce and business development. These activities complemented housing initiatives and the connection of neighbourhoods to the regional economy. During 1997, PPND had an annual budget of $3 million with funding from local and national foundations, banks and corporations plus income from interest, fees and other activities. Most of the funds supported the CDCs, and the

PPND administered a $2 million Ford Loan fund. Organizational changes in 1997 and 1998 mainly concerned the efficient management of PPND's funding and the support of strong high-impact initiatives in local communities. Previously, most of PPND's support to the CDCs was by way of unrestricted annual operating support, but the new policy provided operational support to the CDCs through a Community Economic Development Organization and programme grants. The development organization provided funds to organizations for community planning and organization through the implementation and management of economic development services. The programmatic support provided assistance for local economic and workforce development and housing. The PPND policy therefore shifted to supporting fewer, but higher capacity, programmes with proficient staff producing high-quality services. The clear message for managers was that local initiatives should stress efficiency and effectiveness and that they should relate to their local contexts in an appropriate manner. Desired outcomes could be attained by recognizing the factors that made partnerships work effectively and the processes that contributed to improving the well-being of communities.

13.8 The Pittsburgh Enterprise Community

Another CCI covered by the present research was the Pittsburgh–Allegheny County Enterprise Community. Although not having been officially reviewed by HUD under a theory of change, the programme is an ideal candidate for such treatment, which is especially so as the policy context and early experience of the Pittsburgh Enterprise Community partnership contrasted with that of the URA and the PPND. The Enterprise Community was established under the federal government's Empowerment Zone–Enterprise Community (EZ–EC) policy. The partnership in Pittsburgh was part of a federal initiative that gave cities the opportunity to compete for federal funds for urban regeneration with EZ or EC status. Nationally, a Community Empowerment Board, chaired by Vice-President Al Gore, assumed oversight of a competitive bidding process where local submissions had to show HUD that bids developed innovative strategies to develop the capacities of communities. Local programme managers were to adopt an integrated approach to economic and community development using a range of public and private funds. The accent was on the overcoming of economic decline, unemployment and crime through public–private partnership. The Pittsburgh partnership, designated as an Enterprise Community, aimed to expand local economic opportunity through sustainable community development. It had the support of the City of Pittsburgh, Allegheny County, the cities of Duquesne and Mckeesport, and the boroughs of Homestead, Rankin and West Homestead. The City of Pittsburgh Department of Planning was the lead agency for the bid, but success depended on the active work of community organizations. The partnership spanned communities with a combined population of 48,713 so there was to be a substantial collaborative effort to overcome the combined problems of high unemployment and social deprivation. The partners were to work with reference to the assumed common interests of the communities involved.

Early research by HUD into the performance of the EZs and ECs provided assessments of the factors that contributed to success in urban revitalization. The reports were based on local performance reviews and monitoring supervised by HUD. A 1995–96 performance report for the Pittsburgh EC (US Department of Housing and Urban Development 1997b) highlighted serious problems associated with the implementation of the objectives of the programme and referred to the difficulties of creating an effective partnership in the EC area. The Pittsburgh EC included communities that were unable to achieve a partnership synergy, which was due partly to lingering suspicions in communities about alleged broken promises by policy makers and the belief among ethnic-minority groups that they faced discrimination in public housing. The EC housing proposals thus met with opposition from sections of the very constituency that the EC was to serve. The HUD performance report consequently revealed that Pittsburgh was one of the poorest performing ECs in the USA, and that up to late 1996 the programme had seriously failed to achieve expected outcomes. The HUD report referred to the lack of local leadership and recommended that partners should make a greater effort to create a clear leadership focus. The programme had a partnership structure, but it failed to produce effective relationships between the very different, often self-contained, communities that had little past practice in mobilizing collective resources. In terms of the theory of change approach, the local communities each had their own theories that defined different pathways to the future. In light of the problems that this created, a 1998 bid to HUD for Empowerment Zone status resulted from a period of strategic reassessment and redirection. Despite the failure of the bid, the experience of those involved highlighted the importance of understanding the dynamics of partnership working and the contexts within which partners successfully, or otherwise, reach their goals.

Nationally, HUD has recently introduced a new Performance Measurement System to assess outcomes and the progress of local initiatives through a new reporting mechanism. In addition, HUD has initiated an Interim Outcomes Assessment to evaluate selected EZs and ECs (not including Pittsburgh). The outcomes assessment evaluation, conducted for HUD by Abt Associates, explicitly adopts the theory of change evaluation model. The evaluation establishes essential baseline indicators for each zone and establishes outcome measures and indicators of community transformation (Hebert and Anderson 1998). The evaluation poses special problems associated with combining an assessment of single sites with cross-site comparisons of the EZ–EC partnerships. It focuses on the theories of change in the partnerships using traditional data-collection methods as well as innovative techniques that compare the different contexts and processes in each zone.

13.9 Conclusion

The theory of change evaluation marks an important departure from traditional output-focused evaluations. The framework is useful for policy practitioners concerned with evaluation and for researchers as a way of analysing partnership processes. It is valuable as a management tool for controlling change and organizational development. The approach has potential in viewing the dynamic aspects of different partnerships (as in Table 13.1), and many of the other partnerships covered in other chapters in this book could lend themselves well to a theory of change. There are possible applications of the approach in economic and community development, education and social policy.

With the theory of change, evaluation no longer involves the production of lengthy *ex post* reports concentrating on measuring inputs and the mechanical attainment of objectives. Instead, the evaluation involves policy makers in the discussion of processes and practices as part of the development of effective partnerships. The evaluation helps to explain how partnerships work and why they sometimes do not work, and it establishes the context of good practice by relating performance to the factors that influence partnerships externally and internally. The evaluator is actively engaged in establishing what the conditions are that lead to good practice and synergy between partners. The evaluation becomes an ongoing learning activity enabling partners to trace their progress during the lifetime of a programme and to make changes in policy direction if things appear to be going wrong.

However, as PPND found, the approach requires the commitment of substantial resources. The PPND ran a pilot theory of change assessment, but at the time of the research PPND proposed a possible application of the evaluation only after a full consideration of the commitment necessary. Apart from resource issues, future development suggests that there will be some common ground with Pawson and Tilley's (1998) realistic evaluation focus on contexts and mechanisms. In Britain, the Pawson and Tilley evaluation links with the theory of change in the recently created government-funded Health Action Zones where central government emphasizes the need for partnership and 'whole systems' working. The National Health Action Zone Evaluation Team is synthesizing the theory of change and realistic approaches (Judge 1998). The exercise demonstrates that evaluation increasingly involves the appreciation of partnerships with reference to the complex processes that influence them and the need to arrive at stakeholder consensus.

Such developments indicate the importance of strategic direction in partnerships and the need for stakeholders to define clear targets and outcomes. For partnerships in general, the theory of change evaluation reflects a concern with gaining an understanding of the factors that make initiatives work successfully. The approach elicits good practice and discovers what produces desired results given particular contexts and internal partnership processes. The recent British preoccupation with holistic, or 'joined-up', government and the adoption of strategic community development means that policy makers will need more effectively to manage complex partnerships and steer them to meet their desired outcomes. Understanding the problems of partnership working and the special conditions that influence individual partnerships produces a more sophisticated conception of strategic performance management where cross-site blueprints for initiatives will no longer be viable. Each local context generates particular local problems and strategic management depends on a combination of the good intuition of managers and their appropriate analysis of local problems. Success, and the achievement of desirable long-term outcomes, require a proper recognition of programme characteristics and organizational development (Table 13.1) and an assessment of the processes at work that bring groups together and bring about their successful collaboration. This implies that as partnerships expand they develop core competencies that lead them to become highly organized (Table 13.1), but which also make them prone to restructure as hierarchies to bring about managerial control and strategic direction. There is thus a trade-off in complex community initiatives between allowing organizational ambiguity and spontaneity and striving for strategic clarity and organizational effectiveness.

13.10 Acknowledgements

I thank senior officials at the URA and the PPND for their co-operation with my research during September 1998. I also thank Dr Ralph Bangs of the Centre for Social and Urban Research at the University of Pittsburgh for his assistance arranging research interviews. Thanks to James Connell, President of the Institute for Research and Reform in Education, Philadelphia, and Scott Hebert, Abt Associates Massachusetts, for information about the national EZ–EC evaluations. I take full responsibility for accuracy and interpretation in this chapter. Special thanks go to David Black (PPND) for introducing me to the theory of change model.

References

Allegheny Conference on Community Development (ACCD) (1993) *Toward a Shared Economic Vision for Pittsburgh and South-western Pennsylvania*, Pittsburgh: ACCD and Carnegie Mellon University.

The Aspen Institute (1997) *Voices from the Field: Learning from the Early Work of Comprehensive Community Initiatives*, Washington, D.C.: The Aspen Institute.

Connell, J. P., Kubisch, A. C., Schorr, L. B. and Weiss, C. H. (1995) *New Approaches to Evaluating Community Initiatives: Concepts, Methods and Contexts*, Washington, D.C.: The Aspen Institute.

Connell, J. P. and Kubisch, A. C. (1997) *Applying a Theory of Change Approach to the Evaluation of Comprehensive Community Initiatives: Progress, Prospects and Problems*, Washington, D. C.: The Aspen Institute.

Connell, J. P. and Kubisch, A. C. (1998) 'Applying a theory of change approach to the evaluation of comprehensive community initiatives: Progress, prospects and problems', in K. Fulbright-Andersson, A. C. Kubisch and J. P. Connell (eds) *New*

Approaches to Evaluating Community Initiatives: Volume 2, Theory, Measurement and Analysis, Washington, D.C.: The Aspen Institute.

Ferman, B. (1996) *Challenging the Growth Machine: Neighbourhood Politics in Chicago and Pittsburgh*, Lawrence, KS: University Press of Kansas.

Ford Foundation (1996) *Perspectives on Partnerships*, New York: Ford Foundation.

Hebert, S. and Anderson, A. (1998) 'Applying a theory of change approach to two national multisite comprehensive community initiatives: Practitioner reflections', in K. Fulbright-Andersson, A. C. Kubisch and J. P. Connell (eds) *New Approaches to Evaluating Community Initiatives: Volume 2, Theory, Measurement and Analysis*, Washington D.C.: The Aspen Institute.

Jacobs, B. (1998) 'Bureau-politics and public–private partnerships in economic development in the British West Midlands', in N. Walzer and B. D. Jacobs (eds) *Public–Private Partnerships for Local Economic Development*, Westport, CT: Praeger.

Jacobs, B. (1999) *Strategy and Partnership in Cities and Regions: Economic Development and Urban Regeneration in Pittsburgh, Birmingham and Rotterdam*, Houndmills, UK: Macmillan.

Judge, K. (1998) 'Health Action Zones target setting', unpublished paper given at the National Health Action Zone Evaluation Seminar, University of Kent at Canterbury, Personal Social Services Research Unit.

Mintzberg, H. (1996) 'The structuring of organizations', in H. Mintzberg and B. J. Quinn (eds) *The Strategy Process: Concepts, Contexts, Cases*, Englewood Cliffs, NJ: Prentice-Hall.

Pawson, R. and Tilley, N. (1998 edition) *Realistic Evaluation*, London: Sage.

Pittsburgh Partnership for Neighbourhood Development (PPND) (1996) *Pittsburgh Manufacturing and Community Development Networks*, Pittsburgh: PPND.

Rosenthal, U., Hart, P. 't, and Kouzmin, A. (1991) 'The bureau-politics of crisis management', *Public Administration*, 69: 211–33.

Taub, R. P. (1994 edition) *Community Capitalism: The South Shore Bank's Strategy for Neighbourhood Revitalisation*, Boston, MA: Harvard Business School Press.

US Department of Housing and Urban Development (HUD) (1996) *America's New Economy and the Challenge of the Cities: A HUD Report on Metropolitan Economic Strategy*, Washington, D.C.: HUD.

Urban Redevelopment Authority of Pittsburgh (URA) (1996) *Development Projects and Financing Status*, Pittsburgh: URA.

US Department of Housing and Urban Development (HUD) (1997a) *The State of the Cities*, Washington, D.C.: HUD.

US Department of Housing and Urban Development (HUD) (1997b) *Enterprise Community Performance Report 1995–1996: Pittsburgh-Allegheny County Enterprise Community Executive Summary*, Washington, D.C.: HUD.

Walzer, N. and Jacobs, B. D. (eds) (1998) *Public–Private Partnerships for Local Economic Development*, Westport, CT, Praeger.

14 Rural Action for the Environment in the UK

Developing partnerships and promoting learning through networks

Mike Tricker

14.1 Introduction

As the Rio Earth Summit emphasized, the resources and expertise needed to make a significant impact on many environmental problems are unlikely to be found in any single agency. Instead, tackling environmental problems requires first, a holistic approach – involving inputs from a wide range of separate agencies – and second needs to involve and engage local communities (United Nations 1992). The Rural Action for the Environment initiative – which was launched by the British Government in the wake of the Rio Summit – represented a radical attempt to establish formal partnerships between several public, private and voluntary agencies at the national and county levels in order to encourage and facilitate community-led environmental improvements.

14.2 The context

Prior to the 1980s approaches to rural development and conservation in the UK were essentially 'top-down', fragmented and compartmentalized. Such approaches generally relied upon the professional officers from a range of specialized agencies identifying what they considered the needs of a locality were, deciding how best to tackle them and then arranging the delivery of initiatives to meet these needs. Moreover, policies were often applied in a blanket fashion and were often not tailored to local circumstances. Not surprisingly, this compartmentalized approach resulted in inherently wasteful contradictions and conflicts in which public funds were being used to fund initiatives which were designed to deal with the undesirable side-effects of initiatives which were themselves funded by taxation (Tricker 1998). As concern over this situation grew during the 1980s, increasing emphasis was placed on the need for the separate rural-development agencies to work more closely with each other at the national level and with the private sector and community groups at the local level in order to identify problems and implement solutions which were tailored to local circumstances.

The shift in emphasis which occurred during this period was due in no small measure to the results of a series of 'Community Action Experiments' initiated by the Countryside Commission in the mid-1980s. These met with varying degrees of success, but the overall results convinced the Commission that local action '. . . could make substantial and sustainable improvements in the local environment' (Countryside Commission 1989 and 1991). This led it to adopt a new policy statement emphasizing local action (Countryside Commission 1990) and to introduce a series of new 'community led' schemes, including the Countryside Initiative and the Community Woodlands Scheme. The Commission was also instrumental in setting up a 'steering group', comprising a number of its own officers and representatives from the Shell Better Britain Campaign (SBBC), the Royal Society for Nature Conservation (RSNC) and the British Trust for Conservation Volunteers (BTCV), which began to develop a model for a national countryside environmental-action scheme on which the subsequent Rural Action initiative was loosely modelled.

In the late 1980s and early 1990s English Nature (and its predecessor the Nature Conservancy Council) also began to move away from a narrow preoccupation with nature conservation *per se* and increasingly stressed the role which local communities could play in safeguarding habitats. In particular, English Nature's strategy for the 1990s advocated a far more 'people-oriented' approach than the agency had previously espoused (English Nature 1993), and this was reflected in the introduction of three new initiatives – the Community Nature Scheme, Community Action for Wildlife and the School Grants Scheme (English Nature 1991; Millward 1995).

The UK Government's 1995 White Paper on Rural England, drafted by the Department of the Environment and the Ministry of Agriculture, reiterated the Government's commitment to encouraging local initiative and voluntary action as a means of identifying needs and solving local problems and its '. . . aim to work in partnership with local people rather than impose top-down solutions' (Department of the Environment and Ministry of Agriculture, Fisheries and Food 1995).

A series of evaluations of attempts to stimulate such 'self-help' initiatives have demonstrated that both the levels of involvement and the perceived benefits have been most substantial where intensive practical support and advice had been provided by local-development agencies (Tricker, M. *et al.* 1992; Osborne and Tricker 1994, 2000a; Millward 1995; Millward *et al.* 1995). Several of these evaluations have also highlighted the importance of so-called 'middle ground' support for community groups in order to improve their access to financial resources, technical advice and expertise which would enable them to carry out projects which translated their ideas into action on the ground. The Rural Action for the Environment experimental initiative, launched in 1992 by the Countryside Commission, English Nature, the Rural Development Commission and their private sector and voluntary sector partners, was specifically designed to improve access to such advice and resources by consolidating and strengthening the networks which a number of county-based agencies had already developed. The original intention was that communities could be signposted and put in touch with sources of technical advice and expertise which could help them plan their projects and carry them out in ways which would maximize the potential environmental benefits and minimize the disbenefits. This initiative also provided small grants which were intended to help local community groups to translate their concerns into practical action on the ground.

This chapter considers the extent to which this attempt to establish multi-level partnerships between public, private and voluntary sector agencies at the national and county levels succeeded and whether these partnerships in turn delivered the intended benefits at the community level.

14.3 Evolution of the initiative

In 1992, this 'experimental' initiative was given an initial budget of £3.2 million over its first three years, provided equally by the then three countryside 'quangos' – the Countryside Commission, English Nature and the Rural Development Commission – in a partnership which was brokered by the Department of the Environment (DoE). The initiative was managed at a strategic level by a national steering group comprising senior officers from these three 'sponsors' and representatives from four national voluntary organizations – the British Trust for Conservation Volunteers (BTCV), the Royal Society for Nature Conservation (RSNC), the National Council for Voluntary Organizations (NCVO) and Action with Communities in Rural England (ACRE) and a representative from the Shell Better Britain Campaign (SBBC). The decisions of this group were informed and implemented by a small national development team (based in ACRE) which was responsible for the operational management of the initiative at the national level – including promoting the scheme and administering the grant aid.

Rural Action was predicated on the notion that local people should take a leading role in developing and implementing conservation and regeneration policies for their areas and it incorporated a number of innovative ways of facilitating this process. It therefore represented a model of rural development which had an enabling/empowering approach aimed at achieving sustainable development at its core (Tricker and Osborne 1998).

14.4 Key elements of the Rural Action approach

At the policy level, two key features marked Rural Action out as an important and innovative initiative. First, it espoused an explicit ideology of empowerment. As one of its key early documents argued:

> Rural Action is not government and its agencies standing aloof from those whose lives it will affect. It is local people themselves who will act to

improve their environment, tackling the problems they have identified, in the way they consider best'.

(Department of the Environment 1992)

Such an approach was in line with commitments to local sustainable development made by the UK Government in response to the Rio Summit Declaration (United Nations 1992).

Second, it emphasized what might be termed 'value adding partnerships' (after Johnston and Lawrence 1988) between the rural development and environmental agencies at national and local levels. Such cooperation and collaboration had been comparatively rare in previous approaches to rural regeneration and no previous initiative had ever attempted to work with such a wide range of partners or to include national voluntary organizations.

At a structural level, this initiative had two key components. First, the establishment of formal partnership agreements between members of county-based public and voluntary sector agencies with expertise in rural and/or environmental issues, and second, the provision of small-scale grants to community groups. These grants were intended to cover part of the costs incurred by the groups in securing the training, advice and materials needed to design and implement projects aimed at improving their local environment. The public and voluntary sector organizations joining the country partnerships were required to demonstrate that they could contribute expertise which was relevant to the aims of Rural Action and to sign a 'commitment' to its principles. These 'commitments' mirrored those signed by the national partners. In order to access funds from the National Development Team, the new county 'networks' had to prepare a network plan which set out a series of proposals for making the expert advice and practical assistance available from their members more accessible to local communities in order to encourage and enable them to undertake projects.

The distinctive operational features developed by Rural Action included:

- the local administration of grant aid (all previous similar initiatives had been administered centrally),
- payment methods aimed at easing the cash-flow problems faced by many community groups,
- an initial emphasis on providing advice, information and training rather than capital programmes focused on materials and equipment,
- an agreement to allow volunteer time (costed at a notional day rate) and contributions 'in kind' to be included as an element of the 'matched funding' which communities were usually required to raise in order to 'lever in' funding from other government schemes, and
- a large degree of autonomy for the public and voluntary-sector partners in the county networks to organize their activities in ways which they regarded as most effective in their local context.

The first nine county networks were established by December 1992. A further nineteen were formed in 1993 and seven more were launched in 1994. By the end of 1995 forty county networks were in place, giving complete coverage of all non-metropolitan counties in England.

Significantly, there was no designated lead agency for Rural Action at the national or county level. At the national level the sponsors and partners shared joint responsibility for its strategic management. Responsibility for chairing the National Steering Group rotated between the three sponsors on an annual basis.

The county networks were also, in theory at least, partnerships of equals – although most were, in practice, initiated by small groups of officers from local authorities, BTCV, county wildlife trusts and the county-wide rural community councils (RCCs). In order to ensure financial accountability and meet the Government's Treasury guidelines, responsibility for administering Rural Action project grants was given to the rural community councils, who already had formal agency agreements with the Rural Development Commission. From the Rural Community Council's perspective this had the important benefits of placing them at the centre of the network of agencies and focusing the attention of emergent community groups on the RCC. This, in turn, has facilitated and promoted the RCCs' 'normal' community development activities.

A small amount of funding was provided from the National Development Team to support a 'network secretariat' in each county and the RCCs received additional fees based on the number of grant payments processed. Network plans could include bids for funding training and promotional events and for the costs of preparing and distributing a county network directory which could be used to help signpost community groups to appropriate sources of advice. There was, however, no funding for full-time development or fieldworkers at the local level. Instead, the emphasis was on utilizing the collective expertise of network members.

In keeping with the emphasis of the initiative on the local determination of priorities, networks had considerable freedom to decide their own composition and modus operandi. As a result, they varied considerably in size and composition. By the end of the third year of operation the mean size of networks was generally between thirty and forty member organizations. However, some of the smallest (e.g. Cleveland, Nottinghamshire, Isle of Wight, Avon and Shropshire) had fewer than fifteen members, whilst the largest (e.g. Cambridgeshire, Hertfordshire and Bedfordshire) nominally had more than 100 members. In addition to publicizing Rural Action, network members were responsible for advising local groups and visiting potential projects (an activity for which they received no direct funding from Rural Action).

Community groups interested in undertaking projects could apply for grants of up to £2,000 through their local RCC, to fund a maximum of half of the total costs. However, in practice, many grants were for smaller amounts and the average size of grants made in the first three years of Rural Action was around £850. During this period, one-third of applications received were from local amenity/conservation groups, a quarter from parish councils, 20 per cent from community-based residents' groups and 15 per cent from other local groups such as churches, youth groups and historical societies (Bovaird *et al.* 1995).

By October 1996, four years after the first county support networks began operating, project grants totalling £2 million had been given to more than 2,500 projects and well over 1,000 organizations were reported to be working together through the county networks. It was estimated that at this stage nearly 100,000 local people had taken part in projects supported by Rural Action (Rural Action National Development Team 1996). By the end of 1997 well over 3,500 projects had been funded throughout rural England.

14.5 The effectiveness of the Rural Action partnership approach

A major evaluation of the first three years of Rural Action (Bovaird *et al.* 1995) provided important insights into the benefits of, and problems associated with, this attempt to establish networks of partner organizations as a means of promoting community-led approaches to sustainable development in rural areas. This evaluation study involved a combination of quantitative and qualitative research, including:

- participant observation, at the National Steering Group and other key meetings,
- a series of semi-structured interviews with the national sponsors and their private and voluntary-sector partners,
- a postal questionnaire survey of all network members,
- face-to-face interviews with representatives of the key partner agencies in a sample of networks,
- a postal questionnaire survey of a large sample of community groups which had received grant aid, and
- site visits to a sub-sample of these projects and interviews with members of the community groups responsible for them.

14.6 The roles of the national partners

The National Steering Group was intended to be 'a partnership of equals'. In practice, however, the level of commitment and the power exercised varied considerably between the partners and fluctuated over time.

It emerged in the early stages of the evaluation that the 'partnership' between the three sponsoring agencies had in fact been brokered by the Department of the Environment (DoE) – the government department which controlled their funding. Moreover, it emerged that the DoE had made it clear that it expected the Rural Development Commission (RDC) to get involved in the initiative – a suggestion which they initially vigorously opposed. From the outset therefore, the RDC was a reluctant partner whose commitment to the initiative was seen by some of the other partners as (at best) lukewarm. This lack of enthusiasm was interpreted as reflecting a fear that not only would this take funding away from other priority areas, but also a perceived risk that the RDC's focus on developing their distinctive contribution to rural development would be blurred. As events later turned out this fear may have been well founded.

In marked contrast, the Countryside Commission was seen by most of the other partners as displaying a strong sense of 'ownership' of the initiative. This was not surprising, since Rural Action represented the culmination of more than a decade of 'community action experiments' which they had sponsored.

The seniority and status of the representatives of the three sponsors on the National Steering Group also varied according to which of them was responsible for chairing it. The underlying tensions between the three sponsors were also exacerbated by the jockeying for position which was occurring during this period and which was triggered by the important changes to agricultural and rural policy which were looming on the horizon in Britain and in the wider European Community.

There were also constant tensions in the relationships between the three sponsors and their voluntary sector partners. The root of these tensions seemed to stem from a perceived failure to regard them as equal partners or to recognize the true value of their contributions. It was particularly ironic that, although the Rural Action initiative was widely acclaimed for incorporating innovatory mechanisms for valuing volunteer time and allowing this to be included as part of the matched funding which community groups needed to raise in order to access project grants, the sponsors seem to have consistently undervalued the access to networks of volunteers and community groups which the voluntary-sector partners brought to the table and the expertise they had in community-development approaches. The consequent feelings of being marginalized and undervalued were reinforced by the fact that the sponsors often met on their own, prior to Steering Group meetings, particularly to discuss funding issues.

14.7 Benefits seen by partners in the county networks

The Rural Action approach seems to have generated far greater enthusiasm and commitment amongst members of the county partnership networks. After just three years of operation only 10 per cent of the partners in county networks believed that their network was not working well and almost two-thirds reported that both the number and the usefulness of both formal and informal contacts between themselves and other partners had increased. More than 60 per cent also believed that their knowledge of the activities and priorities of other partners had improved and 25 per cent felt that working relationships had been strengthened. In particular, the establishment of Rural Action was seen as having helped to break down barriers between those agencies concerned primarily with social or community-development issues, such as the RCCs, and environmental agencies, such as BTCV and the county wildlife trusts (Bovaird *et al*. 1995).

14.8 Benefits on the ground

The detailed evaluation of the sample of projects implemented by community groups indicated that the establishment of the national and county partnership networks had been successful in stimulating a wide range of additional community-led projects. In particular:

- 60 per cent of the projects which had been assisted were unlikely to have gone ahead without the funding and advice provided by the Rural Action partnerships,
- 82 per cent of all the projects were considered to have been successful by the members of the local groups which had been involved in them,
- most projects resulted in modest sustainable environmental improvements,
- many had involved collaboration between large numbers of local volunteers who had no previous experience of environmental action,
- nearly all projects were seen as having raised local awareness and enhanced the skills of the people.

In addition to the primary environmental benefits, many projects had produced other important social and economic benefits, such as increasing the confidence of local people to take further action in their community and developing facilities or services which enhanced local tourism. Overall, more than 60 per cent of groups which received Rural Action grants moved on to develop further community initiatives. This indicates a substantial degree of success for the partnerships in establishing sustainable community action.

The ability of community groups to access the initiative through any of the partners in the county networks helped to create a 'seamless service'. Local-community groups also seem to have particularly welcomed the local administration of grants, which they felt facilitated a rapid response to requests for assistance – thus helping to sustain local enthusiasm for projects. They also regarded the ability to include the value of volunteer time as an element of their 'matched funding' as a critical success factor. Finally, they particularly welcomed the fact that, unlike some other initiatives, Rural Action did not just provide 'pump priming' grants but rather allowed them to apply for additional funding in the future, to enable them to carry out further phases of their projects, which had helped to cement the partnerships at the community level and develop considerable momentum.

14.9 Problems with the Rural Action partnership arrangements

Despite these positive lessons, this evaluation also highlighted a number of systemic problems in the partnership arrangements at the county level (Martin 1995). Five are particularly important for their impact on the ability of partnership working to provide an effective basis for encouraging and supporting community-based initiatives.

First, the detailed regulations regarding the types of projects which were eligible for grant aid under Rural Action were in practice ambiguous and incomprehensible to many agencies and local communities. This arose, in part, from the vagueness of the initial stated objectives of the initiative and the broad definition of environmental action as any activity which '... improves, enhances, protects or promotes enjoyment of all aspects of the natural and human environment' (Rural Action Steering Group 1993). It became apparent from discussions with the national partners that these statements had deliberately been couched in the most general terms so that they could be interpreted in different ways to suit the fairly narrowly defined remits of each of the funding partners as well as the local-community groups who it was hoped would be involved in Rural Action. As a result, rather than providing '... a set of simple, nationally agreed criteria' (Rural Action Steering Group 1993), these statements allowed Rural Action to become (in the words of a senior official from one of the sponsors) 'a green initiative bound up in red tape' which, instead of empowering local people, arguably reinforced their dependence on professional experts to interpret the emerging and evolving rules.

Second, and more crucially, the funding partners failed to win commitment to Rural Action from many of their own regional staff. As noted earlier, the attempt to achieve shared ownership of the initiative rotating the Chair of the National Steering Group each year meant that in practice the apparent commitment of the individual sponsors fluctuated and their behaviour suggested that none of them felt they were ultimately responsible for ensuring its success. Moreover, at a time of cutbacks in other budgets, many front-line officers from the separate agencies saw the commitment to the Rural Action partnership as a threat to their own established programmes. This ambiguity was, not surprisingly, also reflected in the views of the partners in the county networks, some of whom had difficulties identifying the immediate benefits of Rural Action projects in relation to their own organizational or departmental objectives. Indeed, nearly half of the network members surveyed believed that the objectives of their own agency were significantly different from those of Rural Action, which reflected a need for a substantial amount of development work at an organizational level in order to move the thinking and approaches of the partners on.

Third, the community-led approach of Rural Action was alien to many of the professional staff representing partner organizations on the county networks. As a result, the very 'top-down' approach to rural development, which Rural Action was a response to, threatened to undermine its success because staff trained for many years in this former approach found it hard to adapt to the more 'bottom-up' approach advocated by Rural Action. Thus, over 60 per cent of the staff involved in the early stages believed that their lack of expertise in working with local people threatened to jeopardize the success of Rural Action in their counties. Again this pointed to the need for development work within the partner organizations.

Fourth, and following on from the above, in the absence of funding for full-time Rural Action field staff to support the initiative locally, the partners in the county networks were often hard pressed to promote it and to support local projects. Thus, more than 70 per cent of representatives in the first nine networks to be established indicated that they felt there had been too little promotion of their work, and 57 per cent highlighted insufficient time to visit potential projects as a serious threat to the success of Rural Action (Martin *et al.* 1994). Moreover, many of the partners who had been most committed to the initiative in its early stages reported that they would be unable to continue to give as much time to it in the future, opening up concerns at a very early stage about the sustainability of this approach.

Finally, three years into the experiment, there was little evidence of the Rural Action partnership networks having learnt from each other. In fact, many of the networks established in late 1993 and 1994 encountered problems which were very similar to those experienced by the networks set up in 1992 and early 1993. Previous studies had found this to be a significant problem in disseminating the lessons of rural development initiatives in the UK (PSMRC 1991). However, a particular problem for Rural Action was the speed with which the initiative was extended across the whole country. This in itself was a product of financial and policy pressures on the three national partners who were sponsoring the initiative. As a result, the original concept of a small number of pilot networks from which lessons could be learned was abandoned before the end of the first year of Rural Action as it became clear that far fewer projects were coming forward than had been budgeted for. In an attempt to reduce the large, and potentially embarrassing, underspend of £400,000 in year one, the National Steering Group accepted many more new counties into the initiative than had originally been envisaged so that they could be allocated network grants and thus reduce this potential underspend. As a result, there was often too little time between the launch of successive waves of networks to allow lessons to emerge and be disseminated. The additional workload involved in establishing large numbers of new networks in 1994 also meant that the National Development Team became overstretched and was unable to facilitate systematic learning between networks or to give sufficient time to development work with the staff of partner organizations.

It is important to note that, in the period following the initial evaluation of the first three years of Rural Action, important changes were made which responded to some of the problems identified above. The most significant of these included:

- The National Development Team was restructured in an attempt to enable it to provide more face-to-face support and advice to the partners in the county networks.
- Formal written guidelines on the appropriate use of the grants provided to networks were produced in an effort to remove some of the ambiguity and uncertainty inherent in earlier guidance.
- Grants were also made available to enable community groups to visit other

groups which have tackled similar projects and thus to encourage networking at the local level.

- The range of projects put forward by local groups also continued to grow – partly as a result of the interest generated by Local Agenda 21. For example, the Countryside Commission, in partnership with English Nature and English Heritage, publicised a guide to conservation initiatives in the local environment which could be funded under the Rural Action initiative (Countryside Commission *et al.* 1996). This produced an encouragingly high level of expressions of interest from parish councils wanting to prepare 'parish conservation plans' (Martin *et al.* 1998).
- The value of the Rural Action networks in providing an effective means of disseminating information about other new policy initiatives to local communities and groups was also recognized by some of the national sponsors. Thus, several of the networks were visited by the officers responsible for managing the Countryside Commission's Millennium Greens initiative.

Nevertheless, significant problems remained. In particular, the partnerships in several counties were still fragile and relied more on the commitment and enthusiasm of often transient collections of individuals rather than established partnerships between committed organizations. Moreover, there was no real sign that the 'bottom-up' community empowerment focus of Rural Action was being reflected in the recruitment criteria and job descriptions for staff for the national or county partners. As a result, many advisors still tended to treat projects referred to them by local communities as narrowly defined technical problems rather than as community-development opportunities.

This problem was exacerbated by the nature of the performance indicators used to judge the effectiveness of the agencies involved in the national and local partnerships. In particular, these did not appear to have evolved to encompass officer involvement in the Rural Action networks or their role in providing support to community groups. Thus, the service-level agreements between the Rural Development Commission and the Rural Community Councils were still specified and monitored in terms of very tangible outputs (such as facilities or services created). Whilst these were undoubtedly important, they did not reflect the time and effort involved in encouraging and equipping communities to engage in local action. As a result, in many localities the professional staff of partner organizations remained diffident about the time commitment involved in supporting local networks and suspicious about the benefits of such approaches. To ease this constraint attention needed to be given to the creation of performance-measurement indicators which accurately and sensitively reflected such developmental work. Possible models for such schema already existed; for example, from the earlier evaluation of the Rural Development Commission's social programmes in the early 1990s (Osborne *et al.* 1995). But these approaches needed to be built on to support such initiatives and to contribute to meaningful sustainable development in rural areas which focuses on the environmental, community and social benefits as well as on the economic benefits.

14.10 Conclusions

The Rural Action for the Environment initiative represented an ambitious attempt not only to establish partnerships between a wide range of public, private and voluntary organizations at the national and sub-national levels, but also, simultaneously, to promote ways of working which were radically different from those previously used by several of the partners.

Its success in establishing functioning support networks and helping to build the capacity of community groups at the local level has been publicly acknowledged and acclaimed by the Government Minister responsible for rural policies in the UK. Why then, despite these undoubted achievements, has it proved so difficult to sustain support for this initiative at the national level? The answers to this question highlight some of the tensions inherent in partnership working and some of the potential pitfalls for organizations seeking to establish similar partnerships in other contexts.

(i) Changing attitudes of partners

The attitudes of the main UK rural development agencies towards community involvement and community-based developments have come a long way in the last decade. The Rural Action partnership initiative must take a significant part of the credit for achieving this shift which has been consolidated by a series of recent policy guidance notes and working papers emerging from the UK National Government (e.g. DETR 1998). However, the research discussed in this chapter has demonstrated that there is still a great deal of nervousness amongst the officers of the funding partners both about the notion of 'community empowerment' in general, and about the difficulties of demonstrating through existing performance indicators the benefits and outcomes of such community-based and community-led development. Concern also remains about the likely slow pace with which these benefits are likely to be manifested compared with the rapid pace of policy development. There has also been a tendency for some of the professionals in the rural development agencies to jealously guard their own territories to seek to protect their own expertise. As a result, they have been slow to commit themselves to meaningful involvement in the Rural Action partnership. This experience is consistent with the experience of other attempts to combine bottom-up approaches to community development with attempts to create stronger partnerships and/or networking arrangements between 'higher level' agencies. Powell (1991) has argued that '... most potential partners approach the idea of participating in [such] a network with trepidation'.

In these circumstances, partnership networks can only survive if they enjoy the wholehearted support of senior managers, if there are rewards for staff who seek to cooperate with other agencies and if a clear idea exists of the mutual, and complementary, benefits to be gained by each of the partners (Campbell and Sommers Luchs 1992). In its early years of operation Rural Action offered little evidence of such incentives. Indeed, there was evidence that equipping local networks and communities to act for themselves was seen by some professional officers as undermining their own positions. One of the national sponsors was in effect forced into the Rural Action partnership by the Government department to which they were accountable. As a result, their commitment to the experiment was constantly in doubt and not surprisingly they do not appear to have 'sold' the initiative effectively or convincingly to their regional staff. Whilst most local agencies now appear to have accepted as a de facto political reality the need to share a degree of power with each other and with local communities in order to gain access to external assistance, in some instances the extent of genuine commitment to partnership continues to be conspicuous by its absence (Osborne and Ross 1999).

(ii) Funding for partnership working

In hindsight it is possible to see that given this nervousness and these tensions, the national Rural Action partnership was built on very shaky foundations. It is not surprising, therefore, that this fragile structure was unable to survive the policy and organizational changes triggered by the election of the New Labour Government.

One of the most significant of these changes was the subsequent dismemberment of the Rural Development Commission – involving the transfer of its business development activities to newly established regional development agencies and its social programmes to the new Countryside Agency based on the former Countryside Commission. At a stroke this removed one leg of the tripartite funding arrangements.

At the time of writing, the new Countryside Agency was reported to be awaiting the outcome of a further evaluation of Rural Action before deciding how to proceed. As a result, most of the county partnerships were in a state of suspended animation pending the outcome of this review. Clearly, in order to be sustainable such national partnerships need more balanced and more robust and broadly based funding arrangements.

(iii) Establishing 'a partnership of equals'

In order to establish a genuine 'partnership of equals' it is vital that the 'funding partners' acknowledge the real value of the non-financial contributions which other partners may make. For network-based organizations this may include providing access to their networks as a means of promoting and supporting the delivery of initiatives and improving their effectiveness. Unless this is done, voluntary sector organizations are likely to experience particular difficulties where (as was the case with the Rural Action partnership) some of the funding partners control a significant part of their funding. In such situations there is likely to be a tendency for them to be regarded as agents rather than as genuine and valued partners. Communities also have to be enabled to become proactive in the identification of their needs and planning to meet them. In this context the village appraisal model (Osborne and Tricker 2000b) is one positive way in which to support positive community involvement in rural-regeneration partnerships.

(iv) *Resolving conflicting timescales*

Another significant source of tension between the national partners stemmed from differences in the timescales to which they were working and, as a result, differences in views on the speed at which the initiative should have been rolled out. Rural Action represented the culmination of more than a decade of painstaking experimentation and development work designed to identify the most effective ways in which government agencies could work in partnerships with local communities. The results of these experiments clearly influenced the emergent Rural Action 'model'. Following the Rio Earth Summit this 'model' appears to have been seized upon as one of the ways in which the British Government could demonstrate that it was discharging the commitments it made. As a result, there was real or perceived political pressure on the funding partners for the initiative to achieve significant momentum and results in its early years. This had two important linked consequences.

First, the sheer pace at which the initiative was rolled out and the pressure to achieve the spend targets of the funding partners were perceived by the voluntary sector partners to conflict with the supposed focus on harnessing community development processes and building the capacity of community groups – which are generally regarded as requiring patient work over fairly protracted periods of time. As a result, many of the community projects which were funded in the early years of the Rural Action initiative were in reality already 'on the shelf' and did not reflect real added value. It was therefore only in the third and fourth year of the initiative that projects which reflected the hoped-for radical shift in thinking and approaches began to emerge in volume – and by then serious questions were being raised about its future.

Second, the speed at which the initiative was launched and rolled out meant that there was little or no time to carry out much needed development work with the staff of the individual partner organizations in order to move their thinking and approaches on.

(v) *Measuring 'performance' and 'success'*

A further source of tension was attributable to differences in the ways in which the partners defined, measured and reported 'outputs', 'outcomes' and 'success'. As noted earlier, the Rural Action partnership approach is widely acknowledged as having been effective in encouraging and enabling communities to carry out a wide range of projects which have provided substantial environmental and social benefits. It is also seen as having been successful in stimulating and supporting substantial amounts of local voluntary effort, building capacity and in widening the potential constituency for further environmental action. These findings have added credibility to the arguments which have been advanced for two decades by advocates of community-based development approaches.

The results from the evaluative studies reported here have also underlined the fact that the *processes* involved in rural development are just as important as any facilities or services that they may develop. In particular, the enhanced skills and confidence of group members, as a result of the successful completion of a project, are likely to have a more significant impact on the sustainability of a community in the future than any individual facility produced. However, the intangibility of such potential benefits and the difficulty in quantifying them has meant that it has been difficult to accommodate them within the current systems for reporting performance in relation to the corporate plans of the funding partners. This difficulty points to the need to continue to press for the development of approaches to performance monitoring and evaluation which can encompass such intangible but essential benefits, as well as the more tangible ones. As noted above, this work has been started elsewhere (Osborne *et al.* 1995) and needs to be built on.

(vi) Funding development work

An obvious, but nevertheless important, lesson from the Rural Action experience is that for such partnership initiatives to be effective, more time, effort and resources need to be allocated to:

- carefully preparing the ground so that the new partners have time to adjust to these new frames of reference and ways of working;
- learning and disseminating the lessons from such experimental initiatives so that approaches can be adjusted;
- developing approaches to performance measurement which can encompass intangible but essential community-development benefits as well as the more traditional tangible and quantifiable ones.

The scale and importance of these tasks and the resources required to successfully complete them should not be underestimated.

14.11 Looking to the future

Despite the problems encountered, the Rural Action initiative has been for many of the participants a valuable learning exercise which has moved thinking on and sensitized many individuals within the partner agency to the potential benefits of community-led development approaches. At the County levels it has served to strengthen working relationships between the partners. Its values and its approaches are already being reflected in a number of other initiatives, but few of these as yet are likely to involve attempts to build such wide-ranging partnerships.

References

Bovaird, A. G., Martin, S. J., Millward, A. and Tricker, M. J. (1995) *Evaluation of Rural Action for the Environment: Three-year Review of Efficiency and Effectiveness*, Birmingham: Public Sector Management Research Centre, Aston Business School.

Campbell, A. and Sommers Luchs, K. (1992) *Strategic Synergy*, Oxford: Butterworth-Heinemann.

Countryside Commission (1990) *Local Countryside Action: Policies and Practice*, CCP 306, Cheltenham: Countryside Commission.

—— (1991) *Countryside Community Action: An Appraisal*, CCP 307, Cheltenham: Countryside Commission.

Countryside Commission, English Heritage and English Nature (1996) *Ideas into Action for Local Agenda 21*, Peterborough: English Nature.

Department of the Environment (DoE) (1992) *David Maclean Launches Rural Action*, London: DoE Press Release 821.

Department of the Environment and Ministry of Agriculture, Fisheries & Food (1995) *Rural England: A Nation Committed to a Living Countryside*, Cmnd 3016, London: HMSO.

Department of the Environment, Transport and the Regions (DETR) (1998) *Community-Based Regeneration Initiatives – A Working Paper*, London: DETR.

English Nature (1991) *Community Action for Wildlife*, Peterborough: English Nature.

Johnston, P. and Lawrence, P. R. (1988) 'Beyond vertical integration – the rise of the value adding partnership', *Harvard Business Review* July/August: 94–101.

Martin, S. J. (1995) 'Partnerships for local environmental action: Observations on the first two years of Rural Action for the Environment', *Journal of Environmental Planning and Management* 38: 149–66.

Martin, S. J., Bovaird, A. G., Green, J., Millward, A. and Tricker, M. (1994) *Rural Action for the Environment: Summary Evaluation of Progress in Selected 'Pacemaker Networks'*, Cirencester: Action with Communities in Rural England.

Millward, A. (1995) *An evaluation of the Community Action for Wildlife Scheme*, Birmingham: Alison Millward Associates.

Millward, A., Tricker, M. and Green, J. (1995) *Jigso Review*, final report to the Countryside Council for Wales, Birmingham: Alison Millward Associates.

Osborne, S., Bovaird, A. G., Martin, S., Tricker, M. and Waterston, P. (1995) 'Performance management and accountability in complex public programmes', *Financial Accountability and Management* 11(1): 19–38.

Osborne, S. and Ross, K. (1999) 'Managing the policy – practice interface in government – nonprofit relations. The case of area regeneration in the UK', Paper given at the Right Conditions for the Development of the Non-profit Organizations Congress, Parma.

Osborne, S. and Tricker, M. (1994) 'Local development agencies: Supporting voluntary action', *Nonprofit Management and Leadership* 5(1): 37–52.

—— (2000a) 'Rural action for the Environment: Building sustainable development in local rural communities in the UK?', *Regional Studies* (forthcoming).

—— (2000b) 'Village appraisals; a tool for sustainable community development in rural areas in the UK?', *Local Economy* (in press).

Powell, W. W. (1991) 'Neither markets nor hierarchy: Network forms of organisation', in G. Thompson, J. Frances, R. Levacic and J. Mitchell (eds) *Markets, Hierarchies and Networks*, London: Sage.

Public Sector Management Research Centre (PSMRC) (1991) *Managing Social and Community Development Programmes in Rural Areas: A Management Review of the Rural Development Commission's Social Programme*, Birmingham: Aston University.

Ross, K. and Osborne, S. (1999) 'Making a reality of community governance. Structuring government – voluntary sector relationships at the local level', paper to the 1999 Public Administration Committee Conference, Civil Service College, Sunningdale.

Rural Action National Development Team (1996) *Bulletin for Network Members*, Autumn 1996, National Development Team.

Rural Action Steering Group (1993) *Rural Action for the Environment: An Introduction*, London: RDC.

Tricker, M. J. (1993) 'The Peak District Integrated Rural Development Project: A catalyst for change?, *Netherlands Geographical Studies*, 172.

—— (1998) 'Community based development initiatives in the U.K.', in A. L. Ontiveros, and F. M. Hernando (eds) *From Traditional Countryside to Postproductivism*, Association of Spanish Geographers.

Tricker, M. J., Martin, S. J. and Soni, S. (1992) *Evaluation of the Taf and Cleddau Rural Initiative*, final report to the Welsh Development Agency, Cardiff: WDA.

Tricker, M. J. and Osborne, S. (1992) 'Promoting sustainable rural regeneration in the UK. Evidence on the effectiveness of government–non-profit partnerships', paper given at the Annual ARNOVA Conference, Seattle.

United Nations (1992) *UN Convention on Conservation of Biological Diversity*, New York: UN.

15 Building 'active' partnerships in aid-recipient countries

Lessons from a rural development project in Bangladesh

David Lewis

15.1 Introduction

This chapter examines the changing relationships between development NGOs, donors and government agencies in the provision of rural development services in Bangladesh. The particular focus is the problematic language of 'partnership' which is increasingly used in social policy and international development policy circles. It seeks to draw lessons from a case study of a rural development project which has attempted to bring government agencies and local and national development NGOs together in order to improve the provision of services provided to low-income rural households engaged in small-scale aquaculture. A model is presented which contrasts 'active' and 'dependent' forms of partnership in an effort to understand why the performance of such partnerships are often variable. Some of the insights gained into the 'processes' of partnership building, it is argued, may offer lessons for researchers and policy makers which could have relevance beyond Bangladesh in other developed and less developed country contexts.[1]

There is a large general literature dealing with interorganizational relationships and it is not possible to summarize this in the present chapter, though much of this literature has been drawn on in earlier chapters of this book. The framework outlined by Robinson *et al.* (1999; see also Osborne 1997) contrasts competition, coordination and cooperation and is useful in providing a set of ideal types through which different types of relationship can be analysed. These authors go on to trace the current rise to prominence of the term 'partnership' in the development field which has moved from being primarily part of development NGOs' discourse in describing relationships between themselves and with communities (arguably sometimes more at the level of rhetoric than reality) to its recent use more widely by aid donors and governments to describe a wide range of relationships within a changing policy framework. In particular, it is noted that the growth of terms such as 'contracting' and 'public–private partnership' imply less intimacy or solidarity in the relationships they describe and may mask the realities of reduced or withdrawn government services and the growth of private provision.

A recent growth of interest by researchers in 'third sector' organizations has resulted in the growth of two 'parallel worlds' of research literatures, one dealing with Western industrialized countries and another with international development work and the 'third world'. There are many common themes discussed in both literatures – such as organizational accountability and effectiveness – but in general there has been very little learning or exchange of ideas between the two research traditions (Lewis 1999).

In Britain and the United States, there has been a growth of interest in the changing relationships between government and voluntary agencies in the delivery of welfare services, particularly since privatization policies pursued since the 1980s have increased the role of non-state actors (Billis 1993; Kramer 1994; Salamon 1995). The rise of what has been termed 'contracting' (a fee for service exchange) has been identified as an important trend in the construction of relationships between voluntary agencies and government, with its impact on both sides still poorly understood (Smith and Lipsky 1993). Kramer's (1994) work, for instance, shows how government and non-governmental agencies may 'need and depend on each other more than ever' (ibid.: 54) and that contracting is central to the institutionalization of interorganizational relationships.[2] The term 'partnership' continues to be used within this policy discourse and is identified and problematized by these authors. For example, Kramer argues that such relationships are complex and unequal and that there is a need

> ... to get beyond the usual rhetoric of collaboration and to recognise not only the mutual dependency but also the significance of the unequal distribution of power in these public–private 'Partnerships'.
>
> (ibid.: 54)

In Smith's (1995) case study of urban partnership, problems were identified around imbalances of power within partnership arrangements in the inner city and one key participant (from the government side) pointed out that:

> ... people must have a common set of values and objectives ... they must be prepared to give up some of their self-objectives in order to achieve common objectives ... different people sitting down together in a room does not constitute partnership.

Billis (1993: 198) has also pointed to the lack of definition around the concept arguing that partnership must be 'something more than the purchase of services, or cosy chats'. In the the US, according to Salamon (1995), the rhetoric of the separateness of the public and non-profit sectors has in reality obscured the largely ad hoc evolution of closer ties or 'partnerships' between the two sectors in recent decades. Salamon goes on to argue the case for a shift from institutions which are 'merely interconnected' towards a situation in which government and third-sector organizations are 'true "partners in public service" ' (ibid.: 13).This brief review lends credence to the view that so far there have been few attempts in the US or UK contexts to provide a systematic conceptual framework for the analysis or evaluation of such public–private partnerships.

Moving away from industrialized country settings, interest in government–NGO relationships in international development during the 1990s has around attempts to build links between government agencies and NGOs in development projects and programmes and in strengthening 'civil society' more widely (Farrington and Bebbington 1993). The increased interest in NGOs as vehicles for service delivery is strongly linked to demands for privatization within what has been termed the 'new policy agenda' with its emphasis on liberalized markets and institutional reform (Robinson 1993). At the same time, the creation of links between government agencies and NGOs has been seen as having implications for strengthening of a transparency in administration and challenging prevailing top-down institutional culture, both of which may contribute to the strengthening of a wider 'civil society' within fragile processes of democratization such as that experienced within Bangladesh (Lewis 1997a). In broad terms, the creation of partnerships is seen as a way of making more efficient use of scarce resources, increasing institutional sustainability and improving beneficiary participation.

For example, a recent World Bank report in Bangladesh advocates partnership between the government and the NGOs under the title 'Pursuing Common Goals' (World Bank 1996). A recent British Government White Paper on international development contains many references to partnerships – between countries, donors, governments, NGOs and business – but offers no real definitions of the 'partnership' and is vague as to the forms such partnerships might take (DFID, 1997). However, as documents such as these indicate, attempts to understand the relationships between government and NGOs have tended to focus in an unproblematic way on complementarities and instrumentalities rather than on the less predictable and frequently conflictual realities of 'partnerships as process'. The reality may well be different from the rhetoric. As a result, Leach (1994) questions whether there is any meaning left in the term 'partnership' at all and prefers instead to develop a model of six different forms of 'collaboration'.

This chapter uses the term 'partnership' to refer to an agreed relationship based on a set of linkages between two or more agencies within a development project, usually involving a division of roles and responsibilities, a sharing of risks and the pursuit of joint objectives, in this case between government agencies, NGOs, donors and farmers, which fits broadly with Postma's (1994) definition which emphasizes mutual trust, joint decision making and a two-way exchange of information. The term 'linkage' is used to refer to specific points of the partnership at which activities are shared between different agencies and stakeholders at different levels of the project. A development project which involves partnership is likely to have a range of interagency linkages at various levels.

15.2 NGO–government partnerships in rural development

The case study discussed here has its roots in an earlier research project on NGOs and government relationships in rural development. This research on government and non-governmental organization linkages documented efforts to bring about poverty-focused technical change in agriculture and drew on case studies collected in Asia, Africa and Latin America (Farrington and Bebbington 1993). A key conclusion was that while partnerships between NGOs and government agencies were certainly taking place, and in many cases generating potentially useful new approaches and insights, a straightforward view of a 'functional' division of agency roles based on static notions of 'comparative advantage' was not appropriate.[3] Social, political and historical contextual factors in different countries were found to be crucial determinants of linkage effectiveness (Farrington and Lewis 1993).

In order to develop these findings further, subsequent research was undertaken with an international agricultural research centre (IARC) involved in an inter-agency aquaculture project in Bangladesh. A research project was designed to build on this earlier work by using the IARC's involvement in aquaculture research and extension in Bangladesh as a case study. With the Government of Bangladesh at both central and local levels and five Bangladeshi NGOs, the IARC is seeking to develop new sets of institutional linkages or 'partnerships' to increase the effectiveness of aquaculture research and extension.

The fieldwork aimed to build an 'institutional ethnography' through which an overall picture of the planned and actual project activities, relationships and outcomes was assembled, and its context analysed, drawing on a range of information sources and combining the often contradictory perceptions of different project actors (Escobar 1995; Bate 1997).[4] After first documenting the linkages envisaged within the planned project framework, it was then possible to explore how these relationships worked (or did not work) in practice and to consider the ways in which they might be strengthened through an 'action research' process. This approach can also be viewed as a form of 'process monitoring', in which a project is not viewed as a simple, controllable event with a beginning and an end, but rather as a series of continuing activities, negotiations and adaptations in which unforeseen problems emerge and course corrections are attempted, often with varying degrees of success (Mosse 1996).[5]

The challenge was to gain an insight into how the project was intended to function and then to document perceptions of how it was working in practice from the various actors taking part. This was carried out at a project workshop with staff from all the participating agencies and through semi-structured interviewing undertaken at headquarters and field level during the subsequent year. This picture was then compared with perceptions of extension workers and farmers at the local and village levels.

15.3 Aquaculture in Bangladesh

Bangladesh is a deltaic, flat country characterized by vast quantities of water with seasonal vulnerability to disastrous flooding. It is also highly dependent on foreign aid, which represents almost 8 per cent of GDP and a total resource transfer of around US$1.8 billion (Hossain 1990). It has a predominantly rural population and more than half of rural households are functionally landless. Fish represent an important part of the local diet and constitute an estimated 75 per cent of animal-protein intake. Fish have in the past tended to be caught (as opposed to cultured) from rivers, lakes and floodplains. As wild sources have declined, the country's extensive water resources are now seen as being ripe for a fisheries-development strategy by the Bangladesh Government and many development agencies (Lewis 1991b). However, while some large landowners have traditionally undertaken extensive fish-rearing practices as a hobby in village ponds, more intensive aquaculture techniques are quite new to most ordinary villagers.

Bangladesh's economic dependency renders it vulnerable to a multi-donor, externally determined 'project culture' which can strongly shape prevailing development strategies and weaken local development institutions. It is within this context that aquaculture (the culturing of fish in ponds) has become a major development objective in Bangladesh. Indeed, it is coming to replace the objective of expanding agricultural production because there is no more uncultivated land available, but there are an estimated two million ponds which are underutilized as far as their potential for aquaculture is concerned. It is widely perceived that Bangladesh contains a wealth of un- or underutilized water resources (Lewis et al. 1996).[6] The reasons for this underutilization remain obscure and complex but may be a consequence of social factors such as the lack of secure access to water bodies by low-income households, multiple and often conflicting use of ponds for activities such as irrigation or washing, instead of the result of a lack among farmers of the technical knowledge required for fish rearing (Worby 1994).

The Government's strategy for aquaculture is primarily production oriented, without much concern for the problem of uneven distribution of economic benefits between rich and poor households. At the central policy level the emphasis is on targets for increased production, while at the local level extension efforts tend to be concentrated on building links with better-off farmers. Furthermore, the Government favours a 'technology transfer' model which places little emphasis on farmers' views and perspectives. In contrast, many NGOs favour the promotion of aquaculture as a potential income-generation activity for Bangladesh's landless and marginal households, which make up more than 50 per cent of the rural population. Many of these NGOs are seeking to include farmers in the joint design and promotion of appropriate technologies.

15.4 The case study

The IARC has in recent years been engaged in a series of aquaculture projects with the Government of Bangladesh, predominantly funded by a large bilateral donor.[7] The main idea is that groups of low-income rural people, particularly women, may be able to utilize local ponds, ditches and other small water bodies to grow fish for their households' subsistence and for sale in the local market. The present Aquaculture Project analysed here aims to develop and provide low-cost, low-input aquaculture technologies mainly in the form of an improved extension message which both carries relevant and useful information to low-income households and engages members of these households, male and female, in a meaningful dialogue about strengthening livelihoods through aquaculture which will produce continuous improvements in the service. The extension message details appropriate pond-management techniques including fish-stocking densities, feeding regimes, pond preparation and appropriate species mixes which can be readily used by low-income rural households towards their income-generation-activity portfolios.

The origins of the project can be found in informal links between a number of NGO field staff and members of the Aquaculture Research Institute (ARI) which emerged during the late 1980s when one of the larger NGOs was starting its aquaculture programme and required some technical assistance. At that time, the IARC was already in contact with ARI. At the same time, the bilateral donor was looking for ways to improve the effectiveness of its work in strengthening national agricultural research institutes (including ARI) in Bangladesh.

The project involves both government agencies and Bangladeshi development NGOs working along with the IARC. It is designed to strengthen ARI's aquaculture-research capacity and responsiveness to farmer needs, along with the capacity of the wider extension system which now encompasses both Government and NGOs. There are three different government agencies taking part in the IARC project. ARI is the public-sector research body responsible for aquaculture. ARI is a relatively new institution without access to adequate resources and with relatively low staff morale, but was judged by the IARC to have the potential to make a contribution to developing relevant technologies if provided with suitable financial support from the bilateral donor and 'technical backstopping' by the IARC.

The Department of Fisheries (DoF) manages the national country-wide extension service but it too lacks sufficient personnel and resources, with only one Fisheries Extension Officer in each *thana* the local government unit which in some areas may contain around a quarter of a million people. The Aquaculture Project therefore seeks to bring NGO fieldworkers into a collaborative relationship with DoF staff, despite the fact that the DoF is driven more by production targets than any real interest in targeted poverty reduction. Finally, the Bangladesh Agricultural Research Council (ARC) is the apex body which co-ordinates research and evaluates the project, although in practice BARC appears to lack a clear function within the project because it has only limited capacity to monitor activities in the field.

For the past decade many of Bangladesh's NGOs have been involved in promoting aquaculture among their organized groups of landless and marginal farmers by providing credit and technical support. There are five Bangladeshi NGOs involved in the IARC project. In order to overcome the constraints of the government agricultural extension system the project has invited NGOs to act as additional extension agents, working in partnership with the DoF, to distribute the technology to their own target groups. The NGOs are also invited to provide feedback on adoption results and research needs to the scientists and trainers at ARI. NGO field staff are trained by ARI and IARC personnel alongside DoF personnel so that this training can then be passed on to the farmers by further demonstration and training. In addition, the NGOs provide credit to their group members which allows them to diversity their household economic portfolios into aquaculture.

In the case of the Aquaculture Project, the two key problems which have generated a perceived need for NGO/Government partnership are both quantitative and qualitative. First, there are resource limitations to the Government's aquaculture extension efforts in terms of numbers of staff, coverage and their mobility; and second there is a relative absence of participatory research and extension linkages in aquaculture between NGOs and government agencies, combined with the need for more 'appropriate' technology packages for low-income farmers.

The concept of potential complementarity between NGOs and government agencies formed the rationale for partnerships within the Aquaculture Project. A further complementary link was founded on the ability of the IARC to provide 'technical backstopping' to the Government and NGOs on the basis of its international research facilities and contacts.

Although this research was by no means intended as a formal project evaluation, some general evidence on performance was collected from existing reports and from new interviews with key actors at both the management and grassroots levels. There was evidence that the project was providing NGOs with the opportunities to gain access to technical assistance with their aquaculture programmes, to report back adoption problems encountered by the farmers with whom they work and to begin to form ties with government agencies in aquaculture for the first time. By late 1994 a total of 3,563 farmers (of which 2,029 were women) had been trained, 900 ponds had been cultivated using the proposed new 'technology package' and the technology appeared to be effective when applied by the farmers.

An initial feedback 'loop' from the farmers, through NGOs, to researchers was created by the project. For example, modifications have been made to the original Aquaculture Project's initially uniform 'technology package' which has now been redesigned into several options in order to take account of different agro-ecological priorities based on feedback from farmers via participating NGOs in different agro-climatic areas. Furthermore, NGOs and government researchers are now, perhaps for the first time, talking to each other about aquaculture. On paper the stated objectives have been largely met.

But there were also a range of problems with the partnerships, particularly once the project was viewed as being embedded in wider processes and context. There were limitations embodied in the contrast between the rhetoric of the project's collaborative approach and the reality of many of the participating agencies' working approaches. This is not the place to provide an exhaustive list of these limitations, but several problems can be briefly mentioned. For example, tensions were evident between the large national NGOs and the small local NGOs, which mitigated against effective sharing of learning and experiences. Also the role of the ARC had become unclear (it did not carry out its agreed project-monitoring activities) and its participation was later brought to an end by the project.

The role of the IARC in supporting ARI, which in practice was under-resourced and under-motivated as a research institution, was far higher profile than had been intended at the outset. There was little evidence of the desired change in the organizational culture of the government agency. ARI had retained a top-down technology transfer approach in its work – characterized by the idea that 'scientist knows best' – in stark contrast to the Aquaculture Project's stated participatory, farmer-centred approach. Nor was learning taking place between this Aquaculture Project and similar initiatives under way with other bilateral donors in other parts of the country.

The full range of identified partnership problems was then highlighted for wider discussion by project staff. Some were raised at monthly project meetings and were identified during the course of the Aquaculture Project, while others were identified by the researcher and discussed at a special workshop. Where possible solutions, along with corresponding 'course corrections', were generated experimentally as part of ongoing activities. For example, new procedures of on-farm demonstration of new techniques were developed to bring researchers closer to farmers, while policy influence by NGO staff and clients was brought about by growing relationships and communication between Government and NGO in the course of the project. Other problems and conflicts, however, have not been satisfactorily solved and the search for solutions and compromises continues.

Such examples help to illustrate the extent to which partnership needs to be viewed as a process in which mechanisms, goals and outcomes must be continually reviewed by all the project's stakeholders. The roots of many of the problems which arose can be found in power imbalances between cooperating agencies. This is reflected in imperfect communication and information flows, differences in organizational culture and approach (e.g. in different levels of participation expected from farmers in the research and extension process) and unequal access to resources. For example, the small local NGOs participating in the project could not command resources on the scale of the large national NGOs and their 'voice' at critical linkage points in the overall project partnership was consequently such smaller. Many of these problems have been solved or at least followed through and the processual approach which was adopted has contributed to the strengthening of the project. However, certain difficulties will of course remain unsolved since, as we have seen, such a process view warns against seeing projects as linear, controllable events. Furthermore, despite the emphasis on technical constraints in the perceptions of the Government and the IARC, it remains likely that the social factors listed earlier may remain important in restricting the growth of small-scale aquaculture in Bangladesh.

15.5 Conclusion: Towards a process model

The use of the word 'partnership' covers a wide range of different relationships between agencies which may have either an active or a passive, dependent character (Table 15.1). This chapter was drawn from a case study of a development project in Bangladesh in order to make some preliminary steps in building a model of partnership based on the idea of partnership as process rooted in 'active' relationships between agency partners.

Active partnerships are those built through ongoing processes of negotiation, debate, occasional conflict and learning through trial and error. Risks are taken and although roles and purposes are clear they may change according to need and circumstance. Dependent partnerships, on the other hand, have a 'blueprint' character and tend to be constructed at the project planning stage according to rigid assumptions about 'comparative advantages' of state and non-state actors and individual agency interests. While there may be apparent consensus among the partners on the surface, this often reflects unclear roles and responsibilities rather than the creative conflicts which emerge within active partnerships. In an aid-dependent context, such as Bangladesh, the likelihood is strong that agencies will come together in 'dependent' partnerships in order to gain access to resources rather than for the purposes of mutual exploration and learning. The project discussed here began with a set of largely dependent partnerships but over time, and with a process of facilitation from both inside and

Table 15.1 Contrasting characteristics of 'active' and 'dependent' partnerships

'Active' partnerships	*'Dependent' partnerships*
Process	Blueprint, fixed term
Negotiated, changing roles	Rigid roles based on static assumptions about 'comparative advantage'
Clear purposes, roles and linkages but an openness to change as appropriate	Some functional division of responsibility in theory, but unclear purposes, roles and linkages in practice
Shared risks	Individual interests
Debate and dissent	Consensus or resignation to role
Learning and information exchange	Poor communication flows
'Activity-based' origins – emerging from practice	Resource-based origins – primarily to gain access to funds

outside the project, built partnerships of a more active character. The task of seeking to generate 'active' partnership is the key challenge for the management of interagency development projects.

To move into the realm of tentative theory building, the process of generating 'active partnership' requires the presence of several key attributes if value is to be added or synergy is to be created, and this process needs to be understood in both functional and processual terms. The five key attributes are as follows.

Communication. The space and time needs to be created which can provide opportunities for channels of communication among different organizational actors.

Risk taking and risk sharing. Not all aims will be achieved, and may change over time. An important part of risk taking is the open discussion and negotiation of conflict and difference.

Acknowledging the importance of personalities. The formation of personal ties between individuals from different partner groups can help build an open exchange of problems and ideas to facilitate learning.

A clear sense of the purposes of the partnership. Understanding of the outcomes which can be achieved jointly, over and above those which might be achieved singly, is essential at the start of the partnership. Equally important is the recognition that these purposes will change over time, requiring redefinition as new opportunities and constraints emerge.

Definition and adaptation. Each specific interagency partnership (and its associated actor linkages) will require new definition and adaptation and it is unlikely, in view of the importance of process, that it can simply be replicated from another context.

Such a process view of partnership has implications for managers in the public, private and the non-governmental sectors. A first step is to identify the goals of partnership, a second is to design a range of mechanisms for achieving the necessary linkages, while a third is to review purposes and progress regularly. Processes of organizational learning (Korten 1990) and techniques of adaptation of successful models (Hulme 1993) will be of central importance. Once these principles are agreed, specific practice can be adapted to local conditions and 'active partnerships' may then be developed based on the principles outlined above. Future research into a sample of both successful and unsuccessful partnership ventures across a range of country contexts would add to the sum of our knowledge and test the tentative hypothesis provided here concerning the crucial elements which make partnerships work.

While there may be common issues in interagency partnerships in any context, there is a set of specific problems created for policy makers and managers in aid-dependent environments. Interagency partnerships need to be analysed within specific historical and political contexts. In a country such as Bangladesh in which the role of foreign aid is predominant in development activity (Sobhan 1982), such partnerships are clearly affected by the level of resource dependence. The flow of resources from the external environment strongly shapes the form and spirit in which partnership links are established.

Under these circumstances, 'partnership' in Bangladesh can be viewed in terms of a discourse in part produced by Bangladesh's dependent position in the provision of international aid and by the changing policy agendas in which this provision is located (Ferguson 1990; Escobar 1995; Gardner and Lewis 1996). External pressures may encourage 'dependent' partnerships to form such that agencies work together based on the availability of resources rather than on common objectives and shared risks. The main danger of course is that within this framework of dependency, such partnerships are unsustainable. But there are other, related problems. In Bangladesh the concept of partnership can be seen to reflect both the technocratic language of instrumentalist solutions to complex development issues centring on power and distribution, and the new donor emphasis on 'civil society' and good governance (Lewis 1997a).

The key challenge for policy makers is therefore to understand more about the process of partnership so that efforts can be made to shift interagency partnerships away from the dependent type towards those with a more 'active' character. In the aquaculture project discussed here, a partial shift was observed in the transformation over time of several of the linkage points. While the functional model of partnership can explain some aspects of successful partnership, it is the process view which illustrates more fully the diverse factors which help to determine partnership outcomes. For example, the high level of effectiveness found in the linkage between farmers and NGO field staff at demonstration sessions can be attributed to the special strengths often found in NGOs in building participatory relationships with clients. On the other hand, the success of the linkage between NGO staff and ARI researchers was the result of a far more complex process of building trust, negotiating conflict and difference and forming personal ties between individuals in which there were tensions and setbacks as well as progress and learning.

References

Bate, S. P. (1997) 'Whatever happened to organizational anthropology?', *Human Relations* 50(9): 1,147–75.

Biggs, S. and Neame, A. (1995) 'Negotiating room for manoeuvre: Reflections concerning NGO autonomy and accountability within the new policy agenda', in M. Edwards and D. Hulme (eds) *Non-Governmental Organizations – Performance and Accountability: Beyond the Magic Bullet*, London: Earthscan.

Billis, D. (1993) *Organising Public and Voluntary Agencies*, London: Routledge.

Dawson, P. (1994) *Organizational Change: A Processual Approach*, London: Paul Chapman.

DFID (1997)*Eliminating World Poverty: A Challenge for the 21st Century*, Department for International Development, London: The Stationery Office Limited.

Escobar, A. (1995) *Encountering Development: the Making and Unmaking of the Third World*, Princeton, NJ: Princeton University Press.

Farrington, J. and Bebbington, A. (1993) 'Reluctant partners?', in K. Wellard and D. J. Lewis (eds) *NGOs, the State and Sustainable Agricultural Development*, London: Routledge.

Farrington, J. and Lewis, D. J. (1993) 'NGOs and the State in Asia', in S. Satish and A. Miclat-Teves (eds) *Rethinking Roles in Sustainable Agricultural Development*, London: Routledge.

Ferguson, J. (1990) *The Anti-Politics Machine: 'Development', Depoliticization and Bureaucratic Power in Lesotho*, Cambridge: Cambridge University Press.

Gardner, K. and Lewis, D. J. (1996) *Antropology, Development and the Post-Modern Challenge*, London: Pluto.

Hossain, M. (1990) *Bangladesh Economic Performance and Prospects*, ODI Discussion Paper, London: Overseas Development Institute.

Hulme, D. (1993) 'Replicating finance programmes in Malawi and Malaysia', *Small Enterprise Development* 4(4).

Korten, D. C. (1990) *Getting to the 21st Century: Voluntary Action and the Global Agenda*, Hartford: Kumarian Press.

Kramer, R. M. (1994) 'Voluntary agencies and the contract culture: Dream or Nightmare?', *Social Service Reviews* March: 33–60.

Leach, M. (1994) *Models of Inter-organizational Collaboration in Development*, IDR Reports Vol. 11, No. 7, Boston: Institute for Development Research.

Lewis, D. (1997a) 'NGOs, donors and the state in Bangladesh', *The Annals of the American Academy of Political and Social Science* 554 (November): 33–45.

—— (1997b) 'Rethinking aquaculture for resource poor farmers: Perspectives from Bangladesh', *Food Policy* 22(6): 533–46.

—— (1998) 'Partnership as process: Building and institutional ethnography of an inter-agency aquaculture project in Bangladesh', in D. Mosse, J. Farrington and A. Rew (eds) *Development As Process: Concepts and Methods for Working with Complexity*, London: Routledge.

—— (1999 (ed.)) *International Perspectives on Voluntary Action: Reshaping the Third Sector*, London: Earthscan.

Lewis, D. J., Wood, G. D. and Gregory, R. (1996) *Trading the Silver Seed: Local Knowledge and Market Moralities in Aquacultural Development*, London: Intermediate Technology Publications and Dhaka: University Press Limited.

Minkin, S. F. and Boyce, J. (1994) 'Development drains the fisheries of Bangladesh', *Amicus Journal* Fall: 36–40.

Mosse, D. (1996) 'Process monitoring and process documentation: Evolving methods for social research and development practice – cases and issues', draft paper, Centre for Development Studies, University of Swansea.

Osborne, S. (1997) 'Managing the coordination of social services in the mixed economy of care: Competition, cooperation or common cause?', *British Journal of Management* 8: 317–28.

Postma, W. (1994) 'NGO partnership and institutional development: Making it real, making it intentional, *Canadian Journal of African Studies* 28(3): 447–71.

Robinson, D., Harriss, J. and Hewitt, T. (eds) (1999) *Managing Inter-Organizational Relationships: Competition, Co-ordination or Co-operation?*, London: Sage.

Robinson, M. (1993) 'Governance, democracy and conditionality: NGOs and the new policy agenda', A. Clayton (ed.) *Governance, Democracy and Conditionality: What Role for NGOs?*, Oxford: INTRAC.

Salamon, L. (1995) *Partners in Public Service: Government–Nonprofit Relations in the Modern Welfare State*, Baltimore: John Hopkins.

Sanyal, B. (1991) 'Antagonistic co-operation: A case study of NGOs, government and donor relationships in IG projects in Bangladesh', *World Development* 19(10): 1,367–79.

Smith, P. (1995) 'The challenge of partnership: A study of the relationship between city challenge and the voluntary sector in a London borough', LSE Centre for Voluntary Organisation, Case Study Paper No. 9.

Smith, S. R. and Lipsky, M. (1993) *Nonprofits for Hire: The Welfare State and the Age of Contracting*, Cambridge: Harvard University Press.

Sobhan, R. (1982) *The Crisis of External Dependence: The Political Economy of Foreign Aid to Bangladesh*, Dhaka: University Press Limited.

Worby, E. (1994) 'Hitting hairs and splitting targets: Anthropological perspectives on fish culture technology transfer through NGOs in Bangladesh', Rockefeller Foundation conference paper, Addis Ababa, mimeo.

World Bank (1996) *Pursuing Common Goals: Strengthening Partnerships between Government and NGOs in Bangladesh*, Dhaka: World Bank.

Notes

1 An earlier version of this chapter was published in *Nonprofit and Voluntary Sector Quarterly* in 1998.
2 In the Bangladesh context, Sanyal (1991), in an exploration of what he terms 'antagonistic co-operation' between NGOs, government and donors, also suggests that these different institutional actors need each other.
3 This point is also made eloquently by Biggs and Neame (1995).
4 A more detailed discussion of the methodology of the research and the conflicts and problems encountered can be found in Lewis (1998).
5 The current interest in viewing development projects in terms of process is to some extent paralleled by recent thinking among organizational-change theorists such as Dawson (1994: 4) who writes '... organizations undergoing transition should be studied 'as-it happens' so that processes associated with change can reveal themselves over time and in context ... This temporal framework of change can also be used to accommodate the existence of a number of competing histories on the process of organizational transition ... The dominant or 'official version' of change may often reflect the political positioning of certain key individuals or groups within an organization, rather than serving as a true representation of the practice of transition management'.
6 'Capture fisheries' (a term which refers to inland fishing in open waters such as lakes and flood plains), despite its potential, has received rather less attention from development agencies and researchers, though an exception is Minkin and Boyce (1994).
7 In order to protect the anonymity of informants, generic acronyms have been used to represent the specific institutional actors involved in the project.

16 Partnership between local government and the local community in the area of social policy

A Hungarian experience[1]

György Jenei and Anna Vári

16.1 Introduction

In 1989, at the beginning of the period of political transition in Hungary, there was no independent social policy system with clear social priorities. Nevertheless, the economy and all branches of the public policy were imbued with social concerns. Full employment, extensive subsidies for basic services, and free or subsidized health services provided all of society with a form of 'social care'. In addition, local social policy supported a very narrow stratum of the population whose members, because of their special needs, struggled with livelihood problems despite the national social policy system.

After 1990, this social policy system was partly disintegrated by itself and was partly dismantled as a result of economic collapse. A new system was built in its place, but only slowly and inconsistently (Ferge 1991). Consequently, it was slow in responding to the social problems accompanying the creation of the market economy.

In 1993, a new Social Welfare Act was adopted. The Act created a qualitatively new situation by establishing a comprehensive legislative framework for social policy making. However, it failed to address important legislative tasks concerning the broader role of government, the budgetary aspects of social policy and the regulation of certain areas (housing policy, childcare, etc.) Nevertheless, it was an important step forward in decentralizing decision making in social policy, thereby giving the local authorities and the local community and organizations the opportunity to play a substantive role both in social matters and in re-establishing civil society in Hungary (Osborne and Kaposvari 1997) .

This chapter describes the background and history of a project aimed at developing a strategic social plan in the city of Eger. This initiative was based upon partnership between the Municipal Government, the local community and civil organizations in Eger. It offers an important perspective on the potential, in the transitional nations of eastern and central Europe, for public–private partnership

[1] This chapter first appeared in 2000 in *Public Management. An International Journal of Research and Theory* 2(2).

as an effective mechanism both to map social needs and to develop policies to address these needs. It also offers one particular approach to the development of such partnerships – the *decision conferencing* model (Phillips 1988). Such an approach takes public–private partnerships into an arena beyond that of policy implementation alone.

16.2 Social changes and challenges in Eger

Eger is a city of around 66,000 inhabitants in north-east Hungary. It is the capital of Heves County, which has a population of 325,000. Since the early 1990s, a plural, multidimensional social structure has been taking shape in the city. The one-dimensional strata structure of the 1980s is shifting in the direction of a two-dimensional structure in which the formation of strata is not only influenced by state redistribution but by the market economy as well. As in other parts of the country, a societal polarization process has taken place, with the slowing down of mobility processes at the 'edges' of society, among the wealthy and the poor. There has been an increase in both the absolute and relative size of the stratum living beneath the minimum subsistence threshold or just above it.

The Local Authority has made enormous efforts to ease social problems and support families and individuals in need of help. Despite this, however, it has not been able to halt the decline in the standard of living of a significant proportion of households which has mainly been caused by problems arising from the transformation of the economic system (restructuring, bankruptcies, etc.).

Because of the economic, social and political pressures, there are ongoing reform steps and innovative efforts in the local government of Eger. The main objective of these actions is to provide more effective and more cost-efficient public services. A shift can be observed from a bureaucratic form of local government to a more entrepreneurial form. The traditional isolation of public administration from civil organizations and private sector companies is blurring. Local officials do not have a monopoly on the provision of public services any more. New forms of interorganizational networks and strategic alliances have been created, and they provide for services based on cooperation and coordination with multiple local governments (Jenei and Palotai 1996; Osborne and Kaposvari 1998).

In Eger the role of civil organizations, as across Hungary generally (Kuti 1996), was quite important in the beginning of this century, especially in the field of education, culture and social policy. A serious attack against civil society during World War II led first to the prohibition of Jewish organizations and then of some trade unions. After 1945 the state socialist system initially prohibited Catholic organizations and later virtually all existing civil organizations. As a consequence of these attacks only a few civil organizations were able to survive through the next 40 years.

By the end of 1996, however, there were again 1,157 civil organizations in Heves County; 241 (21 per cent) of these were located in Eger. Approximately 35 civil organizations have become very well known in Eger, and they take increasingly important initiatives and play a significant consultative and decision-making role in the city.

In order to use the human and material resources of local government, civil organizations and business organizations in the most efficient way, cooperative arrangements need to be established between them. However, as a legacy of centralized planning systems and top-town approaches, there is very little tradition of cooperation between these sectors in Hungary, and local government officials lack expertise in this field. The need for support in developing such cooperation was recognized by the leaders of the Eger City Government in 1996. They decided to invite the authors of this chapter, who are affiliated to the Center for Public Affairs Studies of the Budapest University of Economic Sciences, and the Institute for Social Conflict Research of the Hungarian Academy of Sciences to facilitate the development of a strategic social plan.

16.3 Developing a strategic social plan

The project, aimed at developing a strategic social plan, was started in January 1996. The work was coordinated by a three-member project-management team including a representative of the Eger City Government and the methodological experts. The contribution of the experts was financially supported by the International Research and Exchanges Board/American Council of Learned Societies (IREX/ACLS).

To facilitate the participatory planning process a series of *decision conferences* were organized. *Decision conferencing* is a group decision-support method which is characterized by the presence of all relevant stakeholders and the use of a combination of problem structuring and group-facilitation techniques. The facilitator, a specialist in the techniques of group dynamics and problem structuring, works directly with the participants and directs the interaction process by eliciting and summarizing ideas, focusing discussion, providing feedback and managing conflict. Decision conferencing has been successfully applied in many countries in a variety of decision-making situations (Phillips 1988; Buede and Bresnick 1992; Fekete-Szűcs 1991; Rohrbaugh 1992; Vári and Vecsenyi 1992; Vári *et al.* 1992; McCartt and Rohrbaugh 1995).

The planning process involved three decision conferences and the collection of supplemental data between the meetings. In total, around sixty individuals were invited. Twenty-nine of these participated in the first conference, thirty in the second and forty-one in the third. The participants included:

- Representatives of the local government political structure (the Deputy Mayor, the Chairwoman and members of the Social Committee, the Chairman and members of the Minority Authority of Gypsies, the Director and members of the Office of Social Affairs);
- Representatives of civil organizations (e.g. classical interest protection groups, charitable organizations, associations and foundations social issues);

- Representatives of agencies of the local government (e.g. the Mental Hygiene Service, the Institute for Family Care, the Day Care Centre for the Elderly);
- Managers of enterprises (e.g. service providers in electricity).

Among the participants certain groups – women, the middle-aged and the elderly were over-represented. Local government representatives had qualifications in public administration, economics or law, while most civil activists had backgrounds in teaching or social work.

The conferences, which were used to build consensus among these groups, consisted of small group discussions and plenary sessions in which participants' ideas, judgements and recommendations were elicited and discussed with the guidance of the project management team and local facilitators. The three conferences focused on the following tasks:

- Identifying the most pressing social problems in Eger;
- Generating proposals for possible interventions to ease these problems;
- Evaluating these proposals in terms of their potential benefits, costs and feasibility;
- Selecting the most cost-effective set of feasible interventions; and
- Developing recommendations for the implementation of the selected interventions.

The series of decision conferences were completed by January 1997 and results were summarized in a report issued by the project management team, which formed the basis for the Strategic Social Plan developed by the Social Committee of the Eger City Government.

16.4 The first conference: identifying the most important social problems

At the first decision conference, participants were divided into two groups. Each group was asked to identify the most serious social problems in Eger within the framework of a brainstorming session. After discussion and clarification, problems were classified into problem areas. Then, based on voting, each group selected the most important problem areas. Lists of the key problem areas were presented by both groups at a plenary session, where they were extensively discussed. After a second round of voting, the following were identified as the most important problem areas:

- Families with children;
- The elderly;
- Mentally or physically handicapped persons;
- Gypsies;
- Poverty; and
- Housing.

At the end of the first decision conference, participants were asked to form groups to work on each problem area. Six working groups were established on a voluntary basis. Leaders of each group were elected by group members. Participants then were requested to develop proposals on the following questions and mail them to their working group leader before the second decision conference:

- What are the most important symptoms and causes of the problems assigned to the working group?
- What kinds of steps should be implemented to mitigate or eliminate these problems?

Between the first and second decision conference, group leaders collected the proposals and forwarded them to the three member project management team. Proposals were then structured by the project management team, and the structured list of steps used as an input in conducting the second decision conference.

16.5 The second conference: selecting cost-effective interventions

At the beginning of the second conference, participants decided to merge the working groups dealing with the problems of poverty and of the gypsies, because of the considerable overlap between the proposals of these two groups. Each working group was facilitated by the group leader, who, prior to the second conference, participated in a short training session on group facilitation. Participants of each working group were presented with the structured list of the proposed interventions and asked to add further proposals. Next, the groups collectively revised the interventions and elaborated them in terms of the following issues:

- What activities should be carried out?
- Who should be responsible for implementation of these activities (e.g. local government, civil organizations)?
- Who should be the beneficiaries?

After clarifying and elaborating the proposals, the working groups evaluated them in terms of three criteria: their potential benefits, their expected costs and their feasibility. Every proposed step was evaluated collectively on each criterion using a three-point scale. After consensus had been reached, proposed strategies of low benefit, low feasibility or high cost were eliminated from further analysis.

The second part of the conference was organized as a plenary session in which each working group presented its selected interventions. This was followed by a general discussion during which participants assessed the results of the first two conferences. After the plenary discussion, participants were requested to generate responses to the following questions and send them to the working-group leaders:

- How should the selected interventions be implemented?
- What role, if any, should the participants' organization take in the implementation process?
- Which organizations could potentially be involved as partners in implementation (such as departments or institutions of the local government, civil organizations, business organizations)?

Following the second conference, responses to these questions were collected. These responses then were used to locate representatives of potential partner organizations who, if they were not already involved in the planning process, were invited to the third meeting.

16.6 The third conference: developing recommendations

The main objective of the third conference was to develop specific recommendations for implementing the policies selected during the previous conference. An analysis of the proposals indicated significant overlap between those suggested by the working group on the elderly and the working group on the handicapped, and those suggested by the working groups on poverty and on housing. Therefore, three working groups were formed to address the problems of families, the elderly/handicapped and poverty/housing. In the first part of the conference, participants in the three working groups were asked the following questions:

- Which interventions should be incorporated in the social plan of the Local Government?
- How can cooperative arrangements be best organized between the civil organizations and the Local Government? How should the tasks be shared? Who should initiate, supervise and implement the proposed policies?
- What kind of resources should be used? How can the fund raising process be best organized?
- What is the best time schedule for implementation?

After generating a series of ideas, participants discussed them in a plenary session and created a list of proposals that addressed each of the critical problem areas. Recommendations for individual problem areas are illustrated in Table 16.1.

16.7 Implementation

After the last decision conference, a task force was created consisting of officials of the Department of Social Affairs and representatives of several civil organizations. This collected additional data both about the demographic characteristics of the most vulnerable groups in Eger and about the most serious problems defined during the conferences – including unemployment, educational and cultural disadvantages, regional differences and public-health issues. Based on the work of

Table 16.1 Recommendations for the problem areas in Hungary

Families with children

- The Local Government should support a social programme for families with children. The programme would be organized jointly by NGOs, parents and teachers.
- The Local Government should organize exchanges of information between civil organizations and the local authorities. An information office should be established.
- The Local Government should reform the social-service system in cooperation with families and the civil organizations.
- The civil organizations should establish voluntary groups that involve women.
- Local Government and enterprises should provide more part-time jobs for women.
- A special service network should be established for families.
- A system should be created to provide support for gifted children coming from low-income families.

The elderly

- The local social statute should be modified to take account of current constraints faced by the local government in serving the elderly.
- Existing special services for the elderly should be expanded to include special products with low prices and special catering networks
- The care-taking responsibilities of families for the elderly should be strengthened.
- Regional differences in the level of social services provided for the elderly should be reduced.
- An open university should be organized for the elderly.

The handicapped

- The Local Government should support the retraining of handicapped persons.
- The Local Government should help in transporting handicapped persons.
- A special club should be organized for the handicapped.
- Cooperation should be strengthened between the local government and civil organizations.
- Day-care service for the handicapped should be expanded by involving civil organizations.

Poverty

- More jobs for low-income groups should be created.
- Affirmative actions should be provided in the schools for the children of gypsies and other minority groups.
- Support should be provided for gypsies and members of other minority groups in resolving housing problems.
- Special tax allowances should be provided for low-income groups.

Housing

- A *social map* of the city should be developed.
- The Local Government should aid the younger generation in purchasing their first home.
- The Local Government and the residents' organizations should establish an information office that would provide information about available housing and thereby increase mobility.
- A long-run programme for improving the quality of housing should be developed.

the conferences and this subsequent data, a detailed plan to address these needs was developed for the Social Committee of the Eger Local Government.

However, because of political tensions within the Committee, it was not willing to discuss the full plan before the Local Government elections of 1998. Nonetheless, although it did not make a formal commitment to implementing this plan, several joint actions were approved by the Local Government. A number of key partnerships concerning social services, for example, were established between the City Government and the civil organizations.

Finally, after the 1998 elections, the newly elected Local Government began to implement the full plan. This latter process has served to continue the dialogue of partnership and collaboration between Local Government, the local community, civil organizations and local businesses, in spite of the continuing politically turbulent environment. The *decision conferencing* approach has thus had a major impact upon public–private partnerships in Eger.

16.8 Conclusions

The collaborative strategic planning process of Eger took place during a period that can be characterized as that of a weakening welfare state and an emerging civil society. While many of the new civil organizations were established in response to the state's inadequate functioning in certain areas, including social services, health care and education, their own financial and human resources have not been sufficient to replace the waning state services in these areas (Kuti 1996). Although some business organizations have also made donations for welfare purposes, the efforts of civil organizations and businesses in mitigating recent negative social changes have not yet been sufficient (Pestov 1995).

By the mid-1990s it was widely recognized that, in order to use most efficiently the human and material resources of local governments, civil society and business organizations, cooperative arrangements need to be established between them. The case of the Eger cooperative strategic-planning process represents an important experiment in this field. Uniquely, it has focused on using a public–private partnership for both the planning and the implementation of much-needed local services.

In the course of the strategic planning exercise, an important social learning process took place. By involving representatives of the full range of local organizations in all stages of the strategy-building process, the empathy, tolerance and understanding of local-government officers for those outside the government has been strengthened. The representatives of the civil organizations have also learned how to be both constructively critical and loyal without being subservient. Furthermore, they have developed an understanding and a more realistic view of the nature of social services and they have learned that important negotiation skills are required for the effective implementation of social programmes through public–private partnerships. Finally, individual civil activists have also learned how to express the interests of their constituencies, how to mediate between their organizations and governmental authorities and how to determine if the interests of their constituencies overlapped with the interests of another group. The participants in the strategic-planning process have thus recognized that success can be reached only by a long-term cooperation and partnership.

It must also be noted that this partnership process in Eger has highlighted that local community cooperation is influenced by a range of structural issues which must be negotiated by the participants if the partnership is to be successful. Effective, goal-oriented partnerships among local agencies and civil organizations are only feasible if the required tasks are clear and if each organization can identify with the tasks it will need to perform. Effective management and delegations of tasks are also required – as is ensuring that the designated actors for each task have the requisite skills to carry them out. This emphasizes the importance of genuine *capacity building* with civil organizations if they are to be serious and genuine partners in community planning.

With respect to the transitional nations in particular, the social planning process in Eger also made clear that there can be significant obstacles to developing the collaborative culture necessary for successful public–private partnerships. The history of paternalistic decision making on the part of public authorities in Hungary, as well as the lack of a tradition of cross-community involvement in service planning, has led to a situation in many parts of Hungary where government officials do not recognize the need for collaboration, which is further aggravated by the frequent conflicts between political parties and factions and by the frequent changes of a large proportion of Local Government agency personnel after each election. These factors result in a turbulent political and organizational environment in Hungary, as well as a general lack of trust among the various players. Finally, the weakeness of civil organizations in Hungary, and the other transitional nations, and the scarcity of human, managerial, organizational and financial resources within them can also present major obstacles to an effective government–civil society partnership – again emphasizing the essential need for capacity building to take place to ensure the success of such initiatives.

However, in the long run and whatever their outcomes in terms of local services, participatory decision-making processes are 'important schools of democracy' (Caddy 1998) for local communities in the transitional nations and an important contribution to the development of civil society in the region. Public officials as well as representatives of civil organizations, managers of business enterprises or other key actors can learn important communication, cooperation and conflict management skills in such processes. The tools of joint decision making and teamwork are of a generic nature. Once learned, it is anticipated that they can be utilized for the development of public–private partnerships both in various areas of public policy making and in the delivery of local services to the community.

16.9 Acknowledgement

We would like to acknowledge the generous sponsorship of IREX/ACLS and the Eger City Government. We wish to express our gratitude to Professor John

Rohrbaugh of the State University of New York at Albany for his continuous methodological support in planning and implementing the project.

References

Buede, D. M. and Bresnick, T. A. (1992) 'Applications of decision analysis to the military systems acquisition process', *Interfaces* 22: 110–25.

Caddy, J. E. (1998) 'Sowing the seeds of deliberative democracy? Institutions for the environment in central Europe: Case studies of public participation in environ mental decision-making in contemporary Hungary; doctoral thesis, European University Institute, Department of Political and Social Sciences, Florence.

Fekete-Szűcs, L. (1991) 'Decision conference for strategic issues: Theory in practice', in H. G. Sol and J. Vecsenyi (eds) *Environments for Supporting Decision Processes*, Amsterdam: North Holland.

Ferge, Z. (1991) 'Recent trends in social policy in Hungary', in J. Adam (ed.) *Economic Reforms and Welfare Systems in USSR, Poland and Hungary*, London: Macmillan pp. 132–55.

Jenei, Gy. and Palotai, Zs. (1996) 'Social problems and social management in Eger', in Straussman-Lévai (ed.) *Innovative Local Authorities*, Budapest: Local Society Research Group, pp. 48–88.

Kuti, E. (1996) *The Non Profit Sector in Hungary*, London: Manchester University Press.

McCartt, A. T. and Rohrbaugh, J. (1995) 'Managerial openness to change and the introduction of GDSS: Explaining initial success and failure in decision conferen cing', *Organization Science* 6: 569–84.

Osborne, S. and Kaposvari, A. (1997) 'Toward civil society? Exploring its meanings in the context of post-communist Hungary', *Journal of European Social Policy* 7(3): 209–23.

—— (1998) 'Nongovernmental organizations and the development of social services. Meeting social needs in local communities in post-communist Hungary', *Public Administration and Development* 18: 365–80.

Phillips, L. D. (1988) 'People-centered group decision support', in G. I. Doukidis, F. Land and G. Miller (eds) *Knowledge Based Management Support Systems*, Chichester, UK: Harwood.

Pestov, V. A. (1995) *Reforming Social Services in Central and Eastern Europe – An Eleven Nation Overview*, Kraców: Kraców Academy of Economics–Friedrich Ebert Stiftung.

Rohrbaugh, J. (1992) 'Cognitive challenges and collective accomplishments', in R. P. Bostrom, R. T. Watson and S. T. Kinney (eds) *Computer Augmented Teamwork: A Guided Tour*, New York: Van Nostrand Reinhold.

Vári, A., Rohrbaugh, J. and Baaklini, A. I. (1992) 'Group decision system for legis lative deliberation: Decision conferencing in the Hungarian Parliament', *Informatization and the Public Sector* 2: 27–45.

Vári, A. and Vecsenyi, J. (1992) 'Experiences with decision conferencing in Hungary', *Interfaces* 22: 72–83.

Part IV

Evaluating public–private partnerships

17 Evaluating the impact of public–private partnerships

A Canadian perspective

Vic Murray

17.1 An anecdote

A government ministry responsible for immigration contracted with a number of non-profit immigrant-aid organizations to deliver 'English as a Second Language' (ESL) training for recent immigrants. As a check on how well these organizations were doing the job it told them that their programmes would be evaluated on the basis of their costs per student and the percentage of those signed up for classes who reached a certain score on a standardized test of English language proficiency at the end of their training. This way the Ministry felt it could carry out a 'cost–benefit' assessment of programme outcomes and thus feel assured that the money spent was being used efficiently and producing the results desired.

This actual scenario seems like a good illustration of what many public officials, media commentators and others have been clamouring for in recent years. It would provide a clear indication of value-for-money in the public sector; something roughly equivalent to the 'bottom line' of profit that investors in the business world can use to decide if their investments are good ones.

But does it really do that? Consider what happened next in this scenario. Several of the non-profit contractors quickly realized that continued funding for their ESL programmes would depend on 'looking good' on the numbers that the Government would be collecting. Since there was no shortage of recent immigrants applying to take these free English classes, they began selecting their students much more carefully. The better the existing knowledge of English possessed by applicants and the more stable their lifestyle was (meaning that they could be counted on to attend all classes), the better the chance they had of passing the critical test at the end. Those who did not seem too bright, who did not speak any English at all and who were likely to drop out because of moving, work demands or family pressures (the latter a special problem for women from certain cultures), were not admitted. The result: these agencies looked great on the Government's figures but the real objective of the ESL training, which was to provide English language skills for as many immigrants as possible irrespective of their prior backgrounds, got lost.

This is just one of the many problems that surround attempts by governments to evaluate the performance of non-profit organizations and their programmes (or, indeed, the performance of public sector organizations as well). This chapter will address these problems by looking at the following questions:

- What does evaluation involve?
- What are the common pitfalls and problems in the evaluation process?
- Why do these occur?
- What is the role of evaluation in the relationship between public sector and non-profit organizations?
- Is it possible to improve the evaluation process in the public–non-profit-sector relationship?

17.2 Evaluation: What is it and how does it work?

Before discussing the specifics of evaluation in public–private partnerships, it is necessary to first have an understanding about what evaluation is and why it is so often fraught with problems. To achieve this understanding we need to know who is involved in it, why it is done, what is evaluated and how it is done (see Forbes 1998; Murray and Tassie 1994; Paton 1998; and Taylor and Sumariwalla 1993 for further discussion of these questions).

Who evaluates?

Fundamental to an understanding of the evaluation process is the realization that it involves two basic roles: that of evaluator and that of evaluatee. In addition, those who will make use of evaluation information may well employ specialists in designing and implementing the process by which that information is gathered. Thus, the evaluator role can be further broken down between those who generate the information and those who use it (Ashford and Clark 1996).

Why evaluate?

There are two basic reasons for undertaking evaluation. The professional litera-ture has called them 'formative' and 'summative' evaluation rationales (e.g. Forbes 1998). The purpose of formative evaluation is to help the evaluatee to do a better job at the evaluatee's own behest. The idea is to provide information that helps indicate where there are problems (or successes), why such problems have arisen and what might be done to improve matters. There is no intention to judge the evaluatee as having succeeded or failed in any way. The evaluator is usually seen as the evaluatee's helper or partner in the process.

Summative evaluation is conducted in order for the evaluator to make decisions as a result of assessing how well the evaluatees have carried out the responsibilities conferred on them. The result of the process is a judgement about the level of success that has been achieved. There are normally consequences to these assess-ments such as keeping or dropping a programme or a change in funding levels.

What is evaluated?

A great deal of confusion can arise between evaluators and evaluatees because the latter do not understand what the former is trying to evaluate. It is therefore crucial to know the *level* of evaluation being undertaken. These levels are:

- Individual;
- Programme, organizational unit or function;
- Organization;
- Larger social system.

Individual evaluation focuses on the performance of individuals in their jobs. The evaluation is usually against standards set down in a job description or goals contained in a personal performance plan.

The next level of evaluation focuses on elements *within* an organization such as a programme, an organizational unit (department, section or subsidiary) or a function such as human resources or marketing. Examples of evaluation at this level are assessing the success of a programme for reducing substance abuse by teenagers, or the effectiveness of a marketing department created to boost attendance at symphony concerts, or the impact of a management function, such as planning, on the operation of the organization.

Non-profit organizations are made up of many programmes and functions all designed to achieve the overall mission of the organization. Certain evaluators are interested in assessing the performance of the total organization in achieving its mission and less in the state of each of its programmes. For example, many private funders want evaluations of the whole organization because that is what they fund. Conversely, certain government departments who contract with non-profits for the delivery of specific programmes will be focused on the programme level of evaluation and care little about the rest of the organization in which the programme resides.

Finally, any given social need or issue is usually addressed by a number of organizations and programmes. The system level of evaluation looks at how the efforts of various actors collectively impact an issue. This broader perspective has two levels of analysis, referred to here as 'jurisdictional' and 'sectoral' evaluation. Jurisdictional evaluation measures processes or results at the geographical or political level. For example, the assessment of the quality of life of residents in a country, region or community is an example of jurisdictional evaluation. Sectors are areas of common activity directed towards a particular social or economic end. Evaluation at the sectoral level focuses on the status of the issue or end goal that the activities are attempting to address. The United Nations' assessment of global child poverty is an example of sectoral evaluation. The Canadian Council on Social Development's annual monitoring of the nature and extent of child health and well-being in Canada is another example. In system-level evaluations, evaluators are not interested in how any one organization deals with an issue but rather in the status of the issue itself.

Governments who fund non-profit organizations are usually most interested in programme and system-level evaluation. However, these often take place at two different levels of state bureaucracy. Programme evaluation is located at the 'front line' level of the hierarchy where officials track the performance of specific programmes and organizations. System-level evaluation occurs in the policy advisory units far removed from the front-line level. All too often the connection between the information generated at one level and that at the other is weak.

What kinds of evaluation are there?

The ideal evaluation process is one that provides clear evidence that something has done what it was intended to do. There are three basic types of evaluation that may be carried out to generate this evidence.

1   *Outcome evaluation.* Outcome evaluation looks at the end results of activities designed to achieve a particular goal (Sheehan 1996). As will be seen, all forms of evaluation have their problems and one of the most serious of these for outcome measurement is that outcomes may differ over time and be more difficult to measure the further they are from the programme or intervention, both in time and causality. One, therefore, has to be aware of long-term, intermediate and short-term outcomes. For example, an organization created to help street youth may have as the outcome the ultimate desire to increase the chances that 'children at risk' today will be self-supporting, emotionally healthy and contributing members of society when they become adults. This long-term outcome may not be feasible to measure in terms of available time and resources. But a more modest intermediate outcome could be the percentage of the organization's clients who complete a high-school education by age 20, compared with a matched sample of other street youth who do not participate in the organization's programmes. Finally, it may be possible only to get at relatively short-term outcomes; for example, the number of the organization's clients who re-establish contact with their families and are not charged with any violations of the law in a 12-month period following programme completion. The other problem with outcome evaluation is that it can be difficult to capture the full intent of goals in one or two indicators. The anecdote that began this chapter, describing the government funder evaluating the performance of the English language training programmes for immigrants, is a case in point. The goal was not just to improve the English of immigrants who already spoke some or who were easiest to reach but that is what the outcome measure unintentionally emphasized.

2   *Process evaluation.* It is intended that outcomes, at least in part, should result from a specific set of processes followed or activities undertaken by the evaluatee. As a result, some evaluations attempt to measure the occurrence

of activities, or clusters of activities.[1] For example, programmes to help fishers who have lost their employment as a result of the decline in fish stocks may measure the number who take special retraining courses, the number and kind of courses available, and the quantity and quality of information provided about alternative sources of employment. The inference is that if these activities are performed well more fishers will manage to make a successful transition to a new kind of employment. The problem with measuring processes, of course, is that it is difficult to 'prove' that the processes actually lead to the intended outcomes. The outcomes may be determined by other conditions which were not measured at all.

3   *Input evaluation.* Processes cannot occur without the initial investment of financial, human and technological resources to make them happen. Therefore, it is possible to perform an evaluation of these inputs. For example, how much money was put into a given project; how many person-hours were devoted to it; how much computer technology was put in place; how much management time was invested in developing the project, etc. Here the inference is that, without the inputs of money, people and technology, the activities cannot occur which, in turn, means that the outcomes cannot be achieved.

For years, many non-profit organizations have depended on measurements of the severity of a problem, as a basis for their demands for funds and claims about the growth in numbers served, as the basis for claiming that the organization has been effective whether or not those served actually benefited from the organization's programmes.

How is evaluation carried out?

In order to answer the question, 'What was the result of past actions?' an evaluator must work through four distinct stages in the evaluation process:

1   Designing the evaluation system;
2   Choosing data-collection methods;
3   Developing standards for interpreting the data;
4   Interpreting and using the results of the evaluation.

---

1   It is common in some of the literature on evaluation to differentiate processes and activities from *outputs*. Outputs are the products of processes: decisions or tangible goods or services provided. They can be counted (e.g. the number of interviews conducted by an employment counsellor, number of reports written, etc.) In applied and practical terms, however, outputs ae often difficult to distinguish from processes; indeed they are simply ways of expressing in shorthand fashion the summation of a set of processes or activities. For example, the key activity of an employment counsellor is interviewing. It is called the interview process. These activities can be counted and the number produced is the counsellor output called 'number of interviews conducted'. Because of this conceptual closeness, therefore, we will include output as a part of process evaluation.

1 Designing the system

- Why is this being done? (e.g. is it for formative or summative purposes?)
- What is to be evaluated? (e.g. programmes/functions, organizations or systems?)
- What type of evaluation will be used? (e.g. outcome, process or input?)
- Who will do it and when? (e.g. will outside evaluation experts be used? Will the evaluatees be involved?)

2 Data collection

- Quantitative (e.g. numerical counts, questionnaire surveys);
- Qualitative (interviews, observations, case studies).

3 Evaluation standards

- How will the evaluator know what the results mean?
- What is success and what is failure?
- What will indicate that a problem exists?

There are two basic kinds of standards:

- *Absolute standards.* These are previously identified targets against which the programme, organization or system is measured. There are clear indications of how close the evaluatee has come to the specified standards.
- *Relative standards.* Rather than using a priori targets, an evaluatee's results may be compared with the results of others or to the evaluatee's results from some previous period. *Benchmarks* are comparisons with results achieved by others. The evaluation result may be better, the same as or worse than the others, but there is no known absolute standard. *Time-based* comparisons look at the results achieved by the evaluatee across a range of time periods (months, years). The evaluation result is a trend in performance over time that is rising or falling.

4 Analysis and action

- Why did this result occur? (Was it because the evaluatees were poorly selected or trained? Was it because of a change in conditions beyond their control? Was it because of inadequate funding? Poor management?)
- Should something be changed? (Should the programme be dropped? More money invested?)
- What do these results tell us about what can be done better?

17.3 Ideal and reality

The ideal evaluation process would involve the following:

1   A clear statement of its objectives. They should be S.M.A.R.T.: Specific, Measurable, Achievable, Relevant and Timebound (specific in terms of the time in which they are to be achieved).
2   A clear statement of the desired outcomes – both positive effects and the absence of negative 'side effects'. This means creating:

    a   Indicators or measures that fully reflect the desired outcomes and possible side effects;
    b   A process for interpreting the results of these measurements; that is, what are 'good', 'average' or 'poor' results? This means there must be one or more pre-established, absolute standards against which performance can be measured in a given time period, or relative standards that allow comparisons with others or with the evaluatee over time.

3   Choice of methods for producing the data on the indicators which are timely and feasible to use in terms of cost and effort. They must also be valid (measure what they intend to measure) and reliable (produce consistently accurate results every time they are used).
4   To carry out the analysis of the results, there should be 'logic models' or conceptual frameworks of two kinds:

    a   'Measurement' logic models make clear the assumed links between input indicators and process indicators, process indicators and outcome indicators and outcome indicators and goals. They should also identify the other factors that affect the indicators at each stage but are not directly controllable by those responsible. (These are known by economists as the 'constraints' within which the evaluatee must work.) Finally, they should attempt to predict possible side effects and show how these will be measured.
    b   'Level of focus' logic models link evaluations between levels; that is, they make explicit the links between evaluations of individuals, programmes or organizational units, organizations and systems or subsystems.

17.4 Problems with the ideal evaluation process

When it comes to the evaluation of people, programmes, functions, organizations or systems in the non-profit world, the pitfalls and difficulties are significant (see Herman 1990; Herman and Renz 1997; Tassie *et al.* 1998). They arise from two basic sources:

1   Those that are due to inherent technical difficulties in the design that can cast serious doubt on the conclusions of the evaluation; and

2   Those that are the result of the psychosocial reactions that occur when people are subjected to evaluation by others.

Technical problems with the evaluation process

While the ideal evaluation process ought to start with a clear statement of goals, in reality arriving at such statements is often very difficult. Developing even clearer statements of outcome indicators that fully and unambiguously reflect these goals is even more difficult. For example, at the system level, the aim of a government department may be to improve the 'quality of citizenship' of the populace by 'ensuring a high level of appreciation of our heritage'. Many museums, ethnic associations, historical-site preservation groups and other organizations exist to help achieve this general goal. But the difficulty of creating a clear and widely shared definition of 'appreciation of our heritage' is formidable. At the very least there will likely be considerable disagreement among evaluators and the various evaluatees about the definition; after which will come the equally difficult problem of identifying the best indicators for measuring this.

Once goals are stated clearly, the connection between goals and outcomes may seem a simple enough technical challenge; yet the history of evaluation is rife with examples of failure at this stage. Again, the anecdote at the beginning of this chapter illustrates the point. A critical evaluation system design problem is that the choice of only a few specific outcome measures often cannot begin to capture the full range and complexity of the effects caused by the programme, organization or system interventions. How does one create measures that fully reflect the mission of an art gallery to 'enliven and enrich the human spirit through exposure to art' or even of a simple programme in a community service agency 'to improve the quality of life of frail elderly seniors' in its district?

Once outcomes are established, methods must be put in place to obtain the desired data, such as statistical reporting systems and attitude measurement systems. These methods are often exceedingly difficult and costly to create and maintain over time. A large percentage of non-profit organizations have little or no money to invest in developing sophisticated evaluation tools, or the skills to implement them. Even when an external evaluator such as a government bureau specifies what information is to be reported many small non-profit agencies do not have to capacity to do this job properly.

While creating evaluation systems is fraught with technical problems, interpreting the results of what they produce is even more difficult because of the logical fallacies identified earlier. This is due to the inherent weakness of the logic models (either implicit or explicit) on which the evaluation systems are based.

Problems with measurement logic models

Sometimes, for practical reasons, all that can be gathered are input and/or process data. However, the connection between engaging in certain activities and producing certain outcomes can be influenced by other conditions not controllable by those carrying out the activities; hence it is difficult to 'prove' that the activities caused the outcomes.

Problems with level of focus logic models

Because of the methodological difficulties of measuring things at the organization-wide and system-wide levels, some evaluators suggest that only programmes should be evaluated because only programmes have sufficiently specific and measurable objectives. The problem is that programmes themselves are ultimately only means to larger ends. They are meant to contribute to the overall mission of an organization, or of a larger social system, usually along with many other programmes. However, these links are often not explicitly stated and therefore frequently not tested, which means that a programme may be shown to be a great success on its own terms, but actually not be of value when compared with other programmes in the organization, or when compared with other programmes contributing to the larger system mission. Finally, even if the interlevel logic model is tested in some way, the problem of the contaminating influence of unknown or uncontrollable variables can arise to confuse the interpretation of the results. So 'proving' that programme x provides more 'bang for the buck' than programmes y or z becomes exceedingly difficult (Schuster 1997).

Psychosocial problems with the evaluation process

There are several variations on this theme.

1 The 'look-good-avoid-blame' phenomenon

Most people prefer to succeed and, if there is a failure, prefer not to be seen as responsible for it. This is the 'Look-Good-Avoid-Blame' (LGAB) mindset. Formal evaluation processes often proclaim that they are not being carried out for the purpose of judging those responsible (i.e. that they are formative rather than summative). The intent is to simply reveal any problems that might exist and provide information to help resolve them. The difficulty is that, in spite of all the assurances to the contrary, many evaluatees believe in their hearts that, if an evaluation reveals problems, they will be blamed; or, conversely, if the evaluation results are positive, they can take the credit. The behaviour of elected officials when economic conditions improve or worsen is only one of the more vivid examples of this tendency.

Therefore, when an LGAB attitude prevails, the evaluation process likely will be a 'political' one. The evaluatees will focus on whatever the evaluation indicators are and will do what they can to show the desired results. Or, if the results look bad in spite of their efforts, they will go to whatever lengths are necessary to explain the results as being beyond their control. This self-serving tendency is well recognized in the system of public auditing of finances. It is predicated on the belief that a certain percentage of people who are responsible for other people's money might be tempted to be less than accurate in accounting for its use. Hence the evaluators have created the separate, specialized and highly controlled profession of public accounting and a system of auditing to provide assurance that money has been spent as the providers intended it to be spent. The problem is that more complex evaluations of goal attainment are not amenable to the application of the kind of rigorous standards that are used in tracking financial expenditures.

As we have seen, outcome indicators often fail to capture the full intent of goals. When the LGAB phenomenon is operating, these inadequate indicators become substitutes for goals as the evaluatees seek to 'look good'. This is known as the 'goal displacement' phenomenon (Herman 1990). The case of the immigrant-aid organization offering English language training discussed above illustrates this point. The indicator chosen to represent the goal – number of successful course completions – became the goal while the real goal of helping as many people as possible learn English was forgotten. In this case, goal achievement was actually harmed by the temptation to admit only those applicants with a high potential for success.

2 *The subjective interpretation of reality (SIR) phenomenon*

The other key psychosocial tendency which creates major problems for evaluation systems arises when evaluation data must be interpreted and explained. We have already seen how frail the logic models are which underlie evaluations. When it comes to analysing almost any aspect of human behaviour, there are too many variables and there is too little control over those variables to permit solid conclusions about causal connections. For every human behaviour, there are many theories offered as explanation; few of which can be conclusively proven, which is one of the reasons for the constant flow of new ideas in fields such as child rearing, managing people, education, how to handle chronic welfare dependency and the treatment of mental illness.

In spite of the lack of fully proven theories, however, decisions about complex social problems must be made. Those who make such decisions would usually say they make them on the basis of empirical evidence, but since such evidence is inevitably inconclusive, they also base them on their pre-existing beliefs and attitudes about 'what works'. In other words, most evaluation results are interpreted subjectively and different people can interpret the same data many ways (Herman and Renz 1997; Tassie *et al.* 1998).

The combination of the LGAB and SIR phenomena makes it likely that the evaluation process will be a 'political' one. Some evaluatees may resist evaluation in the first place because of the fear that it will reveal poor results for which they will be blamed. Others may attempt to distort the evaluation data once the process is implemented so the data will make them look good. And, both evaluatees and evaluators may interpret the final results to support predetermined positions (Tassie *et al.* 1996).

17.5 What is the role of evaluation in the public–non-profit sector relationship?

When the public sector provides money to non-profit organizations an account-ability relationship is created. This relationship also exists when governments pass laws which in any way regulate the behaviour of non-profits. Being account-able requires that one attempts to show that the resources with which one has been entrusted have been effectively and efficiently used to achieve the purpose for which they were given or, in the case of the law, that one has complied with it. The evaluation process is simply the means by which accountability manifests itself. Thus, evaluation occurs in government–non-profit sector relationships whenever there is a contract, grant or law in place and it involves the government making judgements about how well the non-profit organizations are doing.

But what about the evaluation of public sector organizations by non-profit organizations? This occurs when the non-profit organization perceives itself as one of the 'publics' which the government organization is created to serve. For example, governments pass laws and create programmes to benefit many different members of society and many non-profits are created to represent the causes of various groups. They constantly make judgements about the effective-ness of government policies and, on the basis of these judgements, advocate for change. Many of these judgements are based on evaluation systems of their own creation which suffer all the problems of systems used by governments to measure non-profits.

In addition, a special kind of problem arises when the non-profit is *also* dependent on government for money. If it feels its funder is not doing a satisfactory job, how much can it afford to bite the hand that feeds it? This means that true reciprocal evaluation between government and non-profits is quite rare.

17.6 Common pitfalls that occur in the public–non-profit-sector relationship

While there is no question that public sector and non-profit sector organizations are constantly appraising one another's actions, the question is *how well do they do it?* We have already seen in a general conceptual way how easy it is for evaluations to go awry. What happens in practice with specific public–non-profit sector evaluations?

Prior research into the nature and impact of effectiveness evaluations in the non-profit sector does not yield an optimistic picture (see Ashford and Clarke 1996; Cutt *et al.* 1996; Forbes 1998; Herman 1990, 1992; Herman and Renz 1977; Paton 1998; Sargeant and Kaehler 1998; Schuster 1997; Sheehan 1996; Taylor and Sumariwalla 1993). The present author's own research with colleagues in Canada (Murray and Tassie 1994; Tassie *et al.* 1996, 1998) confirms the general situation found in the other literature cited above.

This research involved the close observation of evaluation efforts by funders of a small group of agencies to which they gave money. One was a provincial-government ministry, one was a municipal government department and one was a private federated funding agency (common in North America but not elsewhere). Four agencies were studied in depth in Toronto and three more in Victoria, British Columbia. The methodology was qualitative and involved observation, interviews and document analysis with both funders and fundees between 1993 and 1996.

Space prohibits a detailed discussion of the results of this research but they can be briefly summarized as follows.

Evaluator pitfalls

- Inferring outcomes from processes/activities/outputs without a prior logic model.
- Drawing unsubstantiated conclusions about the state of larger systems from lower level indicators; about organizations from programme-level indicators; or about programmes from individual-level indicators.
- Conversely, failing to think about the connections between levels; for example, failing to predict side effects or evaluating a programme with no thought given to the implications of the evaluation for the organization's overall mission.
- Use of weak methods for gathering data (e.g. too quantitative, too qualitative, invalid, unreliable).
- Overemphasis on informal methods of gathering data such as personal impressions and 'reputation' (the unsystematically gathered comments of others).
- Biased interpretation of evaluation results because of prior ideological beliefs and personal connections with evaluatees.
- Use of evaluation results to criticize the evaluatees instead of indicating problems which should be addressed.

Evaluatee pitfalls

- 'Information snowjobs' – providing an excess of information in a disorganized and confusing state to the evaluator.
- Delay – taking excessively long periods to gather the information desired by the evaluator.
- Distortion – providing deliberately misleading information or withholding pertinent information.
- Personalization – obscuring the bigger picture by focusing on a few individual cases; for example, bringing forth one or two people who will claim to have been helped by a particular programme while avoiding statistical data dealing with all those the programme was intended to serve.
- Dependence on symbols and metaphors – instead of 'hard data', using emotional and colourful language to sell an image of the programme or organization as successful.

- Substituting needs for outcomes – trying to substitute a focus on results with a focus on the great need there is for the services provided by a programme or organization.
- Buck-passing – if evaluations produce negative results, placing the cause for them on others or conditions beyond one's control (the LGAB phenomenon).

17.7 Is it possible to improve the evaluation process between public and non-profit sector organizations?

Evaluation will always be a political process, especially in government–non-profit relationships. Technical problems, faulty logic models and the LGAB and SIR phenomena will always exist. Some infer from this conclusion that there is therefore little point in attempting to mount formal evaluation systems. These cynics (or realists, depending on one's viewpoint) would argue that whether it is government organizations evaluating non-profits, or vice versa, each will gather only the information they want (overlooking information they think might be inconvenient) by whatever means is easiest and then use it to support whatever story they want to tell.

On the other hand, without denying all the problems identified in this chapter, it is still possible to argue that it is worth at least trying to improve the level of discourse between evaluators and evaluatees by obtaining more and better information on performance, which can be done in two ways: coercively or cooperatively. Using the coercive approach, government funders simply insist on certain predetermined evaluation systems and standards as part of the contract covering the funding. The approach is much the same as that applied for financial accountability by means of the laws and professional codes governing auditing and accounting practices. For programme or organization evaluation government-appointed 'professional' evaluators descend on the organization or programme being evaluated and carry out the preset evaluation procedure.

As might be imagined, this is the least preferable way of formalizing evaluation, in part because of the always formidable technical difficulties in creating the system but mostly because distorting the data to 'look good and avoid blame' is so tempting when one is being coerced. It is also much more easy to do than falsifying the records required for a simple financial audit. Again, the anecdote at the beginning of this chapter illustrates the point.

By far the better approach is a cooperative one which begins with evaluators and evaluatees agreeing that a jointly developed evaluation system is desirable. The following conclusions are offered as guidelines for future efforts of this kind.

17.8 Conclusions

The introduction to this chapter pointed out that the problems with evaluation systems could be clustered under two headings: 'technical' and 'psychosocial'. To improve the process requires work in both areas.

Fixing the technical problems

It is necessary to realize that the logical fallacies that plague the evaluation process can never be overcome, only minimized. The 'perfect fix' requires knowing the causes of things and, in the realm of human behaviour, there is far too little known about causes. Indeed, many argue that deterministic theories of behaviour are not possible (Herman and Renz 1997). So, at best, one can only hope to make the evaluation process somewhat more conscious, transparent and rational. How to do that?

1   It is probably too soon to promulgate absolute standards of performance and 'best practices' for non-profit programmes and organizations. Too little is known to warrant proclamations such as: 'organizations that spend less than 60 per cent of their income on direct programme costs are inefficient'; or 'all persons working in a counselling capacity must have a Master of Social Work degree'. Premature promulgation of best practice guidelines as the one best way to perform will likely end up supporting fads and fashions rather than achieving real improvement in performance.

2   Rather than setting absolute standards, the emphasis should be on developing more and better kinds of relative standard – benchmark comparisons with others and trends over time.

3   To develop better relative standards there should be more emphasis placed on building infrastructure within the non-profit sector – the equivalent of industry associations, and boards of trade within the commercial sector. In countries such as the UK, US and Canada, there are a few geographically oriented bodies concerned about local communities such as district social planning councils. There are also some sectorally oriented bodies such as the associations of theatres or of organizations that work with youths at risk or the disabled. But many sectors have no intermediary body and those that exist have few resources for gathering information on performance effectiveness in their area of interest. New bodies need to be created and more support given to helping them create databases on the issues they deal with (Osborne 1999).

4   These intermediary bodies should also take a lead in developing standardized methods for gathering information on the performance of organizations and programmes in their area and reach out to help them measure their own performance to compare with others.

5   Much more work needs to be done by evaluators in addressing the logical fallacies that distort the value of most evaluation systems, which means more training in how to think through, in advance, the connections between programmes/functions and organization-wide missions and between organizations and results at larger system levels. It also means more research into how processes/activities connect to outcomes, how to establish the validity and reliability of measurement indicators and how to predict and detect harmful side effects.

Fixing the psychosocial problems

The 'Look Good, Avoid Blame' phenomenon will always be present when evaluatees believe the results will be used to make decisions affecting their lives. It may be *reduced* if evaluatees have influence in deciding the following critical elements of the evaluation process:

- What will be evaluated?
- How will it be done?
- What standards will be applied to the data?
- How will the final results be interpreted and used?

This latter element also addresses the 'Subjective Interpretation of Reality' (SIR) problem in that both evaluatee and evaluator agree beforehand on how to analyse and act on the results of the evaluation.

Finally, for evaluation to succeed, attention must be paid to creating an entire 'culture of accountability' (Connors and Smith 1999) in which acceptance of responsibility is not something that is seen as threatening but is energizing and an incentive to learn and change. The *experiences* of all those connected with a programme, organization or larger system must be based on mutual competence, trust and respect between evaluators and evaluatees. These experiences then create *beliefs* that this atmosphere will exist in the future. These beliefs then drive *actions* aimed at constant improvement and the actions produce *results*.

17.9 Evaluation and the public–non-profit partnerships: a final word

A large proportion of the formal relationships between government and non-profit organizations involve government money going to support non-profit-organization programmes. Whatever the official or legal arrangements, this creates an accountability relationship in which evaluation occurs either formally or informally. At present this relationship is predominantly characterized by:

- Minimal formal evaluation systems beyond financial controls;
- A focus on process rather than on outcome measures;
- A tendency by evaluatees to 'look good and avoid blame' and for evaluators not to want to do much to change this situation.

It is unlikely that attempts to produce new and better tools for evaluation which external evaluators can impose on non-profits to produce a 'report card' on their performance will be successful. Evaluators can always subvert such systems to their own ends.

On the other hand, the *process* of engaging in a periodic dialogue about performance can often be as beneficial as a measurement system that emerges from it, which holds *provided* the process is carried out jointly by both evaluators and eva-luatees in an atmosphere of mutual trust and respect.

References

Ashford, J. and Clarke, J. (1996) 'Grant monitoring by charities: The process of grant-making and evaluation', *Voluntas* 7: 279–99.

Connors, R. and Smith, T. (1999) *Journey to the Emerald City: Achieve a Competitive Edge by Creating a Culture of Accountability*, Paramus, NJ: Prentice-Hall.

Cutt, J., Bragg, D., Balfour, K., Murray, V. and Tassie, W. (1996) 'Non-profits accommodate the information demands of public and private funders', *Non-profit Management and Leadership*, 7: 45–67.

Forbes, D. P. (1998) 'Measuring the unmeasurable: Empirical studies of non-profit organization effectiveness', *Non-profit and Voluntary Sector Quarterly* 27(2): 159–82.

Herman, R. (1990) 'Methodological issues in studying the effectiveness of nongovern-mental and non-profit organizations', *Non-profit and Voluntary Sector Quarterly* 19: 293–306.

Herman, R. and Renz, D. (1997) 'Multiple constituencies and the social construction of non-profit organization effectiveness', *Non-profit and Voluntary Sector Quarterly* 26: 185–206.

Murray, V. and Tassie, W. (1994) 'Evaluation of the effectiveness of non-profit orga-nizations', in R. Herman (ed.) *The Jossey-Bass Handbook of Non-profit Management and Leadership*, San Francisco: Jossey-Bass, pp. 303–24.

Osborne, S. (1999) *Promoting Local Voluntary Community Action*, York: Joseph Rowntree Foundation.

Paton, R. (1998) Performance Measurement, Benchmarking and Public Confidence, London: Charities Aid Foundation.

Sargeant, A. and Kaehler, J. (1998) *Benchmarking Charity Costs*, London: Charities Aid Foundation.

Schuster, R. (1997) 'The performance of performance indicators in the arts', *Non-profit Management and Leadership* 7: 253–69.

Sheehan, R. (1996) 'Mission accomplishment as philanthropic organization effective-ness', *Non-profit and Voluntary Sector* 25: 110–23.

Tassie, W., Murray, V. and Cutt, J. (1998) 'Evaluating social service agencies: Fuzzy pictures of organizational effectiveness', *Voluntas* 9(1) 53–68.

Tassie, W., Murray, V., Cutt, J. and Bragg, D. (1996) 'Rationality and politics: What really goes on when funders evaluate the performance of fundees?', *Non-profit and Voluntary Sector Quarterly* 25: 347–63.

Taylor, M. and Sumariwalla, R. (1993) 'Evaluating non-profit effectiveness: Overcoming the barriers', in D. Young (ed.) *Governing, Leading and Managing Non-profit Organizations*, San Francisco: Jossey-Bass, pp. 93–116.

18 What makes partnerships work?

Chris Huxham and Siv Vangen

18.1 The collaboration dilemma

Whatever the reason for the initiation of a partnership, the essence of partnership rhetoric may be summed up in the notion of *collaborative advantage*. We have developed this concept to capture the idea that the advantage to be gained when members from one organization act collaboratively with members of another organization occurs only when *something is achieved which could not have been achieved without the collaboration* (Huxham and Macdonald 1992; Huxham 1996a). It can be argued that the achievement of collaborative advantage is the ultimate goal for all partnership initiatives and that this can be an extremely powerful way of addressing social issues. For example, the director of a not-for-profit organization recently described to us in graphic detail the story of how she had convened and led a major multi-sectoral initiative in a deprived locality of her city. The primary aim of this was to provide childcare facilities for those living in the area. Indirectly, this was intended as a significant contribution to tackling economic issues in the area through encouraging parents into employment.

Many partnerships, however, do not get near to achieving collaborative advantage. Some typical symptoms were encapsulated eloquently by the manager of an economic and social regeneration partnership with whom we worked:

> The partnership was set up with government funding ... By the time I was appointed nine months later people were refusing to come to meetings because they were not achieving action ... There was a lot of conflict between two of the key agencies ... My predecessor left after nine months *and I think I know why* ...

We understood the manager's comment about her predecessor to imply that managing this tense situation was not a comfortable or rewarding experience. The key agencies to which she referred were the local authority and the local economic development agency, which were apparently vying for the leadership role. Other involved agencies, with responsibilities for housing, the natural environment, health and so on each came with their own sense of what the partnership should be aiming to achieve. A clear divergence of views eventually emerged between whether it should maintain (only) a strategic role or whether it should also be involved in community-based activities.

Those involved in partnerships frequently comment that little is being achieved. We regularly hear people complain that they are forever attending meetings but that there is little in the way of material output. Where achievements are made, they comment that the process of getting there has been slow and painful in the sense that the various parties have found it difficult to agree on actions, responsibilities and so on. It is not uncommon for people to argue that the positive outputs have happened *despite* the partnership rather than because of it! We have called this phenomenon *collaborative inertia* (Huxham 1996b).

This then poses a dilemma for those who wish to promote collaborative activity. If collaborative advantage is the hoped-for outcome, why is collaborative inertia so often the practical result?

Throughout this chapter, concepts aimed at capturing our current understanding of collaboration are presented along with snapshots of examples provided by many of the partnerships with which we have worked. In the next section, we start by providing an overview of our research approach and the way in which it has shaped our understanding of collaboration. We then explore some process-oriented factors – *managing aims, managing language and culture,* and *managing trust and power* – and features inherent in the structure of partnerships – *ambiguity, complexity and dynamics* – which tend to drive them towards inertia. Our aim is to provide an understanding of the forces that tend to cause inertia and to provide a sense of the associated tensions that need to be juggled in order to move forward. The chapter concludes by indicating the broad nature of the challenges faced when working in partnerships.

18.2 Exploring collaborative inertia: our approach to understanding partnership

Our understanding of the management issues facing those involved in partnerships has been built over a prolonged research period involving many projects, both large and small. Our approach has been inspired by the action-research paradigm described by Eden and Huxham (1996) though not all aspects strictly fit within the criteria for action research presented there. Much of the research data has been gained through interventions in partnerships or with individual members of them. In these, we have taken the role of 'consultants', facilitators or workshop leaders. Many of these have been one-off, single-day affairs but others have run over many months or years. In addition to these formal interventions, we have had many informal conversations with practitioners involved in partnership. Typically, they provide us with rich, if short, snippets of description of their experiences and feelings. During or immediately after each of these formal or informal interactions, we have recorded – primarily in the form of notes but sometimes also using computer-stored cause maps, flip charts, video and tape recordings – the expressed experiences, views, action-centred dilemmas and actual actions of the practitioners involved. Through these interventions and conversations we have thus been able both to develop a conceptual understanding of the issues involved in managing partnerships and to test out the relevance and usefulness of our conceptualization for practitioners.

Our conceptualization is structured in terms of a set of interrelated collaboration *themes*. Each theme represents a broad category of issues that have relevance to the management of partnerships. Most themes arise out of concerns *repeatedly* mentioned by practitioners as causing pain and reward (Huxham and Vangen 1996), but others arise because we, as researchers, perceive a conceptual linkage between comments made by practitioners in totally different contexts from each other (Huxham and Vangen 1998a). For each theme we have built up a structured description of what *can* happen in partnerships in relation to the theme issues. These descriptions recognize that there are linkages between the themes. Our intention is to capture the complexity inherent in the reality of partnership management, while presenting a picture that will be immediately recognizable to practitioners. This is in contrast to other approaches to understanding what makes partnerships work, which typically either focus on the identification of a range of success factors (see e.g. Doz 1994; Gray 1985; Long and Arnold 1995; Lorange and Roos 1993; Mattesich and Monsey 1992; Pearce 1997) or seek to identify stages or phases in the process of collaborating (Das and Teng 1997; Kanter 1994; McCann 1984). Although we shall only be able to cover a subset of the themes and discussion of these will necessarily be limited to a summary of some key issues, the intention is to provide a *sense* of the forces which tend to promote *collaborative inertia* and hence of the challenges facing those determined to achieve *collaborative advantage*. Further discussions of our approach to theory building can be found in Huxham and Vangen (1998a, b).

18.3 Aspects of managing partnership

Managing aims

Of all the issues raised by the practitioners with whom we have worked, the most frequently heard concerns the agreement of collaborative aims. Typically, practitioners assert that having a common, agreed and/or clear set of aims helps partners to work together to operationalize policies. They also, however, quote endless examples of experiences in which they have not been able to reach satisfactory agreement on what the aims should be. We see many practitioners who express a great deal of frustration over this problem. They seem to imply that if only the partners could agree on what to do, actually doing it would be a simple matter. What is it then that gets in the way of agreement?

Paradoxically, the very principle of collaborative advantage is central to this. It is usually the bringing together of the *different* resources of each partner that provides the potential for advantage. The different resources are, however, the result of differences in organizational purpose (Eden and Huxham 1999;

Vangen *et al.* 1994). Thus, although partners may ostensibly agree on a broad label for a partnership's purpose – at least to the extent that they are willing to be involved – they will each have different reasons for being there. Commonly, some will have much less interest in it than others and thus be less willing to commit to aims that have significant resource implications. Some will only be involved at all as a consequence of external (usually governmental) pressure. Some partners will be looking to the partnership to help satisfy agendas that are relevant only to their organization and some individuals will be looking to satisfy personal agendas this way. Many of these organizational and individual agendas will be 'hidden'. With all this in the background, it is commonly difficult for individual representatives simply to grasp what may be motivating (or not) others to take part; let alone to find a way to address the different concerns of all involved.

The history of the relationship between partners also sometimes gets in the way of agreeing mutually beneficial aims. For example, in the UK, changes in government policies over the past decade have meant that many public organizations have been deconstructed, partially privatized and thrown into competitive supply-chain relationships, through competitive tendering arrangements, with organizations which were previously constituent parts of themselves. These same organizations are now sometimes being required to act collaboratively. A manager with whom we worked from one such organization, who was concerned to make a partnership of this sort work, not surprisingly found herself grappling with the huge tensions which arose when the two organizations tried to develop collaborative aims, given their history of enforced competition.

There is a dilemma here in terms of the extent to which partners should try to tie down collaborative aims. Although there are obvious potential benefits to be had from bringing discussions about this openly into the partnership forum, there is also the potential danger that irreconcilable differences will be unearthed. Sometimes the pragmatic solution has to be to find a way to move on without explicit agreement about exactly where it is going. In this case, what is needed is *enough of* a sense of direction for initial actions to be taken, but, as one partnership manager argued, any statement of aims must be 'vague enough that none of the parties involved can disagree with it'.

Managing language and culture

Managing aims is thus likely to be a difficult task. The process of doing this is often made much more difficult because of differences between the organizations or professional groups in terms of their embedded professional languages and in terms of their organizational cultures. There are some obvious, stereotypical differences between the commercial language and cultural norms and values of business as compared with the socially oriented language and associated cultural norms and values of public service organizations. Not-for-profit organizations – which now play such an important role in service delivery and regeneration –

may be stereotyped as different again with values associated with empowerment and equality embedded in their language and culture.

Whether or not these sectoral stereotypes are real, they are only a small part of the picture. Significant misunderstandings can happen between business organizations, between public organizations and between not-for-profit organizations because of the different professional languages and associated values that they work with. For example, in the early days following the Community Care Act of 1990 in the UK which required the social services departments and the Health Service to work together to care in the community for those with certain categories of illness, there was evidence of differences in understanding between health care professionals and social services professionals over such basic terminology as 'care management' and 'purchasing' (OPM 1991). Representatives on partnerships from community organizations – who may not be employed in professional roles in their normal jobs – sometimes express extreme frustration and real anger at what they view as professional jargon being used in meetings. Though this may be seen by the speaker as normal, non-specialist, articulate language, it can have the practical effect of excluding community representatives from discussion.

Any loss in subtlety of mutual understanding is likely to hinder the progress in many ways. The difficult process of discussing aims, which was the subject of the last section, will certainly be effected by this. It is not only language that causes frustration, however. Embedded in organizational culture is a mass of organizational procedures – the way an organization does things (Martin 1992; Schein 1985). Formal procedures can add to the problem of reaching formal agreement by making the process tedious. For example, if decisions relevant to the partnership have to be approved through established committee structures of a large bureaucratic public organization or by the head office of a multinational company or charity, there can be considerable delay; by which time the moment of relevance may have passed. This can be particularly problematic if decision cycles are out of synchrony in the partner organizations, especially if any organization refuses to approve the decision in its initial form. Clearly, these kinds of organizations are unnatural bedfellows, in this respect, for the Small and Medium Sized Enterprises (SMEs), small community organizations or relatively autonomous public agencies with which they are often in collaboration.

Decision-making processes are not the only respect in which organizational procedures may differ in ways that hamper progress. Often it is the substance of the decision that would be different in each organization. One situation often encountered, for example, is the employment of staff to the partnership. In this context we have encountered differences in norms about trade union recognition, salary scales, whether to advertise externally as well as within the organizations and so on.

Managing trust and power

The difficulties of communication and progress described above can, if not managed, characterize and dominate the entire working of a partnership. A conclusion drawn both by many authors and by many of the practitioners, with whom we work, is that it is essential that the parties involved have a trusting relationship with each other (Das and Teng 1998; Lane and Bachmann 1998). While there is little doubt that such a relationship would make a significant difference, there are, in practice, many obstacles to achieving it.

One significant category of obstacles to achieving a trusting relationship arises out of issues concerned with power relationships. Power struggles are one aspect of this. For example, the manager from the economic and social regeneration partnership, quoted in Section 18.1, commented that the two major public agencies in the area were continuously 'fighting' over which should take the lead. One of these was the elected local authority, the other a central government agency with a responsibility for economic development in the area. Both could reasonably argue that it was their role to lead any regeneration initiative in the area.

Perceptions about the power differences play a very significant role in hampering trust building. The power is often seen to be tied to the 'purse strings' or to any 'lead organization' formally nominated by a funding body such as government. Individuals from community organizations, for example, often express extreme frustration over feelings of disempowerment when working with large public agencies. It is our observation that those who hold the purse strings or formal 'lead' positions generally do behave as though they hold the power.

Viewed from the outside, however, the power relationships do not always seem so unidirectional. It is often the case that apparently weaker partners are uniquely able to provide some form of essential – though not financial – resource. Minimally – but very powerfully – this may be simply that their involvement allows the partners to satisfy a condition of the funding body that an organization of this type be involved. They may also have resources in the form of, for example, expertise or access to communities or markets that other partners could not substitute. The 'threat of exit' is therefore frequently available. The not-for-profit-sector director who led the childcare partnership described in the opening paragraphs of this chapter was very conscious of the access she had to this source of power. She seemed skilled at knowing when and how to use the threat of walking out to gain ends she regarded as socially important. Most individuals involved in partnerships are, however, less experienced and less skilled. So long as some members of some partner organizations perceive themselves to be vulnerable, and members of others perceive themselves to be powerful, they will act as though this is the reality, which is unlikely to foster a cooperative or trusting attitude.

In some public–private partnerships, however, the facility for exiting is not equally available to parties. For example, the UK Government's Private Finance Initiative makes provision for private sector business organizations to fund, on a commercial basis, aspects of public projects or service delivery (HM Treasury 1995, 1997). School or hospital buildings are examples. Officials from public sector organizations involved in such initiatives have argued that such situations feel very unequal, because while the private sector organization may, for example, sell on its share of the business, the public organization does not have this freedom. Thus even though initial contracts may be negotiated with a great deal of care and attention, those in the public sector organizations remain suspicious about whether any future private sector partner imposed on them would honour the many unwritten aspects of the initial agreement.

Our experiences with those working in private sector partnerships would suggest that public officials have reason to be cautious in presuming that their partners can be fully trusted to behave as they would wish, which is not intended to imply that business organizations, or their managers, inherently lack the appropriate level of goodwill. However, despite the arguments about the value of alliances in recent business strategy literature (see e.g. Doz and Hamel 1998; Bergquist *et al.* 1995), the commercial pressures on business organizations do seem to militate against fully cooperative behaviour. One production manager in an engineering firm told us, for example, that while he was actively working in a formal cooperative relationship with one key part supplier, he was also looking out for alternative suppliers. While he recognized both ethical and practical dilemmas in this, he felt that this dual approach was the only practical way of ensuring that he would be able to secure supplies at a price that would allow his company to produce at costs which their market would bear.

Many authors write about trust as though it were a precondition for successful collaboration (Kumar 1996; Sydow 1998). From a practical point of view, this presents a dilemma to those considering setting up a partnership where there is no history of relationship between (at least some of) the participating organizations or where previous relationships have not engendered mutual trust. In such circumstances, it is probably worth collaborating only if very significant ends are envisaged. In many cases, however, externally imposed constraints or incentives are perceived to remove the luxury of considering the option not to collaborate. This then begs the further question of how trust can be built and maintained in situations where, on the one hand, the power relationships are perceived to be uneven and, on the other, they are seen as too equal, because no individual or organization has any hierarchical authority to enforce action (Vangen and Huxham, 1998).

Comments about trust building by those involved tend to relate to all of the collaboration themes. Typical suggestions are that it is important to: 'have clarity of purpose and objectives'; 'deal with power differences'; 'have leadership but do not allow anyone to take over'; 'have patience and understanding'; 'resolve different levels of commitment'; 'have equal ownership and no point scoring'; and so on. These suggestions are mirrored by researchers (Leifer and Mills 1996; Lewicki and Bunker 1996). While these provide good reminders of the variables which contribute to trust building, they do not provide much in the way of pragmatic help since each piece of advice brings with it its own collection of complications and dilemmas. As with the issue of managing aims, the pragmatic solution sometimes has to be to move on without dealing with all aspects of trust building. This probably means aiming for modest, but achievable, outcomes, in the first instance, becoming more ambitious only as success breeds a greater level

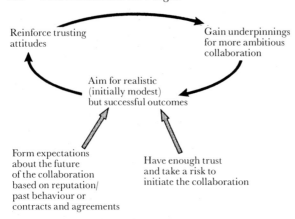

Figure 18.1 The trust-building loop

of trust. We have captured this process in the trust-building loop of Figure 18.1. It has to be recognized, however, that this 'small wins' approach (Bryson 1998), may be in contradiction to the demands of external funding bodies for demonstrable output. It may also be difficult to maintain the necessary stability for the cycle to continue, as Section 18.4 will demonstrate.

18.4 Partnership structure

Our discussion of the previous three themes has aimed to demonstrate that there are a number of forces that tend to drive partnership processes towards collaborative inertia rather than collaborative advantage. If space permitted, it would be possible to elaborate on many other themes of this type: balancing autonomy and accountability; managing the tensions surrounding democracy, equality and the sharing of credit; managing appropriate working processes; and so on (see Huxham 1993, 1996b; Huxham and Vangen 1996). Each of these themes identifies forces that could, alone, explain why participants often struggle to form joint agendas, let alone satisfactorily implement them. *In combination*, these forces can create a powerful barrier to effective joint working.

These process-oriented forces are, however, only a part of the picture. There are also a number of structural features that act to amplify the barrier. In broad terms, we have argued that partnerships tend to have ambiguous, complex and dynamic structures (Huxham and Vangen 1999a).

Ambiguity

A rather surprising characteristic of many situations is the lack of clarity about who the members are. For example, one of the authors has been attending, in an advisory capacity, the management committee meetings of a partnership of three member organizations. At the most recent meeting, a representative from a fourth organization was present. She had not attended – or been mentioned as absent from – the two previous meetings attended by the author. Although her organization's remit clearly lay in the area of the partnership's concern, it had never been mentioned as a partner and it did not appear in the partnership's documents. Nevertheless, she seemed well informed about the partnership, involved with its activities and appeared to have relevant paperwork dating back over the period of its existence. Representatives of the other three organizations treated her as though she was an accepted member of the committee. Exactly how they regarded her status and that of her organization is, as yet, still unclear to the author.

In another situation, the partnership administrator was unable to respond to an urgent request to list the partners without referring to documentation even though she had dealt with its day-to-day administration for over two years and even though the partners are clearly denoted in its publicity brochures, fairly small in number (nine) and listed on its headed letter paper. The reasons were almost certainly: first, that the partner organizations had differing statuses on the partnership, with two organizations being centrally involved and others taking a much more peripheral role and, second that organizations that were not officially members were also involved in its activities.

These examples are typical of the ambiguities that arise. Variety in status of individuals and organizations, and lack of clarity about what individuals represent is common and often leads members to be confused – or, at least, to lack mutual understanding – about who their partners are. Obviously this is not likely to help the process of negotiating aims or that of developing mutual understanding and trust.

Complexity

The problems of ambiguity can be exacerbated when, as often occurs, the structure is immensely complex. Figure 18.2 depicts the structure of an area regeneration partnership by way of illustration. The figure is based on a situation that we have been involved with; but we have many times been told that this diagram is typical of partnerships that others have experienced. The membership included a number of relevant local organizations such as the Housing Agency, the Health Board, the Chamber of Commerce, large local businesses and so on (represented by the circle on the left in Figure 18.2). The interests of 'the community', however, were represented by the Umbrella Group (represented by the circle near the centre towards the top of Figure 18.2) which was initiated, at the request of the Partnership, solely for this purpose. The Umbrella Group was thus both itself a collaboration of community organizations and part of the wider collaboration, the Regeneration Partnership. To complicate matters further, many of the organizations represented on the Umbrella Group were themselves collaborations, comprised of a mixture of community activists

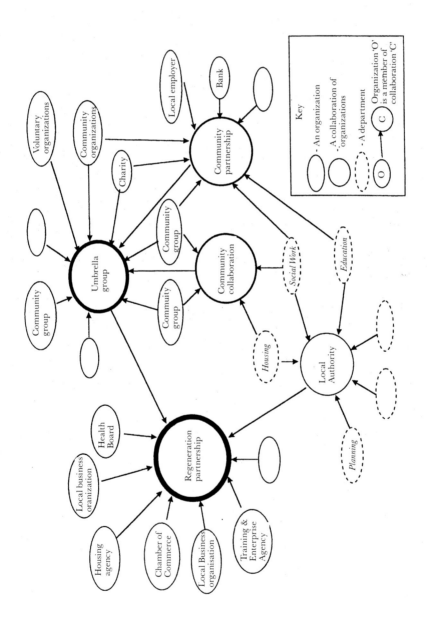

Figure 18.2 Typical structure of a regeneration partnership.

and officers of statutory and voluntary organizations (represented by the circles on the middle right of Figure 18.2). The local authority (represented by the circle at the bottom centre of Figure 18.2) was also a member. However, departments of the local authority, such as Social Services and Education, generally acted as autonomous units almost independently of each other. Representatives from these departments were involved in many of the community collaborative initiatives that were members of the Umbrella Group. Thus the Local Authority was represented both directly and indirectly through a large number of community collaborations and the Umbrella Group.

Despite the complexity of Figure 18.2, the depiction is a vast simplification of the reality of the situation it claims to describe. It is clear, however, even from this simplified representation, that the individuals involved are unlikely to be certain about what organization, collaboration or other constituency (if any) they and others represent or where the accountabilities of the partnership lie. It is thus very difficult for them to make sensitive judgements about how to act and how to interpret the actions of others.

Complex hierarchies of collaboration of this type are a common feature of partnerships. Additional complexities often arise out of concerns to be democratic and accountable as well as to tackle a wide range of related problem areas. For example, partnerships are sometimes designed with multiple layers of committees and steering groups or boards and often initiate (or co-opt) a range of cross-organizational working groups to tackle different aspects of the partnership agenda. Often the latter include individuals and organizations that are not formally a part of the collaboration. We have encountered working groups in which some or most of the members are unaware of the group's formal link to the parent partnership.

To make matters worse, there is a strong trend towards an increase in the number of partnerships set up to tackle public issues. In the UK, for example, the Government's focus on 'joined-up government' has led to a mass of policy incentives for local level partnerships (Cabinet Office 1999) to add to the already prolific EU funded schemes. Not surprisingly, we hear, repeatedly, people telling us that their initiative was set up in response to a funding availability. In some cases this has been a serendipitous means of helping the partner organizations to address a gap in their activities that they would like to fill. However, we have several times heard the comment:

> . . . 'this partnership was set up (only) to spend that government money that was on offer.'

The result in many localities has been the initiation of a large expansion in the number of cross-relating partnerships. The more eloquent of those with whom we have worked have alternatively described this situation as 'partnershipitis' and 'mad zone disease'. Many have expressed weariness with the situation and one complained of 'partnership fatigue'. More formally Stewart (1998) refers to 'pluralism in partnership' – the emergence of overlapping leadership roles as key local figures are present at evermore local meetings of separate but interlocking partnerships. Current research in Bristol (Sweeting *et al.* 1999) demonstrates just how complex the arrangements for partnership can be for some individuals. Figure 18.3 illustrates how twenty-two key people occupy fifty-six places on nine of the major Bristol partnership or joint-working structures.

Pluralism brings with it many other effects in addition to weariness. Where externally stimulated new initiatives overlap with activities that are already being carried out in a locality, they tend to shake up the established relationships. Often such initiatives specify – or at least suggest – not only which organizations should be involved but also which should take the lead. If this is in contradiction to the existing accepted roles for organizations in the area, then incentives intended to promote good relationships can instead be very destructive to social capital. One key player in a new government collaborative initiative put the problem succinctly:

> … 'this is a very good initiative in principle, but if I wanted to get there I wouldn't start from here.'

Clearly, if individuals participate in many partnerships, this significantly exacerbates the difficulty of interpreting what they are representing, and what they are accountable to, in any particular one. Our experience would suggest that individuals themselves are often unclear about their own representativeness and some have commented on the difficulty of juggling their 'multiple hats'. A consequence is bound to be a lack of clarity about the aims and values that they do – or could be expected to – bring. In addition, where the same representatives meet in several fora, they can move a partnership agenda forward in between formal meetings. Whether this is a deliberate power ploy or simply the consequence of ad hoc conversation, it can leave less connected partners – such as those indicated by the ovals in Figure 18.3 – in the cold. One community representative complained that the Social Work Department and Health Board representatives were forever doing this, because they met frequently in other contexts.

Dynamics

Coping with the ambiguity and complexity inherent in structures therefore provides a significant challenge to participants. In practice, the challenge is magnified because the structures tend to be dynamic. Government policies, for example, promote not only totally new initiatives, but also changes to the purposes of existing ones. Even without external pressures, the natural evolution of partnerships leads to changes in their purpose, if only because the initial joint purpose has been successfully addressed. Government policies also, frequently, lead to changes in the nature of the partner organizations. In the UK, for example, policies in the last decade alone have led to a new set of local authorities with new boundaries to both their physical locations and remits. They have also

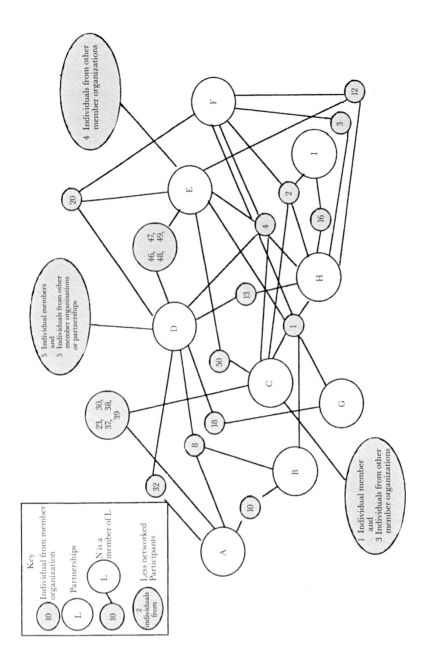

Figure 18.3 Multiple individual membership of urban partnerships (based on Sweeting *et al.* 1999)

306   *Chris Huxham and Siv Vangen*

led to several incarnations of Health Service organizations and development organizations. Business organizations are also affected by government policies, not the least in their responses to collaborative initiatives. Acquisitions, mergers and new start-ups, sell-offs, demergers and closures, together with restructuring are also common characteristics of business life.

The complex structures described in the last section (Section 18.4) are therefore relatively transitory. Organizations come and go either in response to changing purpose or because they themselves have changed. Not infrequently, key organizations cease to exist, and new relationships have to be developed to address the particular social issue. Individual representatives also come and go as they take on new roles within their organizations or move in or out of them altogether. The possibility of maintaining continuity is thus rare and so processes of building mutual understanding and trust must be continuously attended to. In many cases it has to be accepted that these will not be fully achieved before a change occurs. In these circumstances, the cycle of trust building suggested in Figure 18.1 is unlikely to be easy to maintain. In the words of one partnership manager:

> 'After two and a half years we are now beginning to get the hang of how to make this partnership work but we now have to assess whether the partners feel that there is a role left for the partnership which they would be prepared to support.'

18.5 The challenge of partnership

As stated at the start of this chapter, we have aimed to provide a sense of the kind of forces that have to be coped with by those aiming for positive outcomes from a partnership. The emphasis, so far, has been on negative influences, so it is worth making the point that these do not always seem to lead to inertia.

Some kinds of partnership seem more likely to be successful than others, because their circumstances lessen the effect of the inertia forces (Huxham 1996b). As mentioned earlier, many authors have tried to identify conditions that lead to success. Our own data suggests that success is often demonstrably claimed when: (a) key players have identified a *single issue* as being of more importance than any other (e.g. as appeared to happen in the childcare example of the opening paragraph) so that competing demands can be ignored; or (b) the collaboration is over a specific project with a defined end output, rather than over strategic issues or having an expectation of a long-term relationship; or (c) there are only a small number of partner organizations – especially if the individuals concerned have a good relationship or have worked successfully together before; or (d) involvement requires partners to give little away (such as in the case of discussion fora or industry associations); and so on. Success almost always seems to be reliant on the involvement of at least one competent individual who champions and nurtures the partnership.

Sadly, the presence of any of the factors above does not appear to be a guarantee of success and even when a positive outcome is reached, we commonly hear those involved comment that there was a great deal of pain on the way. Our research programme has included a focus on the leadership activities that participants take in order to shape and implement partnership agendas. The picture that has emerged is one in which partnership managers, champions from within partner organizations or, sometimes, external participants become involved in 'leadership' activities which are intended to take the collaboration forward in directions they regard as appropriate, but in which they are frequently thwarted by dilemmas and difficulties so that the outcomes are not as they intend (Huxham and Vangen 1999b). Paradoxically, it is often the requirements of funders for particular types of output that get in the way of efforts to address issues seriously.

It seems clear, therefore, that involvement in partnerships is challenging. We will conclude this chapter, by summarizing, in broad terms, the nature of challenge.

In general it is not easy to take hard-and-fast conclusions from the preceding discussion, but one implication can be firmly stated. Put succinctly, our advice to potential partnership initiators – given the strength of the forces that act against success – is *don't do it unless you have to*; or, more formally, ... *unless you can see the potential for significant collaborative advantage*. One challenge is thus in knowing when *not* to use the collaborative approach and in being able to assess when doing so would really make a difference, which may mean being selective in responding to policy incentives. Being able to judge where these have a sufficiently close fit to existing activities must be an important skill, which means making a judgement not only about the importance of the substance of the policy, but also about how the partnership itself will relate to existing ways of working. It may also mean persuading others who might potentially be involved that it would be unwise to go ahead. The other side of this coin is the challenge to policy makers in the shape of finding a way to devise incentives which allow potential recipients the flexibility to adapt the initiative to their local circumstances.

If the decision to go ahead is made, then a whole raft of further challenges presents itself to those involved in finding ways to cope with the forces described briefly in this chapter. Keeping activity moving even though nothing will be done perfectly and knowing how and when to compromise are obviously key challenges. Finding a workable level at which to agree aims, getting started in the trust-building cycle, gaining mutual understanding and dealing with the effects of changing membership are other examples of challenges. It would be possible to continue with this list ad infinitum. The list can be summarized by our second piece of advice: *if you are seriously concerned to achieve success in partnership, be prepared to nurture ... and nurture ... and nurture*. All of the activities associated with partnership require sensitivity and attention to detail (Carley and Christie 1992; Huxham 1996b; Webb 1991) and because of the dynamics, this can never be relaxed, which means accepting that significant resources and personal energy need to be allocated to the partnership.

It is tempting to search for prescriptive advice on how to meet these challenges, and a continuous stream of 'how to do it' practice guides have emanated from research institutes, organizations that have partnership experience and consultants (see e.g. Winer and Ray, 1994; Wilson and Charlton 1997). Indeed, we have had discussions with three groups considering producing such guides in the past week. Our own view, however, is that there can be no easy rules of best practice, partly because – as we have illustrated previously – the demands of partnership pull in contradictory directions and partly because the sheer volume of activity that needs to be attended to is greater than most available resources would allow for (Huxham 1996b; Vangen 1998).

Our conclusion, therefore, is that making partnerships work requires a sophisticated approach. At this level, the challenge is to identify, for any particular situation, the key areas in which energy is required and to have some sense of the issues involved in tackling that area. Looked at from this perspective, practice guides can be helpful in highlighting areas to consider, and possible ways of addressing them. Our *themes* approach has deliberately aimed only to be descriptive of the kinds of issues that can face those involved and to raise some of the choice dilemmas that face practitioners. From a practical perspective, our aim is that this should first reassure practitioners that any difficulties they face are normal rather than the result of particular awkwardness or incompetence and then provide a basis for consideration of future actions.

18.6 Acknowledgements

This paper results from our involvement over the last decade in a very wide variety of collaborations. Each involvement has influenced our thinking and we thank all of you with whom we have worked. A part of the research which informs this paper was funded by grants from the Economic and Social Research Council in the UK.

References

Bergquist, W., Betwee, J. and Meuel, D. (1995) *Building Strategic Relationships*, San Francisco: Jossey Bass.

Bryson, J. (1998) 'Strategic planning: Big wins and small wins'. *Public Money and Management* Autumn.

Cabinet Office (1999) *Modernising Government*, White Paper, London, Stationery Office.

Carley, M. and Christie, I. (1992) *Managing Sustainable Development*, London: Earthscan.

Das, T. and Teng, B. (1997) 'Sustaining strategic alliances: Options and guidelines'. *Journal of General Management* 22(4), 49–64.

—— (1998) 'Between trust and control: Developing confidence in partner cooperation in alliances', *Academy of Management Review* 23: 491–512.

Doz, Y. (1994) 'Partnerships in Europe', in B. de Witt and R. Meyer (eds) *Strategy: Process, Content and Context*, Minneapolis, MN West.

Doz, Y. and Hamel, G. (1998) *Alliance Advantage: The Art of Creating Value Through Partnering*, Boston, MA: Harvard Business School Press.

Eden, C. and Huxham, C. (1996) 'Action research for the study of organizations', in S. Clegg, C. Hardy and W. Nord, (eds) *Handbook of Organization Studies*, London: Sage, pp. 526–42.

Eden, C. and Huxham, C. (1999) 'Understanding the negotiation of purpose in multi-organizational collaborative groups through action research', to appear in *Journal of Management Studies*.

Gray, B. (1985) 'Conditions facilitating interorganizational collaboration', *Human Relations*, 38: 911–36.

HM Treasury (1995) 'Private opportunity, public benefit', HM Treasury, London.

HM Treasury (1997) 'Partnerships for prosperity', HM Treasury, London.

Huxham, C. (1993) 'Pursuing collaborative advantage', *Journal of the Operational Research Society* 44: 599–611.

Huxham, C. (ed.) (1996a) *Creating Collaborative Advantage*, London: Sage.

Huxham, C. (1996b) 'Advantage or inertia: Making collaboration work', in R. Paton, G. Clark, G. Jones, J. Lewis and P. Quintas, (eds) *The New Management Reader*, London: Routledge, pp. 238–54.

Huxham, C. and Macdonald, D. (1992) 'Introducing collaborative advantage: Achieving inter-organizational effectiveness through meta-strategy', *Management Decision* 30: 50–6.

Huxham, C. and Vangen, S. (1996) 'Working together: Key themes in the management of relationships between public and non-profit organizations', *International Journal of Public Sector Management* 9: 5–17.

—— (1998a) 'What makes practitioners tick? Understanding collaboration practice and practising collaboration understanding', paper given at the Workshop on Interorganizational Collaboration and Conflict at McGill University, Montreal, April, Strathclyde Graduate Business School Working Paper 98/3.

—— (1998b) 'Action research for understanding collaboration practice: Emerging research design choices', paper given at the 24th International Congress of Applied Psychology, San Francisco, August, Strathclyde Graduate Business School Working Paper 98/5.

—— (1999a) 'Ambiguity, complexity and dynamics in the membership of collaboration', *Human Relations* [forthcoming].

—— (1999b) 'Perspectives on leadership in collaboration: How things happen in a (not quite) joined up world', paper given at the International Research Symposium on Public Sector Management, Aston University, March.

Kanter, R. M. (1994) 'Collaborative advantage: Successful partnerships manage the relationship, not just the deal', *Harvard Business Review* July–August: 96–108.

Kumar, N. (1996) 'The power of trust in manufacturer–retailer relationships', *Harvard Business Review* 74(6): 92–106.

Lane, C. and Bachman, R. (eds) (1998) *Trust Within and Between Organizations, Conceptual Issues and Empirical Applications*, Oxford: Oxford University Press.

Leifer, R. and Mills, P. (1996) 'An information processing approach for deciding upon control strategies and reducing control loss in emerging organizations', *Journal of Management* 22: 113–37.

Lewicki, R. and Bunker, B. (1996) 'Developing and maintaining trust in work relationships', in R. Kramer and T. Tyler (eds) *Trust in Organizations Frontiers of Theory and Research*, London: Sage, pp. 114–39.

Long, F. and Arnold, M. (1995) *The Power of Environmental Partnerships*, Fort Worth, TX: The Dryden Press.

Lorange, P. and Roos, J. (1993) *Strategic Alliances: Formation, Implementation and Evolution*, Oxford: Blackwell.

McCann, J. (1984) 'Design guidelines for problem solving interventions', *Journal of Applied Behavioural Science* 19: 177–92.

Martin, J. (1992) *Cultures in Three Organizations: Three Perspectives*, Oxford: Oxford University Press.

Mattesich, P. and Monsey, B. (1992) *Collaboration: What Makes It Work?*, St Paul, MN: Amherst H. Wilder Foundation.

Pearce, R. (1997) 'Towards understanding joint venture performance and survival: A bargaining and influence approach to transaction cost theory', *Academy of Management Review* 22: 203–25.

OPM (1991) 'Futures for community care', Southwest Thames Regional Health Authority and Office for Public Management, London.

Schein, E. (1985) *Organizational Culture and Leadership*, San Francisco: Jossey Bass.

Stewart, M. (1998) 'Partnership, leadership and competition in urban policy', in N. Oatley (ed.) *Competition and Urban Policy*, London: Paul Chapman Publishing.

Sweeting, D., Stewart, M. and Hambleton, R. (1999) 'Leadership in urban governance', paper given at the ESRC Cities: Competition and Cohesion Convention, Birmingham, June.

Sydow, J. (1998) 'Understanding the constitution of interorganizational trust', in C. Lane and R. Bachmann (eds) *Trust Within and Between Organizations*, Oxford: Oxford University Press, pp. 31–63.

Vangen, S. (1998) 'Transferring insight on collaboration into practice', PhD thesis, University of Strathclyde, Glasgow.

Vangen, S. and Huxham, C. (1998) 'The role of trust in the achievement of collaborative advantage', paper given at the 14th EGOS Colloquium in Maastricht, July.

Vangen, S., Huxham, C. and Eden, C. (1994) 'Performance measures for collaborative activity', paper given at the Annual Conference of the British Academy of Management, Lancaster University, September.

Webb, A. (1991) 'Co-ordination: A problem in public sector management', *Policy and Politics* 19: 229–41.

Winer, M. and Ray, K. (1994) *Collaboration Handbook: Creating, Sustaining and Enjoying the Journey*, St Paul, MN: Amherst H. Wilder Foundation.

Wilson, A. and Charlton, K. (1997) *Making Partnerships Work: A Practical Guide for the Public, Private, Voluntary and Community Sectors*, York: Joseph Rowntree Foundation.

19 NGO partners

The characteristics of effective development partnerships

John Hailey

19.1 Introduction

Over the last twenty years shifts in policy have changed the relationship between governments and non-government development organizations (NGDOs). This 'new' relationship is marked by increased collaboration and dialogue, new patterns of working, the introduction of new reporting systems and a greater emphasis on cost-effectiveness and accountability. More importantly there has been an increase in funding to the NGDO sector as a whole; and in particular an increase in funds directed to NGDOs in the South. Both multilateral and bilateral donors recognize the importance of developing civil society and a strong Third Sector, and have consequently invested in building institutional capacity and promoting new partnerships.

Most politicians and policy makers emphasize the importance of developing new partnerships as an integral element of official government aid policy, which is well exemplified in the tone and content of the British Government's White Paper reviewing current policy on international development which was published in 1997. This new statement of policy emphasized the key role of partnerships in the development process and poverty elimination. Although much has been written about the changing nature of relations between donors and NGDOs, there has been little analysis of the organizational and personal implications of implementing such partnerships. This chapter analyses the development, dynamics and character of NGO partner relationships, identifies some of the conditions for effective partnership and concludes that personal dimensions based on trust and clarity of purpose are as important as institutional relations based on power and money.

19.2 NGDOs: growth and dependency

NGDOs are now recognized as key players in the development arena. There has been a dramatic expansion in their work. Some focus on emergency relief, others provide specialist technical assistance, while others promote social change or are engaged in advocacy. Some have grown considerably: World Vision has an income of over half a billion dollars per year, and the Bangladeshi NGDO,

BRAC, now employs over 50,000 staff. An increasing proportion of official aid is now channelled through such NGDOs (Smillie and Helmich 1999). Official figures suggest that aid channelled through NGDOs trebled in the decade after 1983; and in India, for example, the World Bank estimates that over a million NGDOs receive over 25 per cent of official aid.

This growth is partly a consequence of the disenchantment with the role and effectiveness of government in the development process, and the dominance of neo-Liberal ideologies and the resulting privatization and the contracting out of government services. But it is also a recognition of the role of NGDOs as effective change agents, and their ability to deliver aid in an appropriate, responsive and participative manner (Korten 1990; Fowler 1997). The consequences of continuing population growth, migration, urbanization, and the aftermath of conflict and civil war suggests that NGDOs have a continuing role. As the United Nations reminds us there are now more than 100 countries worse off today than they were 15 years ago. Such indicators of poverty are more striking because of the obvious economic success of some hitherto poor countries, notably in South-East Asia. This situation was graphically described as being one where:

> a rising of tide of wealth is supposed to lift all boats, but some are more seaworthy than others. The yachts and sea liners are rising in response to new opportunities, but the rafts and rowboats are taking on water – and some are sinking fast.
> (United Nations Development Programme (UNDP) 1997: 9)

The environment that NGDOs find themselves in is turbulent and demanding. They are expected to work in increasingly difficult circumstances, notably conflict and post-conflict environments, as well as in such non-traditional settings as the transitional economies of Eastern Europe and Central Asia, even China and North Korea. They are also increasingly involved in non-traditional sectoral activities such as environmental regeneration, credit and micro-finance, and conflict resolution. As a result they are under pressure from donors and beneficiaries alike to expand their project base, scale up and build sufficient capacity to have an impact in these diverse areas (Edwards and Hulme 1992; Farrington and Bebbington 1993; Smillie 1995a). This demanding environment requires that organizations make best use of limited resources by building on their strengths, and collaborating with others to complement their weaknesses, which has resulted in donors, government departments and NGDOs negotiating a variety of partnership arrangements and alliances. Partnerships can therefore be seen as a contemporary solution to present-day problems.

However, despite these ambitious expectations and the expansion of direct funding of NGDOs, the overall pool of aid funds available to development agencies is under increasing threat as the total amount of official aid and foreign investment to the developing world has declined in real terms. Aid from the twenty-one countries belonging to the OECD has fallen to 0.22 per cent of their combined GNP – the lowest-ever level since records began 45 years ago in 1950 (German and Randel 1998).

Aid funds are a scarce resource. Donors have considerable leverage as to how recipient agencies should operate and what performance criteria should be met. There is an extensive debate about the impact of such donor conditionality on the independence and legitimacy of NGDOs (Farrington and Bebbington 1993; Smillie 1995b, Chambers 1997; Manji 1997). There is concern about the way donors abuse their power, the lack of transparency of donor agendas and the impact of the donor conditionality. The evidence suggests that over-dependence on donor funding is counter-productive and corrupting, and that some NGDOs are more geared to the demands of donors than the needs of beneficiaries (Edwards and Hulme 1995). Yet the political, operational and economic reality is that donors can, and do, impose conditions and shape the development agenda. Among other things they look for value for money and demonstrable impact, but also evidence of collaboration, networking and the creation of new 'partnerships'.

19.3 Partnership: the new policy imperative

The use of the term 'partnership' in the context of development has a mixed genesis. On the one hand, there are those who point to the 1968 World Bank report, 'Partners in Development', which was produced under the auspices of ex-Canadian Prime Minister Lester Pearson. This report expressed dissatisfaction with existing aid relations, and argued that future development strategies should emphasize cooperation between donor and recipient (Hately 1997). On the other hand, there are those who suggest that 'partnership' has its roots in the radical solidarity movements of the 1960s and 1970s, typically found in Latin America, and the belief that international solidarity lay at the heart of development ideology (Fowler 1997; Martella and Schank 1997).

However, as governments, donors and different development agencies and NGDOs have adopted the term, the concept of 'partnership' has lost its original ideological legitimacy. It is increasingly used in a pragmatic way to describe and define a variety of development relationships. The term is commonly found in policy documents, and the language of partnership is now central to the development agenda. For example, the 1997 DFID White Paper emphasizes the centrality of partnership to Britain's aid relationship with the developing world:

> We shall work closely with other donors and development agencies to build partnerships with developing countries to strengthen the commitment to the elimination of poverty.

> (DFID 1997: 22)

> The Government believes that genuine partnerships . . . are needed if poverty is to be addressed effectively in a coherent way.

> (ibid.: 37)

These DFID statements should be seen as part of an ongoing process whereby government departments and official donor agencies have adopted the concept of partnership to support their development agenda. Thus, for example, official Canadian aid policy suggests that equity and shared learning are key elements of their mutual partnership with the South:

> partnership is intended to help Canadians build a more equitable relationship with the people of developing countries by helping bring Canada's cooperation into line with major improvements that have taken place not only in the ability of developing countries to carry out development on their own, but also on the capacity of Canada's domestic and international partners as well.
>
> (CIDA 1993)

In the United States USAID issued a statement in 1995 which noted that complementarity compatibility and shared responsibility were essential ingredients of America's relations with development partners:

> partnership is a two way street based upon shared rights and responsibilities. Each partners bring different, but complementary, skills, expertise and experiences to a common objective. Each contributes to areas of comparative advantage that complement each other and are fundamentally compatible.
>
> (USAID 1995)

Multilateral agencies like the World Bank and the United Nations have also prioritized partnership development. In November 1997 the World Bank advertised for a partnerships coordinator, who was expected to strengthen partnerships and build broader scope for joint action with other institutions, as well as develop the Bank's 'partnerships agenda'. The UNDP sees partnerships with civil-society organizations as a way to meet three specific objectives. First, to promote dialogue among the government, civil society organizations and private sectors to help define policies that support sustainable development. Second, to meet critical needs of civil society organizations for training and capacity building. Third, to strengthen UNDP's own capacity and operations through the increasing involvement of civil-society organizations in the design, implementation and monitoring of UNDP's programmes and projects (UNDP 1997).

In the late 1990s there is also a growing momentum among many northern NGDOs to decentralize their operations, and work through local partners. As a consequence they have attempted to redefine their relationships with their Southern partners so that they can ensure levels of effectiveness and accountability, while maintaining their own values and integrity, and still meeting the needs of the beneficiaries, partners and donors. Such NGDOs see partnership as an integral part of their work. For example, Norwegian Church Aid's Global Plan states that partnership is about 'entering into a long-term, binding cooperation with like-minded organizations. The cooperation shall be characterized by equality and mutuality.' The Geneva-based International Council of Voluntary Agencies (ICVA) has introduced guidelines recommending that partnerships should be based on 'an equality of commitment and involvement', and that collaboration between Northern and Southern NGOs should be:

> equitable and genuine partnerships that grow out of mutual respect and trust; compatible purposes, strategies and values; and a two-way exchange of information, ideas and experience.
>
> (ICVA 1995)

19.4 Partnership: definitions and typologies

Thus, we have a picture whereby governments, official donors and NGDOs in both the North and South use the language of partnership to articulate policies and define their development relationships. Unfortunately, as Kamal Malhotra comments, 'partnership' is one of those 'something nothing' words of indeterminate meaning (Malhotra 1997). In other words it suffers from a multitude of interpretations, is easily abused and exploited to disguise the real power dynamics of an unbalanced relationship.

Hately (1997) notes that the language of partnership is often contradictory, while Fowler (1997) suggests the usefulness of the term has been eroded in part because of the ways donors have reinterpreted meaning but also because of the 'medley of names' used to describe relationships between NGDOs including 'partnership, networks, alliances, coalitions, consortia, and coordination bodies' (Fowler 1997: 107). Faced with the concern that partnership is just a convenient 'something nothing word' that can be used all too promiscuously, a number of commentators have attempted to refine, define or create typologies that identify the characteristics of successful partnerships.

These definitions and typologies commonly emphasize the mutuality and synergy between NGDOs. A key element of mutual partnership is trust, and the mutual recognition that each organization needs each other to accomplish their aims and objectives. Alan Fowler refers to such relations as 'authentic partnerships', which he suggests is based on: trust and commitment; shared beliefs, values or culture; accepted standards of legitimacy, transparency and accountability; and common approach to gender issues (Fowler 1997: 109).

Other commentators have attempted to define partnership in terms of distinct polarities. Hately has identified 'conventional partnerships', and 'reciprocal partnerships'; while Lewis talks of 'active partnerships' and 'dependent partnerships'. Conventional partnerships are commonly short term, bureaucratic, one way and unequal, with the Northern agency driving the agenda; whereas reciprocal partnerships attempt to change the traditional way of working by creating two-way, horizontal relationships based on solidarity and equality (Hately 1997). Active partnerships are those based on a negotiated process, with common purpose, shared risks, marked by debate, learning and information exchange; whereas dependent partnerships are based on fixed-term blueprints with rigid roles and static assumptions, poor communication, and are commonly motivated by access to funds and individual interests (see Chapter 15).

Muchunguzi and Milne (1995) identified an alternative typology suggesting that partnerships can be defined by four different purposes. First, partnerships that exist in order to enable donors, counterpart agencies and project holders to better manage local NGDOs and allocate resources. Second, partnerships established to encourage linkages between people in both the North and South and promote awareness and understanding. Third, partnerships between Northern NGDOs and other agencies for the purpose of combining and coordinating resources to support new initiatives in both the North and the South. Fourth, partnerships created to support and permit local advisory committees and networks to provide effective advice (Muchunguzi and Milne 1995).

Another purpose-based typology was proposed by Martelia and Schank (1997). They suggest that the structure and dynamics of any partnership will depend on its purpose, and that partnerships are either a 'contracted resource', 'a way of working', or for 'acquiring critical consciousness'. Thus, if a partnership is seen merely as resource based it is about contracted delivery of tangibles with emphasis on cost-effectiveness and implementation. If the purpose is to develop a 'way of working' then it is intended to build linkages, decentralize responsibility, promote sustainability and empower staff and beneficiaries through shared decision making. The third type of partnership exists to promote a critical consciousness of the development process. One consequence of this is that Southern NGDOs need to take more responsibility for the design and progress of the development process in which they are involved, while Northern NGDOs adopt more of a 'consulting' role (Martelia and Schank, 1997).

Such typologies and definitions all provide useful insights, but little clarity. Any review of the different models suggests that there is a 'spectrum of partnerships'. At one extreme are 'resource', 'dependent', or 'conventional' partnerships, commonly simple contracting relations between a donor and a local-service-providing organization. While at the other end of the spectrum can be found 'authentic', 'active', or 'reciprocal' partnerships which are marked by mutuality, trust, and shared governance, dialogue and learning.

19.5 Partnership: the benefits

The benefits of building effective or 'authentic' partnerships are multifold. Partnership should be seen as a way of making more efficient use of scarce resources, increasing institutional sustainability, improving participation, and sharing skills, knowledge and learning. There is also evidence to suggest that successful partnerships can reduce administrative overheads and associated transaction costs resulting in more cost-effective projects and programmes (Brett 1993). Fowler (1998) also argues that effective partnerships contribute to building 'social capital' because they help develop a range of trustworthy, reciprocal relationships which bind individuals, groups, communities and society together.

Such partnerships also encourage local ownership, facilitate the growth and development of local institutions and promote shared learning. Operational evidence from NGDOs suggests that effective partnerships result in a greater spread of activity and skills resulting in increased impact, shared risk, greater local involvement and ability to handle complex problems. For example, Katalysis, a well-respected US-based NGDO working with partners in Latin America, justifies its investment in building partnerships on the grounds that traditional Northern-dominated top-down assistance has failed to provide sustainable improvements in the lives of the poor, and that Southern partners need to assume ownership of their development. They see partnering as about building 'close, equitable and hopefully lifelong relationships between and among northern and southern development agencies' (Jones 1993: 6).

Partnerships, when they work well, are seen as a valuable component of the development process. In particular, they help build local capacity, facilitate the transfer of skills and knowledge, and encourage mutual dialogue. They can generate and motivate more cohesive and committed teams, and promote shared learning. Effective partnerships encourage better quality decision making because they introduce a wider perspective, spread the ownership of the decision-making process and ensure that there is broader accountability for actions taken. In particular, links with government and other public institutions can foster greater levels of transparency and accountability within their administration, and so reduce the wastage, nepotism, corruption and abuse of power which has become virtually institutionalized.

19.6 Partnership: the problems

However, both researchers and practitioners recognize that there are a number of problems inherent in partnerships formed between Northern and Southern NGDOs. These commonly result from the power imbalance between partners. It is all too common for one partner to have access to money, expertise and political power, while the other (commonly based in the South) has few resources to act as a counterweight. There are also tensions because of the inbuilt biases and paternalistic behaviour of the staff of some Northern NGDOs who are anxious about loss of control and fearful for their reputation. This in turn is aggravated by: the inherent lack of transparency among many development agencies; the organizational weaknesses of many Southern NGDOs and their lack of self-criticism; dependence on one funding source; and deep-rooted suspicions as to the motives of Northern agencies. This state of affairs is often exacerbated by the differences in language, culture and mores; and the fact that many Northern agencies employ relatively young, inexperienced staff to handle partner relations and liaise over major policy issues with senior staff of their Southern partners (Fowler 1998; Manji 1997; James 1996).

Some of the most serious criticism is saved for government–NGDO 'partnerships'. The reasons given are commonly that such partnerships are merely contractual relations with clear power imbalances between partners, aggravated by the extent of the cultural and resource gap between official donors and NGDOs, and the way government-sponsored donor agencies in the North impose their own conditions and agenda subvert the independence of NGDOs (Farrington & Bebbington 1993; Edwards and Hulme 1995; Brown and Ashman 1996; Pinzas 1997). Ian Smillie commented that the relationship between official donors and NGDOs is akin to that between prisoner and prison warder (quoted in Malhotra 1997), while Farrington and Bebbington highlighted the vulnerability of many NGDOs because of their growing dependence on official donors, referring to them as 'reluctant partners' (1993).

The power imbalance between articulate, wealthy Northern NGDOs having international experience with small local institutions can also result in a variety of tensions and unforeseen slights. This is partly a product of the way powerful donors or government departments try to coerce smaller, less powerful NGDOs and other civil society organizations to adopt strategies, introduce new working practices, or implement projects in specific ways. But it is also a product of the self-perpetuating feeling of inferiority that besets so many organizations that have become dependent on external stakeholders. There are also tensions because of the ill-defined nature of the language of partnerships and misunderstanding as to their purpose and objectives. Furthermore, the degree of mythologization and mystification that has come to be associated with the term creates confusion and delusions as to the real purpose of many partnerships (Martelia and Schank, 1997). In general, the problems facing many partnerships arise when both parties are unable to negotiate a relational balance which adds any value and empowers both partners.

19.7 The characteristics of effective partnerships

Different commentators have highlighted a variety of different characteristics of effective partnership. For example, a recent review of NGO–private-sector partnerships suggests that the key criteria for success are focused on meeting a specific need or resolving a particular problem; and as such they are not based on ill-defined generalities. Also that efforts are made to understand each partner's needs and interests, and that personal relations are supported by organizational structures and sufficient resources (Heap 1998). However, evidence from the partnerships formed between NGDOs, such as Katalysis with its Latin American partners, suggests that structural and institutional issues are less important than personal relations and process issues. The experience of Katalysis suggests that the key characteristics of effective partnering are: open and effective communication; willingness to address difficult decisions; sharing cultures, building friendships and investing in a long-term relationship; as well as respecting institutional autonomy (Jones 1993).

Similarly, Malhotra (1997) in his overview of the characteristics of successful partnerships between NGDOs emphasizes the importance of a process marked by openness and reciprocity. He picks out: shared vision; adequate time to build relations; mutual transparency and accountability; and the willingness for both partners to accept criticism as the key characteristics of successful partnerships. Fowler (1997) emphasizes mutuality and trust as the key ingredient of 'authentic partnerships'. Operationally this is reflected in joint-performance measures, partner-based financing, shared governance, open decision making and time spent in building mutual trust through a process of 'organizational empowerment'.

The personal experience of this author and analysis of the existing research into effective partnerships suggests there are five key principles that characterize successful partnerships:

1   *Clarity of purpose*. This helps to ensure that any partnership is driven by a clear and shared vision of the purpose and objectives of the partnership, and what is to be accomplished. This enables partners to understand what is expected of them and work together to resolve problems when things go off track or disappointing results begin to develop. Clear goals make it easier for partners to work together and raise sensitive issues about each other's role and performance. Practical experience also suggests that partnerships based on shared interests or expertise are more likely to succeed and not be deflected by extraneous issues (see Chapter 18, also, for the limitations of too much charity).

2   *Mutual trust and respect*. Trust and respect lies at the heart of partnering. Where mutual trust and reciprocity exists it is much easier to negotiate issues, resolve problems and work towards a common purpose. Trust and respect facilitates communication, the sharing of sensitive information and promotes learning. It also means that partners have some flexibility in their approach, or the way they allocate resources, because of their trust in their partners' reliability and the integrity of their decision-making processes.

3   *Investment of time and resources*. Time, effort, and resources need be invested in building personal relationships and trust, negotiating strategies and procedures, sharing experiences and concerns. All the evidence points to the importance of setting realistic time-frames for proposal development and submission, programme implementation and evaluation, feedback and shared learning. Sufficient time also needs be allocated to develop networks of collaborators, build local constituencies and work with key stakeholders – all of which are essential to the success of most NGDOs.

4   *Negotiation of roles and responsibilities*. Systems and procedures need be established early in the life of the partnership to plan joint activities, identify distinct roles and responsibilities, negotiate mutually acceptable indicators of performance and milestones of success, etc. Regular meetings need to be scheduled for feedback and shared reflection on programmatic or institutional issues. The evidence suggests that too many partnerships fail because of false expectations as to the roles of different partners, unwillingness to take responsibility for specific activities or failure to accept feedback.

5   *Long-term sustainability*. Plans need be considered as to the lifespan of the partnership, how it will be funded and what are the organizational and staff

implications of maintaining a partnership at an optimum level. All partners need to budget for the overheads associated with maintaining the partnership, and design a diversified funding plan to ensure partnership costs do not devour project funds. They also need to be explicit about indicators of the success of the partnership, and their expectations for the phase down or exit from the partnership.

19.8 Building effective partnerships

Efforts to establish effective partnerships have resulted in the introduction of a variety of capacity building initiatives, and organization development processes in both the North and the South. Ian Smillie (1995a) argues that the creation of strong organizations with sufficient institutional capacity, and management systems and skills are an essential prerequisite for effective development. Rick James (1996) argues convincingly that partnership and capacity building are inextricably linked, and that strong partnerships can only be implemented through a coherent capacity building programme.

The challenge is to identify how best to develop the key characteristics of effective partnering. Any analysis of these characteristics highlights the importance of clarity of purpose, mutual trust, respect and commitment as key ingredients of an effective partnership. However, the danger is that such terms are all too often reduced to 'motherhood and apple-pie' exhortations of little practical or operational values to staff struggling to build partnerships across international borders and cultures.

The issue of how best to ensure common purpose, maintain trust and build commitment in different locations and diverse environments is one that many international organizations and multinational companies face. It is a particular issue for those involved in creating international partnerships because they are so dependent on the ability of a relatively small cadre of key staff to form effective working relationships based on personal trust and mutual commitment to the goals of the partnership. Furthermore, the reality is that personal agendas, frustration, internal politics and mistrust of colleagues all combine to threaten the clarity of purpose and relationship of trust needed in organizations and international partnerships (Hailey 1996). As a result new strategies and work practices have been introduced to bridge the gap between staff working in diverse locations and partnerships. These are commonly based on due process, participative decision making, effective communication, team building and knowledge-management systems designed to share understanding and build trust (Bartlett and Ghosal 1989, Chan Kim and Mauborgne 1993).

Thus, we have a situation developing where personal relationships, shared understanding, effective communication and mutual trust are as important as institutional concerns and other structural imbalances, such as uncertain funding, issues of power and control, governance and accountability. Any review of the literature and research on the operational characteristics of effective partnerships highlights the importance of personal rather than institutional issues, with process being more important than procedure.

In practical terms this means that effective partnerships need to incorporate some of the elements essential to facilitating personal relationship and good partnering. These include: recognition of the impact of personal and cultural biases and behaviour on sustainable partnerships; an appreciation of the importance of interpersonal behaviour in building trust and promoting dialogue; also some shared understanding of language and commonly used terms or concepts. There also needs to be an appreciation of the stress, anxiety and insecurity inherent in many partnerships where there is a degree of uncertainty and latent conflict arising from an imbalance of power or resources. New strategies and innovative work practices should be considered with the specific intention of reducing insecurity and anxiety in order to promote sustainable and healthy partnerships. Similarly there needs to be clarity about the expectations arising from the partnership, and an understanding of the different roles, responsibilities and obligations expected of each partner.

We also need to know more about the motives and dynamics behind successful partnerships. Research is needed to assess the characteristics of successful partnerships and analyse the operational reality of building effective partnerships. There is also a need to analyse the personal and organizational dynamics of building mutual trust within partnerships spanning different cultures. Among other issues researchers should also: review the practical experience of funding partnerships; identify the different stages in the partnership life cycle, indicators of growth and effective exit strategies; and analyse the impact of government policies and donor-funding strategies on the establishment of viable and legitimate partnerships between NGDOs and donors.

19.9 Conclusion and discussion

This chapter was written with the intention of analysing the development, dynamics and characteristics of effective NGDO partnerships. There are clearly a multitude of definitions, as well as a complex debate as to the history and policy implications of promoting 'partnerships'. The current development environment with its emphasis on accountability, cost-effectiveness and impact assessment means that NGDOs are looking to have more impact and make better use of resources by working through new alliances and partnerships. However, there is also a growing consensus that we need develop partnerships that reflect the values of the sector and the needs of beneficiaries with whom they work. As a result there has been greater emphasis on promoting 'authentic' or 'reciprocal' partnerships which are not only based on common objectives and issues of mutual concern, but also shared values, mutual learning, equity, participation and personal respect.

Partnerships based on paternalistic, mechanistic and financially driven strategies are clearly ill-suited to the contemporary environment. Furthermore, researchers who merely concern themselves with the institutional, structural or political dimensions of partnership run the risk of overlooking key elements of the partnering process. Evidence from both the private and the non-profit sector highlights the importance of personal relations, trust and clarity of purpose in successful partnerships, which suggests that process-based initiatives should be introduced which promote common values, and facilitate shared decision making, interpersonal communication, mutual learning, and, above all, reaffirm the role of trust in building authentic and reciprocal partnerships.

However, possibly most important of all, is for partners to define and clarify the purpose of the partnership in which they are engaged. To what degree is it merely based on some ill-defined, all-encompassing, policy jargon of politicians and policy makers? Does the partnership exist merely to promote some vague notion of solidarity? Or is there a specific goal and purpose? As has been so aptly pointed out the success of any viable partnership depends on much more than a symbolic display of 'launch, lunch and logo'. Success is based on negotiation and common objectives, mutual respect, shared commitment, and trust. For the relationship of trust, which appears to be such an essential characteristic of effective partnerships, to thrive there needs to be clarity of purpose and a genuine understanding of mutual expectations, and agreement on the different roles and responsibilities expected of each partner.

References

Bartlett., C. and Ghoshal, C. (1989) *Managing Across Borders*, Harvard Business School Press.

Brett, E. A. (1993) 'Voluntary agencies as development organisations: Theorising the problem of efficiency and accountability', *Development and Change* 24(2): 264–303.

Brown, D. and Ashman, D. (1996) 'Participation, social capital, and intersectoral problem-solving', *World Development* 24(9): 1,467–79.

Chambers, R. (1997) *Whose Reality Counts: Putting the First Last*, London: IT Publications.

Chan Kim, W. and Mauborgne, R. (1993) 'Making global strategies work', *Sloan Management Review* Spring: 11–27.

DFID (1997) *Eliminating World Poverty: A Challenge for the 21st Century*, London: DFID.

Edwards, M. and Hulme, D. (1992) *Making a Difference: NGOs and Development in a Changing World*, London: Earthscan.

—— (1995) *NGOs: Performance and Accountability*, London: Earthscan.

Farrington, J. and Bebbington, A. (1993) *Reluctant Partners: NGOs, the State and Sustainable Agricultural Development*, London: Routledge.

Fowler, A. (1997) *Striking a Balance: A Guide to Enhancing the Effectiveness of NGOs*, London: Earthscan.

—— (1998) 'Authentic NGO partnerships in the new policy agenda for international aid', *Development and Change* 29(1): 137–59.

German, T. and Randel, J. (1998) *Reality of Aid*, London: Earthscan.

Hailey, J. (1996) 'The expatriate myth: Cross-cultural perceptions of expatriate managers', *The International Executive* 38(2): 255–71.

Hately, L. (1997) 'The power of partnership', in L. Hately and K. Malhotra (eds) *Essays on Partnership in Development*, Ottawa: North South Institute.

Heap, S. (1998) *NGOs and the Private Sector: Potential for Partnerships*, Oxford: INTRAC.

James, R. (1996) 'The organisational strengthening needs of European NGOs', *Journal of International Development* 9(4), June.

Jones, R. E. (1993) *Choosing Partnerships, The Evolution of the Katalysis Model*, Stockton, CA: North/South Development Partnerships.

Korten, D. (1990) *Getting to the 21st Century: Voluntary Action and the Global Agenda*, West Hartford, CT: Kumarian.

Lewis, D. (1998) 'Inter-agency partnerships in aid-recipient countries: Lessons from an aquaculture project in Bangladesh', *Non-Profit and Voluntary Sector Quarterly* 27(3): 323–38.

Malhotra, K. (1997) 'Something nothing words: Lessons in partnership from southern experience', in L. Hately and K. Malhotra (eds) *Essays on Partnership in Development*, Ottawa: North South Institute.

Manji, F. (1997) 'Collaboration with the South: Agents of aid or solidarity', *Development in Practice* 7(2): 175–8.

Martelia, P. and Schank, J. (1997) 'Partnership: New name in development cooperation', *Development in Practice* 7(3): 283–5.

Muchunguzi, D. and Milne, S. (1995) *Perspectives from the South: A Study on Partnership*, Dar es Salaam: AFREDA.

Pinzas, T. (1997) *Partners or Contractors: The Relationship Between Official Agencies and NGOs in Peru*, Oxford: INTRAC.

Smillie, I. and Helmich, H. (eds) (1999) *Stakeholders: Government–NGO Partnerships for International Development*, London: Earthscan.

Smillie, I. (1995a) *The Alms Bazaar: Non-Profit Organisations and International Development*, London: IT Publications.

Smillie, I. (1995b) 'Changing partners: Northern NGOs, northern governments', *Voluntas* 5(2): 155–92.

UNDP (1997) *Human Development Report*, New York: United Nations.

Conclusions

A one-way street or two-way traffic? Can public–private partnerships impact on the policy-making process?

Kathleen McLaughlin and Stephen P. Osborne

C.1 Introduction

Throughout this book authors have examined, in international perspective, both the pivotal role of public–private partnerships (PPPs) in providing public services and the nature of their governance arrangements. One issue which has been raised in these analyses, but only received direct discussion in Chapter 16 of this book by Jenei and Vári, is the extent to which PPPs can influence the policy-making process as well as being a product of it. This raises important issues about whether it is realistic or desirable for the partners in PPPs to have an impact on policy making. On the one hand, the *community governance* perspective (Clarke and Stewart 1998) argues that such involvement is an essential pre-requisite for effective and responsive policy making. On the other hand, such involvement can raise the spectre of *incorporation* of the independent organs of society into a corporate state (Wilson and Butler 1985) and, in the case of the voluntary sector, the loss of important mediating forces against the meta-institutions of society (Berger and Neuhaus 1977). This debate is the subject of this final chapter, in which we consider the impact of PPPs on the policy-making process.

The chapter focuses on one specific form of PPP, namely Government–non-profit partnerships (GNPs) in the UK, in which the State and voluntary and community organizations (VCOs) formally interact within partnership settings. It draws on evidence from recent and current research about GNPs and area regeneration in the UK.

GNPs are increasingly advocated by Governments for a variety of reasons – including engaging the involvement of citizens in policy making in order to enhance the quality of policy decision making and its implementation (Hall and Mawson 1999; Ross and Osborne 1999). This objective is frequently portrayed within the UK and the EU as a means of 'combating social exclusion' and as a vehicle for addressing complex social and economic problems (Social Exclusion Unit 1998; Jones 1998).

Such aspirations are at odds with the approach of the previous Conservative Government in the UK, which restricted its vision of the role of VCOs in GNPs to the more narrow role of policy implementation. The dissonance between this earlier model and the community governance aspirations of the current Labour

Government in the UK has created problems and tensions in respect of broadening the role of VCOs into the policy-making process. This chapter will argue that such tensions can be resolved, if not solved, by locating this debate away from the new public management framework and within the theoretical framework of *public governance* (Kickert *et al.* 1997a). This offers a framework, based on a plural model of public policy making and implementation, for considering the issues which PPPs raise by taking on a proactive role in policy formulation as well as implementation.

The chapter will begin by exploring the evolving context of GNPs in the UK in general, and in particular of GNPs for local area regeneration. It will highlight the extent to which the model of plural policy making is a break with the dominant model of the last two decades, by drawing on this field of local area regeneration. It will conclude by using the public governance perspective to draw out key lessons for the successful achievement of plural policy making through GNPs, as well as highlighting some of its dangers.

C.2 Context: changing relations between the State and voluntary and community organizations

The nature of relationships between government and VCOs is currently undergoing fundamental review across the world, with governments exploring new mechanisms for relations between VCOs and government (Phillips 1999; Ross and Osborne 1999). In part this reflects dissatisfaction with the working relationships, and their impact, of the past two decades (Osborne and Ross 1998). However, it is also a product of the institutional shift from *government* to *governance* (Philips 1999) in these relationships, and by which the State seeks to work collaboratively with VCOs in order to enhance its own legitimacy within an increasingly pluralistic society.

As a result of these changes there is a need to consider the nature of the potential role played by VCOs in the sphere of public policy making, which can be conceptualized along two dimensions:

- the recognition of the range of roles that such organizations can play in this process; and
- the awareness that institutional frameworks are also required to cultivate such an involvement in policy making.

This context has created the potential of an enlarged role for VCOs not just as public service providers, but also as agents for the creation and sustenance of *social capital* within local communities (Putnam 1995; Fisher 1996). Within the transitional economies of Eastern Europe, for example, this has been posed as an effective mechanism for dealing with the so-called *democratic deficit* of these states (Osborne and Kaposvari 1997), whilst in the UK it has been posed as part of the drive to *modernize* local government and to enhance its legitimacy in plural local communities (Cabinet Office 1999; see also Ross and Osborne 1999).

Addressing the challenge of involving VCOs in the policy process

While it is generally acknowledged, therefore, that GNPs can have important benefits for all parties involved, including the broadening of the level of community involvement in the policy process and the empowering of local communities, the achievement of such benefits through PPPs is beset with difficulties (Huxham and Vangen 1996). Their development and management is fraught with challenges which require to be resolved if they are to deliver their anticipated benefits. Too often discussions of PPPs and GNPs have been undertaken in the absence of any clear analysis of what might be expected of them, of what contribution they can make to the goal of community empowerment, and of how we distinguish between good and bad partnerships. These issues cannot be ignored, though, if governments are seriously committed to involving VCOs as genuine partners in the co-production of policy.

Given that PPPs are therefore of interest to governments as such multi-purpose policy tools, with the potential for spanning both the process of policy formulation and for policy implementation, this raises the question of how to structure and manage such partnership arrangements. Before addressing this issue, it is necessary to establish the context of GNPs within the prevailing model of public management in the UK.

GNPs within UK public management

Over the past two decades, partnership thinking in the UK has developed within the context of the *new public management* paradigm, which has advocated a clear distinction between policy formulation and policy implementation (Stewart 1996). In this model, government was presumed to maintain control over policy formulation whilst a plurality of providers were invited into the domain of service provision. Relationships between governmental and non-governmental organizations (including VCOs) within this framework could be viewed as that of *service agency*, with the latter operating to contract, and with the contract providing the core governance mechanism for regulating relationships between the so-called partners (Walsh 1995; Ferlie *et al.* 1997). This model of GNP implied governmental control over policy formulation and with other partners, both voluntary and business oriented, being confined to involvement in policy implementation. Thus GNPs were advocated solely as a tool for enhancing the implementation of a policy agenda predetermined by government.

By way of contrast to this model, in the UK, the 'New Labour' Government has, since its election in 1997, sought to create a new role for GNPs which cuts across the established policy making–implementation divide. In this model, GNPs are developed from a standpoint which emphasizes the desire to use them as policy-making mechanisms, as part of the espoused project to modernize government in the UK (DETR 1998b). The overarching policy drivers for such partnerships now view VCOs as critical actors who can help to breakdown endemic departmentalism within government and fragmentation in the policy-making process, in order to produce the much desired model of *joined up government* (Labour Party 1997; Cabinet Office 1999). As one government minister has observed:

> ... I'm relying on [VCOs] to teach us a thing or two about 'joined up working'. You've been doing it with each other for years – years when parts of government were still ploughing their own furrows in isolation'.
>
> (Cabinet Office Press Release 23/11/99)

The idea of using partnership as a vehicle for involvement of VCOs in the policy process is not unique to the UK, though. As previously mentioned, the EU has advocated this model for some time. Jones (1998) and Teisman and Klijn (Chapter 10 in this book) have expounded some of the tensions inherent in this approach at a European level. However, in spite of the appeal of this model, the role of PPPs and GNPs as dynamic forces in the creation of policy still remains 'relatively under-theorised' (Scott 1998) with little attention paid to 'cutting beneath the rhetoric of partnership' (Peck and Tickell 1994) or to any clear recognition of the conceptual or practical challenges associated with making a reality of involving VCOs in the policy process. The evolving policy context to area regeneration in the UK provides a useful nexus for exploring such challenges and their implications for the management of GNPs.

C.3 GNPs in area regeneration policy in the UK

PPPs in general have been a key feature of area regeneration initiatives in the UK, and in the EU, for several decades. Diverse regeneration programmes in the UK, such as the UK Single Regeneration Budget (SRB) in urban areas and the Priority 5(b) Programme of the European Union in rural areas, are predicated on belief in the significance of partnership by government with both the VCO and the business sectors. Indeed, partnership has fast become the buzzword to sprinkle liberally through any funding application in order to improve its chances of success. Such applications can cover projects as diverse as local-training initiatives, the redevelopment and utilization of abandoned buildings, and the use of projects with their own distinctive ends in order to further economic development (such as by providing employment or small business opportunities). An example of the latter could be heritage and conservation projects in rural areas which incorporate opportunities for the development of small businesses based on the preservation and utilization of traditional rural skills.

Within this broad emphasis upon PPPs for regeneration there has been a particular interest in local partnerships with the VCO sector through GNPs, which are perceived to offer benefits to all parties. For government, especially at the local level, GNPs can offer a seductively easy route into genuine local and community experience and views (and particularly of disadvantaged sections of the community). At their best, they can offer an independent voice not linked to political or commercial ends and they can provide specialist expertise in areas ranging from community care through to conservation and the environment. For the local voluntary and community groups themselves, they can offer a valuable source of funding for them. Finally, for local communities they can offer a chance to influence the shape of initiatives aimed at their local communities (Osborne 1998a).

However, the last two decades have seen such partnerships situated within the service agency paradigm discussed above. In its extreme form this approach to GNPs resulted in an instrumental agenda through which they came to be used, not because of their potential to promote organizational synergy and genuine involvement of VCOs in the development of local initiatives, but rather because of their ability to introduce service providers, and particularly the VCO sector, to the discipline of the market (MacKintosh 1992). This dominant thinking created barriers to realizing the full potential of GNPs for local area regeneration.

Within the area regeneration field it is possible to chart over the duration of the Conservative Administration of the 1980s and early 1990s the continuance of this agency paradigm of GNPs, in spite of a shift in attitude regarding the broader role that GNPs might play in the regeneration process. The top-down model of economic regeneration imposed on GNPs during the 1980s (Colenutt and Cutten, 1994), with its focus on private sector dominance and on property and physical regeneration, failed to produce the hoped-for 'cascade' impact on local communities (Audit Commission 1989). This ultimately led in the 1990s to a resurgence of the importance attached to *community empowerment* as an essential tool of area regeneration – in the City Challenge and SRB schemes, for example. Despite this shift in terminology, however, the hegemony of government within these schemes remained. Colenutt and Cutten (1994) commented at the time that

> ... community involvement in these initiatives is thus carefully circum-scribed. Neither City Challenge nor SRB are designed to empower local communities to any significant extent but to keep local communities 'on side' as far as possible. Most community organisations take the pragmatic view that if they do not cooperate they will not get the money.
>
> (ibid.: 138)

Other analysts have also questioned the degree to which the SRB actually enhanced VCO participation to the extent that it claimed it would. Instead, it has been argued that the competitive bidding arrangements which characterized the SRB were 'constructed with a view to getting one over the competition and, above all, getting the money' (Peck and Tickell 1994: 253). Mawson (1995), NCVO (1995) and Tilson *et al.* (1997) have all highlighted the low level of success of VCO sector bids in the first round of the SRB Challenge Fund and the low level of participation in other bids, compared with private and public sector partners.

Under the Conservative Government, therefore, GNPs became associated with an inherently centralist agenda, which emphasized their role in delivering government policies and allowed the separation of the policy-making process from implementation. This, it has been argued, conveniently deflected attention away from government underfunding of regeneration policies as a whole and depoliticized the issue of area regeneration by requiring partners to demonstrate external compliance with 'effective partnership' as a condition of funding, thus engendering an uncritical consensus perspective on local problems (De Groot 1992).

This recent history of regeneration policies under the Conservative Government in the UK thus raises a number of issues about the position of GNPs in area regeneration policies and the role(s) that VCOs can play within them. It also raises broader questions about the potential contribution of GNPs to plural policy making in the UK. Critically, in spite of a rhetorical commitment in the UK to community empowerment through partnership as an essential component in effective policy delivery, little attention or recognition was given to the conditions for effective partnership or the institutional challenges this posed to the machinery of government. It is precisely these challenges which the New Labour Government has argued latterly that it is seeking to address.

The election of the New Labour Government in the UK in 1997 undoubtedly led to a broadening of the overall policy context of GNPs. As identified above, a key theme in the early years of this government has been the pursuit of *joined-up government* as a response to complex social and economic problems. VCOs have been identified by the Labour Party as having an important contribution to make to this initiative, because of their potential to focus on identifying unmet needs in a way which transcends the traditional departmental boundaries and professional specialisms of local and central government (DETR 1998b). Their input is therefore being increasingly sought by Central Government to promote its agenda of cross-sectoral policy making and implementation in response to social and economic issues and problems. Whilst in the past, the campaigning and advocacy roles of VCOs were devalued by Government because of their potential to add costs to service contracts and to bring VCOs into conflict with Government over contested policy initiatives, these roles are now being valued precisely because of the 'challenging' qualities that they bring to decision making within the public policy process.

This perspective undoubtedly offers opportunities for VCOs to influence the direction and content of regeneration policies. Crucially, and in contrast to the previous administration, it also emphasizes *their potential formative role* in the policy process, rather than seeing them solely as agents of implementation. Within such a model, emphasis in government policy is increasingly being placed on the contribution that the VCO sector can make to mobilizing local communities and in giving voice to minority views (Labour Party 1997; Working Group on Government Relations 1998).

Such a positive view of the potential contribution of GNPs to the policy-making process in not universally held, though. Miller (1999), for example, has argued that political interest in GNPs derives not from their capacity to improve the policy-making process but rather from their potential to legitimate controversial decisions 'where real issues of power are at stake and trust and solidarity are essential for success'. Attention has to be paid, therefore, to the key challenges of embedding policy-making considerations as a feature of GNP management processes at a local level if such charges are to be refuted.

C.4 Involving VCOs in policy formulation at the local community level

As has been argued above, the involvement of local VCOs has many advantages to offer to the process of area regeneration. Despite such advantages, however, the partnership process is also one fraught with dangers for all parties. Osborne (1999) has suggested that a number of challenges require to be addressed if GNPs are to offer an opportunity to enhance the policy-making process rather than a threat to the articulation of independent and critical perspectives on government policies. One especial issue is the sheer diversity of local VCOs and the problems which this raises for local government in identifying which organization to involve in any particular policy initiative. Government can frequently be guilty of idealizing the nature of the VCO sector (e.g. Home Office 1990) and of assuming that it can speak with one voice. The idea of the VCO sector as a united and easily identified entity in a locality is far removed from reality. Just as local communities in the UK are plural, diverse and sometimes conflictual, so is the VCO sector (Osborne 1999). This diversity is often argued by the Labour Government as an essential contribution of the VCO sector to plural policy making. It is important, therefore, that any initiative aimed at harnessing this strength does not ultimately undermine it, either by the incorporation of this sector into the local state (Wilson and Butler 1985) or by the eradication of its diversity through a process of isomorphism (DiMaggio and Powell 1988). This is a real danger, as the history of government attempts to harness the innovative potential of VCOs to improve the quality of mainstream social services in the UK has demonstrated (Osborne 1998b).

C.5 Two-way traffic? Using GNPs to improve the policy making process at the local level

The preceding discussion has focused upon the involvement of VCOs in GNPs for area regeneration at the local level. It has highlighted some of the broad dilemmas of management that such partnerships pose. The question still remains, however, of the extent to which such partnerships are able to actually impact on the local policy making process. This section takes this debate forward, by focusing on the local community level in the UK.

One concrete way in which the current Labour Government is trying to take forward this role is through the development of *voluntary sector compacts* between the key stakeholders at the local level (Stowe 1998). These compacts are jointly agreed statements of the duties and responsibilities both of Government and of the VCO sector within GNPs, as well as processes to resolve disagreements within them.

This approach offers the potential for a break with the unidirectional service-agency model which has dominated GNPs for the last two decades and a real option for GNPs to be involved in mapping community needs and planning to meet them, as well as being agents of implementation. This has certainly been recognized, in theory at least, by the *New Commitment for Regeneration* initiative announced by the DETR in partnership with the Local Government Association (Local Government Association 1997; DETR 1998a; see also Hall and Mawson 1999).

If the challenge of creating and sustaining such 'mutual benefit' GNPs which have an impact on the local policy-making process is to be met then it is important to realize that the nature of such partnerships is not homogenous. Rather there is a range and implications of possible local GNPs. Ross and Osborne (1999) have developed a typology to understand the variety of such GNPs. It emphasizes both that local government has a diversity of relationships with the VCO sector, dependent upon its own political agenda (Leach and Wilson 1998) and that differing governance mechanisms have different impacts on the development of GNPs (Osborne 1997). It is argued here that the *service agency* model of GNPs has little to offer in helping to understand or maximize the contribution of such diverse partnerships to the policy-making process. An alternative, more helpful, approach is provided by the public governance model of Kickert *et al.* (1997a).

GNPs and the 'public governance' perspective

The main argument of the *public governance* perspective

> ... is that public policy of any significance is the result of interaction between public and private actors. Public policy is made and implemented in networks of interdependent actors ... Public management should therefore be seen as network management.
>
> (Kickert *et al.* 1997a: 2–3)

Kickert *et al.* (1997a: 8–11) contrast *public governance*, as a theoretical model, to the limitations of the public management model, especially as developed in the Anglo-American model of the *new public management* (Hood 1991; Ferlie *et al.* 1997). They argue that the latter contains two visions of the policy process, both of which are flawed. In the first, government simply uses other bodies as implementation agents. In this vision, 'management is a top-down activity based on a clear authority structure'. The second vision offers a 'radial plea for decentralization ... and privatization' and 'the retreat of ... government from the public domain' and from the policy arena, with its surrender to what has been known as *private interest government* (Streeck and Schmitter 1985).

Public governance, by contrast, emphasizes the interdependency of the actors in policy formulation networks and emphasizes that central control or management is not possible because there is 'no clear authority structure'. Policy making is thus an interactive process which takes place within policy networks. Although Government is still a significant actor in such networks it is not the 'network controller'. Rather power exists in a number of different sites and forms. The managerial role in such policy networks is thus directed at sustaining interaction between the different actors involved in a policy network and at unifying their goals and aspirations:

> Public 'governance' is the directed influencing of societal processes in a network of many other co-governing actors. These actors have different and sometimes conflicting objectives and interests. Government is not the single dominant actor that can unilaterally impose its will. Hierarchical, central top-down steering does not work in networks, which have no 'top'.
>
> (Kickert and Koppenjan 1997: 39)

Kickert *et al.* (1997a: 9) are at pains to point out that they are not talking about 'the existence of policy networks in the real world' but rather 'the network approach as a theoretical framework'. They acknowledge the force of recent critiques of currently existing policy networks, such as that of Marsh and Rhodes (1992) that they are 'non-transparent and impenetrable structures of interest representation which prevent necessary innovation in public policy and form a threat to the effectiveness, efficiency and democratic legitimization of the public sector'. However, they counter that this is not a fault of such plural networks, per se, but rather of their ineffective management. The contribution of the theoretical framework of *public governance* can be to improve both their management and their contribution to public-policy making, by clarifying the key managerial challenges to be addressed (Kickert *et al.* 1997b).

This debate is an highly significant one for the role of GNPs in the 'community governance' debate about the role of such partnerships in plural-policy formulation in local communities in the UK – though one which sadly has had only limited exposure in the UK (Rhodes 1997). It offers crucial lessons both to central and local government, as well as to VCOs, as to how to move GNPs away from the policy agency model which we have argued has dominated them over the last decade and toward genuine *community governance*, where policy making and implementation are both approached on an inclusive and plural, rather than top-down, basis. Whilst it is clear that this latter model has much to offer public policy making in the UK, it has also been argued here that these benefits are unlikely to be achieved unless there is a genuine paradigm shift in behaviour by Government rather than simply a change of language. Drawing on the lessons of this perspective, we would conclude by offering five challenges for local government in the UK, if they are to make a reality of the policy formulation potential of GNPs. These challenges, we would argue, have an import for GNPs and PPPs across the world.

C.6 Final comments

Making a reality of GNP involvement in policy formulation

We would highlight five key challenges for local government if it is to make a reality of GNP involvement in the policy formulation process. First, it is important to understand partnership with the VCO sector as a *process* rather than as a document or structure. Partnerships are dynamic rather than being a steady state (see Chapter 4 by Osborne and Murray in this book). The core component of successful partnerships, as the literature on clans makes clear, is trust (Ouchi 1980). However, trust is not an easily obtainable commodity. It is something which has to be nurtured and developed. It is the product of previously successful working relationships (Ring and Van de Ven 1992; Davis and Walker 1997). These prior relationships, for which the term 'networks' is often used as a proxy, should not be confused with actual partnerships. Rather, they are the essential prerequisite for the trust that is an essential component of genuine partnership (Lowndes and Skelcher 1998).

Second, as Leach and Wilson (1998) make clear, the values on which a relationship is based are central to this relationship. In order to make the shift from service agency to policy making partnerships it is essential therefore that local government embarks on initiatives to change the values of its staff, as well as its structures and processes. Such cultural change exercises are notoriously difficult. At least one recent attempt to create a rural regeneration programme based on a comparatively modest conception of community governance (*Rural Action*) foundered because the professional training and values of the local authority community development staff were wedded to top down planning processes rather than the bottom up ones required for such a shift (Osborne and Tricker 2000; see also Colville *et al.* 1993).

Third, such policy making partnerships also require the reformulation of the role of local politicians, away from being the sole sources of policy initiatives and representative democracy and towards being their facilitators and supporters, which is at the heart of much of the current modernization programme for local government (Cabinet Office 1999). Such a change will not be easy, though Klijn and Koppenjan (1999) have argued that the current trend in Europe toward network-based policy making can only reinforce the development of such a 'new, but no less prominent' role for politicians in local government.

Fourth, the logic of such GNPs requires that local government cede part of its powers and role to the VCO sector. As Huxham and Vangen (1996) have shown, such action by the more powerful participant in a relationship is at the core of successful partnership. Unless local government is prepared for such real power sharing then genuine plural policy making will only ever remain part of the political rhetoric discourse rather than become a reality. Examples of such power sharing are to be found across the UK, if sporadically at present. In one of our own ongoing longitudinal case studies of the local implementation of the Voluntary Sector Compact in the UK, for example, a senior local government officer argued that this process had to be led by the voluntary-sector, rather than by local government:

> The CVS [Council for Voluntary Services] will lead the process and co-ordinate it on behalf of the voluntary sector. If it's to work it needs to be wider than just the council and not just another name for our strategy ... We don't see it as our job to say 'follow us' – that's not partnership. We have to be prepared to be led by others.

Finally, plural policy making requires a real commitment from local government to build the capacity of local VCOs to participate in planning and implementation fora (Harrow and Alcock 2001). This has also been identified as a core goal for the *Agenda 21* initiative to build sustainable communities for the future (LGMB 1994). As the research discussed previously has argued, the lack of such capacity building was a significant cause of the failure of many government regeneration programmes with aspirations toward partnership. Again, such capacity building is not easy, not least because the concept itself is a nebulous and ill-defined one. Osborne (1999) has suggested that true capacity building involves using concrete projects and activities as vehicles

> ... to achieve sustainable development in the local voluntary sector and community, by enabling the individuals and/or organizations concerned to develop skills that they can use again in the future
>
> (ibid.: 26)

Examples of such skills include establishing local needs, negotiating funding packages and creating and supporting local networks.

The existing literature offers a number of potential models for addressing these challenges. A typology for understanding these approaches is offered in Table C.1. Along one dimension, this typology clarifies whether the approach is seeking to effect the structure or the processes of GNPs. Along the other dimension it clarifies whether the approach is utilizing rational or relational approaches (derived from the 'rational' and 'natural' systems perspectives on organizations – see Scott 1990) to the management of these partnerships. This produces four alternative approaches to enhancing the plural policy-making model, called here Type I through to Type IV.

Table C.1 A typology of approaches to managing plural policy making

Partnership focus	Management focus	
	Rational	*Relational*
Process	Type I	Type III
Structure	Type II	Type IV

Type I approaches seek to offer rational guides to the management of the process of the involvement of GNPs in plural policy making. Examples of this include the *group decision support* model (Huxham and Vangen 1996) and the *decision conferencing* model presented by Jenei and Vári (Chapter 16 in this book). Type II approaches, by contrast, offer rational approaches to structuring both the composition of GNPs and the competing objectives of these participants. Examples of this include *stakeholder strategies* (Finn 1996) and the *Chelsea Charter Consensus Process* (Podziba 1998).

Type III approaches shift the attention toward relational management. These approaches seek to offer guidance as to how to manage the process of developing and maintaining organizational relationships within plural policy making arrangements – the public-governance perspective being the most significant literature here (e.g. Klijn *et al.* 1995; Klijn and Teisman 1997; O'Toole *et al.* 1997). Finally, Type IV approaches look to provide guidance about how to structure organizational relationships within a GNP, in order to maximize its policy making potential. Examples of this approach include *community governance* itself (Clarke and Stewart 1998) and the *Voluntary Sector Compact* (Stowe 1998).

. . . *And the dangers of plural policy making*

In an ideal world, plural policy making would offer the best of all solutions to social inclusion and to meeting needs in local communities. Inevitably, reality does not match such ideals. We would highlight four dangers that it poses for local communities. First, the clan mode of governance, which we argued above is inherent to this model, carries threats for local communities as well as opportunities. Building as it does upon mutuality and interdependence there is a danger of a lack of openness – clans can exclude people and groups as much as they include others (Ouchi 1980; Osborne 1997).

Second, Murdoch and Abram (1998), drawing on evidence from the field of housing, have argued that plural models of policy making can lead to strategic drift and a lack of direction in the development and support of local services because no one agency has ultimate responsibility for programme outputs and outcomes. 'Joined up government', they contend, requires from government a clear lead and 'dominant strategic line [which] can link together actors in a whole variety of spheres and scales' (ibid.: 49).

Third, there is a danger that the creation and sustenance of the networks required to underpin plural policy making will become an end in itself. 'Networking' can consume resources vital for the development and support of local communities and, without a proper context and purpose, can become a sterile and time-consuming exercise (Osborne and Tricker 1994).

Finally, as detailed above, such plural modes of governance carry the dangers of incorporation and isomorphism for the local VCO sector (Wilson and Butler 1985; DiMaggio & Powell 1988). If either of these dangers were to prevail then the potential benefits of the plural policy making model would be fatally undermined.

References

Audit Commission (1989) *Urban Regeneration and Economic Development: The Local Government Dimension*, London: HMSO.

Berger, P. and Neuhaus, R. (1977) *To Empower People. The Role of Mediating Structures in Public Policy*, Washington: American Enterprise Institute for Public Policy Research.

Cabinet Office (1999) *Modernising Government*, London: HMSO.

Clarke, M. and Stewart, J. (1998) *Community Governance, Community Leadership and the New Labour Government*, York: YPS.

Colenutt, B. and Cutten, A. (1994) 'Community empowerment in vogue or vain', *Local Economy* 9(3): 236–50.

Colville, I., Dalton, K. and Tomkins, C. (1993) 'Developing and understanding cultural change in the HM Customs and Excise: there is more to dancing than knowing the next steps', *Public Administration* 71: 549–66.

Davis, H. and Walker, B. (1997) 'Trust based relationships in local government contracting', in *Public Money and Management* 17(4) 47–54.

De Groot, L. (1992) 'City challenge: Competing in the urban challenge game', *Local Economy* 7(3).

Department of Environment, Transport and the Regions (DETR) (1998a) *Community-Based Regeneration Initiatives: A Working Paper*, London: DETR.

—— (1998b) *Modern Local Government*, London: DETR.

DiMaggio, P. and Powell, W. (1988) 'The iron cage revisited' in C. Milofsky (ed.) *Community Organizations*, New York: Oxford University Press, pp. 77–99.

Ferlie, E., Ashburner, L., Fitzgerald, L. and Pettigrew, A. (1997) *The New Public Management in Action*, Oxford: Oxford University Press.

Finn, C. (1996) 'Utilizing stakeholder strategies for positive collaborative outcomes', C. Huxham (ed.) *Creating Collaborative Advantage*, London: Sage.

Fisher, J. (1996) 'Civil society, political development and all that', paper given at the 1996 ARNOVA Conference, New York.

Hall, S. and Mawson, J. (1999) *Challenge Funding: Contracts and Area Regeneration*, York: Joseph Rowntree Foundation.

Harrow, J. (2001) 'Capacity building as a public management goal: Myth, magic or main chance?,' *Public Management Review* [Forthcoming].

Home Office (1990) *Efficiency Scrutiny of the Voluntary Sector*, London: HMSO.

Hood, C. (1991) 'A public management for all seasons?', *Public Administration* 69: 3–19.

Huxham, C. and Vangen, S. (1996) 'Managing inter-organizational relationships', in S. Osborne (ed.) *Managing in the Voluntary Sector*, London: International Thomson Business Press, pp. 202–21.

Jones, R. (1998) *The European Union as a promoter of public–private partnerships'*, in L. Montanheiro, B. Haig, D. Morris and N. Horovatin (eds) *Public and Private Sector Partnerships. Fostering Enterprise*, Sheffield: Pavic Press, pp. 183–94.

Kickert, W. and Koppenjan, J. (1997) 'Public management and network management: An overview' in W. Kickert, E-H. Klijn and J. Koppenjan (eds) *Managing Complex Networks. Strategies for the Public Sector*, London: Sage, pp. 35–61.

Kickert, W., Klijn, E-H. and Koppenjan, J. (1997a) 'Introduction: A management perspective on policy networks', in W. Kickert, E-H. Klijn and J. Koppenjan (eds) *Managing Complex Networks. Strategies for the Public Sector*, London: Sage, pp. 1–13.

—— (1997b) 'Managing networks in the public sector: findings and reflections', in W. Kickert, E-H. Klijn and J. Koppenjan (eds) *Managing Complex Networks. Strategies for the Public Sector*, London: Sage, pp. 166–91.

Klijn, E-H., Koppenjan, J. and Tremeer, K. (1995) 'Managing networks in the public sector: A theoretical study of management strategies in policy networks', *Public Administration* 73: 437–54.

Klijn, E-H. and Teisman, G. (1997) 'Strategies and games in networks', in W. Kickert, E-H. Klijn and J. Koppenjan (eds) *Managing Complex Networks. Strategies for the Public Sector*, London: Sage, pp. 98–136.

Klijn, E-H. and Koppenjan, J. (1999) 'Interactive decision making and the primacy of politics: in search of new roles for politicians', paper given at the Luton Conference, Luton.

Labour Party (1997) *Building The Future Together: Labour's Policies for Partnership Between Government and the Voluntary Sector*, London: Labour Party.

Leach, S. and Wilson, D. (1998) 'Voluntary groups and local authorities: Rethinking the relationship', *Local Government Studies* 24(2): 1–18.

Local Government Association (1997) *A New Deal for Regeneration*, London: LGA.

Local Government Management Board (LGMB) (1994) *Community Participation in Local Agenda 21*, Luton: LGMB.

Lowndes, V. and Skelcher, C. (1998) 'Dynamics of multi-organisational partnerships: An analysis of changing modes of governance', *Public Administration* 76: 313–33.

MacKintosh, M. (1992) 'Partnership: Issues of policy and negotiation', *Local Economy* 7(3): 210–24.

Marsh, D. and Rhodes, R. (1992) *Policy Networks in British Government*, Oxford: Clarendon Press.

Mawson, J. (1995) *The Single Regeneration Budget: The Stock-Take*, Birmingham: University of Birmingham/Local Authority Association.

Miller, C. (1999) 'Partners in regeneration: Constructing a local regime for urban management?', *Policy and Politics* 27(3): 343–58.

Murdoch, J. and Abram, S. (1998) 'Defining the limits of community governance', *Journal of Rural Studies* 14(1): 41–50.

National Council for Voluntary Organisations (NCVO) (1995) *A Missed Opportunity: An Initial Assessment of the 1995 Single Regeneration Budget Approvals and their Impact on Voluntary and Community Organisations*, London: NCVO.

Osborne, S. (1997) 'Managing the coordination of social services in the mixed economy of care: Competition, cooperation or common cause?', *British Journal of Management* 8: 317–28.

—— (1998a) 'Partnerships in local economic development. A bridge too far for the voluntary sector?', *Local Economy* 12(4): 290–5.

—— (1998b) *Voluntary Organizations and Innovation in Public Services*, London: Routledge.

—— (1999) *Promoting Local Voluntary Action*, York: Joseph Rowntree Foundation.

Osborne, S. and Kaposvari, A. (1997) 'Towards a civil society? Exploring its meaning in the context of post-communist Hungary', *Journal of European Social Policy* 7(3): 209–22.

Osborne, S. and Ross, K. (1998) 'Local development agencies and public private partnerships in local communities. The policy–practice interface', paper given at the XXth Anniversary Conference of the Centre for Voluntary Organisation, LSE.

Osborne, S. and Tricker, M. (1994) 'Local development agencies: Supporting voluntary action' *Nonprofit Management and Leadership* 5(1): 37–52.

—— (2000) 'Rural Action for the Environment. Building sustainable development in local rural communities in the UK', *Regional Studies* [in press].

O'Toole, L., Hanf, K. and Hupe, P. (1997) 'Managing implementation processes in networks', in W. Kickert, E-H. Klijn and J. Koppenjan (eds) *Managing Complex Networks. Strategies for the Public Sector*, London: Sage, pp. 137–51.

Ouchi, W. (1980) 'Markets, bureaucracies and clans' *Administrative Science Quarterly* 25(1): 129–41.

Peck, J. and Tickell, A. (1994) 'Too many partners ... the future for regeneration partnerships', *Local Economy* 9(3): 251–65.

Phillips, S. (1999) 'Voluntary sector–state relations in transition: Canada's reform process as a model for realigning relationships', paper given at the ARNOVA Conference 1999, Washington, DC.

Podziba, S. (1998) *Social Capital Formation, Public-Building and Public Motivation. The Chelsea Charter Consensus Process*, Dayton, OH: Kettering Foundation.

Putnam, R. (1995) 'Bowling alone', *Journal of Democracy* 6(1): 65–78.

Ring, S. and Van de Ven, A., (1992) 'Structuring cooperative relations between organizations', *Strategic Management Journal* 13: 483–98.

Rhodes, R. (1997) 'Forword', in W. Kickert, E-H. Klijn and J. Koppenjan (eds) *Managing Complex Networks. Strategies for the Public Sector*, London: Sage.

Ross, K. and Osborne, S. (1999) 'Making a reality of community governance. Structuring government – voluntary sector relationships at the local level', *Public Policy and Administration* 14(2): 49–61.

Scott, J. (1998) 'Law, legitimacy and EC governance: Prospects for partnership', *Journal of Common Market Studies* 36(2): 175–94.

Scott, R. (1990) *Organizations. Rational, Natural and Open Systems*, Englewood Cliffs, NJ: Prentice Hall.

Social Exclusion Unit (1998) *Bringing Britain Together*, London: HMSO.

Stewart, J. (1996) 'A dogma of our times: The separation of policy making and implementation', *Public Money and Management* July–September: 1–8.

Stowe, K. (1998) 'Compact on relations between government and the voluntary and community sector in England and Wales', *Public Administration and Development* 18(5): 519–22.

Streeck, W. and Schmitter, P. (eds) (1985) *Private Interest Government: Beyond Market and State*, London: Sage.

Tilson, B., Mawson, J., Beazely, M., Burfitt, A., Collinge, C., Hall, S., Loftman, P., Nevin B. and Srbljanin, A (1997) 'Partnerships for regeneration: The Single Regeneration Budget Challenge Fund round one', *Local Government Studies* 23(1): 1–15.

Walsh, K. (1995) *Public Services and Market Mechanisms: Competition, Contracting and the New Public Management*, London: MacMillan.

Wilson, D. and Butler, R. (1985) 'Corporatism in the British voluntary sector', in W. Streeck and P. Schmitter (eds) *Private Interest Government: Beyond Market and State*, London: Sage.

Working Party on Government Relations (1998) *Consultative Document on the Development of a Compact between Government and the Voluntary and Community Sector*, London: NCVO.

Index